AUTOPSY IN ATHENS

AUTOPSY IN ATHENS

RECENT ARCHAEOLOGICAL RESEARCH ON ATHENS AND ATTICA

Edited by

MARGARET M. MILES

Oxbow Books

Oxford & Philadelphia

Published in the United Kingdom in 2015 by
OXBOW BOOKS
10 Hythe Bridge Street, Oxford OX1 2EW

and in the United States by
OXBOW BOOKS
908 Darby Road, Havertown, PA 19083

Hardcover Edition: ISBN 978-1-78297-856-5
Digital Edition: ISBN 978-1-78297-857-2

A CIP record for this book is available from the British Library

Library of Congress Cataloging-in-Publication Data

Autopsy in Athens : recent archaeological research on Athens and Attica / edited by Margaret M. Miles.
      pages cm
  Includes bibliographical references and index.
   ISBN 978-1-78297-856-5 (hardcover) -- ISBN 978-1-78297-857-2 (digital) 1. Athens (Greece)--Antiquities. 2. Attike (Greece)--
      Antiquities. 3. Excavations (Archaeology)--Greece--Athens. 4. Excavations (Archaeology)--Greece--Attike. 5. Salvage archaeology-
      -Greece--Athens. 6. Salvage archaeology--Greece--Attike. 7. Social archaeology--Greece--Athens. 8. Social archaeology--Greece-
      -Attike. I. Miles, Margaret M.
   DF275.A88 2015
   938'.5--dc23
                                      2015014203

Printed in the Malta by Melita

For a complete list of Oxbow titles, please contact:

UNITED KINGDOM
Oxbow Books
Telephone (01865) 241249, Fax (01865) 794449
Email: oxbow@oxbowbooks.com
www.oxbowbooks.com

UNITED STATES OF AMERICA
Oxbow Books
Telephone (800) 791-9354, Fax (610) 853-9146
Email: queries@casemateacademic.com
www.casemateacademic.com/oxbow

Oxbow Books is part of the Casemate Group

Front cover: Temple of Poseidon, Sounion. (Photograph: M. M. Miles)
Back cover: Votive relief from Piraeus Asklepieion, ca. 350 BC. Piraeus Archaeological Museum Inv. 405.
(Photograph © Piraeus Museum, Piraeus)

Contents

List of Contributors

JOHANNA BEST is a Fellow at the American School of Classical Studies, Athens, where she is writing a dissertation for Bryn Mawr College. Her research focuses on the roadside religious sites in Athens and Attica, landscape, and the history of religion. She has excavated at Nemea and Despotiko in Greece.

SYLVIAN FACHARD is a Swiss National Science Foundation Senior Research Associate at the University of Geneva. He was the Assistant director of the Swiss School of Archaeology in Greece (2002–2011) and a Postdoctoral Fellow at the Center for Hellenic Studies and the Joukowsky Institute for Archaeology & the Ancient World (Brown University). He has conducted extensive research in Eretria and its territory, and published *Eretria* XXI (2012), which focuses on the defense of the *chora*. His current research project is about the Attic borderlands.

MARYA FISHER is a Ph.D. candidate at the Institute of Fine Arts, NYU and a Regular Member of the American School of Classical Studies at Athens, writing a dissertation which examines the intersection of architecture and cult in the non-peripteral temples of South Italy and Sicily. She is currently involved in field projects in Selinunte, Sicily, and Samothrace, Greece, working on architectural documentation and analysis.

NANCY KLEIN is Associate Professor in the Department of Architecture at Texas A&M University. Her research explores the relationship of architecture and society in Late Bronze Age and Early Iron Age Crete, the development of the Doric order, and the architecture of the Athenian Acropolis in the Archaic and early Classical periods.

RACHEL KOUSSER is Professor at the City University of New York, Brooklyn College and the Graduate Center. Her first book, *Hellenistic and Roman ideal sculpture: The allure of the Classical* was published by Cambridge University Press in 2008. Her current monograph, *The afterlives of monumental sculptures in Classical and Hellenistic Greece: Interaction, transformation, destruction* is forthcoming from Cambridge University Press.

JESSICA LAMONT is completing a Ph.D. at the Johns Hopkins University. Her dissertation focuses on healing cults in Athens in the late 5th century BC. She has held fellowships from the American School of Classical Studies at Athens and the Alexander Onassis Public Benefit Foundation. She has taught at the College Year in Athens (CYA), and has excavated at Pylos-Iklaina, the Athenian Agora, Corinth, and Molyvoti (Thrace).

CAROL LAWTON is Professor of Art History and Classical Studies at Lawrence University. She is the author of *Attic Document Reliefs: Art and Politics in Ancient Athens* (Oxford 1995) and articles on document and votive reliefs. Her volume on the votive reliefs from the excavations of the Athenian Agora is forthcoming.

KRISTIAN LORENZO is a Visiting Lecturer at the University of Richmond. He held an ACM-Mellon Post-doctoral fellowship in Classical Archaeology at Monmouth College. His research focuses on dedications for victories at sea, the cross-cultural adaptation of victory imagery, and early imperial usage of traditional commemorative practices for propagandistic purposes. He has excavated at Old Fort Niagara in western New York, the town of Salemi, Sicily, the Athenian Agora and ancient Corinth.

BRIAN A. MARTENS is a DPhil candidate in classical archaeology at the University of Oxford. His research focuses on the production, uses, and reuses of marble divine statuettes in Roman and late antique Greece, with materials from the Athenian Agora as a case study for understanding wider regional practices. He is a supervisor at the Agora Excavations, where he has worked since 2008.

MARGARET M. MILES is Professor of Art History and Classics at the University of California, Irvine. She served as the Andrew W. Mellon Professor of Classical Studies at the American School of Classical Studies in Athens during 2008–2014. Her publications include a study of the Temple of Nemesis at Rhamnous (*Hesperia* 1989), *The Athenian Agora* XXXI: *The City Eleusinion* (1998), *Art as Plunder: the Ancient Origins of Debate about Cultural Property* (Cambridge, 2008), and (as Editor) *Cleopatra: A Sphinx Revisited* (2011).

JACOB MORTON is a PhD candidate in the Graduate Group in Ancient History at the University of Pennsylvania and a Fellow at the American School of Classical Studies at Athens. He is currently writing his dissertation, which explores the effects of the initial Roman military presence in Greece, while continuing research on the practicalities of Greek religion.

JENIFER NEILS is the Ruth Coulter Heede Professor of Art History and Classics at Case Western Reserve University, and currently the Chair of the Managing Committee of the American School of Classical Studies at Athens. She has written extensively on Attic art and archaeology, including *Goddess and Polis: The Panathenaic Festival in Ancient Athens* (1992), *The Parthenon Frieze* (2001) and *The Parthenon from Antiquity to the Present* (co-author and editor, 2005).

JESSICA PAGA is an Andrew W. Mellon Postdoctoral Fellow at Washington University in St. Louis, where she is appointed in the Interdisciplinary Project in the Humanities as well as the Classics Department. Her research focuses on Greek architecture, particularly of the Archaic and Classical periods, and ritual theory and democratic theory. She is a Senior Archaeologist with the Samothrace Excavations, where she has worked since 2012. She joins the Department of Classics at The College of William & Mary in 2015.

DANIELE PIRISINO is a PhD student in archaeology at Durham University. He is writing a dissertation on the overland sacred route from Athens to Delphi, with a focus on its course across Attica. He has taken part in excavations of Prehistoric, Phoenician, Greek, and Roman sites. He is a supervisor at the Athenian Agora, where he also conducts the 3D modeling survey of the excavations.

DEREK REINBOLD received his Bachelors in Art History, International Studies, and Political Science at Case Western Reserve University in 2014. His honors thesis in Art History examined the interplay of Helios, the Greek god of the sun and Hephaistos, the Greek god of fire and the forge, on the Parthenon's east metopes.

ANGELE ROSENBERG-DIMITRACOPOULOU is a PhD candidate in the Department of Art History at the University of Chicago. Her dissertation examines the cultural meanings of youth and nudity in the fifth and fourth centuries BCE and the relationship between personal and period style. She has excavated at Corinth and Pylos.

RACHEL STERNBERG is Associate Professor of Classics and History at Case Western Reserve University. She studies compassion. Her edited volume, *Pity and Power in Ancient Athens*, was published by Cambridge University Press in 2005; her monograph, *Tragedy Offstage: Suffering and Sympathy in Ancient Athens*, by University of Texas Press in 2006.

BARBARA TSAKIRGIS is Associate Professor of Classics and Art History at Vanderbilt University. She studies ancient Greek houses and households around the Mediterranean world and is the author of several articles and a forthcoming book on the Hellenistic and Roman houses at Morgantina. Currently she is completing a synthetic study of Greek houses around the Mediterranean and the final publication of the houses excavated around the Athenian Agora.

Introduction

Autopsy has long been a driving force for people interested in ancient Athens: already in the Hellenistic period, Attalid princes came to Athens for polish, as did notables from Rome (Cicero and Aulus Gellius are among the better known students who flourished as a result). Everyone wanted to see the famous city for himself, bask in its glory, and perhaps eventually contribute to it. In the early modern era, Athens and Attica came under a new, antiquarian and archaeological eye when Cyriacus of Ancona traveled to Athens in the 1430s, copied many ancient inscriptions, and kept extensive diaries of his visits to Greece and the eastern Mediterranean. His efforts and observations in effect founded the study of Athens and Attica, and the new field of archaeology.

A small but ever-increasing number of intrepid early travelers from western Europe braved the difficult conditions and political obstacles to travel in the eastern Mediterranean then under Ottoman rule. Jacob Spon and his fellow traveler Sir George Wheler published accounts of their travels in 1675, but two of their traveling party did not survive.[1] In the eighteenth century, David Le Roy and the British team James Stuart and Nicholas Revett traveled with the goal of understanding and documenting ancient Greek architecture. Up until then, Greek architecture in Italy provided exemplars for students of architecture, particularly the temples at Paestum and in Sicily, but even those temples had not yet been fully explored and documented.

In the coffee houses of Rome, Stuart and Revett eagerly talked about going to Athens. Le Roy's account was published first, much to the chagrin of Stuart and Revett, but it caused great excitement in France. His book and a few years later, Stuart and Revett's *Antiquities of Athens,* were read avidly in western Europe and their drawings much admired. *The Antiquities of Athens* has gone through many printings since the initial volume of 1762 and is still in print. Their work had a huge influence on contemporary architecture, as the authors and their sponsor the Society of Dilettanti hoped. Above all, Stuart and Revett took pride in accuracy of measurement and recording, and their drawings were useful to practicing architects of their time, and are still useful to archaeologists today. They set a new standard of representation for ancient buildings and monuments.[2]

The ongoing Napoleonic Wars made Greece an attractive alternative destination to the more typical Grand Tour of Italy that was so popular for gentlemen of means in the 18th century. The British artist Edward Dodwell and his Italian assistant Simone Pomardi made numerous watercolors during his travels in Greece beginning in 1805, many of them based on views provided by a *camera obscura*; hence they provide accurate rather than merely impressionistic views of sites and monuments. In the years leading up to the Greek War of Independence, Col. Martin Leake walked or rode much of the Greek countryside and brought extensive military experience and acumen in his observations as a topographer. Like Dodwell, he was steeped in ancient texts and a keen student of Pausanias. A more scholarly view of Greece's past was emerging and is noticeable, for example, in C. R. Cockerell's account of his work at Aigina and Bassai in 1811 (published in 1860), which could be regarded as one of the earliest proper excavation reports.[3]

With the founding of the new modern state of Greece, interest in archaeology intensified. This era saw increasing diligence in recording, salvaging, protecting and collecting antiquities, with the island of Aigina initially serving as a depository for a new national collection, founded under the initiative of Ioannis Kapodistrias, the first Governor of the new Greek state. The choice of Athens, rather than Nafplion, as the capital resulted in an extensive program of building within the city and at Piraeus, and soon the population of Athens doubled and tripled.

After 1832, the young new King Otto, son of the philhellenic King Ludwig I of Bavaria, attracted German architects to Athens, and one result was renewed attention to the Akropolis. Karl Friedrich Schinkel developed plans for a palace on the Akropolis (fortunately not carried out!). A style modeled on ancient Greek buildings influenced much of his other work in Berlin and elsewhere. Among important early studies of the time was that of the Temple of Athena Nike; it had been dismantled by the Ottomans and incorporated into a fortification wall, but now Ludwig Ross, Eduard Schaubert and Christian Hansen measured and drew it so that it could be set up again.[4] This work gave them the opportunity to study ancient construction and sculpting methods in detail.

The Greek Archaeological Service was formed in 1833 as the first such national body in Europe, and became responsible for management of the whole of the archaeological heritage of Greece. Greek scholars such as K. S. Pittakys undertook to document as many inscriptions as possible, laying part of the groundwork for epigraphical volumes to come later in the century. In 1848, he became General Ephor of Antiquities, thus head of the Greek Archaeological Service. A new Archaeological Society at Athens, founded in 1837 by Greek scholars and politicians, took a very active role in encouraging the study, collection and restoration of monuments and antiquities of all sorts. With private funding, the Society sponsored excavations and accomplished important archaeological documentation which continues today.[5] A third interested body was the National and Kapodistrian University of Athens, officially founded on April 14th, 1837. It was the first university founded in the Balkan peninsula and the Eastern Mediterranean. The study of the classical heritage of Greece, and efforts to protect and conserve it, were underway.

After the foundation of modern Greece, the physical remains of the Greek past were becoming more a matter for scholarship than ownership: the era of widespread "collecting" of antiquities did not start with Lord Elgin but certainly was punctuated by his depredations, and now was coming to a close.[6] While looting continued, and occasionally still does, more effort was made to halt it. The new government bodies were organizing the various aspects of archaeological heritage with control over ownership, excavation and study. The Parthenon itself was becoming a focal point and symbol for ancient Greek achievement.

Western European governments sponsored schools or institutes of archaeology in Athens: the first was the French School of Archaeology (1846), followed by the German Institute of Archaeology (1872), and the British School at Athens (1886). These institutes, largely funded by their respective governments, sponsored excavations with permission from the Greek government, founded libraries, and served as a base to connect the countries' home universities with research in Greece. They were founded at a time when everyone regarded Greek history and ancient Greek culture as the fundamental underpinning of western civilization. The significance and importance of Greek history and Greek archaeology were unquestioned, and it was felt that all of Europe was the heir of Greece: a general sense of philhellenism had fostered European intervention in the Greek War of Independence. Today there are seventeen foreign Schools of archaeology in Athens.

The American School of Classical Studies at Athens, founded in 1881 as the third of the foreign schools in Greece, is exceptional among the seventeen in two ways: it was founded by private donors committed to Classical Studies, and continues to be funded with its endowment and donations, plus occasional grants; and it sought from the beginning to provide an academic program for graduate students in Greece. This was felt to be especially important for North American students, who live at a much greater distance from Greece compared to their European counterparts, who could easily journey there when they wished.

A year abroad at "the School" (as its denizens refer to it) was soon regarded as a necessity for any young American scholar wishing to study Greek history, literature, or archaeology, as it continues to be today. It was believed then, and we still do, that there is no substitute for personal autopsy: to understand the literature, history, and material culture of ancient Greece, one must experience the landscape, walk through the mountains, sail on the seas, visit its museums. Today the School provides an intensive, year-long academic program for North American graduate students, houses two superb research libraries, sponsors excavations in the Athenian Agora and ancient Corinth, supports other excavations and affiliated research projects, and houses the Weiner Lab for archaeological scientific study.

In the course of the 20th century, archaeological research contributed by members and faculty of the School expanded enormously our knowledge of Athens and Attica. The excavations of the Athenian Agora were inaugurated in May, 1931, and since then have revealed the very heart of the ancient city, a whole complex of civic and sacred buildings, law courts, monuments, and roadways. The Stoa of Attalos was reconstructed as authentically as modern engineering standards allowed to serve as a museum for the public, under the leadership of Homer A. Thompson.[7] Excavations are still ongoing, and the excavated ancient site is now a shady archaeological park, replanted with trees and shrubs known to have been part of ancient landscapes, and a major attraction for birds, as well as modern visitors. Some 60 books and more than 400 articles have been published on the results of the excavations.

The rural demes and countryside of Attica were thoroughly explored by Eugene Vanderpool during his many years as Professor of Archaeology at the School; he published extensively on the plain and topography of Marathon and its environs, and the northwestern areas of Attica, including border forts. William B. Dinsmoor, Jr. also took on many topics of architectural interest both within the Agora and outside it, such as a major study of the Temple of Athena Sounias at Sounion.[8] Merle Langdon has contributed extensive studies of mountaintop sanctuaries in Attica, and the rupestral inscriptions he found on the slopes of Hymettos and in the area of Laurion. John Camp, Josiah Ober and Mark Munn have elucidated further the border defenses of Attica, not only through excavation, but also extensive hiking and personal observation, a strong tradition in the School.

As we move forward in the 21st century, fresh examination of old material in Athens and Attica brings new perspectives and answers. One approach is to take on a specific, knotty chronological problem and bring every shred of known evidence to elucidate it, such as Andrew Stewart's close reading of the chronology for art production around the time of the Persian Wars.[9] Another approach is to make good use of previously published data that is quite scattered and difficult of access: examples of recent articles that follow this method with great success are Merle Langdon's study of the quarries in Piraeus, Nathan Arrington's location of the *demosion sema*, and Anna Theocharaki's thorough investigation of the walls of Athens.[10] Another project gathers a research team of scholars to tackle a large body of material: thus John Travlos's now classic *Pictorial Dictionary of Athens* (1971) is being supplemented by an ambitious eight-volume series on the topography of Athens, led by Emanuele Greco of the Italian School of Archaeology in Athens, with thorough coverage of each area of the ancient city.[11] Perhaps the most vigorous area within Classical Archaeology is the study of ceramics, with ongoing new interpretations in types, sources, production and distribution, uses and iconography. Chronologies established by ceramics are essential for the study of everything else, and continue apace with important results. An example is the refined dating for the beginning of Athenian Red-figure pottery, argued by Ulf Kenzler and Susan Rotroff.[12]

Other new directions have resulted from changes in the scholarly consensus formed in the previous generation: an example is the now dropped "rule of the three-barred sigma," a shorthand description for overly prescriptive dating of inscriptions by letter forms. Those rules had developed over the course of decades of study of the inscribed lists of *aparchai* offered to Athena (the "Athenian tribute quota lists") that had emerged in the course of excavations of the Agora and environs, and other Athenian inscriptions. The history of Athenian *arche* in the 5th century BC, a seemingly closed subject until recently, attracts fresh interpretation from every direction, especially when inscriptions from elsewhere, as from Delos, are brought into the discussion.[13]

What finally persuaded everyone in the early 1990s to take a less rigid view of letter forms was the application of new laser technologies that enhance autopsy and enable new ways of viewing.[14] New technologies continue to enhance interpretations in Classical studies; all of ancient Greek literature may be searched digitally on the Thesaurus Linguae Graecae (TLG). Laser scanning has wonderful applications for architecture and architectural terracottas, as we may see in the digital reconstructions by Philip

Saperstein. In Athens, new interpretations of the sculpture of the Parthenon and its visibility have been undertaken by Jenifer Neils and Bonna Wescoat, and like the TLG, are easily available on the internet.[15] These supplement fresh studies of the details of the Parthenon's frieze, and other new studies of Athenian sculptural production.[16]

While students of Athens and Attica are eager to apply new technologies, we still are in frequent dialogue with earlier travelers. Thanks to Cyriacus' close observation and careful records of his visit in 1436, for example, it was possible in a study published in 2005 to redate and reinterpret the significance of the Little Metropolitan church (Panagia Gorgoepikoos) in the center of Athens. Bente Kiilerich shows that Cyriacus saw an inscription in the area of the ancient Agora, which later was moved and built into the south wall of the church, along with many other spolia.[17] Rather than viewing the small church as typical of late 12th century Byzantine plans, whose builders used large quantities of old marble blocks because it was cheap and convenient, we now see that the church was carefully constructed of ancient material with new meanings attached to their imagery, probably around 1460. The Parthenon (then known as the Panagia Athenotissa) had just been converted from a Christian church to a mosque after the Ottoman capture of Athens in 1458. Under the new Ottoman regime, Greek Orthodoxy was nonetheless able to make a public statement about inherited traditions by virtue of the recycled blocks. Thus fresh research, based on Cyriacus' record of his own autopsy, has added a new layer to Athens' history.

Why focus on classical Athens and Attica, and why now, after so many centuries? Philhellenism, of course, is still alive and flourishing. The large body of prestigious literature written in antiquity encourages further exploration. The enormous amount of information available about ancient Athens and Attica may be paralleled only in the study of ancient Rome, so that many historical questions may be posed, and have the potential for satisfactory answers. The excavation of the Athenian Agora, and other sites in Athens and Attica, have yielded a large corpus of inscriptions that are critical for understanding details of ancient religion, social institutions, political history, and daily life. Despite the ongoing tensions between the needs of a modern city situated over the ancient remains of interest to archaeologists, much material of all sorts is available for fresh study, and older finds may be further elucidated by younger eyes.

The "rescue" excavations of recent years, conducted by the Greek Archaeological Service during construction of the Metro system, of the highway known as the Attiki Odos, and of other sites in anticipation of the 2004 Olympics, have also contributed significant new finds. These excavations have added greatly to our knowledge of mortuary practices and ancient populations, about houses, and road networks. The ongoing, meticulous restoration projects on the Akropolis have yielded much new information about its architecture, some of it surprising, such as the windows in the Parthenon.[18] Faculty and visitors at the seventeen foreign schools, plus the staff of the Greek Archaeological Service, the members of the Archaeological Society of Athens, and the faculty of the University of Athens fill the year with lectures, symposia, and conferences: an energetic and effervescent international community of persons interested in antiquity has fully superceded the lone pioneering travelers of centuries ago. This is an exciting time to study in Athens.

The authors in this volume have all had some association with the American School, and several "generations" of students are represented here, as well as many decades' experience in Athens. The papers, while brief, contribute new findings that result from intensive, first-hand examinations of the archaeological and epigraphical evidence. They illustrate how much may be gained by re-examining material from older excavations, and from the methodological shift from documenting information to closer analysis and larger historical reflection. Several of the papers were given in an earlier form at the annual meetings of the Archaeological Institute of America, held in Chicago in January, 2014.

The papers here offer a variety of perspectives on a range of issues: the ambience of the ancient city for passers-by, filled with roadside shrines, is discussed by Johanna Best. The metopes on the east front of its major temple, the Parthenon, are elucidated by Jenifer Neils, Rachel Sternberg, and Derek Reinbold. Techniques of construction and of sculpting are discussed by Nancy Klein and Barbara Tsakirgis. Aspects of religious expression in Athens include cults of Asklepios and Serapis, investigated here by Jessica Lamont, Carol Lawton, and Brian Martens, and the precise procedures for Greek sacrifice are explained by Jake Morton, based on practical experiments. How damaged statuary could be treated reverently or not is investigated by Angele Rosenberg-Dimitracopoulou and Rachel Kousser. Jessica Paga looks outward to the borders of Attica and how they were defined over time, and its road-system has been walked by Sylvian Fachard and Daniele Pirisino. In the deme sites, a stoa at Thorikos is treated by Margaret Miles, and a spectacular dedication at Sounion by Kristian Lorenzo. With a broad perspective, Marya Fisher urges us not to be overly fascinated by columnar orders if we want to understand better the purposes of Greek architecture.

Collectively, the authors of this volume owe warm thanks to the American School of Classical Studies, for fostering and nourishing our scholarship. We are also grateful to our Greek hosts who generously share access to ancient material so that we may study it. On behalf of the authors, I thank in particular past Director of the School Jack Davis and current Director James Wright, and the staff at the School for making our studies possible and encouraging them over the past few years when the work presented here took shape. I myself as Editor add personal thanks to the many friends and colleagues who were willing to drop everything to read drafts of these papers, often at very short notice, so that this could be a peer-reviewed volume. You know who you are, and I thank you so much for improving our work and helping us move it forward. As the School continues to train younger generations of scholars, the tradition of autopsy pioneered by Cyriacus of Ancona is thriving.

Margaret M. Miles
Andrew W. Mellon Professor of Classical Studies
American School of Classical Studies, Athens
June 2, 2014

Notes

1 Spon 1678, Wheler 1682; one man became ill and died near Delphi, and a second was captured by pirates, enslaved, and later murdered (Arbuthnott 2006, 68).

2 Middleton 2004, Le Roy 2004 [1770], Stuart and Revett 1762–1812, Watkin 2006.

3 Dodwell 1819, 1834, Leake 1821, Cockerell 1860, Eisner 1993, Camp 2013.

4 On the initial archaeological work on the Akropolis and the ideological views then at play, see Hamilakis 2007, pp. 85–99.

5 Petrakos 2007.

6 Miles 2008, pp. 307–319.

7 For an illustrated overview of the excavations, see Mauzy and Camp 2006.

8 His manuscript is soon to be published by Barbara Barletta, with her additional observations.

9 Stewart 2008a, 2008b.

10 Langdon 2000[2004], Arrington 2010, Theocharakis 2012.

11 Greco 2010, 2011.

12 Kenzler 2007, Rotroff 2009.

13 Warnings had been sounded early on by H. Mattingly (papers collected in 1996). See the essays in Ma, Papazarkadas, Parker 2009; Marginesu 2010; Delos: Chankowski 2008; overview on the stelai with *aparchai*: Miles 2011.

14 Chambers, Galluci, Spanos 1990.

15 TLG: http://www.tlg.uci.edu; Saperstein: http://sites.museum.upenn.edu/monrepos/; Neils: https://www.youtube.com/watch?v=hUZhApnYbGc; Wescoat: https://www.youtube.com/watch?v=RauBAZYLJ2A; see also Wescoat http://www.samothrace.emory.edu/visualizing-the-sanctuary/

16 Neils 2001, Marconi 2009, Palagia 2006, 2009.

17 Kiilerich 2005.

18 Korres 1984.

References

Arbuthnott, C. 2006. "The Life of James "Athenian" Stuart, 1713–1788," in *James "Athenian" Stuart, 1713–1788. The Rediscovery of Antiquity*, ed. S. Soros, 59–101. New Haven.

Arrington, N. 2010. "Topographic Semantics. The Location of the Athenian Public Cemetery and Its Significance for the Nascent Democracy," *Hesperia* 79, pp. 499–539.

Berger, E., ed. 1984. *Parthenon-Kongress Basel: Referate und Berichte*, Mainz.

Camp, J. McK., II. 2013. *In search of Greece: Catalogue of an exhibit of drawings at the British Museum by Edward Dodwell and Simone Pomardi from the Collection of the Packard Humanities Institute*, Los Altos, CA.

Chambers, M., R. Galluci, and M. Spanos. 1990. "Athens' Alliance with Egesta in the Year of Antiphon," *Zeitschrift für Papyrologie und Epigraphik* 83, pp. 38–60.

Chankowski, V. 2008. *Athènes et Délos à l'époque classique: recherches sur l'administration du sanctuaire d'Apollon délien*, Athens.

Cockerell. C. R. 1860. *The Temples of Jupiter Panhellenius at Aegina, and of Apollo Epicurius at Bassae near Phigaleia in Arcadia*, 4 vols., London.

Dodwell, E. 1819. *A Classical and Topographical Tour through Greece: 1801, 05, 06*, London.

Dodwell, E. 1834. *Views and Descriptions of Cyclopian or Pelasgic Remains in Italy and Greece*, London and Paris.

Eisner, R. 1993. *Travelers to an Antique Land: The History and Literature of Travel to Greece*, Ann Arbor.

Greco, E. 2010. *Topografia di Atene: Sviluppo urbano e monumenti dalle origini al III secolo d. C.* Vol 1, *Acropoli, Areopago, Tra Acropoli e Pnice*, Athens and Paestum.

Greco, E. 2011. *Topografia di Atene: Sviluppo urbano e monumenti dalle origini al III secolo d. C.* Vol 2, *Colline sud-occidentali ed valle dell'Ilisso*, Athens and Paestum.

Hamilakis, Y. 2007. *The Nation and Its Ruins. Antiquity, Archaeology and National Imagination in Greece*, Oxford.

Kelly, J. 2009. *The Society of the Dilettanti. Archaeology and Identity in the British Enlightenment*, New Haven and London.

Kenzler, U. 2007. "Hoplitenehre: ein Beitrag zur absoluten Chronologie attischer Vasen der spätarchaischen Zeit," *Hephaistos* 25, pp. 179–207.

Kiilerich, B. 2005. "Making Sense of the *Spolia* in the Little Metropolis in Athens," *Arte medievale* 4, pp. 95–114.

Korres, M. 1984. "Der Pronaos und die Fenster des Parthenon," in *Parthenon-Kongress Basel*, ed. E. Berger, Mainz, pp. 47–54.

Langdon, M. 2000 [2004]. "The Quarries of Peiraieus," *Archaiologikon Deltion* 55, A': 35–250.

Le Roy, Julien-David. 2004 [1770]. *The Ruins of the Most Beautiful Monuments in Greece*, introduction by Robin Middleton, trans. David Britt, Los Angeles.

Leake, W. M. 1821. *Topography of Athens*, London.

Ma, J., N. Papazarkadas, and R. Parker, eds. 2009. *Interpreting the Athenian Empire*, London.

Marconi, C. 2009. "The Parthenon Frieze: Degrees of Visibility," *Res: Anthropology and Aesthetics* 55/56, pp. 156–173.

Marginesu, G. 2010. *Gli epistati dell'Acropoli:. Edilizia sacra nella città di Pericle 447/6–433/2 a.C.*, Athens and Paestum.

Mattingly, H. 1996. *The Athenian empire restored. Epigraphic and historical studies*, Ann Arbor.

Mauzy, C. and J. Camp. 2006. *Agora Excavations, 1931–2006. A Pictorial History*, Athens.

Middleton, R. 2004. "Introduction," in Le Roy, Julien-David. 2004 [1770], *The Ruins of the Most Beautiful Monuments in Greece*, Los Angeles, pp. 1–199.

Miles, M. M. 2008. *Art as Plunder. The Ancient Origins of Debate about Cultural Property*, Cambridge.

Miles, M. M. 2011. "The *Lapis Primus* and the Older Parthenon," *Hesperia* 80, pp. 657–675.

Neils, J. 2001. *The Parthenon Frieze*, Cambridge.

Palagia, O., ed. 2006. *Greek Sculpture. Function, materials, and techniques in the archaic and classical periods*, Cambridge.

Palagia, O., ed. 2009. *Art in Athens during the Peloponnesian War*, Cambridge.

Petrakos, B. 2007. Τα 170 χρόνια της Αρχαιολογικής Εταιρείας, 1837–2007, Athens.

Pittakys, K. S. 1835. *L'ancienne Athènes, ou, La description des antiquités d'Athènes et ses environs*, Athens.

Rotroff, S. 2009. "Early Red-figure in Context," in *Athenian Potters and Painters* II, ed. J. Oakley and O. Palagia, Oxford, pp. 250–260.

Soros, S. W., ed. 2006. *James "Athenian" Stuart 1713–1788. The Rediscovery of Antiquity*, New Haven and London.

Spon, Jacob. 1678. *Voyage d'Italie, de Dalmatie de Grece et du Levant fait 1675*, Lyon.

Stewart, A. 2008a. "The Persian Invasions of Greece and the Beginning of the Classical Style: Part 1, The Stratigraphy, Chronology, and Significance of the Acropolis Deposits," *American Journal of Archaeology* 112, pp. 377–412.

Stewart, A. 2008b. "The Persian and Carthaginian Invasions of 480 B.C.E. and the Beginning of the Classical Style, Part 2, The Finds from Athens, Attic and Elsewhere in Greece, and on Sicily, Part 3, The Severe Style: Motivations and Meaning," *American Journal of Archaeology* 112, pp. 581–615.

Stuart, J. and N. Revett. 1762–1812. *The Antiquities of Athens*, London.

Theocharaki, A. M. 2011. "The Ancient Circuit Wall of Athens: Its Changing Course and the Phases of Construction," *Hesperia* 80, pp. 71–156.

Tsigakou, F.-M. 1981. *The Rediscovery of Greece: Travellers and Painters of the Romantic Era*, Athens.

Watkin, D. 2006. "Stuart and Revett: The Myth of Greece and Its Afterlife," in *James "Athenian" Stuart, 1713–1788. The Rediscovery of Antiquity*, ed. S. Soros, New Haven, pp. 19–57.

Weber, S. H. 1952–1953. *Voyages and travels in Greece, the Near East, and adjacent regions: made previous to the year 1801; being a part of a larger catalogue of works on geography, cartography, voyages and travels, in the Gennadius Library in Athens*, Princeton.

Wheler, George. 1682. *A Journey to Greece*, London.

Architectural Repairs of the Small Limestone Buildings on the Athenian Acropolis in the Archaic Period

Nancy L. Klein

This examination of architectural blocks found on the Athenian Acropolis identifies several different methods that were used to patch, stabilize, and fill in damaged areas. In the 6th century BC, lead was used for repairs in both solid (pins) and molten form, but the subsequent replacement of lead pins with iron suggests a better understanding of each metal's properties. These techniques are seen in other limestone and marble buildings from the Archaic and Classical periods and contribute to the body of evidence (including 4th century BC building inscriptions) that documents an important aspect of Greek construction.

Introduction

In ancient Greece, the construction of a temple was an expensive undertaking. The cost to quarry, transport, and dress the stone blocks was significant and there were many opportunities for damage. Building inscriptions from the 4th century BC inform us that blocks were inspected upon arrival in the sanctuary, and officials could levy fines and require repair to, or replacement of, pieces that were damaged.[1] Archaeological excavations provide us with examples of architectural elements that have been damaged and repaired during their functional lifespan.[2] In the late 19th century, excavators on the Athenian Acropolis discovered fragments of sculpture, architecture, inscriptions, pottery, bronzes and small finds in layers of fill.[3] Hundreds of limestone architectural elements from Archaic and Early Classical buildings present a particularly useful body of evidence for studying techniques of construction and repair. The architectural blocks come from several limestone buildings from the 6th and 5th centuries BC, including two large Doric temples, known as the H-Architecture and the Old Temple of Athena, and several smaller buildings (A–E and others).[4] The blocks found in the fill had been deliberately broken up into relatively small pieces before being discarded, but with careful inspection it is possible to differentiate between the final act of demolition and earlier damage that was repaired. Among the hundreds of pieces that remain, over

a dozen limestone architectural elements from Building A and Building E have repairs that took place during the lifetime of the building and provide information about the nature and location of damage (what parts of the building were damaged, and what parts of individual blocks), and methods used to repair the blocks. Three different categories of intervention can be discerned: a replacement patch added to a damaged block where a piece had broken off, attempts to stabilize a block that had cracks or faults in its stone, and filling in the flaws on the surface of a finished block.

Type 1: replacement patch

The relatively soft limestones used for the small buildings are vulnerable to injury from a variety of causes, manmade and natural. The techniques of dressing blocks by hand and raising them into position on a building require care and expertise. The upper parts of the building, especially the entablature, were particularly vulnerable during construction because the blocks were completely finished before being lifted into position and projecting elements such as the geison seem to have been damaged quite frequently. In most cases, a small area was affected and was repaired by preparing a separate piece of limestone to serve as a patch and securing it with a piece of lead. Building A is a small Doric building dating to ca. 560–550 BC and over 60 blocks from its

Figure 1.1 Athens, Acropolis, Building A, reconstructed corner entablature (Acr. Inv. 4503). Photo N. L. Klein

Figure 1.2 Athens, Acropolis, Building A. Detail of repair to geison (Acr. Inv. 4503). Photo N. L. Klein

superstructure have been identified. Today, the best pieces of the entablature are on display in the new Acropolis Museum and the remaining blocks are in storerooms on the Acropolis (Figure 1.1). Among these are a dozen blocks with evidence of repair. As seen in the corner of Building A (Acr. Inv. 4503), a small piece was broken out of the geison crown molding on the flank and was repaired with piece of limestone attached with two lead pins, still in situ (Figure 1.2).

Other geison blocks show similar damage and repair. One lateral geison (Acr. Inv. 4390) was damaged at the edge of the soffit, and a piece of the mutule was fitted into place and secured with a lead pin (Figure 1.3). Another lateral geison (Acr. Inv. 7395) sustained damage along its lower front edge and a cutting was made into the lower taenia for a patch (Figure 1.4). Although the stone patch is now missing, a curved piece of lead still occupies an angled cutting (Figure 1.5). Given the malleability of lead and the softness of the limestone, it does not seem likely that a piece of lead could be threaded through such a cutting. This suggests that molten lead was poured into a hole made by two intersecting drill channels to secure the piece.[5] The position of the repair on the lower edge of the block and the hole drilled from the

Figure 1.3 Athens, Acropolis, Building A. Detail of repair to geison (Acr. Inv. 4390). Photo N. L. Klein

lower surface (which would have been inaccessible once the block was in place on the building) suggest that the repair was carried out before the block was lifted into position.

Building E, a small Doric structure from the early 5th century BC, was also made from limestone, although the quality of its stone is finer than Building A. Here, a lateral geison block (Acr. Inv. 4388) bears evidence of damage in three places: the crown molding and two sections of the face, including the drip, upper taenia and mutule (Figure 1.6).[6] The uppermost repair is visible as a cutting to hold pieces of the crown molding in two places, along the left

joint and further to the right, although the actual patches are now missing. In between these cuttings, the crown molding is present, indicating that it was usually cut from the same block. The second repair is a rectangular patch replacing the lower drip edge, upper taenia, and mutule along the left joint. The third repair is to the drip and lower taenia above the right mutule and via. In all three examples, stonemasons cut out the damaged section and inserted a patch. The lack of drill holes or traces of lead in the repair to the crown molding where the patches are missing suggests that mortar or stucco was used to keep them in place, although no trace of this remains. The patch above the right mutule and via is inserted into the face of the block and is supported from below, so it too may have needed only an adhesive to remain in place. The repair along the left joint had no support from below, although the adjacent geison would apply lateral pressure, so this patch would have required a stronger method of attachment. Unfortunately, there are no signs of drill holes,

Figure 1.4 Athens, Acropolis, Building A. View of geison soffit (Acr. Inv. 7395). Photo N. L. Klein

Figure 1.5 Athens, Acropolis, Building A. Detail of repair to lower edge of geison (Acr. Inv. 7395). Photo N. L. Klein

Figure 1.6 Athens, Acropolis, Building E. Detail of repair to geison (Acr. Inv. 4388). Photo N. L. Klein

lead, or stucco here either. While it is possible that some form of lead pin was used and is hidden by the patch, it would have been a different method of attachment than the molten lead used elsewhere to accomplish a similar repair.

Type 2: stablization of flawed stone

There are several blocks from Building A where lead pins or other means were used to hold together a block with a flaw in the stone, typically a crack running through it. Acr. Inv. 7390 is lateral geison block with the characteristic cavetto crown molding decorated with recurving leaves and mutular soffit below (Figure 1.7). The block is broken at back and left and has a crack running from top to bottom a few inches from its left side, so one could assume that the crack is associated with the destruction and disposal of the building, but a view of the top surface suggests otherwise. The preserved top surface is smoothly finished along the front edge and the crack can be seen continuing back from the face of the block (Figure 1.8). To the right of the crack is a small hole (ca. 2.0 cm from front, 0.5 cm wide) and further back is a slightly larger pair of holes (5.5 cm apart and 0.8–1.0 cm wide), which once held metal dowels to secure the lateral sima. Marks from a claw chisel at the right may also indicate a final dressing of the top surface to ensure the correct position of the sima. But the smaller

hole closer to the front edge cannot have had the same function and may indicate that the stonemason was aware of the crack and attempted to strengthen the block. Based on its size and position, this may have been one of a pair of holes into which a metal "staple" was placed to prevent the front edge of the block from fracturing along the fault line. Traces of stucco on the front of the block that cover the crack, the taenia, and mutule suggest that the block was flawed from the beginning, but that the metal "staple" and stucco made such defects less apparent.

Another lateral geison block from Building A (Acr. Inv. 4436) offers an example of a similar repair (Figure 1.9). This block also had several faults in the stone that are visible as faint lines running diagonally from top left to bottom right, especially through the taenia, diagonally across the via, and then back through the partial mutule at left. An attempt was made to stabilize the block on either side of the crack using molten lead. Three horizontal drill holes on the upper taenia, still filled with lead, are matched by three holes in the via below, but on the other side of the crack (Figure 1.10). This type of repair must have been done by drilling the holes and filling them with molten lead when the block was upside down, thus as the block was being finished and before it was raised into position. Traces of red paint on the taenia indicate that the repair was painted over in an attempt to hide it. In this case, the technique was successful since the

Figure 1.7 Athens, Acropolis, Building A. View of geison face (Acr. Inv. 7390). Photo N. L. Klein

Figure 1.8 Athens, Acropolis, Building A. View of geison top surface (Acr. Inv. 7390). Photo N. L. Klein

Figure 1.9 Athens, Acropolis, Building A. View of geison face (Acr. Inv. 4436). Photo N. L. Klein

Figure 1.10 Athens, Acropolis, Building A. View of geison soffit (Acr. Inv. 4436). Photo N. L. Klein

crack did not expand and the part of the block at risk for breaking away is still in place today.

A similar attempt is seen in another lateral geison (Acr. Inv. 4509) which has several visible cracks running through the block from top to bottom (Figure 1.11). A closer look at the mutule shows that a piece of lead with several branching arms was anchored in the bottom surface. One arm leads toward the via and another forward toward the face. By comparison with the previous block, it appears that the repair was also intended to hold the front of the mutule together. Intersecting drill holes spanning the crack were filled with molten lead while the block was upside down and prior to it being lifted into position on the building. Today, one part of the stone has broken away, but it is impossible to know if this is due to a failure of the repair or the final demolition and disposal of the block.

Type 3: filling

The third type of repair is where molten lead has been used to fill in the voids or surface flaws on an otherwise complete block. As currently reconstructed in the new Acropolis Museum, the corner triglyph of Building A (Acr. Inv. 4503) illustrates this exceptional technique. Voids on the upper taenia and interior of the glyphs have been filled with molten lead to create a smooth surface (Figure 1.12).

Figure 1.11 Athens, Acropolis, Building A. View of geison face (Acr. Inv. 4509). Photo N. L. Klein

Once again, this must have been done while this surface of the block was horizontal and thus before it was lifted into place. A dark patch at the bottom of the triglyph may be a trace of blue paint that was traditionally applied to triglyphs. Once the finished block was painted, the blue color would have successfully concealed the repair.

Figure 1.12 Athens, Acropolis, Building A. View of corner triglyph (Acr. Inv. 4503). Photo N. L. Klein

Architectural comparanda

In the Archaic period, other examples of architectural repairs are found on the earliest limestone temples on the island of Aegina as well as on the marble Siphnian Treasury at Delphi. Fragmentary remains from the sanctuary of Apollo at Kolonna attest to an early Doric temple made from limestone and dated ca. 600 BC.[7] A corner geison block from this temple has a stone patch on the soffit that appears to be attached with mortar, since there are no drill holes or pins visible.[8] On the eastern side of Aegina, the first temple of Aphaia, which Schwandner dates before 570 BC, is also made of limestone. Blocks from the geison, architrave, and anta capital show signs on having been damaged and repaired during the initial construction process.[9] As on the Acropolis, three different techniques were used to attach small patches to the blocks: lead pins, molten lead, and mortar. The lateral geison blocks typically have mutules with guttae carved from the same stone, but two examples have repairs to a single gutta. One geison block (Nr. 159) has a cylindrical gutta that was carved separately and attached with a central lead pin.[10] A second example (Nr. 171/172) has a square patch held in place with mortar.[11] One architrave

block from the exterior entablature (Nr. 137) with damage to the taenia along the right joint has a small patch secured with mortar in a manner very similar to that seen on Building E.[12] A second architrave block from the interior entablature of the temple (Nr. 263) has a gutta attached with a lead pin, similar to the repair to geison Nr. 159.[13] Finally, the crown molding of an anta capital (Nr. 113/114) had broken off and was patched with molten lead.[14] Schwandner described the attempt to join the two pieces with two drilled channels, one passing through the patch and into the block with the second channel rising vertically. Whatever the intention, the result was not completely successful, since the lead appears to have flowed into a space between the two pieces and it was decided to leave the exterior lead pieces in place to secure the patch. In his evaluation of the use of lead pins or mortar to attach a patch, Schwandner suggests that lead was used for delicate repairs to the blocks before they were in position on the building, while those inserted with mortar could have been done once the block was in place. The Siphnian Treasury at Delphi, a marble Ionic building dating before 525 BC, shows evidence of a similar technique used to repair a marble block. Here a block with an elaborate Ionic egg-and-dart molding was repaired with molten lead.[15] The position of the patch and the direction in which the lead was poured indicate that the repair took place while the block was upside down, before it was lifted into position. These examples suggest that the techniques for attaching a piece or patch to a damaged block seen on the Acropolis, lead pins, molten lead, mortar, were commonly used for both limestone and marble construction in the 6th century BC.

In the Classical period, the next generation of temple builders would replace lead pins with ones made of iron. In the last quarter of the 5th century BC, an egg-and-dart molding in the entablature of the Erechtheion was repaired with a marble patch secured with an iron dowel.[16] The late fifth century BC temple at Segesta used molten lead to attach a patch to a corner geison, but iron pins for individual guttae.[17] Although molten lead would continue to be used as a covering for iron dowels and clamps, iron pins and dowels replaced lead, perhaps because the builders had learned from experience that lead was not strong enough to resist any significant force in tension or compression.[18]

Evidence from building inscriptions

Of the extant blocks that preserve evidence of repairs, many of the examples discussed above belong to the geison course and were damaged during the building process. Building inscriptions of the 4th century BC from the sanctuaries of Athena Alea at Tegea, Zeus at Lebadeia, and Apollo on the island of Delos provide further evidence of the risk of damage to architectural blocks during the construction process as well as the oversight and penalties assessed to the contractors.[19] An inscription from Delos, *ID* 104 (24), describes the damage to one temple including several places where the geison was damaged (exterior corners, raking geison, interior porch) and repair required, along with a monetary fine in some cases.[20] One of the extant corner geison blocks from the Great Temple of Apollo sustained damage to the crown molding along the front edge and a separate piece of marble was carved and attached using iron Pi-clamps.[21]

Conclusions

This examination of architectural repairs identifies several different methods that were used to patch, stabilize, and fill in damaged areas of individual blocks in the Archaic and Classical periods. Evidence from the archaic limestone buildings on the Acropolis, the early temples of Apollo and Aphaia on Aegina, and the Siphnian Treasury at Delphi, demonstrate a preference for mortar or small pieces of worked or molten lead. Although lead's intrinsic properties of malleability and low melting temperature make it easy to use, they also make it a weak and unsatisfactory means to join architectural pieces. Builders were experimenting with mortar in the 6th century and, by the end of the 5th BC, lead pins were subsequently replaced by iron in the Erechtheion and the unfinished temple at Segesta in Sicily. The location of the repairs and the use of molten lead (which must respond to gravity) support the hypothesis that some blocks were damaged during construction and required repair before they were lifted into position on the building. Building contracts, which are typically created during the construction process, also testify to oversight of supervisors in the sanctuaries who required a repair or patch to damaged blocks already in position on the building.

The contribution of this study goes beyond documentation of repair techniques. By paying close attention to individual blocks and distinguishing between damage that occurred during the construction process and the final demolition or disposal of a building, we can now assemble several cases studies to determine more precisely the timing and methods of architectural repairs. The evidence suggests that craftsmen had to respond to less than perfect stone as well as injury to blocks, either as a consequence of a mistake in cutting or lifting, or perhaps later damage that required a significant effort to dismantle, remove, and repair parts of a building. Subsequent application of paint and stucco would have hidden the repairs from view, but it is clear that not every piece of a building could be declared flawless. The examples of early Greek architectural repairs reflect the expertise and ingenuity of the craftsmen who worked to create buildings that would be acceptable not only to sanctuary officials, but perhaps also the deities to whom they were offered.

Notes

1 See Burford 1969, pp. 91–100, for summary of buildings inscriptions from Tegea, Delos, Delphi, and Lebadeia that include fines for damage and work being redone at the expense of the contractor.
2 Hellmann 2002, pp. 95–98, discusses many examples of architectural repairs with illustrations and references.
3 Kavvadias and Kawerau 1906; Bundgaard 1974. See also discussion of stratigraphy and dating of layers in Stewart 2008, with summary of previous scholarship.
4 The primary publications of the architectural remains from the small limestone buildings are Wiegand 1904 and Heberdey 1919.
5 Wright 2005, p. 235, comments on the low melting point of lead, which facilitated its use in a fluid state; p. 278, Melting point 327°C, Hot Working Temperature ~20+°C, Specific gravity 11.37, Hardness (Moh's Scale) 1.5, Relative Compressive Strength (-), Relative Tensile Strength (-).
6 Wiegand 1904, p. 171 and fig. 170.
7 Hoffelner 1999.
8 Hoffelner 1999, p. 24, pl. 33, 1.
9 Schwandner 1985, pp. 130–131.
10 Schwandner 1985, Nr. 159, pp. 43, 130, fig. 26; pl. 12,1. All other guttae were carved directly from the same stone as the mutule.
11 Schwandner 1985, Nr. 171/172, pp. 50, 130, fig. 31, pl. 14,1.
12 Schwandner 1985, Nr. 137, pp. 33, 130, fig. 18, pl. 10.1.
13 Schwandner 1985, Nr. 263, pp. 60–62, 130, fig. 40; pl. 18,1.
14 Schwandner 1985, Nr. 113/114, pp. 22, 25, 130, fig. 12, pl. 33,5.
15 Hellmann 2002, p. 72, *FdD* II, p. 165 no. B5, fig. 78.
16 Hellmann 2002, p. 97, fig. 113; Paton et. al. 1927, pp. 206–215, figs. 141–142.
17 Mertens 1984, p. 24, pl. 36,6 (repair to corner geison); p. 38, pl. 36, 4 (guttae attached with iron pins).
18 See discussion in Orlandos 1968, pp. 117–118; Schwandner 1985, pp. 131–132. Observing the use of lead clamps at the corner of the first temple of Aphaia, Schwandner expresses his amazement: 'Das Vetrauen in dieses weiche Metall kann uns heute nur verwundern.'
19 See above, note 1. Tegea: *IG* V 2,6, ll. 15ff.; Lebadeia *IG* VII, 3073.15, 29ff.; Delos *ID* 104 (24)
20 Summarized in Hellmann 2002, pp. 96–97.
21 *EAD* 12, fig. 48; see also Hellmann 2002, fig. 62.

References

Bundgaard, J. A. 1974. *The excavation of the Athenian Acropolis 1882–1890: the original drawings, edited from the papers of Georg Kawerau*, Copenhagen.

Burford, A. 1969. *The Greek Temple Builders at Epidauros. A social and economic study of building in the Asklepian sanctuary, during the fourth and early third centuries B.C.*, Liverpool.

EAD 12 = F. Courby, *Les temples d'Apollon (Exploration Archéologique de Délos* 12), Paris, 1931.

FdD II = G. Daux and E. Hansen, *Le Trésor de Siphnos (Fouilles de Delphes* II), Athens, 1987.

Heberdey, R. 1919. *Altattische Porosskulptur. Ein Beitrag zur Geschichte der archaischen griechischen Kunst*, Vienna.

Hellmann, M.-C. 2002. *L'architecture grecque 1. Les principes de la construction (Les Manuels d'Art et d'Archéologie Antiques)*, Paris.

Hoffelner, K. 1999. *Das Apollon-Heiligtum. Tempel, Altäre, Temenosmauer, Thearion (Alt-Ägina I,3)*, Mainz am Rhein.

Kavvadias, P. and G. Kawerau. 1906. *Die Ausgrabung der Akropolis vom Jahr 1885 bis zum 1890*, Athens.

Mertens, D. 1984. *Der Tempel von Segesta und die dorische Baukunst des griechischen Westens in klassischer Zeit*, Mainz am Rhein.

Orlandos, A. K. 1968. *Les matériaux de construction et la technique architecturale des anciens Grecs. Première et Seconde partie (École Française d'Athènes Travaux et Mémoires XVI bis)*, Paris.

Paton, J. M., G. P. Stevens, L. D. Caskey, and H. N. Fowler. 1927. *The Erechtheum*, Cambridge, MA.

Schwandner, E.-L. 1985. *Der ältere Porostempel der Aphaia auf Aegina (Deutsches Archäologisches Institut Denkmäler Antiker Architektur Band 16)*, Berlin.

Stewart, A. 2008. "The Persian and Carthaginian Invasions of 480 B.C.E. and the Beginning of the Classical Style: Part 1, The Stratigraphy, Chronology, and Significance of the Acropolis Deposits," *American Journal of Archaeology* 112, pp. 377–412.

Turner, L. A. 1994. "The History, Monuments and Topography of Ancient Lebadeia in Beoetia, Greece" (diss. Univ. of Pennsylvania).

Wiegand, T. 1904. *Die archäische Poros-Architektur der Akropolis zu Athen*, Cassel and Leipzig.

Wright, G. R. H. 2005. *Ancient Building Technology (Technology and Change in History vol. 7/1)*, Leiden and Boston.

Tools From the House
of Mikion and Menon

Barbara Tsakirgis

Small finds from a house on the edge of the Athenian Agora indicate that the house was used by sculptors. The evidence for this is presented here: worked marble fragments, and working tools, in particular lead strips. This new evidence was obtained by examining the contents of storage tins in the basement of the Stoa of Attalos, the storage facility of the excavations of the Athenian Agora, and a close reading of the original excavators' notebooks.

Excavation of the House of Mikion and Menon

In 1932, in the second season of American excavations in and around the Athenian Agora, Dorothy Burr (Thompson) explored the edge of the northwest slope of the Areopagos, southwest of the ancient public square. While her primary focus was an oval hut which she interpreted as a Geometric period house that was later converted to a Proto-Attic shrine, Burr also investigated an adjacent area very disturbed by Roman-period construction, robbing, and modern intrusions.[1] There she excavated a cistern filled in the early Hellenistic period, referred to as the "Demeter Cistern" because of numerous terracotta figures in the deposit.[2] The late Classical building containing the cistern was so roiled up by the later activities that Burr's excavations in the region were abandoned after only one season. The area was not excavated again until 1968, when Stella Grobel (Miller-Collett) returned to reveal the building now known as the "House of Mikion and Menon," a house named for inscribed objects found in its earliest and latest contexts.[3] Mikion's name is punched on a bone stylus recovered from the first occupation of the house just before the mid 5th century BC, while Menon's name is written on several vessels in the deposit in a second cistern and a well that were used in the first half of the 3rd century BC.[4] Thus the House of Mikion and Menon had about two centuries of use before it was demolished (Figure 2.1).

The House of Mikion and Menon sits at the crossroads where one street which exits the southwest corner of the

Agora intersects with a second which runs east-west, ultimately to the Piraeus Gate; the house has an irregular footprint because the streets do not cross at right angles.[5] A triangular shrine lies on the other side of the street from the house, and to the south lies the so-called Industrial District, where there is much evidence of stone working.[6] The walls of the House of Mikion and Menon are founded on a substantial layer of broken pottery and debris dated to the first quarter of the 5th century BC; a few sherds date this layer slightly later than the debris normally encountered in the deposits associated with the immediate clean-up of the city in the aftermath of the Persian sack.[7] The building is one of the many residential and industrial structures built in the vicinity of the emerging Classical Agora in the wake of the Persian invasion of Athens.[8] The central element of the house's layout is a roughly trapezoidal courtyard where two cisterns were constructed, the Demeter Cistern and a second, later cistern, published by Grobel (Miller-Collett) as Menon's cistern. No vestibule was found, but an entrance directly from the street and into the courtyard has been posited, correctly in my opinion. Rooms open to the northeast and southwest of the courtyard, and a second courtyard may have opened to the north of the first. This second central space has rooms dependent on it to the northeast, but since the entire house was not excavated and the remains of this part of the house are exiguous, the complete layout of this northern segment is unknown.

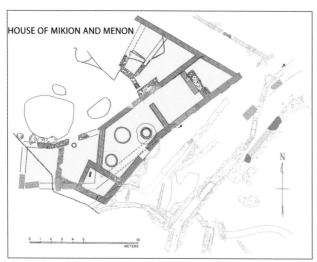

Figure 2.1 Athenian Agora, House of Mikion and Menon, plan. Courtesy American School of Classical Studies at Athens: Agora Excavations

Many of the rooms of the House of Mikion and Menon were found by both Burr (Thompson) and Grobel (Miller-Collett) almost carpeted with marble dust and chips and the same material made up some of the fill of the Demeter Cistern; in her publication of the cistern's contents, Burr speculated that "sculptors lived nearby."[9] Several works of unfinished sculpture and fragments of a marble basin were recovered from the rooms of the house and from the Demeter Cistern. They likely were practice pieces or intended for reuse for smaller works of sculpture.[10] In and among these products of the marble worker's trade were also recovered a number of tools, some of which were recognized at the time of excavation. Others only recently came to light after I reexamined the tins in which the context pottery has been stored. In this paper, I present the tools, discuss their possible use in the craft of carving and finishing marble sculpture, and I consider the context of the house as it was used in the daily life of the resident sculptors.

The two cisterns in the courtyard of the house appear to have been roughly contemporaneous in their use, although the Demeter Cistern was probably filled a little before its neighbor.[11] While Menon's cistern was very full of pottery and packed at its top with debris from the house after its destruction and abandonment, the Demeter Cistern contained relatively little material. Much of the fill consisted of terracotta figurines, associated by Burr (Thompson) with a shrine of Demeter, thus the name she gave to the cistern.[12] Yet such a sanctuary is not to be seen in the simple dwelling containing the cisterns: the closest confirmed sanctuary of Demeter is the City Eleusinion above the opposite corner of the Agora. Given all the available evidence of its size, construction and contents, the building is undoubtedly a house and a workshop.

Tools and Related Finds

Catalogue:

IL 1507 Lead Strip[13] (Figure 2.2)
Find spot: House of Mikion and Menon, pit E
L 0.154 m.   Max Th 0.007 m.
Strip of lead, square in section. One end flattened with rounded edge. Other end pointed but slightly blunted with signs of use.
IL 1508 Lead Strip (Figure 2.3)
Find spot: House of Mikion and Menon; embedded on top of layer of crushed stone (layer 3)
L 0.086 m.   Max Th 0.005 m.
Strip of lead similar to IL 1507. One end flattened with curved edge. Other end broken.
IL 1509 Lead Strip
Find spot: House of Mikion and Menon (Area E, layer 5)
L 0.128 m.   Max Th 0.009 m.
Strip of lead similar to IL 1507 but irregular in section. One end flattened with rounded edge. Other end pointed with rounded tip.
IL 1510 Lead Strip (Figure 2.4)
Find spot: House of Mikion and Menon (Area E, layer 3)

Figure 2.2 Athenian Agora, lead strip IL 1507. Courtesy American School of Classical Studies at Athens: Agora Excavations

Figure 2.3 Athenian Agora, lead strip IL 1508. Courtesy American School of Classical Studies at Athens: Agora Excavations

Figure 2.4 Athenian Agora, lead strip IL 1510. Courtesy American School of Classical Studies at Athens: Agora Excavations

Figure 2.5 Athenian Agora, lead strip IL 1511. Courtesy American School of Classical Studies at Athens: Agora Excavations

Figure 2.6 Athenian Agora, lead strip IL 1513. Courtesy American School of Classical Studies at Athens: Agora Excavations

L 0.076 m.   Max Th 0.005 m.
Strip of lead similar to IL 1507. Square in section. One end narrows to a blunted point. Other end curved into a hook and narrowing to a point. Pointed end is striated on several sides.
IL 1511 Lead Strip (Figure 2.5)
Find spot: House of Mikion and Menon, (Area B, layer 2)
L 0.147 m.
Strip of lead similar to IL 1507. Square in section at center. Both ends narrow to blunted points.
IL 1513 Lead Strip (Figure 2.6)
Find spot: House of Mikion and Menon (Area A, below floor 2)
L 0.094 m.   Max Th 0.006 m.
Strip of lead similar to IL 1507. Roughly square in section at center. One end narrows to round section with point. Point blunted with use. Other end broken. Tool is slightly bent and curved.
IL 1514 Lead Strip
Find spot: Street outside of the House of Mikion and Menon; above road 2a, at intersection of streets.
L 0.045 m.   Max Th 0.003 m.
Strip of lead similar to IL 1507. One end tapers to a point. One end broken.
IL 1943 Lead Strip (Figure 2.7, 2.8)
Find spot: Demeter Cistern. Recovered from box of context pottery in 2000.
L 0.069 m.   Max Th 0.006 m.
Strip of lead similar to IL 1507. Square in section. Slightly flattened at one end. Tapered to other end.
ST 983 Stone Pounder (Figure 2.9)
Find spot: Demeter Cistern. Recovered from box of context pottery in 2000.
Pres. L 0.076 m. Pres. W 0.065 m.   Th 0.037 m.
Dark grey stone with smooth surfaces and rounded end. Other edge broken in numerous small planes.
ST 984 Pumice Polisher

Figure 2.7 Athenian Agora, lead strip IL 1943. Courtesy American School of Classical Studies at Athens: Agora Excavations

Figure 2.8 Athenian Agora, lead strip, IL 1943, detail of end. Courtesy American School of Classical Studies at Athens: Agora Excavations

Figure 2.9 Athenian Agora, stone pounder ST 983. Courtesy American School of Classical Studies at Athens: Agora Excavations

Find spot: Demeter Cistern. Recovered from box of context pottery in 2000.
Pres. L 0.028 m.   Pres. Th 0.021 m.
Piece of pumice with a flattish base. Smoothed into several planes toward a rounded end.
ST 933: Stone Polisher
Find spot: House of Mikion and Menon, above floor 3
Pres. L 0.104 m.
Dense grey stone. Oblong stone with one rounded end. Other end broken into rough plane. Broad sides smoothed from rubbing.
BI 819 Bone Stylus
Find spot: House of Mikion and Menon, Area B, layer IV
L 0.05 m. W 0.005 m.   Th 0.003 m.
Flat strip of bone, sharpened into a point at one end. Blunt at other end. Punched into surface on one side:]ΟΜΙΚΟΝΕΠΟΙΕ[ΣΕ , with faintly incised lines separating each letter.
ο Μικιων εποιε[σε
BI 817 Bone Stylus
Find spot: House of Mikion and Menon, trench A, road IIa
L pres. 0.083 m. Diam 0.003 m.   W (flat end) 0.007 m.
Thin, round sectioned piece of bone. Long spatulate end.
BI 818 Bone Stylus

Find spot: House of Mikion and Menon, below floor IV
L 0.064 m.   Diam 0.0045 m.
Thin, round sectioned piece of bone. One end is pointed. Other
   end broken away.
S 195 Unfinished Sculpture[14]
Find spot: House of Mikion and Menon, Demeter Cistern (Deposit
   F 16:1)
H: 0.135   W: 0.078   Th: 0.055
marble
Unfinished seated figure, possibly the Mother of the Gods
S 201 Unfinished, possibly practice Sculpture[15]
Find spot: House of Mikion and Menon, Demeter Cistern (Deposit
   F 16:1)
PL: 0.125   PW: 0.098   Th: 0.044
marble
Fragment of a basin, reused as a practice piece. On the convex
   exterior surface of the fragment, a head facing left is carved
   in relief. The outline of the head is rendered with a point and
   the surface has been roughly smoothed with a claw chisel.

How were the Tools Used?

While the working equipment used by ancient sculptors is
known from gravestones of the Roman period, few actual
tools have been recovered from the excavations of sculptors'
workshops in the Greek world.[16] The dearth of evidence
for chisels and other metal objects is hardly surprising; a
sculptor or even a scavenger would have taken away any
bronze or iron equipment when a workshop was abandoned;
old tools and bent or broken pieces could be melted down
and recast into new tools or other objects.[17] From the
examination of the surface of surviving Greek sculpture
and the funerary monuments of Roman sculptors we are
fairly certain of the form of the punches, points, and chisels
used by ancient artists, although debate has been focused
on the configuration and the date of introduction of certain
tools, especially the claw chisel.[18] Olga Palagia and Carl
Nylander have studied the surfaces of both early Greek
and late period Egyptian sculpture to determine when and
where the claw chisel was invented.[19] In lieu of surviving
metal tools, scholars are forced to refer to modern chisels
when illustrating the equipment of a sculptor's workshop.[20]

The workshop of Pheidias, discovered to the west of the
Temple of Zeus at Olympia, is exceptional for the detailed
view it gives us of a sculptor's studio.[21] The workshop
contained both detritus from the creation of the great image
of Zeus and some discarded tools. The excavators recovered
from the remains flat lead objects with complex curved edges,
probably templates, and numerous lead strips very similar to
those catalogued above.[22] Similar lead tools have been found
at a number of sites around Greece, and because the strips
are so humble in material and form, probably many more
have been recovered than have been published. In several
cases the strips have been recovered in contexts where craft
activity is evident, such as in the working layers of the Temple

of Aphaia at Aegina, the Temple of Poseidon at Isthmia,
and both in a bronze workshop near the sanctuary of Zeus
at Nemea and in the construction levels of the 4th century
temple.[23] At Aigina, based on associated stone working chips,
Bankel determined that the strips were used while working
the stone for the temple; he was the first to propose that the
lead strips were pencils. At Isthmia, because of associated
metal debris, Rostoker and Gebhard assumed that the lead
strips were used in the manufacture of metal objects; Zimmer
assumed the same for Nemea, although the context for the
lead tool cited by Miller suggests a use similar to that of
the lead strips recovered from the Athenian Agora. The
lead strips are not chisels; lead is too malleable to be struck
with a mallet and is too soft to cut either the hard crystals
of marble or softer limestone. A similar lead strip, although
thinner in form, was recovered from the fill of the Keyhole
Foundry of the Athenian Agora, and another is noted in a
discussion of Hellenistic pottery production at Pergamon.[24]

In his study of the lead strips found at Aegina, Bankel
suggests they were used by the architects and sculptors
as pencils, in order to make preliminary sketches on the
stone.[25] This identification of the lead strips as pencils has
been accepted by Schiering and Zimmer in their respective
publications of Pheidias' and bronzeworkers' sculpting
studios.[26] The findspots of the lead strips in Athens, within
a house and workshop clearly occupied by stone sculptors,
provides further support to the association of the lead strips
with stoneworking. A magnified view of the tip of one of
the lead strips shows how the point is blunted, possibly
from having been drawn along the hard surface of the
marble (Figure 2.8). Several other lead strips were recovered
from the area of the Athenian Agora and at least two of
these strips were found in association with stone chips, in
contexts similar to that of the strips found in the House of
Mikion and Menon.[27] If the strips are pencils, as yet no
sculpture or unfinished works from Athens or elsewhere
in Greece has been seen to bear the marks of lead pencils.
Such preliminary sketches would be removed very early in
the sculpting process as the artist carved away the topmost
layers of marble on which he drew.[28] No stone reliefs bearing
traces of sketches are preserved in the Greek world, but
the analogous process of rendering a preliminary drawing
for a relief carving is known from numerous examples in
the Egyptian world. In these sketches, the drafting is done
with black paint.[29] An alternative type of drawing tool in
the Mediterranean was likely a charcoal stick (made from
a grapevine), used by artists for many centuries and still in
use today. Such sticks provide fine, consistent points for
drawing, ease of use, are inexpensive and readily available.

Several of the lead strips found at the Aphaia Temple
were rolled at one end to form a loop. Bankel suggests that
this allowed the sculptor to wear the strip on a string, perhaps
around his neck or on his belt. None of the examples from
the House of Mikion and Menon is bent in this way, nor are

any of those at Olympia. A single lead strip (IL 1842, Figure 2.10) found in the Agora excavations, in the industrial and commercial zone north of the public square, is fashioned with a rolled end.

Since some lead strips were recovered in workshops other than those belonging to stone sculptors, likely they were used widely and for many purposes. Zimmer speculates that the lead strips found in a bronze-working context at Nemea could have been used either as pencils or as raw material for use in creating the bronze alloy.[30] It seems an unnecessary step to form the lead into narrow, square-sectioned strips if it is only to be used as an ingredient in the molten metal to be cast, yet perhaps it was molded into units in preparation for sale. Such preparation might have been a convenience for marketing (presumably by weight), even though in some instances they were only to be melted into and around the clamps used in monumental architectural construction. The tapered form obviates any use of the strips as a straight edge, to be employed in the finishing of a block.[31] Yet lead was sometimes pounded into a template, such as the one found in excavation at Mon Repos on Corfu.[32] The lead strip from the Keyhole Foundry in Athens has bits of bronze embedded in its spatulate end; Mattusch suggests this may indicate its use as a material for inlays.[33]

The identification of the lead strips as pencils is by no means certain; as noted above, the Egyptians drew on stone with paint and more modern sculptors produce preliminary sketches with charcoal. Actual pencils are fashioned with graphite, a soft carbon, but never lead, as both the English term "lead pencil" or German "Bleistifte" implies (the modern terms are a result of an early misunderstanding about the chemical composition of graphite, an allotropic form of carbon). If the lead strips are not pencils as Bankel has suggested, then what are they? Their common square section and tapering shape prove that they are not simply stray fragments of lead, leftover after some process; they were clearly fashioned into a regular and repeated shape. Their common association with the debris left after stone, metal, and pottery working (especially the first), both in Athens and elsewhere, demands that their function be associated with stoneworking, and occasionally other craft activity. The lead strips may have been used as tools for sculpting material softer than stone. Their pointed and spatulate ends would have served for molding and providing detail to the wax or clay models with which the sculptors first thought out their compositions and designs. These *typoi* would have preceded the sculptures, stone or metal, in their creation, but would have been crafted in the same workshops where the final images were made.

Nancy Klein's paper in this volume details numerous repairs evident in Athenian monumental stone architecture and many of which were achieved with lead. The lead strips could have served as the raw form of the repairs Klein has noted in the monumental blocks, the pointed or spatulate

end of the strips perhaps prefashioned by either the stone workers or the metal workers who separated the lead from silver during the refining process near silver mines. The pointed end of the strip could have served to be inserted into a hole drilled for the purpose of the repair and the spatulate end could have been inserted into the interstices between two pieces of marble used in a repair; however, Klein notes that most of the replacement patches, stabilization of flawed stone, and the filling of voids was rendered with molten lead rather than with pre-formed strips. Also indicative that the strips were seen as tools rather than as simply raw material are the loops fashioned at the end of some of the strips and the fact that two of them, one from Isthmia and one from Athens were inscribed. The lead strip (IL 242) found in the construction debris at Nemea bears the inscription ΛΑΚΤ and a lead pencil recovered in the Agora from an unknown context in inscribed (ΜΙΠΝ [N.B. N is retrograde]).[34] At present, the weight of the evidence suggests to me that the lead strips were used as some kind of tool, perhaps a multipurpose one, in the creative process. Given the common practice of sketching on stone with charcoal, Bankel's explanation of their use as pencils is the least convincing. More likely, the strips were used variously by artists working in different media for shaping or pressing soft materials like clay or wax. When the need arose, sculptors might even have melted the strips in order to repair broken or flawed stonework.

The two large stone tools (ST 983, ST 933) recovered from the House of Mikion and Menon are more enigmatic in their use (Figure 2.9). Both are too heavy to have been used to strike the marble directly; such action would only shatter the marble's crystalline structure and thus bruise it. Using either stone as a mallet with which to strike now missing chisels is also unlikely, as the resulting vibration caused by stone hitting metal would quickly tire the sculptor. Small, delicate strokes against a chisel may have been achieved with such a tool to add detail to a small area, but large portions of a sculpture cannot have been worked with the stones as mallets. That both stones show damage at one end indicates that they may have been used for striking, but there is no way to determine what was hit with them. Alternatively, the stones may have served as polishers. Stones with similar dimensions have been recovered from numerous building sites in Egypt, and on the basis of funerary reliefs which depict sculptors at work, the stones have been recognized as polishers.[35] The stones can be identified as tools, but their use uncertain.

The faceted piece of pumice is more easily identified. As a soft abrasive, it represents the end of the sculpting process, just as the pencils represent the commencement of the artistic enterprise. After the preliminary sketches, after the carving with punch and ever finer chisels and rasps, the sculptor would have smoothed his finished work with abrasives.[36] Two stone abraders, made of sandstone, were

Figure 2.10 Athenian Agora, lead strip IL 1842. Courtesy American School of Classical Studies at Athens: Agora Excavations

found in a Roman period sculptor's workshop not far from the earlier residence of Mikion and Menon and represent the tools used in the early stages of smoothing and finishing sculpture.[37] The pumice, with its softer fabric, is evidence of the final steps in the production of sculpture. Like the sandstone polishers, the pumice is worked into a faceted form, perhaps intentional, so that each small side could be used to polish a limited area, or perhaps accidental, so that the facets are similar to the flat planes left on a rubber eraser after extensive pencils marks are removed from paper.[38]

The bone styluses, including that labeled with Mikion's name, are of a type ubiquitous throughout the ancient world; they are found in ordinary houses as well as in industrial establishments, in public as well as private contexts.[39] Whether flat, like BI 819, or round in section, like BI 817 and B 818, the styluses could have been used on a wax tablet, the pointed end for writing and the blunt end for erasing the words and images scratched into the wax of a tablet. Since the bone is far softer than marble, it would have served no purpose in the carving or finishing of stone sculpture. Whether Mikion or his relations sketched designs for their sculptures on such wax tablets, we can only guess. Mikion's desire to identify his bone stylus by punching his name in its surface is possibly paralleled by the inscribed lead tool (IL 1079) cited above.

The House of Mikion and Menon as a Workshop

The combining of a house and a workshop is known from both literary and epigraphical sources.[40] Demosthenes, when taking account of his purloined inheritance, notes that his father owned both furniture and sword factories connected with houses (Dem. 27.9), and the father of Lysias had a shield factory, also connected to a house (Lys. 12.18). Numerous inscriptions, many of them *horoi* pertaining to mortgages, refer to houses and their attached *ergasteria*; the House of Mikion and Menon appears to be just such a house, combining spaces for both living and working (Figure 2.1).[41] The absence of a vestibule in the house is likely a response to the dual identity of the building; as a place of residence, it should have a vestibule to serve as a buffer between the outside world and the interior of the house, but in a place of work and probably also of commerce, the

vestibule would be superfluous. The courtyard in which the cisterns are located is unencumbered by colonnades which would limit the amount of space and light necessary for the sculptors to work comfortably on their pieces. If Alison Burford is correct that the artists generally had some ready made goods on hand, such pieces to be bought off the shelf might have been stored in the court or the rooms which opened off of it.[42] The rooms which open onto the court were found paved, as is the open yard, with marble chips and dust; they served as work spaces for the artists when the weather was inclement. The putative second court may have served as a focus for the private life of the generations of sculptors, but too little of this space was excavated to be confident of its form and use. That people lived in the building, in some comfort, is suggested by the fragments of painted and drafted stucco which was recovered from the Demeter Cistern and which once must have adorned the walls of a room there.[43]

The plan of the House of Mikion and Menon as it is so far revealed has distinct similarities both to the Roman era sculptor's workshop at Aphrodisias and to several industrial establishments excavated on the periphery of the Athenian public square.[44] Peter Rockwell describes this 3rd century AD studio as "cramped," with a decided lack of space and privacy and a difficult access for large blocks of stone.[45] All of these descriptors fit equally well for the rooms and working conditions in the House of Mikion and Menon, where the sculptors may have had the slight advantage of working on small pieces, such as the unfinished plaque of the Mother of the Gods and the votive relief which were recovered from the Demeter Cistern.[46] That Mikion, his successors in the house and his contemporaries elsewhere near the Agora had no commodious space in which sizeable blocks of stone could be stored may mean that this family of sculptors specialized in smaller works, or that blocks of marble were stored elsewhere and brought to the sculptor's studio only when a large statue was to be created.

The lead strips associated with this workshop could support the idea that the family worked largely on small scale works. While large-scale sculptures typically were blocked out at the quarry, as we see with the famous unfinished *kouroi* in the quarries on Naxos, smaller works were started only in the studio itself. A sketch (with charcoal) may have helped the artist conceive of his work on the surface of the stone, especially when the finished piece was to be a relief, a hybrid between a two and three dimensional sculpture. Preliminary sketches could be especially necessary for carving to be done from re-used pieces of stone, such as the marble basin recovered from the House of Mikion and Menon. The sculptor may have preferred to sketch an image on the curved surface of the basin before he started carving away the stone. **The somewhat linear composition of relief sculpture may have called for preliminary sketching more than was deemed necessary for free-standing sculpture.**

Another similarity between this Classical era Athenian house and the Roman Imperial studio at Aphrodisias is its ready access to the street. Rockwell conjectured that the sculptors of Aphrodisias worked in a studio which was also a shop, and the same conclusion can be drawn about the House of Mikion and Menon. Passers-by on the main road out of the Agora could stop to purchase a ready made work or easily find the artists in order to commission them to create a specific piece. The later workshop in Aphrodisias has an analogous position, near the Agora of Aphrodisias and the Odeon.

Conclusion

The House of Mikion and Menon has not yet been fully excavated, and what has been found was rather fragmentary. Nonetheless the scant remains provide a unique look at the working and living quarters of Classical Greek stone carvers. The contemporaries of Polykleitos and Pheidias who lived there built their house along a major thoroughfare which exited the Agora and ran through a densely populated area of the ancient city. Close to both the Acropolis and the Kerameikos cemetery, the sculptors who lived and worked in the building could have easily and quickly served both public and private commissions. While the unfinished works recovered from the house were undoubtedly intended to be purchased by private individuals, living in such a centrally located house the members of this artisanal family could easily walk to the site of public as well as private projects. Given the discovery of both marble debris and humble equipment for the commencing and the completion of the sculpting process, some of the work was accomplished in the relative comfort of home. How comfortable that home was with gritty marble dust in the air and sharp shards of marble underfoot is questionable, and the conditions lead one to conclude that with the open drains of antiquity and the *koprones* located in public streets outside houses, residential districts were decidedly less comfortable in antiquity than they are today.

Acknowledgements

Exploring this unusual topic has led me to seek the help of the many scholars working in and around the Athenian Agora. I would like to express my gratitude to Kathleen Lynch, Susan Rotroff, and Andrew Stewart for their help with Classical deposits, the manufacture of Hellenistic pottery, and sculptors, respectively. Thanks also to our editor Margie Miles for her invitation to include my paper in this volume and to Rocco Leonardis for his comments on an earlier draft. Any problems and mistakes that remain are my own. Lastly, I offer this short article as a belated but heartfelt thank-you to Jerome J. Pollitt, my undergraduate advisor. While I will never equal his heights in the study of Greek sculpture, I can present this bit of evidence for how some of that sculpture might have been produced.

Notes

1   The oval building and its contents: Burr 1933; her interpretation has been questioned (Papadopoulos 2003).
2   The contents of the Demeter Cistern (Agora deposit F 16: 1): Thompson 1954, pp. 87–107. An early assessment of the date of its fill is found in Thompson 1934, p. 317. The date of its fill is confirmed in Rotroff 1983, p. 263; Thompson, Thompson and Rotroff 1987, pp. 184–185; Rotroff 1997, p. 451.
3   For the initial publication of the house, Shear 1969.
4   Second cistern and its well (Deposit F 16:8): Miller 1974; Rotroff 1997, p. 451. Plutarch (*Per.* 31) names Menon as the assistant of Pheidias who accused the great sculptor of theft of gold intended for the image of Athena Parthenos. If Pheidias's assistant was a member of the family resident in this house, he could have been the grandfather or some other predecessor of the Menon who scratched his name into several vessels found in the second cistern.
5   For the street system of ancient Athens and these two streets, see Costaki 2006, pp. 300–302 and Theocharaki 2011.
6   For the abaton, Lalonde 1968; for the Industrial District, Young 1951.
7   See Shear 1993 for a detailed discussion of the post Persian clean-up.
8   Other houses around the Agora of similar date include the House of Simon (Thompson 1960), the classical block on the north slope of the Areopagos (Thompson and Wycherley 1972, pp. 177–179), and many of the houses and shops in the Industrial District (Young 1951).
9   Burr 1933, p. 87.
10 The unfinished sculptures from the Demeter Cistern include a seated figure, possibly depicting the Mother of the Gods (S 195) and a head in relief (S 201). Votive sculptures, including these pieces, from the area of the Agora will be published by C. Lawton.
11 Miller 1974, p. 196. The relative and absolute dating of the material in the cisterns is confirmed in Rotroff 1997, p. 451.
12 Thompson 1954, p. 105.
13 Julie Unruh, former Agora conservator, confirmed that the metal of the strips is lead.
14 Thompson 1954, p. 88, fn. 2; Shear 1969, 389, fn. 11.
15 Shear 1969, p. 389, fn. 11.
16 A few metal tools have been found from Roman sculptors' studios, e.g. punches from a workshop at Aphrodisias (Rockwell 1991, p. 127) and points from Pompeii (Strong and Claridge 1976, p. 197).
17 *IG* II² 1673 refers to old iron tools being sold as scrap for new tools.
18 Durnan 2000.
19 Palagia and Bianchi (1994) argue that the claw chisel was invented in Egypt in the seventh century and then was introduced to Greece (contra, Nylander 1991, p. 1040, who argues Greeks invented the claw chisel in the sixth century). For an excellent survey of the techniques of creating classical sculpture, Palagia 2006, pp. 243–279. See now J. Paga 2015.

20 Blümel 1969 argued for a pick-hammer, a mallet, and a point as the Archaic sculptor's only tools. By careful examination of the surfaces of sculptures, Adam (1966, *passim*) has shown that the variety of tools, especially chisels, employed by Greek sculptors was far greater than assumed by Blümel. See Palagia 2006, p. 246.

21 Schiering 1991.

22 Schiering 1991, plate 61; plate 60a.

23 For the lead strips from the Temple of Aphaia, Furtwängler 1906, p. 424 and Bankel 1984. The two lead strips (IM 458, IM 459) from Isthmia were found in temple trench C9 (Rostoker and Gebhard 1980). Zimmer (1990, p. 56) catalogues three lead strips from a bronze workshop at Nemea; for the temple construction, Miller 1979. For lead strips from Rhamnous, see Petrakos 1999, pp. 267–269.

24 For the strip in the Agora foundry, Mattusch 1977, pl. 86. The lead strip from Pergamon is slightly different in form from the Agora examples, triangular rather than rectangular in section. Hübner (1993, p. 31) speculates that it could have been used like a reed, to work the side of Hellenistic vessels into the mold.

25 Bankel 1984. Stewart (1990, p. 34) notes the practice of making a preliminary sketch before sculpting.

26 Schiering 1991; Zimmer 1990.

27 IL 535 was found in a pit containing marble chips on the north slope of the Kolonos Agoraios. The associated pottery dates to the 5th century BC. IL 668 was recovered from the working chips of the Stoa of Zeus. IL 1753 was found in a layer of compacted poros limestone chips, below the robbing fill of an early altar. At least two other lead strips (IL 1751, IL 1755) were found nearby. A bronze stylus (BI 511) was recovered from a well filled with the debris of a sculptor's workshop (Deposit BB 17:1). In a photograph the strip looks very like the lead strips discussed here, but since the strip has been misplaced, it cannot be checked for its composition.

28 Just such a step of preliminary sketch is assumed by Carpenter (1960, pp. 37–40); Blümel (1969, p. 71); Ridgway (1969, p. 101).

29 E.g. the 4th Dynasty tomb of Senenuke in the Boston Museum of Fine Arts (number 07.1000–1001; Giza tomb G2041).

30 Zimmer 1990, p. 56.

31 As was suggested to me by H. Nick Eiteljorg.

32 Shear 2001.

33 Mattusch 1977.

34 IL 1079.

35 Clarke and Engelbach 1930, pp. 198–199. Depictions include the 18th dynasty tomb of the vizier Rekhmirē. Parallels for the polishers: Metropolitan Museum, New York, 11.151.733 (Dynasties 12–13); Petrie Museum of Egyptian Archaeology, UC 3147, UC 72860, UC 44073.

36 For this step and the use of pumice as an abrasive, see Rockwell 1993, p. 48.

37 ST 456 and ST 464 are both elongated prisms in shape and are made of sandstone, a material cited by Rockwell 1993, p. 48 as an abrasive used in stone sculpture. For the early Roman workshop in which they were found, Young 1951, p. 270.

38 Pumice was used also to polish cast bronze objects (Mattusch 1977, p. 353).

39 E.g. dedications depicting scribes writing with styli on wax tablets are found on the Athenian Acropolis: Keesling 2003.

40 For *ergasteria* and whether they should be seen as separate establishments from shops and houses, see Bettalli 1985.

41 IG II² 2677, 2746, 2750, 2752, 2759, 2760. IG II² 2747, 2748, 2749, 2751. Structures of this type are discussed in Hopper 1979, p. 131.

42 Burford 1972, p. 60.

43 Pritchard (1999) posits a fairly substantial service of black glaze pottery in the house. Given that the context pottery is highly fragmentary and incomplete and largely the result of secondary and even tertiary deposits, such conclusions should be regarded with some caution.

44 Rotroff 2014 *passim*.

45 Rockwell 1991, p. 141. The shape and arrangement of the rooms in the Aphrodisias studio are reminiscent of the cells of the Poros Building or so-called prison in Athens, cubicles arranged in a line with doors all on one side. For a recent reassessment of the building as an industrial establishment, Rotroff 2014. Because the Poros Building was found with a considerable fill of marble chips, it is reasonable to ask whether it too might have been a workshop for sculptors, rather than a place of incarceration and execution. It is not worthwhile to compare the stone sculptor's studio with the work spaces used by contemporaneous bronze sculptors, as the heat and possible danger of the foundries required them to be larger and different in layout than the rooms used by marble workers.

46 There is a marked contrast between the work spaces in the House of Mikion and Menon with that of the workshop of Pheidias at Olympia; however, Pheidias created a colossal image which so filled the Temple of Zeus that Strabo (8.3.30) feared that the image, should it stand, would take the roof off with his head.

References

Adam, S. 1966. *The Technique of Greek Sculpture in the Archaic and Classical Periods*, London.

Bankel, H. 1984. "Griechische Bleistifte," *Archäologische Anzeiger,* pp. 409–411.

Bettalli, M. 1985. "Case, Botteghe, *Ergasteria*: Note sui luoghi di produzione e di vendità nell'Atene classica," *Opus* 4, pp. 29–42.

Blümel, C. 1969 *Greek Sculptors at Work*, 2nd ed., London.

Burford, A. 1972. *Craftsmen in Greek and Roman Society*, Ithaca.

Burr, D. 1933. "A Geometric House and a Proto-Attic Votive Deposit," *Hesperia* 2, pp. 542–640.

Carpenter, R. 1960. *Greek Sculpture: A Critical Review*, Chicago.

Clarke, S. and R. Engelbach. 1930. *Ancient Egyptian Masonry. The Building Craft*, London.

Costaki, L. 2006. "The *intra muros* Road System of Ancient Athens" (diss. University of Toronto).

Durnan, N. 2000. "Stone Sculpture," in *Making Classical Art. Process and Practice*, ed. R. Ling, Stroud and Charleston, pp. 18–36.

Furtwängler, A. 1906. *Aegina: Das Heiligtum der Aphaia*, Munich.

Hopper, R. J. 1979. *Trade and Industry in Classical Greece*, London.

Hübner, G. 1993. *Die Applikenkeramik von Pergamon: Eine Bildersprache im Dienst des Herrscherkultes*, Berlin.

Keesling, C. 2003. *The Votive Statues of the Athenian Acropolis*, Cambridge.

Lalonde, G. V. 1968. "A Fifth Century Hieron Southwest of the Athenian Agora," *Hesperia* 37, pp. 123–33.

Mattusch, C. C. 1977. "Bronze- and Iron-Working in the Area of the Athenian Agora," *Hesperia* 46, pp. 340–79.

Miller, Stella G. 1974. "Menon's Cistern," *Hesperia* 43, pp. 194–245.

Miller, Stephen G. 1979. "Excavations at Nemea," *Hesperia* 48, pp. 73–103.

Nylander, C. 1991. "The Toothed Chisel," *Archeologia classica* 43, pp. 1037–1052.

Paga, J. (forthcoming 2015)."The Claw-Tooth Chisel and the Hekatompedon Problem: Issues of Tool and Technique in Archaic Athens," Mitteilungen des Deutschen Archäologischen Instituts, Athenische Abteilung 127.

Palagia, O. ed. 2006. *Greek Sculpture, Function, Materials and Techniques in the Archaic and Classical Periods*, Cambridge.

Palagia, O. and R. S. Bianchi. 1994. "Who invented the claw chisel?" *Oxford Journal of Archaeology* 13, pp. 185–197.

Papadopoulos, J. 2003. *Ceramicus redivivus. The early Iron Age Potters' Field in the area of the Classical Athenian Agora* (*Hesperia* suppl. 31), Princeton.

Petrakos, B. 1999. Ο Δῆμος τοῦ Ραμνοῦντος, I, Athens.

Pritchard, D. M. 1999. "Fool's Gold and Silver: Reflections on the Evidentiary Status of Finely Painted Attic Pottery," *Antichthon* 33, pp. 1–27.

Ridgway, B. S. 1969. "Stone Carving: Sculpture," in *The Muses at Work: Arts, Crafts and Professions in Ancient Greece and Rome*, ed. C. Roebuck, Cambridge MA, pp. 96–117.

Rockwell, P. 1991. "Unfinished Sculpture associated with a Sculptor's Studio," in *Aphrodisias Papers 2: The Theater, a Sculptor's Workshop, Philosophers, and Coin-types*, ed. R. R. R. Smith and K. T. Erim, Ann Arbor, pp. 127–43.

Rockwell, P. 1993. *The Art of Stoneworking. A Reference Guide*, Cambridge.

Rostoker, W. and E. R. Gebhard. 1980 "The Sanctuary of Poseidon at Isthmia: Techniques of Metal Manufacture," *Hesperia* 49, pp. 347–63.

Rotroff, S. I. 1983. "Three Cistern Systems on the Kolonos Agoraios," *Hesperia* 52, pp. 257–97.

Rotroff, S. I. 1997. *The Athenian Agora*, XXIX. *Hellenistic Pottery. Athenian and Imported Wheelmade Tableware and Related Material*, Princeton.

Rotroff, S. I. 2014. *Industrial Religion: The Saucer Pyres of the Athenian Agora*, Princeton.

Schiering, W. 1991. *Die Werkstatt des Phidias in Olympia, zweite Teil: Werkstattfunde* (*Olympische Forschungen*, Vol. XVIII), Berlin.

Shear, T. L., Jr. 1969. "The Athenian Agora: Excavations of 1968," *Hesperia* 38, pp. 382–417.

Shear, T. L., Jr. 1993. "The Persian Destruction of Athens: Evidence from Agora Deposits," *Hesperia* 62, pp. 383–482.

Shear, T. L., Jr. 2001. "A Template for Carving Moldings," in ΚΑΛΛΙΣΤΕΥΜΑ. Μελέτες προς τιμην της Ὄλγας Τζάχου-Αλεξάνδρη, Athens, pp. 395–402.

Stewart, A. 1990. *Greek Sculpture*, New Haven.

Strong, D. and A. Claridge, 1976. "Marble Sculpture," in *Roman Crafts*, ed. D. Strong, London, pp. 195–208.

Theocharaki, A. M. 2011. "The Ancient Circuit Wall of Athens: its Changing Course and the Phases of Construction," *Hesperia* 80, pp. 71–156.

Thompson, D. B. 1954. "Three Centuries of Hellenistic Terracottas, I, A, B and C," *Hesperia* 23, pp. 72–107.

Thompson, D. B. 1960. "The House of Simon the Shoemaker," *Archaeology* 13, pp. 234–40.

Thompson, H. A. 1934. "Two Centuries of Hellenistic Pottery," *Hesperia* 4, pp. 311–476.

Thompson, H. A., D. B. Thompson and S. I. Rotroff. 1987. *Hellenistic Pottery and Terracottas*. Princeton.

Thompson, H. A. and R. E. Wycherley. 1972. *The Athenian Agora*, XIV. *The Agora of Athens*, Princeton.

Young, R. S. 1951. "An Industrial District of Ancient Athens," *Hesperia* 20, pp. 135–288.

Zimmer, G. 1990. *Griechische Bronzegusswerkstätten*, Mainz.

3

More Than the Time of Day:
Helios to the Rescue

Jenifer Neils, Derek Reinbold and Rachel Sternberg

The identification of the individual gods fighting the giants in the fourteen East metopes of the Parthenon is fairly secure, but the unusual iconography of the last two metopes featuring Hephaistos and Helios merits further study. The charioteer Helios (East 14) is commonly interpreted in a temporal sense as representing dawn and thus the end of the nocturnal Gigantomachy. An overlooked passage in the Argonautika *(3.232–234) suggests that Helios should be interpreted instead as driving his chariot to the rescue of the lame smith-god in East metope 13. This reading has important resonance with other scenes of warriors coming to the aid of their comrades in the Parthenon's sculptural program. The East metopes' evocation of pity is in accord with an emerging moral universe in classical Athens.*

Introduction

The Gigantomachy is a venerable theme in Greek art and is especially popular in Attic vase painting of the 6th century BC.[1] It is represented in Parian marble at Delphi in the Siphnian Treasury, and in a pediment of the Old Temple of Athena on the Acropolis, and was the standard scene woven

Figure 3.1 East façade of the Parthenon. Photo: M. M. Miles.

into the peplos presented to the goddess at the Panathenaic festival. In Athenian vase-painting, Zeus, Athena and Herakles are the chief protagonists and in more expanded versions Poseidon, Apollo, Ares, Hermes and Dionysos often join the battle. Besides Athena, other goddesses take part as well, notably Artemis alongside her brother, or Hera in the vicinity of Zeus.

One of the more expansive representations of this cosmic battle appears on the fourteen East metopes of the Parthenon (Figures 3.1 and 3.2), carved around 447–442 BC.[2] The ten divine combatants are badly effaced, but are identified as follows: East 1= Hermes, East 2= Dionysos, East 3= Ares, East 4= Athena, East 6= Poseidon, East 8= Zeus, East 9= Apollo, East 11= Herakles, East 12= Aphrodite, and East 13= Hephaistos. There are several distinctive and unusual aspects of this representation of the Gigantomachy, examined in greater detail below: the prevalence of chariots (East 5, 7, 10, and 14); the inclusion of the lame smith-god Hephaistos (East 13); and the appearance of the sun-god Helios (East 14) without his usual counterpart Selene.

Anomalies

Four of the East metopes feature deities in chariots with

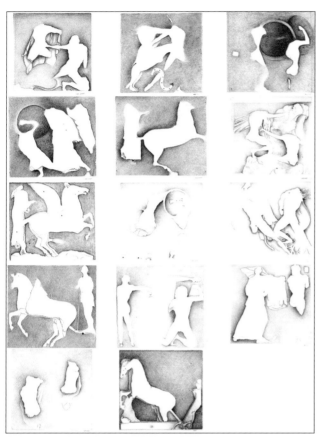

Figure 3.2 Drawing of the East metopes of the Parthenon, Gods battling Giants: 1 Hermes, 2 Dionysos, 3 Ares, 4 Athena and Nike, 5 Amphitrite, 6 Poseidon, 7 Hera, 8 Zeus, 9 Apollo, 10 Artemis, 11 Herakles and Eros, 12 Aphrodite, 13 Hephaistos, 14, Helios. © Drawing by K.A. Schwab.

Figure 3.3 Attic red-figure cup attributed to the Brygos Painter, ca. 490 BC. Interior: Selene or Nyx. Berlin, Antikenmuseum F 2293. After CVA Berlin 2 (Germany 21) pls. 67.2 and 70.3.

Figure 3.4 Exterior of Figure 3.3: Hephaistos and Poseidon fighting giants.

their charioteers, as does the next metope around the corner to the north (North 1) as well as South 15 (where it is part of the wedding preceding the centauromachy). Perhaps this is not surprising as chariots are so ubiquitous in the Parthenon's sculptural program. Upon entering the Acropolis the viewer was confronted with the chariots of Athena and Poseidon prominently featured in the West pediment. In the East pediment the chariots of Helios and Selene flank the dramatic birth of Athena, as they do at the creation of Pandora on the base of the *Athena Parthenos*.[3] The Ionic frieze above the wall of the cella of the Parthenon abounds with quadrigas, ten on the south side and eleven on the north; these are the tribal participants in the famous *apobates* race held at the Panathenaic festival in honor of Athena.[4] Yet chariots and their teams of horses are an unusual choice for the square format of metopes, where the space is more typically filled with compositions of two to three figures.[5] Representations of chariots from the front do appear on some Archaic metopes, but the Parthenon may well feature their first appearance in profile.[6]

What role do these chariots play in the narrative? Clearly three of them are driven by the consorts of the gods. Thus, the female in East 5 is identified as Amphitrite because of her proximity to Poseidon who is wielding the island of Nisyros as a weapon in East 6. The charioteer reining in the winged horses on East 7 must be Hera because Zeus appears in the adjacent metope to the north. Since East 9 has been identified as Apollo, the female charioteer in the next metope is usually identified as Artemis. Familiar from the frequent descriptions of Homeric warfare, charioteers ferry warriors into battle and wait for the successful completion of the duel to carry them off to the next encounter. These "taxi" chariots form an integral part of the paired compositions of god and consort, and add variety to the two-figure compositions of the majority of the East metopes.

The chariot of Helios, however, is usually interpreted differently. His presence is thought to be a temporal indicator, marking the sunrise when the Gigantomachy came to an end.[7] But the battle is not over on the East front. Contradicting this interpretation are the on-going duels in the other metopes where a giant has yet to be killed. Moreover, Helios is usually paired with Selene (or Nyx), as in the pediment above, yet here in the East metopes he is without his dual opposite. Another interpretation of his presence as charioteer, more in keeping with the other charioteers, seems warranted.

A solo Helios, without his usual counterpart Selene, is unprecedented in the Gigantomachy and in the iconography of the Parthenon. On a red-figure krater in Naples which is often used for the reconstruction of the Gigantomachy on the interior of the Parthenos' shield, Helios rises on one side while Selene descends on the other – not unlike the pair of the East pediment. Selene (or Nyx) appears alone on the interior of a cup in Berlin where she clearly represents the extended nocturnal aspect of the battle of the gods and giants which is depicted on the exterior. (Figures 3.3 and 3.4).[8] Some scholars have identified the charioteer in the adjacent metope North 1 as Helios rising, but Schwab has argued persuasively that this charioteer is in fact Athena pulling her horses to a halt.[9]

Another anomaly in the Parthenon's Gigantomachy is the inclusion of Hephaistos.[10] He is markedly absent from depictions of this battle in relief sculpture. When he does appear, as on the West frieze of the Siphnian Treasury at Delphi, he is shown at the far end working the bellows to assist his side, but not personally battling giants like the other gods.[11] Only on the Attic red-figure cup in Berlin (F 2293, Figure 3.4) and a krater in Basel is he shown in an extended Gigantomachy wearing battle armor and wielding his red-hot tongs as he attacks a giant.[12] More frequently, Hephaistos is shown seated at his forge, or riding a donkey in his return to Olympus and not in the context of a battle at all.

Hephaistos in Athens

Hephaistos' representation in the Gigantomachy is especially meaningful in the context of Athenian myth and cult. In the overall sculptural program of the Parthenon his prominence is notable. He must have made an appearance in the now-lost central section of the East pediment since he was instrumental in the birth of Athena from the head of Zeus. On the East frieze he is seated next to Athena, a crutch under his right arm, in the assembly of gods. He was also prominent on the now-lost base of the *Athena Parthenos* where he,

together with Athena, is responsible for the creation of the first woman, Pandora. His close association with Athena is emphasized by the designers of the Parthenon's architectural sculpture and they thrust him into a prominence among the other Olympians that he did not enjoy previously. Earlier literary depictions in the *Iliad* (1.599–600) have his limp as a subject of laughter to the other Olympians, and a source of shame to his mother Hera (*Homeric Hymn to Pythian Apollo* ll. 316–318).[13]

The likely explanation for this new presentation relies on the god's status in Athenian religious life. Hephaistos held a prominent place in the cults of Athens, paralleled elsewhere in Greece only on the island Lemnos. He was linked closely with Athena, the city's patron goddess, not only for his midwife-like role in her birth and their joint parentage of the Attic king Erichthonios, but also through their common patronage of the arts and crafts.[14] Further, the two shared the Hephaisteion, above the ancient Athenian Agora, which contained monumental bronze sculptures of both gods. That temple was likely begun about 460, when preliminary design work and planning for the Parthenon was underway.[15]

East Metopes 13 and 14: Hephaistos and Helios

All that is left of metope East 13 is a badly scarred surface with no indication remaining of any identifiable attributes. Schwab calls it "one of the most intractable" of the Parthenon's metopes.[16] One can make out a giant who has fallen to his knees at the left and an attacking god at the right. Although most scholars have followed Praschniker in identifying the god as Hephaistos, some have argued for Herakles.[17] Schwab has reconstructed Hephaistos holding tongs with a red-hot lump of iron and moving violently toward a fallen giant (Figure 3.5).[18] Hephaistos' opponent is presumably the giant Mimas who was felled by red-hot missiles which were hurled at him, according to Apollodoros in his later account of the episode (1.6.2): Μίμαντα δὲ Ἥφαιστος βαλὼν μύδροις ("Mimas [slain] by Hephaistos with red-hot metal".)

What is Hephaistos' role within the narrative of the Gigantomachy on the East front of the Parthenon? An answer is provided by his neighbor in East 14. Reconstruction work undertaken by M. Korres and K. Schwab has conclusively established the charioteer in East 14 as Helios, the titan god of the sun (Figure 3.6).[19] Early reconstructions conveyed a "relatively quiet scene with a small figure of Helios driving his chariot pulled by two horses truly at the periphery of [the Gigantomachy]."[20] Korres' reconstruction reveals that Helios rode atop his iconic quadriga, rather than the biga present in earlier restorations.[21] Schwab's work, which relies on the placement of extant drill holes that would have supported gleaming metal attachments, imparts a far greater aura of luster and brightness to the metope. The presence of two leaping fish at the hub of the chariot wheel not only

Figure 3.5 Parthenon East metope 13: Hephaistos fighting a giant, proposed reconstruction. © Drawing by K.A. Schwab.

Figure 3.6 Parthenon East metope 14: Helios drives a chariot, ascending above Okeanos, proposed reconstruction. © Drawing by K.A. Schwab

suggests the sea from which Helios is emerging but also his swift voyage.[22]

Helios' role as representing the dawn sun, signifying victory over the giants (the traditional understanding of his presence) is characterized by M. Tiverios' statement that "Helios was most likely shown in the East metopes of the Parthenon because he too contributed, in an indirect way, to the victory of the gods. If Helios is present, then Metope 14 pictures him just as he is starting to shine, and implies that Zeus is already in possession of the magic potion and that the annihilation of the giants has already begun."[23] Schwab echoes this interpretation, presenting East 14 as a signifier of Olympian victory, and drawing on Apollodoros' *Bibliotheca*.[24]

The claim that Helios was presented solely as a landscape or temporal element seemed to be supported by his position on the periphery, i.e. at the far north end of the metope series. This minimal interpretation proves unconvincing in the face of Schwab's new reconstruction. If Helios is not symbolic in East 14 of the dawning sun, why is he there? A largely ignored passage from *Argonautika* (3.232–234) seems to offer the likeliest solution.[25] Apollonios wrote, "such were the marvelous works that subtle craftsman / Hephaistos had made ... / as a repayment for Helios, who'd picked him up / in his chariot when he was weary from battling the Giants" (Πρὸς δὲ καὶ αὐτόγυον στιβαροῦ ἀδάμαντος ἄροτρον / ἤλασεν, Ἡελίῳ τίνων ὅς ῥά μιν ἵπποις / δέξατο, Φλεγραίῃ κεκμηότα δηιοτῆτι).[26] Hephaistos had collapsed from the physical strain of the epic battle, and Helios, seeing the struggling god, rushed to his rescue. Thus, East metopes 13 and 14 can be understood as a pair acting out this dramatic rescue mission.

Given what we know about the Parthenon, this interpretation is compelling. First, Hephaistos and Helios were not singletons at the end of the metopes. They can be aligned with the pairings proposed by Schwab based on her identification of the figures in the East metopes: "East 1–2: Hermes and Dionysos (Birth of Dionysos); East 3–4: Ares and Athena/Nike (war, victory in battle); East 5–6: Amphitrite and Poseidon (consorts); East 7–8: Hera and Zeus (consorts); East 9–10: Apollo and Artemis (brother-sister); East 11–12: Herakles/Eros and Aphrodite (archers, mother/son); East 13–14: Hephaistos and Helios (Helios assists Hephaistos twice)."[27] Within these pairs of adjacent metopes are four figures driving chariots, Helios and three female charioteers – Amphitrite (East 5), Hera (East 7) and Artemis (East 10) – and all three may be interpreted as assisting the god in the adjacent metope.

All four charioteers are not directly fighting in the battle, but are racing towards gods who are. They are acting as helpers, a novel motif found elsewhere on the Parthenon. On the exterior of the shield of the *Athena Parthenos* there are two groups of helpers within the Amazonomachy (Figure 3.7).[28] There are both a Greek helper pair and an Amazon helper pair, each consisting of one healthy combatant helping a fallen compatriot from the field of battle.[29] The shield represents the first appearance of this conceit in Greek art, and it is echoed in later monuments.[30]

A broader consideration of Hephaistos and Helios' role in the legendary battle of the Olympian gods and the giants may illustrate how these two figures could have been paired together for the ancient Athenian viewer. The visual dynamism of the two panels, revealed in recent reconstructions, bolsters this claim. The pairing of the fire god and the sun god was a trope inherited from myth, applied on the Parthenon, and continued later. The Parthenon was a site for artistic experimentation, where the Classical style was perfected, and the pairing of the fiery gods Helios and Hephaistos is one such example of this innovation.

The Pity Motif

In the moral universe of Classical Athens, the 5th century witnesses the development of concern for others and an increasingly positive valuation of pity, probably in reaction to numerous abuses of power perpetrated by democratic Athens during its memorable decades as an imperial power.[31] The genre of tragedy repeatedly explored and developed this theme, a process culminating in Sophocles' *Philoctetes,* where the title character, a warrior suffering from an incurable snakebite, wins the pity of young Neoptolemos, thus thwarting the callous designs of heartless Odysseus. At the crux of the action, Neoptolemos says (lines 965–966, trans. D. Greene):

> A kind of compassion,
> a terrible compassion, has come upon me
> for him. I have felt for him all the time.

As M. B. McCoy posits in *Wounded Heroes,* we may see the development of vulnerability as a virtue in the *Philoctetes.* She points to the evolving concern for the wounded as seen in literature and philosophy.[32] Other texts of the period also reflect emerging concern with the rescue of wounded warriors from the field of battle or, later at Syracuse in 413 BC, with their removal from the theater of war, an unachieved desideratum painfully captured by Thucydides (7.75.2–4).[33]

Indisputably the Athenians were constantly at war, and battlefield comportment mattered. If wounded, would you be left behind to die – slowly, perhaps, of your wounds, or more quickly from trampling or enemy action? Or would you be rescued and brought to safety? The single most famous example of a battlefield rescue is the one found in Plato's *Symposium* (220E), where he has Alcibiades credit Socrates with having rescued him (wounded) at the battle of Delion (in 424 BC): τετρωμένον οὐκ ἐθέλων ἀπολιπεῖν ἀλλὰ συνδιέσωσε καὶ τὰ ὅπλα καὶ αὐτὸν ἐμέ.

The tragic plays of Athens, taken as a whole, furnish an education in pity.[34] The Athenians accepted that the spectacle of suffering in tragic plays and in art might play a role in the cultivation of pity.[35] Drama could also furnish models for active intervention. A. Ajootian, commenting on a statue group of Prokne and her pitiful young son Itys that Pausanias describes on the Acropolis (1.24.3), writes that such works

Figure 3.7 Reconstruction drawing of the exterior of the shield of the Athena Parthenos by E. B. Harrison.

"had the ability to inscribe the experience of suffering on the public landscape and perhaps on the civic conscience."[36]

The image of Helios rushing to the rescue of the exhausted Hephaistos, therefore, furnishes a conspicuous paradigm for this newly emerging theme of pity and other-concern. Presumably, compassionate action in the divine realm would set an example for mortals. Parallel to this phenomenon in public sculpture is the nearly contemporary literary invention of *philanthropia,* the love of humanity, which begins as an attribute of the gods but by the fourth century is touted as a virtue *par excellence* of the Athenians.[37] Athenians, we are told (Demosthenes 25.87), live in "mutual *philanthropia* [τὴν κοινὴν φιλανθρωπίαν] which you have by nature toward one another". In warfare again, it was *philanthropia* that prompted the generals at Arginousai in 406 BC to order the rescue of some 2,000 shipwrecked warriors, as Xenophon (*Hellenica* 1.7.18) tells us. The rescue attempt was thwarted by storms, but the Athenians expressed their anger at the failure to rescue despite the weather by condemning six of the eight generals to death.

Conclusion

Greek art features a long tradition of depictions of dead warriors being carried from the battlefield, from the Geometric period onward. No doubt inspired by scenes in the *Iliad*, such vivid representations show the terrible aftermath of battle.[38] On the Parthenon, we see a different aspect of the experience of war. The East metopes present the first exemplars of aid for the war-weary and wounded. In the divine sphere Helios comes to relieve Hephaistos in the East metopes. The shield of the deity herself inside the temple also illustrates heroes and even opponents in the Amazonomachy carrying their wounded comrades to safety. This new motif had an impact on later sculptors, for it is found on later sculptural monuments depicting battle scenes such as the east and south friezes of the Temple of Apollo at Bassai.[39] The moral concept of compassion even in great duress gains momentum in fourth-century rhetoric and historiography, and also pragmatically, since in the course of the 4th century BC, Greek generals were increasingly expected to assume responsibility for the evacuation of wounded combatants.[40] With sculpture that ennobles the concept of pity and *philanthropia*, the Parthenon presents for its Athenian viewers models of high-minded virtue put into action by gods and heroes.

Notes

1   This paper began as an undergraduate honors papers researched and written by Derek Reinbold and directed by Jenifer Neils at Case Western Reserve University. Reinbold is responsible for the central thesis; Neils supplied the supplementary material on the Parthenon sculptural program; and Rachel Sternberg provided the coda on the motif of pity. On the Gigantomachy in Greek art see *LIMC* 4 (1988) s.v. Gigantes. Still useful is Vian 1951.

2   For detailed studies of the Parthenon East metopes see Praschniker 1928, pp. 142–223, pls. 14–27; Brommer 1967, pp. 22–38, 196–209; and Berger 1986, pp. 55–76. For more general overviews see Schwab 2005, pp. 168–173 and Choremi-Spetsieri and Mavrommatis 2004, pp. 94–99.

3   For the chariots in the West pediment see Palagia 1992. For the base of the Athena Parthenos, see Leipen 1971, pp. 24–27, and Kosmopoulou 2002, pp. 111–117.

4   Schultz (2007) discusses the importance of chariots and charioteers and in particular the *apobates* race in the imagery of the Parthenon. See also Neils and Schultz 2012.

5   On the relative widths of the East metopes see Yeroulanou 1998, pp. 413–16. She notes that the East metopes do not follow the 5th century norm of being equal, and in fact those with chariots are relatively wider (average 1.306 m) compared with those without (average 1.265–1.274 m). The Helios metope (width 1.275 m) is the exception but this chariot is depicted on a diagonal unlike the other three.

6   On the frontal chariot in metopes of Archaic temples in Sicily, see Marconi 2007, pp. 104–109, 138–142.

7   E.g. Choremi-Spetsieri and Mavrommatis 2004, p. 100: "The Sun evidently rises when the battle has been decided in favour of the gods. The presence of personified celestial bodies on the Parthenon is known also from the east pediment, the north and the south metopes, and reflects the contemporary philosophers' interest in astronomy."

8   Naples Archaeological Museum 81521; BAPD 217517. For a drawing of the vase see Leipen 1971, fig. 84. Berlin,

Antikenmuseum F 2293; BAPD 203909. See *CVA* Berlin 2 (Germany 21) pls. 67–68 and 70.

9   Schwab 1994.

10   On Hephaistos in Greek art see *LIMC* 4 (1988), s.v. Hephaestus and Brommer 1978.

11   Moore 1977.

12   See Brommer 1978, p. 39 and pls. 14, 2 and 18, 1. He makes a solo appearance on a black-figure lekythos in Athens attributed to the Theseus Painter. BAPD 352527; see Marangou 1996, p. 84, no. 121.

13   See Bremer 2010.

14   See Shapiro 1989.

15   Wyatt and Edmonson 1984; Lippolis et al. 2007, pp. 565–566.

16   Schwab 2004, p. 162.

17   Tiverios 1982, p. 229 and Berger 1986, p. 70. Tiverios (p. 228) identifies the god in East 3 as Hephaistos, although the figure is universally identified as Ares. Berger argues that East 11 and East 13 could be either Hephaistos or Herakles.

18   Schwab 2004, pp. 162–63.

19   Brommer 1967, pp. 204–208, identified the charioteer as Poseidon because he believed that Helios would not be shown twice, i.e. back-to-back with himself on North 1. However, this argument no longer holds if North 1 is correctly identified as Athena (cf. Schwab 1994).

20   Schwab 2009, p. 79.

21   Korres 1994, p. 62.

22   The fish have been identified as grey mullet, a fish which according to our ancient sources was known for its *dike* in that it did not consume other fish. See Thompson 1947, pp. 110–112. Could it be an oblique reference to Helios' role as a helper rather than a fighter?

23   Tiverios 1982, p. 228.

24   Schwab 2009, p. 85.

25   Praschniker 1929, p. 222 mentions the passage in the context of the Helios metope, and it is again referenced in Berger 1986, p. 72, and Schwab 1996, p. 89, n. 41.

26   Trans. Green 1997, 3.228–234. In his note on this passage Green 2007, p. 260 states: "His rescue by Helios is not elsewhere attested in our surviving sources, though he is placed near Helios's chariot on the Parthenon metopes."

27   Schwab 1996, p. 89. In n. 41 Schwab mentions two instances in which Hephaistos is aided by Herlios: the gigantomachy and his notification of his wife's affair with Ares.

28   Harrison 1966, p. 121 and pls. 36b, 38, 38a–d.

29   Harrison 1981, pp. 290–292 and pl. 29.

30   E.g. the interior frieze of the Temple of Apollo at Bassai (ca. 400 BC) which shows influence from the Parthenon. In the left-most slab depicting the Trojan Amazonomachy (BM 539) a squire or slave is assisting a wounded Greek off the battlefield (while at the other end of the slab a dead comrade is being carried off). In the Heraklean Amazonomachy the motif appears three times: an Amazon helping a wounded comrade (BM 531), a Greek drags away a fallen comrade (BM 540), and another Amazon comes to the aid of her wounded comrade (BM 542). See Madigan 1992, pp. 74–76.

31   Sternberg 2005, pp. 98–122

32   McCoy 2013.

33   Sternberg 2006, pp. 104–145.

34   Sternberg 2005, pp. 123–192.

35 See Munteanu 2012. For the imagery of wounded warriors on Attic vases see Kephalidou 2011.
36 Sternberg 2005, pp. 223–252.
37 Sternberg 1998, pp. 110–116.
38 Ahlberg-Cornell 1992, pp. 35–38, 71–72. Greeks regularly carry their own war dead off the field, while foreigners like Sarpedon and Memon are carted off by the gods; see Neils 2009.
39 On the Bassai temple, see Madigan 1992.
40 Sternberg 1999.

References

Ahlberg-Cornell, G. 1992. *Myth and Epos in Early Greek Art: Representation and Interpretation*, Jonsered.

BAPD = Beazley Archive Pottery Database

Berger, E. 1986. *Der Parthenon in Basel: Dokumentation zu den Metopen. Studien der Skulpturhalle Basel* 2, Basel.

Bremmer, J. N. 2010. "Hephaistos Sweats or How to Construct an Ambivalent God," in *The Gods of Ancient Greece, Edinburgh Leventis Studies* 5, ed. J. N. Bremmer and A. Erskine, 193–208.

Brommer, F. 1967. *Die Metopen des Parthenon*, Mainz.

Brommer, F. 1978. *Hephaistos, der Schmiedegott in der antiken Kunst*, Mainz.

Brommer, F. 1979. *The Sculptures of the Parthenon*, London.

Choremi-Spetsieri, A. and S. Mavrommatis. 2004. *The Sculptures of the Parthenon*, Athens.

CVA = Corpus Vasorum Antiquorum

Green, P. 2007. *The Argonautika by Apollonios Rhodios*, Berkeley.

Harrison, E. B. 1966. "The Composition of the Amazonomachy on the Shield of Athena Parthenos," *Hesperia* 35, pp. 107–33.

Harrison, E. B. 1981. "Motifs of the City-Siege on the Shield of Athena Parthenos," *American Journal of Archaeology* 85, pp. 281–317.

Kephalidou, E. 2011. "A Wounded Warrior from Kamarina and Some Notes on the Iconography of Battlefield Doctors," in *Veder greco a Camarina dal principe Boscari ai nostri tempi*, vol. 2, ed. G. and E. Giudice, Catania, pp. 97–104.

Korres, M. 1994. "The History of the Acropolis Monuments," in *Acropolis Restoration: The CCAM Interventions*, ed. R. Economakis, London, pp. 35–51.

Kosmopolou, A. 2001. *The Iconography of Sculptured Statue Bases in the Archaic and Classical Periods*, Madison.

Leipen, N. 1971. *Athena Parthenos, A Reconstruction*, Toronto.

LIMC= Lexicon Iconographicum Mythologiae Classicae

Lippolis, E., M. Livadiottti, and G. Rocco. 2007. *Architettura greca. Storia e monumenti del mondo della* polis *dalle origini al V secolo*, Milan.

Madigan, B. C. 1992. *The Temple of Apollo Bassitas, Vol. 2. The Sculptures*, Princeton.

Marangou, L. I. 1996. *Ancient Greek Art in the N. P. Goulandris Collection*, Athens.

Marconi, C. 2007. *Temple Decoration and Cultural Identity in the Archaic Greek World: The Metopes of Selinus*, Cambridge.

McCoy, M. B. 2013. *Wounded Heroes: vulnerability as a virtue in ancient Greek literature and philosophy*, Oxford.

Moore, M. 1977. "The Gigantomachy of the Siphnian Treasury: Reconstruction of the Three Lacunae," *Bulletin de Correspondence Héllenique* 4, pp. 305–35.

Moore, M. 1979. "Lydos and the Gigantomachy." *American Journal of Archaeology* 83, pp. 79–99.

Munteanu, D. 2012. *Tragic Pathos*, Cambridge.

Neils, J. 2001. *The Parthenon Frieze*. Cambridge.

Neils, J. 2009. "The 'Un-heroic' Corpse: Re-reading the Sarpedon Krater," in *Athenian Potters and Painters*, vol. 2, ed. J. H. Oakley and O. Palagia, Oxford, pp. 212–219.

Neils, J. and P. Schultz. 2012. "Erechtheus and the Apobates Race on the Parthenon Frieze (North XI–XII)." *American Journal of Archaeology* 116, pp. 195–207.

Palagia, O. 1992. *The Pediments of the Parthenon. Monumenta Graeca et Romana* 7. Leiden.

Praschniker, C. 1928. *Parthenonstudien*, Augsburg and Vienna.

Schultz, P. 2007. "The Iconography of the Athenian Apobates Race: Origins, Meanings, Transformation," in *The Panathenaic Games*, ed. O. Palagia and A. Choremi-Spetsieri, Oxford, pp. 59–72.

Schwab, K. 1994. "The Charioteer in North Metope 1," *Archaeological News* 19: 7–10.

Schwab, K. 1996. "Parthenon East Metope XI: Herakles and the Gigantomachy," *American Journal of Archaeology* 100, pp. 81–90.

Schwab, K. 2004. "The Parthenon East Metopes, the Gigantomachy, and Digital Technology," in *The Parthenon and Its Sculptures: Their History, Iconography and Interpretation*, ed. M. B. Cosmopoulos, Cambridge, pp. 150–165.

Schwab, K. 2005. "Celebrations of Victories: The Metopes of the Parthenon," in *The Parthenon from Antiquity to the Present*, ed. J. Neils, Cambridge, pp. 159–96.

Schwab, K. 2009. "New Evidence for Parthenon East Metope 14," in *Structure, Image, Ornament: Architectural Sculpture in the Greek World*, ed. P. Schultz and R. von den Hoff, Oxford, pp. 79–86.

Shapiro, H. A. 1989. *Art and Cult Under the Tyrants in Athens*, Mainz.

Sternberg, R. H. 1998. "Pity and Pragmatism: A Study of Athenian Attitutudes Toward Compassion in Fifth- and Fourth-Century Historiography and Oratory" (diss. Bryn Mawr College).

Sternberg, R. H. 1999. "The Transport of the Sick and Wounded in Classical Greece," *Phoenix* 53, pp. 191–205.

Sternberg, R. H. 2006. *Tragedy Offstage*, Austin.

Sternberg, R. H., ed. 2005. *Pity and Power in Ancient Athens*, Cambridge.

Thompson, D. W. 1947. *A Glossary of Greek Fishes*, London.

Tiverios, M. 1982. "Observations on the East Metopes of the Parthenon," *American Journal of Archaeology* 86, pp. 227–229.

Vian, F. 1951. *Répetoire des gigantomachies figuées dans l'art grec et romain*, Paris.

Yeroulanou, M. 1998. "Metopes and Architecture: The Hephaisteion and the Parthenon," *Annual of the British School at Athens* 93, pp. 401–425.

Wyatt, W. and C. N. Edmonson, 1984. "The Ceiling of the Hephaisteion," *American Journal of Archaeology* 88, pp. 135–167.

4. Asklepios and Hygieia
in the City Eleusinion

Carol L. Lawton

This article argues that in addition to his sanctuary on the south slope of the Athenian Akropolis, Asklepios was worshipped in a shrine in the City Eleusinion. The archaeological, epigraphical, and literary evidence suggests that it was established there by officials of the Eleusinion shortly after the arrival of Asklepios in Athens in 420/19 BC and that it was the focal point for the celebration of the Epidauria, *the festival in honor of Asklepios that was celebrated within the festival of the Greater Eleusinian Mysteries.*

Asklepios in the City Eleusinion

Although it has long been known that Asklepios and Hygieia had an important Athenian sanctuary on the south slope of the Akropolis, the number and findspots of votive reliefs and related sculpture and inscriptions from the excavations of the Athenian Agora and the surrounding area suggest that they also received dedications on the north slope of the Akropolis, in the City Eleusinion.[1] The area of the Eleusinion has been only partly excavated, and the precise location of a shrine to Asklepios and Hygieia within it must remain conjectural, but the archaeological evidence, together with literary and epigraphical testimonia, strongly points to the worship of Asklepios in the City Eleusinion, probably in the forecourt of the sanctuary, from about the time of his arrival in Athens in 420/19 BC.[2]

The presence of Asklepios and Hygieia in the City Eleusinion is supported not only by the archaeological record but also by the epigraphical and literary sources for the introduction of their worship to Athens. The primary account of their arrival is inscribed on the Telemachos Monument, the large and elaborately decorated stele commemorating the role of Telemachos, a private citizen, in the establishment of the sanctuary of Asklepios on the south slope of the Akropolis.[3] Its inscription says that after his arrival in the harbor at Zea, Asklepios came to the Eleusinion during the celebration of the Greater Eleusinian Mysteries, and from there he and Hygieia were escorted

by Telemachos to the south slope of the Akropolis where, in the archonship of Astyphilos of Kudantidai of 420/19, Telemachos set up a sanctuary and altar to Asklepios, Hygieia, and his other children. The inscription goes on to describe the improvements made to the sanctuary over the years, including the construction of a peribolos and the rebuilding of a wooden gateway, with the last recorded work, the planting and adornment of the sanctuary, occurring in 413/12; the archon of 412/11 is mentioned where the inscription breaks off, without listing what happened in that year. Although the fragmentary inscription is often interpreted as saying that Telemachos was responsible for bringing Asklepios all the way from Epidauros and then up from the harbor to the Eleusinion, the text actually credits Telemachos only with moving Asklepios from the Eleusinion to the sanctuary on the south slope.[4]

In fact, it seems very unlikely that a private citizen alone could have been responsible for bringing Asklepios to Athens in the first place and for taking him to the City Eleusinion. Wickkiser has persuasively argued that it was a constellation of strategic and political factors as much as the consequences of the plague and warfare that prompted the Athenian state to import the cult.[5] The introduction of the new cult must have required the sanction of the demos.[6] Officials of the Eleusinion were also surely involved, since Asklepios arrived there in the midst of the celebration of the Greater Mysteries, and his arrival was henceforth commemorated annually in Athens in the *Epidauria*, a one-day festival in honor of Asklepios held within the longer festival of the Mysteries (Paus. 2.26.8; Philostr., *VA* 4.18).[7] Officials of the sanctuary of Asklepios in Epidauros must also have played a role. Both the name of the festival and a late-5th-century Athenian law concerning it that apparently lists Epidaurian officials led Clinton to conclude that not only did officials from the sanctuary of Asklepios in Epidauros participate in the Athenian festival, but that they were also at least partly responsible for the journey of Asklepios from Epidauros to the Eleusinion that the festival commemorated.[8] Wickkiser has outlined the strategic and economic benefits that may have motivated the Epidaurians to export their cult to Athens.[9]

From all these considerations it would seem that, although Telemachos took credit for bringing Asklepios to the south slope of the Akropolis and establishing a sanctuary there, the state and the Eleusinian and Epidaurian officials had been involved from the outset and his welcome at the Eleusinion carefully planned. Whatever may have happened to prompt the establishment of a sanctuary of Asklepios on the south slope of the Akropolis, the arrival of Asklepios in Athens and his reception at the Eleusinion nevertheless continued to be celebrated annually with the state-sponsored festival that included a sacrifice, a *pannychis*, and a procession.[10] The procession, which was organized by the eponymous archon, probably re-enacted the initial arrival of Asklepios and his journey from Zea to the Eleusinion.[11] Wickkiser imagined that the procession continued beyond the Eleusinion and ended at the Asklepieion on the south slope,[12] but if the procession was a re-enactment of the original journey, it seems more likely that its destination was the Eleusinion, which was also the focus of the activities during the Mysteries.[13]

The Shrine in the Eleusinion

Whether it ended there or not, the annually celebrated presence of Asklepios in the Eleusinion must have required a shrine as its focus, the shrine that attracted the numerous dedications that have been found in the area. The shrine is most likely to have been located in the forecourt of the sanctuary, since only those initiated into the Mysteries were permitted access to the inner sanctuary.[14] The sanctuary of Demeter and Kore at Eleusis similarly had shrines dedicated to others in its forecourt, a temple to Triptolemos and another to Artemis Propylaia and Father Poseidon (Paus. 1.38.6–7).[15] Given the probable original extent of the Athenian forecourt, it is unlikely that any shrine to Asklepios in the City Eleusinion could have been large, certainly not on the scale of his healing establishment on the south slope.[16] It would have needed only enough space for the altar required for the celebration of the *Epidauria* and for votives such as the reliefs that have been found in the vicinity.

What happened after the arrival of Asklepios is unclear because Telemachos' inscription is fragmentary and apparently exclusively concerned with his role in founding the sanctuary on the south slope. But the Telemachos Monument itself suggests that almost from the time of his arrival, Asklepios had two shrines in Athens. The first sentence of its inscription says that Telemachos was the first to establish a *hieron* and set up an altar to Asklepios and Hygieia. Telemachos' emphasis upon his priority suggests that by the time he set up his monument, ca. 400 BC, a second sanctuary and altar had already been established, perhaps the sanctuary proposed here for the Eleusinion.[17] This seems to be borne out, at least by the Roman period, by the existence of two thrones for priests of Asklepios in the proedria of the Theatre of Dionysos, one for the priest of Asklepios and another for the priest of Asklepios Paieon.[18]

Sophocles and Asklepios

The second shrine that can be inferred from the account of Telemachos has often been associated not with the Eleusinion but rather with the establishment of an altar to Asklepios by the poet Sophocles.[19] Plutarch says that Sophocles received Asklepios as a guest (*Moralia* 14. 22 (1103B) = *TrGF* 4 T M 68 Radt, and *Numa* 4.6 = *TrGF* 4 T M 67 Radt), and a 9th-century Byantine lexicon says that Sophocles was heroized after his death and given the name Dexion or Receiver because he had received the god in his own house and set up an altar to him (*Etymologicum Genuinum* 256.6 = *TrGF* 4 T M 69 Radt). The altar would have been erected before his death in 406. Some scholars have placed the altar in or by the house of Sophocles, the location of which is unknown.[20] Others have located it in the sanctuary of Amynos on the south slope of the Areopagos, where the presence of Asklepios is attested by several votives dedicated to him and where honorary decrees of the *orgeones* of Amynos, Asklepios, and Dexion were found.[21] But several scholars have recently argued that the connection of Sophocles with the hero Dexion and of Sophocles with the Amyneion is tenuous, and that the entire story of the heroization of Sophocles and his role in the arrival of Asklepios might have been Hellenistic fictional biography, based upon Sophocles own works and especially upon the evidence that the poet had written a paean for the god.[22]

The initial connection of Sophocles with Asklepios in the Amyneion arose when Körte published two honorary decrees of the *koina* of the *orgeones* of Amynos, Asklepios, and Dexion, which had been found along with dedications to Amynos and Asklepios in the excavations of the sanctuary, and identified the Dexion of the decrees as the heroized Sophocles.[23] Körte then sought to strengthen the association of Sophocles with the sanctuary by emending the *Vita Sophoclis*, which says that Sophocles was a priest of Halon or Alon (*Vita Sophoclis* 11 = *TRGF* 4, T A 1, lines 39–40 Radt), to read that the poet had instead been a priest of Amynos.[24] A few scholars initially rejected Körte's emendation,[25] but it soon became the widely accepted basis for the activities of Sophocles in the Amyneion. Even though the decrees clearly indicate that there was a group of individuals who gathered to worship Amynos, Asklepios, and Dexion, nothing has ever been found in the Amyneion that would associate this Dexion with Sophocles; the only testimony linking Sophocles and Dexion is the late entry in the Byzantine lexicon. Furthermore, one of the decrees of the *orgeones* (*IG* II² 1252+999, lines 14–17) stipulates that one copy of the decree was to have been set up in the *hieron* of Dexion and another copy in the *hieron* of Asklepios and Amynos, which seems to indicate that the shrines were separate.[26] Finally, several scholars have suggested that the name Dexion might originally have referred not to reception but rather to the right hand and its healing power and to a minor Attic healing hero with no connection at all to Sophocles.[27]

Whatever may have been the relationship between Sophocles and Dexion, none of the epigraphical evidence placing Asklepios in the Amyneion can be dated earlier than the 4th century; the only altar dedicated to Asklepios that has been found there is dated to the 1st century BC.[28] The shrine of Amynos was established in the 6th century, and Asklepios appears to have arrived there too late for Sophocles to have had anything to do with his presence.[29] Thus it would seem that if there is any truth to the tradition that Sophocles set up an altar to Asklepios, it would have been a modest household altar unlikely to have been seen as competition by Telemachos and a shrine unlikely to have merited a seat for its priest in the theatre. Such a private shrine apparently did exist by the second half of the 4th century, in a house and garden dedicated to Asklepios by Demon, son of Demomeles (*IG* II² 4969), which Despinis has located in the area between Kolonos Agoraios and the Kerameikos.[30]

Votive Reliefs Found in the Vicinity of the Eleusinion

A more likely candidate for the second shrine that prompted Telemachos to claim that his was the first would be the more prominent one I postulate in the Eleusinion. A survey of the findspots of the votive reliefs from the Agora excavations representing Asklepios, Hygieia or both produces a scatter of eight reliefs certainly depicting them and one relief possibly depicting Asklepios from the Eleusinion and the area immediately south and west of it, as well as a number of reliefs from the Agora square and its environs.[31] The eight or nine reliefs representing Asklepios and Hygieia from this vicinity are a relatively large number, almost equal to the eight certain and four possible votive reliefs depicting the Eleusinian deities that have been found there. The pattern of the findspots of the reliefs is also similar to that

of the Eleusinian reliefs. One of the reliefs and the relief possibly depicting Asklepios were found in the area of the Eleusinion itself, three were found on the north slope of the Areopagos west of the Eleusinion, and four were found just north and downhill from the Eleusinion (Figure 4.1).[32] None of the reliefs were found in situ; as with much of the sculpture found in the Agora excavations, they had either been discarded or reused in later building. However, five of the nine reliefs certainly or possibly depicting Asklepios and Hygieia from the Eleusinion area were found in ancient or medieval contexts, suggesting that they had not wandered far from their original locations.[33] Some of the reliefs may have been damaged in the Herulian sack of AD 267 and then, along with fragments of destroyed buildings, inscriptions and other sculpture, thrown into the construction of the Post-Herulian Wall, a section of which ran in a north-south direction just to the west of the Eleusinion.[34] Any reliefs that survived the Heruli could have been damaged in the invasion of Alaric and the Visigoths, in which the Eleusinion itself was probably finally destroyed.[35]

In addition to the votive reliefs depicting Asklepios and Hygieia, two other types of relief found in Asklepieia in Athens and elsewhere, anatomical reliefs and reliefs depicting banqueting heroes, were also found in the excavations in the vicinity of the Eleusinion (Figure 4.1). The inscription on one of the five anatomical reliefs from the area, depicting a female pelvis, is possibly to be restored as a 2nd-century AD dedication to Asklepios (Figure 4.2).[36] Two of the other anatomical reliefs also depict female body parts, the lower part of a torso and a breast.[37] Women constituted a high proportion of the dedicators listed in the inventories of the Asklepieion on the south slope of the Akropolis, and among the anatomical votive reliefs actually found there, reliefs depicting breasts far outnumber those depicting other parts of the body.[38] Another anatomical votive relief from the area of the Eleusinion depicts eyes.[39] The inventories of the Asklepieion on the south slope list numerous dedications of eyes in the form of metal *typoi*, and blindness is the most common ailment in all of the *iamata* recording cures in Asklepieia generally.[40] The fifth anatomical votive from the area, probably Roman, depicts a leg, a very common dedication in the Asklepieion on the south slope.[41]

The other type of votive relief found in Asklepieia and shrines of other healers that is well-represented in the area of the Eleusinion are reliefs dedicated to banqueting heroes.[42] Of the forty-nine reliefs depicting banqueting heroes from the Agora excavations, fourteen dating from the late 5th and 4th centuries BC came from the immediate area of the Eleusinion, the north slope of the Areopagos just west of the Eleusinion, or the north slope of the Akropolis (Figures 4.1 and 4.3).[43] Banqueting heroes are seldom named, and in general little is known about them, but there are strong indications that at least some of them had healing powers that could explain their association with Asklepios.[44] One

Figure 4.1 Distribution plan of finds related to Asklepios in the vicinity of the Eleusinion. Drawing by Richard C. Anderson and Craig A. Mauzy

relief from the Agora excavations actually depicts Asklepios with a banqueting hero and his accompanying heroine, although it was found not in the area of the Eleusinion but rather in a cluster of dedications that seem related to another healer, Heros Iatros, in the residential and industrial area outside the southwest corner of the Agora (Figure 4.4).[45] Heros Iatros is himself depicted as a banqueting hero.[46] At least six reliefs depicting banqueting heroes have been found in the sanctuary of Asklepios on the south slope of the Akropolis or its immediate vicinity.[47] A banqueting hero is also depicted on the Telemachos Monument.

In addition to these votive reliefs, a number of other finds relating to Asklepios and Hygieia have come to light in the area of the Eleusinion (Figure 4.1). An altar dedicated to Hygieia (*IG* II² 4539) and dated to the Roman era, came from the church of Agia Kyra, on Polygnotos Street north of the Eleusinion.[48] A large Roman-period dedication (*SEG* 21.776), possibly to Asklepios, by a group of patients (θερα[πευθέντες]), was found in the wall of a modern house just southwest of the Eleusinion.[49] A fragment of a large base dating from the 4th century BC and apparently depicting the family of Asklepios was found in the wall of a modern house on the north slope of the Areopagos just southwest of the Eleusinion (Figure 4.5).[50] And a small early Roman statue of Asklepios came from late Roman destruction debris or fill in the vicinity of the large Roman houses on the north slope of the Areopagos.[51] A large number of statuettes of Asklepios have been found in the Agora excavations, but most of them do not come from the area of the Eleusinion, and they have limited significance as evidence for the location of a shrine.[52] As with statuettes of other deities from the excavations, some of them are unfinished, and many came from the residential and industrial area southwest of the Agora proper, where they were probably being made in some of the sculptors' workshops there.[53]

Probably the most intriguing discovery from the area of the Eleusinion is a boundary marker of the 2nd century BC for a *temenos* of Asklepios and Hygieia found in an ancient dump on Polygnotos Street.[54] Although Telemachos in his inscription concerning the founding of the sanctuary of Asklepios on the south slope of the Akropolis refers to the new sanctuary as both a *hieron* and a *temenos*, Clinton doubted that this newly discovered boundary marker came from that sanctuary because the term *temenos* generally refers to a more modest shrine.[55] By the time this boundary marker was inscribed, the sanctuary on the south slope was no longer a private establishment, if indeed it ever had been;[56] it had been under state control since at least the mid-4th century,[57] and it was now called a *hieron*.[58] The term *temenos* would, on the other hand, be appropriate for the marker of a shrine to Asklepios within a larger *hieron* such as the City Eleusinion.[59]

One of the reliefs from the excavations in the area of the Eleusinion is among the earliest Athenian votive reliefs dedicated to Asklepios (Figure 4.6), and its date, ca. 420, suggests that Asklepios was worshipped there soon after his arrival in Athens.[60] Although the relief is fragmentary and lacks an inscription, the identity of its figure as Asklepios seems assured by comparison with a nearly identical figure of Asklepios on a votive relief from the Asklepieion on the south slope (Figure 4.7).[61] In both reliefs Asklepios is shown in his familiar casual stance, his right hand propped on his hip, wearing his usual himation with triangular overfold; as often in 5th-century reliefs he is without his staff. Harrison, tracing the evolution of patterns in the triangular overfall of the himation in the late 5th century, compared the drapery of the figure in the Agora relief to that of the Dresden "Zeus," which she dated to just after 420.[62] The himation of Aphrodite on the relief of the honorary decree for Proxenides of Knidos, now securely dated to 422/1 (*IG* I³ 91 Add.), has a very similar treatment of the folds.[63] A second relief depicting Asklepios from the Agora excavations may also date from the last quarter of the 5th century (Figure 4.8). The relief, recovered from the foundations of the Church of Panagia Vlassarou in the middle of the Agora square, shows Asklepios with a similar triangular overfall, but its thinner, more transparent cloth calls for a date of 410 or a little later.[64] In this relief he holds his staff.

The Relationship to Telemachos' Shrine on the South Slope

If one or both of these reliefs were dedications from a shrine of Asklepios in the Eleusinion, and if we can believe Telemachos when he says that he was the first to set up a *hieron* and an altar, then the dates of the reliefs suggest that the shrine in the Eleusinion was established very soon after Telemachos set up his shrine on the south slope in 420, soon enough for Telemachos to have felt that he had competition. The inscription of the Telemachos Monument also hints at what that competition might have been. In lines 20–23, the text states that when Archeas was archon (419/18), "the Kerykes disputed the land and hindered some actions" (trans. Wickkiser) – and then there is an unfortunate lacuna in the inscription. The text is usually understood to read that the Kerykes, one of the two clans with priestly jurisdiction over the Eleusinion and the Mysteries, raised some objections about the site on the south slope of the Akropolis where Telemachos had set up his sanctuary. Many scholars have speculated about the reasons for the dispute,[65] but surely the most obvious would have been that the Eleusinian officials, having gone to a great deal of trouble to bring Asklepios to the Eleusinion, were loathe to turn him over to a privately established shrine on the other side

Figure 4.2 Anatomical relief from the Agora excavations possibly inscribed to Asklepios. Agora I 5721. 2nd c. AD. Courtesy American School of Classical Studies at Athens, Agora Excavations.

Figure 4.4 Relief depicting a banqueting hero and heroine, with the left hand, staff, and snake of Asklepios on the left, from the excavations of the Athenian Agora. Agora S 1258. Second half 4th c. BC. Courtesy American School of Classical Studies at Athens, Agora Excavations.

Figure 4.3 Relief depicting a banqueting hero from the excavations of the Athenian Agora in the area of the Eleusinion. Agora S 1006. Mid-4th c. BC. Courtesy American School of Classical Studies at Athens, Agora Excavations.

Figure 4.5 Fragment of a large base depicting Hygieia and probably one of the sons of Asklepios, from the Agora excavations in the area of the Eleusinion. Agora S 1103. 4th c. BC. Courtesy American School of Classical Studies at Athens, Agora Excavations.

of the Akropolis. In 419/18, Asklepios had been in Athens for at most only a year, and it is not unreasonable to assume that the Kerykes were already constructing an altar for him in the Eleusinion and making plans for the establishment of the *Epidauria*, which were inaugurated sometime before 404.[66] If they had tried to stop Telemachos from establishing his shrine, they were clearly unsuccessful, but Telemachos would have been powerless to do anything about what had

been constructed or planned for Asklepios in the Eleusinion; in the end, all he could do was to claim that his shrine and altar had been the first.

If the finds relating to Asklepios and Hygieia from the area of the Eleusinion came from a shrine dedicated to

Figure 4.7 Votive relief dedicated to Asklepios by a cart-driver, from the Asklepieion on the south slope of the Akropolis. Athens, National Archaeological Museum 1341 (IG II² 4356). Ca. 400 BC. Courtesy National Archaeological Museum (photographer: Giannis Patrikianos).

Figure 4.6 Votive relief with Asklepios, from the excavations of the Athenian Agora in the area of the Eleusinion. Agora S 2050. Ca. 420 BC. Courtesy American School of Classical Studies at Athens, Agora Excavations.

Asklepios there, their dates also suggest that the shrine continued in use into Roman times, probably until the destruction of the Eleusinion itself in the late 4th century AD. But the association of Asklepios with the Eleusinians was not confined to the proposed shrine in the Eleusinion and the annual observation of the *Epidauria*. A 4th-century BC relief from the Asklepieion on the south slope indicates that the connection was observed there as well. It depicts six male worshippers in the presence of Asklepios, Demeter and Kore.[67] The inscribed crowns beneath the relief apparently indicate that it honored five men, three of whom are known to have been physicians or sons of physicians.[68] A very poorly preserved relief without provenance in the Akropolis Museum that possibly depicts Asklepios with Kore and Athena might have come either from the south slope or a shrine in the Eleusinion. Walter restored Demeter in the missing right part of the relief and suggested that the combination of deities referred to the *Epidauria*.[69]

Figure 4.8 Votive relief with Asklepios, from the excavations of the Athenian Agora. Agora S 621. Ca. 410 BC. Courtesy American School of Classical Studies at Athens, Agora Excavations.

Asklepios and Demeter: Conclusions

After the introduction of Asklepios into the Eleusinion at Athens, the association of Asklepios with Demeter was also established at Eleusis, where by the late 5th or early 4th century there was apparently a shrine of Asklepios and Hygieia situated on the Kephissos River about 1 k north of the sanctuary of Demeter and Kore.[70] The worship of Asklepios spread rapidly, often to sites where Demeter was also worshipped.[71] The affinities between Asklepios and Demeter are notable: their civilizing gifts to mankind, the

hope they offered for triumph over death, Asklepios in life and Demeter in the afterlife, and even similarities in their rituals.[72] Whether there was a perceived connection between them before Asklepios' arrival in Athens is unclear, but quite probably their frequent later association throughout the Greek world was an acknowledgment of their relationship in Athens, cemented ritually by the integration of the *Epidauria* into the Mysteries. In Athens itself the popularity of the cult of Asklepios and Hygieia continued to grow and flourish in multiple locations, not only in their sanctuary that Telemachos established on the south slope of the Akropolis, but also in private shrines such as that of Demon and perhaps of Sophocles, and in the very place where Asklepios was first welcomed into Athens, the City Eleusinion.

Notes

1   This article originated in a lecture given at the International Congress of Classical Archaeology in Amsterdam in July, 1998: Lawton 1999. The votive reliefs from the Agora excavations will be published in a volume of the series *The Athenian Agora, Results of the Excavations*. I am very grateful to the late Homer A. Thompson, T. Leslie Shear, Jr., and John McK. Camp II, former and present Directors of the Agora Excavations, and to the late Evelyn B. Harrison for permission to study the reliefs. My research on the Agora votive reliefs has been funded by the National Endowment for the Humanities, the Solow Foundation for Art and Architecture, the John Simon Guggenheim Memorial Foundation, the Kress Foundation, and Lawrence University. For their advice and suggestions on specific points, I would like to thank the late Judith Binder, John Camp, Alkestis Choremis, Kevin Clinton, Jesper Jensen, Margaret M. Miles, Olga Palagia, Dimitris Sourlas, Ronald Stroud, Jere Wickens, and Bronwen Wickkiser. I am grateful to two anonymous readers for their helpful suggestions, and to Craig A. Mauzy for making the distribution plan.

2   The connection of the Agora reliefs with the Eleusinion was first tentatively suggested by Clinton, but he ultimately concluded that the Amyneion was a more likely location for them: Clinton 1994, p. 33, n. 67. For Asklepios and Hygieia in the Amyneion, see Körte 1893, pp. 231–256; Körte 1896, pp. 287–332; Judeich 1931, pp. 289–291; Travlos 1971, p. 76; Aleshire 1991, pp. 223–239; Riethmüller 2005, vol. 2, pp. 12–17. Harrison (1982, p. 45, n. 16) had perhaps already hinted at the connection when she wrote with reference to the votive relief Agora S 2050 (Figure 4.6) that it was "interesting to have a fragment of an Asklepios relief from the area of the Eleusinion which can be dated by its style to the time between the initial introduction of Asklepios into the Eleusinion in 420/19 BC and his establishment in his permanent sanctuary on the south slope of the Acropolis in 413/12 BC." See also Harrison, pers. comm. in Riethmüller 2005, vol. 2, p. 11, where he too (vol. 1, p. 245, vol. 2, pp. 11–12) concluded that some of the reliefs, statuettes, and inscriptions from the Agora concerning Asklepios and Hygieia came from the Eleusinion. Although Geagan (2011, pp. 296–297, 305) recognized that there was probably a *temenos* of Asklepios in or near the Eleusinion, he concluded that many of the dedications from the Agora came from the Asklepieion on the south slope. Despinis (2001, p. 216) thought that some of the Agora material might have come from a shrine of Asklepios north of the Akropolis, but he did not suggest a specific location. The Eleusinion originally occupied a far greater area than has been exposed by excavation. For the extent and identification of the excavated portion of the site, see Miles 1998, pp. 1–9. For the identification of at least part of the forecourt with the area of the Eleusinion already excavated, see Miles 1998, pp. 50–52.

3   *SEG* 25.226 = *IG* II² 4960 + 4961; *SEG* 47.232 (lines 1–26 only). The monument is now displayed in the Akropolis Museum under the inventory number EAM 2490 +. For the reconstruction of the monument, see Beschi 1969a; Mitropoulou 1975; Beschi 1982; Beschi 1985; Wickkiser 2008, pp. 67–72.

4   Clinton 1994, p. 24; Wickkiser 2008, p. 71. For the Asklepieion in Piraeus, see Chapter 5 by J. Lamont in this volume.

5   Wickkiser 2008, pp. 62–66, 90–101.

6   Clinton 1994, pp. 24–25; Wickkiser 2008, pp. 71–72. For the necessity of the approval of the demos for the introduction of new cults, see Rudhardt 1960, pp. 92–93; Garland 1984, p. 78; Garland 1992, pp. 19–20; Parker 2011, pp. 273–277.

7   For the *Epidauria* and the role of the Eleusinian cult in the arrival of Asklepios, see Deubner 1932, pp. 72–73; Parke 1977, pp. 64–65; Garland 1992, pp. 123–124; Clinton 1994; Wickkiser 2008, pp. 71–75, 101–105.

8   Clinton 1994, pp. 18–21, 24. He cites Agora I 7471, a fragment of a late-5th-century law concerning the *Epidauria*, which he restored to include *phr*[*ouroi*], a term for officials in the Epidaurian cult of Asklepios not known in Attica, and *hier*[*omnemones*], a term unattested for officials of the Mysteries or the Asklepieion on the south slope of the Akropolis.

9   Wickkiser 2008, pp. 97–98.

10 For the sacrifice and *pannychis*, see *IG* II² 974.11–13; *IG* II² 975.5–8; Philostr., *VA* 4.18. For the procession, see Arist. *AthPol.* 56.4.

11 Parke 1977, pp. 64–65; Clinton 1994, p. 29; Wickkiser 2008, pp. 74, 101–105.

12 Wickkiser 2008, p. 104.

13 Clinton (1994, p. 27) thought that the procession, before going to the Eleusinion, went to the house of Sophocles and, after the death of Sophocles, to the sanctuary of Dexion. For the involvement of Sophocles and Dexion in the arrival of Asklepios, see below.

14 For the exclusion of non-initiates from the inner sanctuary of the Eleusinion, see Paus. 1.14.3 and Miles 1998, p. 12, n. 6.

15 Miles 1998, pp. 50–51.

16 Clinton, pers. comm., has pointed out to me that none of the financial accounts and inventories of Eleusis and the City Eleusinion list valuables such as the *typoi* characteristic of Asklepios found in the inventories of the Asklepieion on the south slope. For the financial records of the Eleusinion officials, see Clinton 2005, nos. 52, 136–179. Stone votives were not included in inventories because they were not salable: Clinton 2008, p. 72.

17 For the date of the Telemachos Monument, see Beschi 1969a, pp. 428–436.

18 *IG* II² 5045 (Asklepios Paieon): Maass 1972, p. 120, pl. 12; *IG* II² 5068 (Asklepios): Maass 1972, p. 133, pl. 18; Aleshire 1989, pp. 83–84. Asklepios is called Paieon in two other inscriptions of the 2nd or 3rd century AD, *IG* II² 3809 and 4533.

19 Foucart 1900, pp. 117–118; Walton 1935, pp. 173–174, Ferguson 1944, pp. 90–91; Aleshire 1989, pp. 10–11; Clinton 1994, p. 31.

20 Kearns 1989, p. 154; Clinton 1994, p. 26; Parker 1996, tentatively, p. 185, n. 15.

21 Körte 1896, pp. 312–313; Travlos 1971, p. 76; Riethmüller 2005, vol. 2, p. 278. Ferguson 1944, pp. 90–91, thought that Sophocles might have set up altars both in his own house and in the Amyneion. An epigram in the *Anthologia Palatina* 6. 145 (= TrGF 4 T Z 182 Radt) refers to altars set up by Sophocles. For doubts about the authenticity of the

epigram, see Connolly 1998, pp. 4–5. Inscribed dedications to Asklepios and Hygieia found in the Amyneion: a marble base of the first half of the 4th century BC with a dedication to Asklepios and Amynos (*IG* II² 4365): Körte 1896, pp. 294–295, no. 1; Travlos 1971, p. 78, fig. 99; a 4th-century BC anatomical votive of a breast dedicated to Asklepios (*IG* II² 4422): Körte 1893, pp. 241–242, no. 6, fig. 3; Travlos 1971, p. 78, fig. 101; and a 1st-century BC marble altar dedicated to Amynos, Asklepios and Hygieia (*IG* II² 4457): Körte 1896, pp. 296–297, no. 4. Honorary decrees of the *orgeones* of Amynos, Asklepios, and Dexion: *IG* II² 1252+999 and *IG* II² 1253.

22 Lefkowitz 1981, pp. 83–85; Connolly 1998; Wickkiser 2008, pp. 66–67. In the early 3rd century AD, the text of a paean by Sophocles (*IG* II² 4510) was inscribed on the left side of the choregic monument of Sarapion of Cholleidai, which had been set up in the Asklepieion on the south slope of the Akropolis: Oliver 1936; Aleshire 1991, p. 51, fig. 1. For other testimonia for a paean to Asklepios by Sophocles, see Pseudo-Lucian, *Demosthenes Encomium* 27 (= TrGF T M 73b); Philostratos, *Vita Apollonii* 3.17 (= TrGF 4, T M 73a); Philostratos the Younger, *Imagines* 13 (= TrGF 4, T Y 174).

23 Körte 1896, pp. 298–303, nos. 6, 7, pp. 310–311 and n. 21 above. Both decrees are usually dated to the second half of the 4th century, but Tracy (2003, p. 152) has recently suggested a date in the first half of the 3rd century for *IG* II² 1253.

24 Körte 1896, pp. 311–312. Meineke (1840, p. 683) had previously suggested the name Alkon.

25 Wilamowitz 1932, p. 225; Kern 1935, pp. 313–314, n. 1. Pfister (1909, p. 121, n. 434) and Schmidt (1909, p. 107, n. 6) noted A. Dieterich's suggestion that the name Halon or Alon was etymologically related to ἅλς, or salt, which led Schmidt (1913, pp. 73–77) to make a case for Halon as a god or hero of healing salt water, a shortened form of the name Halirrhothios, the hero associated with one of the springs in the Asklepieion on the south slope of the Akropolis. He was followed by Judeich 1931, p. 320, n. 2; Walter 1953, pp. 472–473; and Beschi 1969a, pp. 434; Beschi 1969b, 512–514. The controversy over the name is neatly summarized in Walter, 1953. Körte's emendation has only recently come under renewed criticism: Connolly 1998, pp. 10–11, n. 50; Wickkiser 2008, p. 136, n. 13.

26 Walter 1953, pp. 473–475.

27 Pfister 1909, p. 121, n. 435; Weinreich 1909, pp. 38–40; Connolly 1998, pp. 5–6. Lefkowitz (1981, p. 84) has noted that it was the usual practice for adult heroes to be worshipped under their own names. No votives to Dexion have been found: Aleshire 1989, p. 11, n. 1.

28 See n. 21 above.

29 Date of the Amyneion: Körte 1893, pp. 234–235; Travlos 1971, p. 76; Riethmüller 2005, vol 2, p. 15.

30 Despinis 2001; Riethmüller 2005, vol. 2, p. 18, no. 5.

31 Three other Asklepios reliefs were found farther afield, two (Agora S 621, depicting Asklepios (Figure 4.8), and Agora S 2741, depicting Asklepios and Hygieia) just west of the Odeion in the Agora proper and one (Agora S 1939, representing Asklepios and Hygieia) in the residential and industrial area southwest of the Agora square. Two other reliefs, one possibly depicting Asklepios and Hygieia (Agora S 593) and the other apparently depicting Asklepios (Agora S

2805) were found in the Agora square. Another relief probably representing Hygieia was found near the Hephaisteion prior to the Agora excavations: Athens, NM 1383, found in 1891 in the construction of the Athens-Piraeus railway (Kavvadias 1891, pp. 88, 90, no. 24; Svoronos 1908–1937, pl. 38:4; Leventi 2003, pp. 151–152, R 66, pl. 43). Edwards (1985, p. 431), noting that the figure is accompanied by a fragmentary horse rather than by Asklepios, identified the figure as a goddess associated with a hero. As many as 17 votive reliefs depicting Asklepios and/or Hygieia are housed in the storerooms of the Roman Agora (pers. comm. A. Choremis, D. Sourlas).

32 From the Eleusinion itself, Agora S 2050, depicting Asklepios (Figure 4.6), was found in packing beside a late Roman wall north of the south stoa terrace of the Eleusinion, and Agora S 2966, which may depict Asklepios, was found in a dump of marbles from the area of the Eleusinion. On the north slope of the Areopagos, Agora S 1179, depicting Asklepios, was found discarded in a dump of the 4th and 5th centuries in a well just southwest of the Eleusinion; Agora S 2323, also depicting Asklepios, came from the abandonment debris of a late Roman house just west of the Eleusinion; and Agora S 800, depicting Asklepios and Hygieia, came from the walls of a modern house further west. Downhill from the Eleusinion, Agora S 1825 and Agora I 4108, both depicting Hygieia, were found in the vicinity of the Church of the Holy Apostles; Agora S 2866, depicting Asklepios, in a marble dump in the vicinity of the South Stoa; and Agora S 2505, depicting Asklepios and Hygieia, in a dump of the 3rd to 5th centuries in a well near the Library of Panainos.

33 See n. 32 for the findspots of Agora S 2050, S1179, S 2323, and S 2505.

34 For the incorporation of material from the Eleusinion in the Post-Herulian Wall, see Frantz 1988, p. 130.

35 For the destruction of the Eleusinion, see Miles 1998, pp. 92–93.

36 Agora I 5721, found in a marble pile southwest of the Eleusinion: Geagan 2011, p. 299, V574, pl. 58.

37 Agora I 5307, a profile view of the lower part of a female torso, probably dating from the 4th century BC, found in the eastern wall of the Church of the Hypapanti in the area of the Eleusinion: Geagan 2011, p. 301, V577, pl. 58 (photo printed backwards). Agora I 3727, depicting a breast, dated by Geagan from the 2nd century BC to the 2nd century AD, found in a dump just north of the Eleusinion: Geagan 2011, pp. 296, 298, V572, pl. 58.

38 For women as dedicators in the inventories of the Asklepieion on the south slope of the Akropolis, see Aleshire 1989, pp. 45–46. For anatomical votive breasts from the Asklepieion, see Forsén 1996, pp. 33–40, nos. 1.5–1.21. Forsén 1996, p. 145, has argued that the frequent dedications of breasts and female pelvises in Asklepieia suggests that Asklepios was not only a healer of women's ailments but also a deity concerned with fertility, childbirth, and childrearing.

39 Agora S 1573, unpublished, found among demolition marbles in the area of the Church of the Holy Apostles northwest of the Eleusinion.

40 For the large number of dedications of *typoi* depicting eyes in the Asklepieion, see Aleshire 1989, p. 42. For the *iamata*, see Wickkiser 2008, p. 59. The relative rarity of stone anatomical

votive reliefs with eyes from the Asklepieion (Forsén 1996, pp. 31–33, nos. 1.1–1.2) led Forsén (1996, pp. 154–157) to conclude that the metal eyes of the inventories are not indications of specialization but rather that metal was the preferred medium for that type of dedication. A 4th-century BC stone votive from Eleusis depicting eyes and dedicated to Demeter (Athens, NM 5256; *IG* II² 4639) differs from other anatomical votives depicting eyes in having on top of it a head of Demeter with painted rays emanating from her head, which may indicate that it is not an anatomical votive but rather a dedication by a person who had been cured of the ritual blindness of the Mystes and was now an Epoptes, "one who sees:" van Straten 1981, pp. 121–122, no. 13.1, fig. 56; Clinton 1992, pp. 86–90, fig. 78; Clinton 2005, pp. 107–108, no. 105, pl. 47. Although there is one recorded instance of a cure for blindness at the Mysteries (epigram of Antiphilus, *Anth. Pal.* 9.298; Clinton 2008, p. 110, no. 105), no other anatomical votives dedicated to the goddesses are known from Attica. For Demeter and Kore as healers, see Rubensohn 1895, pp. 360–367; Forsén 1996, pp. 143–144.

41   Agora S 2513, found in late fill over the Library of Pantainos. For anatomical votives of legs from the Asklepieion, see Forsén 1996, pp. 47–53, nos. 1.37–1.46.

42   For banqueting heroes in general, see Dentzer 1982. For banqueting reliefs from the Asklepieion on the south slope of the Akropolis, see Dentzer 1982, pp. 463–464; Riethmüller 2005, vol. 2, p. 248, n. 38. A late-5th-century BC relief from Piraeus depicting a banqueting hero (Athens, NM 1501) may have come from the Asklepieion there: Svoronos 1908–1937, pp. 528–529, pl. 83; Dentzer 1982, pp. 593–594 (R 222), pl. 79, fig. 477; Kaltsas 2002, p. 136, no. 261. Reliefs depicting a banqueter have also been found in the sanctuaries of the healers Amynos, who is associated with Asklepios (Dentzer 1982, pp. 468, 591 (R 206)), and Herakles Pankrates (Vikela 1994, p. 29 (A 22), pl. 17).

43   Immediate area of the Eleusinion: Agora S 103 + 1010 (fragment S 1010 only), S 713, S 1006, S 1018, S 2628. North slope of the Areopagos west of the Eleusinion: Agora S 982, S 986, S 988, S 1101, S 1152, S 2891, S 3180, S 3334. Marble pile on the north slope of the Akropolis: Agora S 2761. S 713 and S 986 may date from the late 5th century BC; the others date from the 4th century.

44   Hausmann 1948, pp. 111–124; Dentzer 1982, p. 464.

45   Agora S 1258: Mitropoulou 1976, pp. 137–138, no. 97, fig. p. 137; Dentzer 1982, pp. 331, n. 282, 334, n. 303, 335, n. 318, 583 (R 134), pl. 68, fig. 397.

46   von Bothmer 1957–1958, p. 187, fig. p. 190.

47   Dentzer 1982, p. 463.

48   Pittakis 1835, no. 51.

49   Agora I 5717: Meritt 1961, p. 273, no. 113; Geagan 2011, p. 56, no. C117.

50   Agora S 1103, unpublished, preserves two figures, Hygieia and a nude male, probably one of the sons of Asklepios.

51   Agora S 1068: Frantz 1988, p, 41, pl. 39:d.

52   Most of the statuettes are unpublished; some are listed in Riethmüller 2005, vol. 2, pp. 11–12, n. 11.

53   For sculptors' workshops in the area, see Young 1951; Shear 1969, pp. 383–394; Lawton 2006, pp. 12–20.

54   Choremis 1995, p. 21, pl. 14:a; *SEG* 44.79; Chaniotis and Stavrianopoulou 1997, p. 264, no. 39. A small statue of Asklepios was found nearby, in a rescue excavation at the corner of Pelopidas and Pan Streets: A. Choremis, pers. comm. in Clinton 1994, p. 33, n. 67.

55   Clinton 1994, p. 33, n. 67.

56   Wickkiser (2008, pp. 5–9, 62–75) questioned the validity of the concept of "private cult" and argued that it was not Telemachos but rather the state and the cult of Eleusinian Demeter and Kore that were responsible for the importation of the cult of Asklepios.

57   Aleshire 1989, pp. 14–15.

58   Clinton 1994, p. 33, n. 67.

59   For a discussion of the terms *temenos* and *hieron* and their use in Athenian documents, see Clinton 1994, n. 58 above. As an example of a *temenos* within a larger sanctuary, he cites the *temenos* of Neleus and Basile within the *hieron* of Kodros, Neleus, and Basile (*IG* I³ 84).

60   Agora S 2050: Harrison 1982, pp. 44–45, pl. 6:d; Lawton 2009, pp. 77, 83, no. 10, fig. 22. See n. 2 above.

61   Athens, NM 1341 (*IG* II² 4356), identified by inscription as a dedication to Asklepios by a cart-driver: Kaltsas 2002, p. 140, no. 267, fig. 267; Leventi 2003, pp. 133–134, R11, pl. 13; Harrison 1982, n. 60 above.

62   Harrison 1982, n. 60 above.

63   Lawton 1995, pl. 36, no. 68.

64   Agora S 621: Harrison 1982, pp. 45–46, pl. 7:a. Cf. the relief on the accounts of the treasurers of Athena of 409/8 (Paris, Louvre MA 831 (*IG* II³ 375)): Lawton 1995, no. 8, pl. 5.

65   For the dispute between Telemachos and the Kerykes, see Körte 1896, pp. 331–32; Kutsch 1913, pp. 21–23; Walton 1935, pp. 172–174; Ferguson 1944, p. 89, n. 36; Clinton 1994, pp. 28–29, 32–33; Connolly 1998, p. 13; Wickkiser 2008, pp. 74–75, 100–101.

66   The *Epidauria* are mentioned in a sacred law (Agora I 7471) dated between 410 and 404: Clinton 1994, pp. 18–19. See n. 8 above.

67   Athens, NM 1332 (*IG* II² 4359): Svoronos 1908–37, pl. 36:2; Kaltsas 2002, pp. 224–225, no. 472, fig. 472; Comella 2002, pp. 110–111, 196 (Atene 77), fig. 110.

68   The men have sometimes been identified as Athenian public physicians, but for the problems in the interpretation of the names in the inscription, see Cohn-Haft 1956, p. 57, n. 13; Aleshire 1989, pp. 94–95.

69   Athens, AM 4726: Walter 1923, no. 56.

70   Skias 1898, pp. 87–90; Kourouniotes 1924–25; Travlos 1988, p. 96; Clinton 2005, pp. 497–499, nos. 680–686, pl. 307; Clinton 2008, pp. 427–428. A 4th-century BC statue of Asklepios and inscriptions concerning him dating from the late 5th century BC to the Roman period were found in a vineyard there, although the excavator, Skias, doubted that this was their original location. The area has not been excavated.

71   Benedum 1986.

72   Edelstein and Edelstein 1945, II, pp. 127–129; Benedum 1986; Garland 1992, p. 124; Wickkiser 2008, pp. 87–89. Cf. Parker 1996, p. 180, n. 96, who calls Garland's comparison of the rituals "exaggerated."

References

Aleshire, S. B. 1989. *The Athenian Asklepieion: The People, their Dedications, and the Inventories,* Amsterdam.

Aleshire, S. B. 1991. *Asklepios at Athens: Epigraphic and Prosopographic Essays on the Athenian Healing Cults,* Amsterdam.

Benedum, C. 1986. "Asklepios und Demeter: Zur Bedeutung weiblicher Gottheiten für den frühen Asklepioskult," *Jahrbuch des Deutschen Archäologischen Instituts* 101, pp. 137–157.

Beschi, L. 1969a. "Il monumento di Telemachos, fondatore dell'Asklepieion ateniese," *Annuario della Scuola archeologica di Atene e delle Missioni italiane in Oriente* 45–46 (n.s. 29 30), 1967–1968 [1969], pp. 381–436.

Beschi, L. 1969b. "Contributi di topografia ateniese," *Annuario della Scuola archeologica di Atene e delle Missioni italiane in Oriente* 45–46 (n.s. 29–30), 1967–1968 [1969], pp. 511–536.

Beschi, L. 1982. "Il rilievo di Telemachos ricompletato," *Athens Annals of Archaeology* 15, pp. 31–43.

Beschi, L. 1985. "Rilievi attici del Museo Maffeiano," in *Nuovi Studi Maffeiani: Atti del Convegno "Scipione Maffei e il Museo Maffeiano,"* 18–19 November 1983, Verona, pp. 13–32.

Chaniotis, A. and E. Stavrianopoulou. 1997. "Epigraphic Bulletin for Greek Religion 1993–1994," *Kernos* 10, pp. 249–314.

Choremis, A. 1995. "Α' Εφορεία Προϊστορικών και Κλασικών Αρχαιοτήτων: Οδός Πολυγνώτου 3," *Archaiologikon Deltion* 45, 1990 [1995] Β'1, p. 21.

Clinton, K. 1992. *Myth and Cult: The Iconography of the Eleusinian Mysteries,* (*Skrifter utgivna av Svenska Institutet i Athen* 8°.11), Stockholm.

Clinton, K. 1994. "The Epidauria and the Arrival of Asclepius in Athens," in *Ancient Greek Cult Practice from the Epigraphical Evidence,* (Proceedings of the Second International Seminar on Ancient Greek Cult, Athens, 1991), Stockholm, pp. 17–34.

Clinton, K. 2005–2008. *Eleusis. The Inscriptions on Stone: Documents of the Sanctuary of the Two Goddesses and Public Documents of the Deme,* 2 vols., Athens.

Cohn-Haft, L. 1956. *The Public Physicians of Ancient Greece* (Smith College Studies in History 42), Northampton, Mass.

Comella, A. 2002. *I rilievi votivi greci di periodo arcaico e classico: diffusione, ideologia, committenza* (Bibliotheca Archaeologica 11), Bari.

Connolly, A. 1998. "Was Sophocles Heroized as Dexion?," *Journal of Hellenic Studies* 118, pp. 1–21.

Dentzer, J.-M. 1982. *Le motif du banquet couché dans le Proche-Orient et le monde grec du VIIe au IVe siècle avant J.-C.,* Rome.

Despinis, G. 2001. "Zum Basisfragment *IG* II² 4417 im Kerameikos," *Mitteilungen des Deutschen Archäologischen Instituts, Athenische Abteilung* 114, 1999 [2001], pp. 207–218.

Deubner, L. 1932. *Attische Fest,* Berlin.

Edelstein, E. J. and L. Edelstein. 1945. *Asclepios: A Collection and Interpretation of the Testimonies,* 2 vols., Baltimore.

Edwards, C. M. 1985. "Greek Votive Reliefs to Pan and the Nymphs" (diss. Institute of Fine Arts, New York Univ.).

Ferguson, W. S. 1944. "The Attic Orgeones," *Harvard Theological Review* 37, pp. 61–134.

Forsén, B. 1996. *Griechische Gliederweihungen: Eine Untersuchung zu ihrer Typologie und ihrer religions- und sozialgeschichtlichen Bedeutung,* Helsinki.

Foucart, P. 1900. *Les Grands Mystères d'Éleusis: Personnel et Ceremonies* (Mémoires de l'Académie des Inscriptions et Belles-lettres 37), Paris.

Frantz, A. 1988. *The Athenian Agora,* XXIV. *Late Antiquity: A.D. 267–700,* Princeton.

Garland, R. 1984. "Religious Authority in Archaic and Classical Athens," *Annual of the British School at Athens* 79, pp. 75–123.

Garland, R. 1992. *Introducing New Gods: The Politics of Athenian Religion,* London.

Geagan, D. 2011. *The Athenian Agora,* XVIII. *Inscriptions: the Dedicatory Monuments,* Princeton.

Harrison, E. B. 1982. "A Classical Maiden from the Athenian Agora," in *Studies in Athenian Architecture, Sculpture and Topography Presented to Homer A. Thompson* (*Hesperia* Suppl. 20), Princeton, pp. 40–53.

Hausmann, U. 1948. *Kunst und Heiltum: Untersuchungen zu den griechischen Asklepiosreliefs,* Potsdam.

Judeich, W. 1931. *Topographie von Athen,* 2nd ed., Munich.

Kaltsas, N. 2002. *Sculpture in the National Archaeological Museum, Athens,* Los Angeles.

Kavvadias, P. 1891. "Δελτίον μηνῶν Αὐγούστου καί Σεπτεμβρίου," *Archaiologikon Deltion,* pp. 85–96.

Kearns, E. 1989. *The Heroes of Attica* (Bulletin of the Institute of Classical Studies of the University of London Suppl. 57), London.

Kern, O. 1935. *Die Religion der Griechen,* II, Berlin.

Körte, A. 1893. "Bezirk eines Heilgottes," *Mitteilungen des Deutschen Archäologischen Instituts, Athenische Abteilung* 18, pp. 231–256.

Körte, A. 1896. "Die Ausgrabungen am Westabhang der Akropolis. IV. Das Heiligtum des Amynos," *Mitteilungen des Deutschen Archäologischen Instituts, Athenische Abteilung* 21, pp. 287–332.

Kourouniotes, K. 1924–1925. "Ἄγαλμα Ἀσκληπιοῦ ἐξ Ἐλευσῖνος," *Archaiologikon Deltion* 9, pp. 105–117.

Kutsch, F. 1913. *Attische Heilgötter und Heilheroen,* Giessen.

Lawton, C. 1995. *Attic Document Reliefs: Art and Politics in Ancient Athens,* Oxford.

Lawton, C. 1999. "Votive Reliefs and Popular Religion in the Athenian Agora: the Case of Asklepios and Hygieia," *Proceedings of the XVth International Congress of Classical Archaeology, Amsterdam, July 12–17, 1998* (Allard Pierson Series, vol. 12) ed. R. F. Docter, E. M. Moormann, Amsterdam, pp. 232–234.

Lawton, C. 2006. *Marbleworkers in the Athenian Agora* (Agora Picture Book 27), Princeton.

Lawton, C. 2009. "Attic Votive Reliefs and the Peloponnesian War," in *Art in Athens during the Peloponnesian War,* ed. O. Palagia, Cambridge, pp. 66–93.

Lefkowitz, M. 1981. *The Lives of the Greek Poets,* Baltimore.

Leventi, I. 2003. *Hygieia in Classical Greek Art* (Archaiognosia Suppl. 2), Athens.

Maass, M. 1972. *Die Prohedrie des Dionysostheaters in Athen* (Vestigia, Beiträge zur alten Geschichte 15), Munich.

Meineke, A. 1840. *Fragmenta Comicorum Graecorum,* vol. 2, Berlin.

Meritt, B. 1961. "Greek Inscriptions," *Hesperia* 30, pp. 205–292.

Miles, M. M. 1998. *The Athenian Agora,* XXXI. *The City Eleusinion,* Princeton.

Mitropoulou, E. 1975. *A New Interpretation of the Telemachos Monument*, Athens.

Mitropoulou, E. 1976. *Horses' Heads and Snake in Banquet Reliefs and Their Meaning*, Athens.

Oliver, J. H. 1936. "The Sarapion Monument and the Paean of Sophocles," *Hesperia* 5, pp. 113–114.

Parke, H. W. 1977. *Festivals of the Athenians*, London.

Parker, R. 1996. *Athenian Religion: A History*, Oxford.

Parker, R. 2011. *On Greek Religion (Cornell Studies in Classical Philology*, vol. 60), Ithaca and London.

Pfister, F. 1909. *Der Reliquienkult im Altertum (Religionsgeschichtliche Versuche und Vorarbeiten* 5), Giessen.

Pittakis, K. S. 1835. *L'Ancienne Athènes, ou la description des antiquités d'Athènes et de ses environs*, Athens.

Riethmüller, J. W. 2005. *Asklepios: Heiligtümer und Kulte (Studien zu antiken Heiligtümern)*, 2 vols., Heidelberg.

Rubensohn, O. 1895. "Demeter als Heilgottheit," *Mitteilungen des Deutschen Archäologischen Instituts, Athenische Abteilung* 20, pp. 360–367.

Rudhardt, J. 1960. "La definition du délit d'impiété d'après la législation attique," *Museum Helveticum* 17, pp. 87–105.

Schmidt, E. 1909. *Kultübertragungen (Religionsgeschichtliche Versuche und Vorarbeiten* 8.2), Giessen.

Schmidt, E. 1913. "Halon," *Mitteilungen des Deutschen Archäologischen Instituts, Athenische Abteilung* 38, pp. 73–77.

Shear, T. L., Jr. 1969. "The Athenian Agora: Excavations of 1968," *Hesperia* 38, pp. 382–417.

Skias, A. N. 1898. "Περί τῶν ἐν Ἐλευσῖνι ἀνασκαφῶν," *Praktika tes en Athenais Archaiologikes Etaireias*, pp. 72–91.

Svoronos, J. N. 1908–1937. *Das Athener Nationalmuseum*, Athens.

Tracy, S. V. 2003. *Athens and Macedon: Attic Letter-Cutters of 300 to 229 BC*, Berkeley.

Travlos, J. 1971. *Pictorial Dictionary of Ancient Athens*, New York.

Travlos, J. 1988. *Bildlexikon zur Topographie des Antiken Attika*, Tübingen.

TrGF 4 = *Tragicorum Graecorum Fragmenta*, vol. 4, ed. S. Radt, Göttingen, 1999.

van Straten, F. T. 1981. "Gifts for the Gods," in *Faith, Hope and Worship: Aspects of Religious Mentality in the Ancient World* (Studies in Greek and Roman Religion 2), ed. H. S. Versnel, Leiden, pp. 65–151.

Vikela, E. 1994. *Die Weihreliefs aus dem Athener Pankrates-Heiligtum am Ilissos: Religionsgeschichtliche Bedeutung und Typologie (Mitteilungen des Deutschen Archäologischen Instituts, Athenische Abteilung, Beiheft* 16), Berlin.

von Bothmer, D. 1957–1958. "Greek Marble Sculptures," *Bulletin of the Metropolitan Museum of Art, New York* 16, pp. 187–192.

Walter, O. 1923. *Beschreibung der Reliefs im kleinen Akropolismuseum in Athen*, Vienna.

Walter, O. 1953. "Das Priestertum des Sophokles," in Γέρας Ἀ. Κεραμοπούλλου, Athens, pp. 469–479.

Walton, F. 1935. "A Problem in the *Ichneutae* of Sophocles," *Harvard Studies in Classical Philology* 46, pp. 167–189.

Weinreich, O. 1909. *Antike Heilungswunder: Untersuchungen zum Wunderglauben der Griechen und Römer*, Giessen.

Wickkiser, B. L. 2008. *Asklepios, Medicine, and the Politics of Healing in Fifth-Century Greece: Between Craft and Cult*, Baltimore.

Wilamowitz, U. von. 1932. *Der Glaube der Hellenen*, II, Berlin.

Young, R. S. 1951. "An Industrial District of Ancient Athens," *Hesperia* 20, pp. 135–288.

5

Asklepios in the Piraeus and the Mechanisms of Cult Appropriation

Jessica Lamont

This article addresses the questions of where, when and how the healing god Asklepios was absorbed into the Attic pantheon, focusing in particular on one understudied Classical sanctuary, the Piraeus Asklepieion. Through the synthesis of excavation reports and a constellation of archaeological, literary, and epigraphic sources, this unpublished sanctuary can be resurrected from the concrete under which it currently lies buried. Crucial to the integration of new cults, it is suggested, was the role of sacrifice, shared altars, and cultic personifications related to health; this ultimately provides a glimpse of personal experience, or "lived religion," within a cultic space.

Introduction

With the Peloponnesian War came great change and tumult. In Athens, the *demos* was confronted by war, plague, and both the overthrow and reinstallation of the democracy. Religion during these dynamic years was not a static backdrop, in front of which historical events and figures performed; religion experienced change alongside other institutions. It comes as no surprise, then, that the last quarter of the 5th century BC witnessed a flurry of activity within the Athenian religious sphere. Although traditional polytheistic systems exhibit a constant ebb and flow of gods within their pantheons, a case can be made that Athens experienced an atypical surge in a new, specialized type of deity at this time: the healing hero and his distinct incubation cult.[1] The sudden emergence of deities concerned with health was striking and deliberate, and reflected a larger phenomenon at work in Athenian society; this was manifest in the near simultaneous foundation of several healing cults across Attica in a period of less than ten years.[2]

This paper addresses the questions of *where*, *when* and *how* the healing god Asklepios was absorbed into the Attic pantheon, focusing in particular on an understudied sanctuary, the Piraeus Asklepieion. By synthesizing excavation reports and a constellation of archaeological, literary, and epigraphic material, this unpublished sanctuary can be resurrected from the concrete under which it currently lies buried. After examining the sanctuary as it reemerged in the late 19th century AD, this paper charts a chronology for the cult's establishment. The workings of the cult and, lastly, the mechanisms by which Asklepios was incorporated into the Attic community will be illuminated. Crucial to his integration, it is argued, was the role of sacrifice, shared altars, and cultic personifications related to health. The repeated, ritual act of sacrifice – or "pre-sacrifice" in this case – would have molded the minds of worshippers and forged links between the deities sharing the *temenos*, regardless of how subconsciously the ritual actions were performed. Sacrifices made on shared altars, or multiple altars grouped within the same space, reveal associations and connections perceived among the gods by their Athenian worshippers. These *sunnaoi theoi* – personifications or otherwise – could affect or color the identity of the "primary" healing deity to whom the sanctuary belonged. By worshipping Asklepios, a non-Attic deity, alongside divinities related to health, worshippers were in effect integrating the new healing god into the Attic pantheon through sacrifice and other sanctuary rituals.

Asklepios in the Piraeus: the Sanctuary

Situated in Zea harbor, the Piraeus Asklepieion is often ignored in scholarly discussion in favor of its well-studied

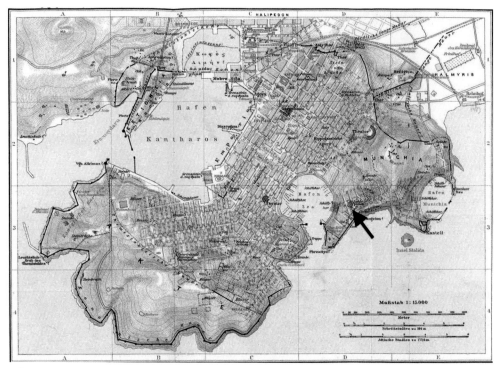

Figure 5.1 Map of Piraeus and Zea Asklepieion (at D3 with arrow). Reprinted from Judeich 1905: Topographie von Athen (München), Plan III

sister sanctuary, prominently located on the Akropolis' southern slope (Figure 5.1).[3] Part of the reason for the sanctuary's obscurity lies in its modern invisibility; remains of sanctuary architecture have been seen by few, with no foundations visible today. The exact location of most structures within the precinct is unknown. Despite these obstacles, the Piraeus Asklepieion can be reconstructed through a synthesis of old and new excavation reports; what emerges is an expansive sanctuary that played an important role in the local religious community.

From 1878–1881, a construction project on the eastern shore of Zea Harbor uncovered numerous votive reliefs depicting worshippers alongside large snakes; based on iconographic parallels from the south slope sanctuary of Asklepios, the existence of another, Piraeus-based Asklepieion seemed likely.[4] This suspicion was confirmed by the discovery of an inscribed Ionic column base dedicated to Asklepios; a few years later, in the vicinity of Tsocha Theater, a Hellenistic dedicatory inscription of a priest of Asklepios and Hygieia surfaced (*IG* II[2] 4453), along with the remains of walls and a 5th century BC boundary stone, inscribed ὅρος τô ἱερô.[5] As construction continued, additional finds from the Asklepieion emerged: a substantial *lex sacra*, inscribed votive reliefs to Asklepios featuring large snakes, architectural elements, and a throne with griffin's feet.[6] Finally in 1888, an over-lifesize Hellenistic statue of Asklepios was discovered, the so-called "Mounychian

Asklepios," named for its recovery on the SW slope of Mounychia Hill.[7] This statue, now a jewel of the National Archaeological Museum in Athens (Figure 5.2), launched an official excavation of the region around Tsocha Theater, under the direction of Jacob Dragatsis. In a very short period, the excavations yielded fragments of statues, statuettes, votive reliefs, and anatomical votives – all associated with Asklepios and Hygieia. Dragatsis also mentions four fragments of a "well-made geison" (suggesting that the temple to Asklepios was of the Doric order), three fragments of snakes from the sanctuary's "great altar," poros limestone blocks, ashlar blocks and roof tiles with snake representations, and a fired clay antefix decorated with serpents, which belonged to the temple's sculptural decoration.[8]

According to the excavation reports, Dragatsis also recovered the ancient *peribolos* wall, in the midst of which stood the foundations of the temple, along with "walls of various ancient buildings and two ancient cisterns" associated with the Asklepieion.[9] These muddled and intermittent excavations left behind no photographs of sanctuary architecture or structural foundations. Most plans of the Piraeus locate the Asklepieion on the modern corner of Odos Serangiou and Odos Kleomanso; according to this placement, the sanctuary would have been south of the major NW–SE road connecting the Hippodamian Agora to the sanctuary of Artemis Mounychia, and roughly 80 m.

Figure 5.2 Hellenistic Statue of Mounichian Asklepios, Athens National Archaeological Museum Inv. 258. Credit line: Εθνικό Αρχαιολογικό Μουσείο/National Archaeological Museum, Athens (φωτογράφος: Κ. Ξενικάκης). Copyright © ΥΠΟΥΡΓΕΙΟ ΠΟΛΙΤΙΣΜΟΥ & ΑΘΛΗΤΙΣΜΟΥ/ ΤΑΜΕΙΟ ΑΡΧΑΙΟΛΟΓΙΚΩΝ ΠΟΡΩΝ/© Hellenic Ministry of Culture and Sports/Archaeological Receipts Fund

northeast of the ship sheds in Zea Harbor (Figure 5.1).[10] The precinct was thus situated alongside or near major roads that accessed the deme agora, Zea Harbor and, climbing in elevation over the southern slope of Mounychia Hill, Mounychia Harbor to the east.

Nothing more was known about the location or layout of the Zea Asklepieion until quite recently, when rescue excavations under the direction of M. Petritaki unearthed a rectangular building and numerous votives along 2–4 Leoforos Vasileos Pavlou Street (Figure 5.1).[11] Discovered ca. 110 m. away from the region in which the sanctuary was thought to have stood, anatomical votives and a named dedicatory inscription (*SEG* 57.196) could associate this region with the worship of Asklepios. Measuring 17.0 m. in length and 3.7 m. in width, the long proportions of the rectangular building could suggest a stoa or incubation

hall. Found amid a new stretch of the Piraeus fortification walls, only the foundations of the rectangular structure were preserved; in the absence of a full publication, the building's function remains speculative. Petritaki believes that this building stood within the sanctuary. Further investigations to the southeast uncovered a group of 13 bases for votive *stelai* and statues, with fragments of offerings dispersed among them; that the new dedication to Asklepios was found here hints that he was also receiving worship in this area (*SEG* 57: 196). These bases and dedications suggest that the precinct incorporated – or at the very least, bordered upon – an area of outdoor, open-air worship. This could correspond to a late 1st century BC inscription that mentions ψιλά, "bare" or "open areas," attached or near to the Asklepieion (*SEG* 26.121.40). Anatomical votive offerings, a fragment of a votive relief, a headless statue of a young girl holding a goose (4th century BC), and the inscribed dedication to Asklepios were also found there.[12] Lastly, near these offerings were discovered a drainpipe and a large rectangular *bothros*, drilled into the rock; unfortunately, the *bothros* was back-filled with modern material, making its original function elusive.

These new excavations shed further light on the invisible Asklepieion, and suggest that the precinct was expansive; in addition to the temple, "great altar," walls, and cisterns noted by Dragatsis, it also likely included an open area in which votives were displayed, a drain and *bothros*, and subsidiary buildings and altars, further discussed below. The sanctuary stretched further to the south and east than previously supposed, into a region long associated with the worship of Zeus Meilichios and Zeus Philios.[13] These new discoveries elucidate excavation reports from the late 19th century, which found dedications to Zeus Meilichios and Zeus Philios in the region of the Asklepieion; the snake-themed iconography of these three deities was so similar that they could only be distinguished with the aid of an inscription, and emerged together from the same area.[14] It seems that on the southwest slope of Mounychia Hill these divinities formed a close network of chthonic cults: within an open-air region in the southeastern part of the Asklepieion precinct, Asklepios was worshipped near to or possibly alongside Zeus Meilichios and Zeus Philios. Perhaps the nearby Serangeion also partook in this religious matrix; the hero's name, Σῆραγξ, means "hollow rock" or "cave," which could suggest that the cult and its baths also had something of a chthonic character.[15] The concentration of cults in this area is striking, though none was more prominent than the bustling Asklepieion.

Asklepios in the Piraeus: a Proposed Chronology

Inscriptions and votives demonstrate that the Piraeus Asklepieion was a thriving healing sanctuary for many centuries, from the Classical period down through the Roman Imperial Era.[16] But when was this sanctuary founded? The chronological order in which the Piraeus and city Asklepieia were established is unclear; for example, Robert Parker states that "a second sanctuary [of Asklepios] was soon founded in the Piraeus (or possibly this came first.)"[17]

I argue that the Piraeus Asklepieion was in fact the first in mainland Attica, established before those in central Athens.[18] The so-called Telemachos Monument (*IG* II² 4960–61) fixes the foundation of the south slope Asklepieion in the year 420/19 BC through a series of archon dates (lines 19–41).[19] Most transcriptions of the monument's text read "Ζεόθεν" in lines 9–10, an indication that the city cult came up "from Zea." Due to abrasions on the surface of the stone, this reading is insecure, as the epsilon and omicron are the only letters actually preserved; possibly Zea is not mentioned at all.[20] Yet above the patchy text a great deal of information is encoded in the monument's reliefs. (Figure 5.3). The iconography visually explicates a version of the cult's history, topography, and social identity. Luigi Beschi and others have noted how the double wooden gates (the tympanum of which carries snakes) are probably referenced in line 36 of the text, the ξ[υλοπύλια] extant by 415/14 BC; the stork (*pelargos*) represents the Pelargikon wall, thus situating the cult spatially through a topographic symbol.[21] The relief also depicts a ship's prow, floating atop a bay rendered by schematic waves; immediately above the prow is a votive relief with an incubation scene, a lounging dog, and a horse protome (Figure 5.3 right fragment). This vignette, formed of clustered iconographic cues, should be understood as an allusion to Asklepios' arrival and precinct in Zea, the harbor just below the sanctuary that lodged Athens' naval fleet. The visual group formed by the ship's prow, horse protome, hound and – most significantly – votive relief with an incubating worshipper, is used to represent a sanctuary near the water and equipped with incubation facilities.[22] This iconographic group stands for the Piraeus Asklepieion. It would thus correspond to and support the reading of "Ζεόθεν" in lines 9–10, while depicting visually the Attic cult's origins at Zea and trajectory through Attica.[23] The reliefs on the Telemachos Monument were uniquely tailored to the sanctuary's history and topography, and the grouping of the horse/dog/incubation imagery nods to the already extant Asklepieion in Zea, using a trireme to situate the cult beside the harbor and its fleet.

Located beside Athens' navy and ship sheds, the cult's appropriation from the Peloponnese was readily apparent. Athenian interest in controlling Epidauros was evident in the failed attack on the city in 430 BC, and through Athens' continued raids into Epidauros' territory five years later (Thuc. 2.56.4–5; 4.45.2). All attacks on Epidauros were carried out by the Athenian navy, which sailed from the Piraeus through the Saronic Gulf en route to the Peloponnese. Wickkiser links Athens' imperial interest in Epidauros to Asklepios' importation to the Akropolis

sanctuary;[24] yet it was in the Piraeus that this connection would have been the strongest. The Piraeus Asklepieion explicitly referenced and commemorated its association with the Epidauros sanctuary through sacrifice to Epidaurian divinities such as Maleatas (*IG* II² 4962, discussed below). Thus Asklepios, a deity appropriated from the Peloponnese, received cult near the powerful Athenian fleet in Zea Harbor.

Additionally, a marble votive relief from the Piraeus Asklepieion itself (Ny Carlsberg Glyptothek 1430, Figure 5.4) supports an early foundation.[25] The dedication has been dated to ca. 420; its highly Classical figures appear almost Parthenonian.[26] This expensive, skilled relief should indicate an established and successful sanctuary by the late 5th century. The boundary stone also supports this early date (*IG* I³ 1081), accepting that it did indeed delimit the sanctuary of Asklepios as Milchhöfer, Judeich, and Riethmüller maintain.[27] Furthermore, an early 4th century BC inscription (*IG* II² 47) inventories select temple dedications, documenting the numerous votives stored [ἐπ]ὶ τῆι τραπέζει (line 1) – metal statuettes, rings, crowns, drinking cups and other sympotic vessels (κύλιξ, κ[ώ]θων, ψυκτήριον, lines 11–12), cupping vessels, a medicine chest, and doctor's tools, such as surgical knives and pincers (μαχαίρια καὶ καρκίνος ἰατρικά, line 17). These dedications, many of which suggest that the sanctuary engaged in incubation and temple healing from an early date, would have taken considerable time to accumulate; it is impossible that the sanctuary had only recently come into existence. They provide a glimpse of a wealthy, prosperous cult that had great success in the realm of healing by the dawn of the 4th century BC, a view confirmed by Aristophanes' contemporary *Ploutos*, set in this same seaside sanctuary.[28] The play offers a comic look at the incubation process within the Piraeus Asklepieion. Although the extant play has a performance date of 388 BC, an earlier iteration was performed two decades prior, in the year 408.[29] Assuming that the comedy's setting had not been altered, Aristophanes' play depicted a bustling precinct that, as early as the late 5th century, was a prominent, highly visible (dare we say primary?) Attic sanctuary of Asklepios.

As the foundation of the Piraeus cult should predate those of the *astu*, I suggest that it arrived between 422 BC, when the nearest accessible Asklepieion was on Aigina (Ar. *Vesp.* 122–3, with scholia), and 419 BC, the foundation year of the south-slope Asklepieion (*IG* II² 4960–1). Presumably Bdelykleon in Aristophanes' *Wasps* would have incubated in the Zea Asklepieion, rather than across the Saronic Gulf at Aigina, had the nearer Piraeus sanctuary been extant at the time of the play's performance in 422 BC. A foundation date, then, between 422 and 419, would fall perfectly within the Peace of Nikias, allowing a window for the cult's acquisition from the mother sanctuary of Epidauros, or possibly, via an intermediary sanctuary like that on Aigina.[30] Amid metics, foreigners, and foreign cults (such as that of nearby Bendis), the Piraeus was a fitting place for the new, non-Attic Asklepios.

Finances, Festivals, and Incubation: The Workings of the Early Asklepieion

The Piraeus Asklepieion likely came under state control before its Akropolis counterpart; this contributed to its high degree of public popularity by the early 4th century BC, the date assigned to *IG* II² 47, the sacred law-*cum*-temple inventory.[31] In addition to cataloguing the cult's property – a tabulation possibly ordered by the *demos* when the sanctuary came under state control – this inscription also sheds light on the workings of the cult. The lengthy inscription is brimming with official terminology, beginning in line 23 with ἔδοξεν τῶι δήμωι. We learn that the *demos* itself voted to approve several 'preliminary sacrifices' within the Piraeus Asklepieion, a newly proposed ritual that was brought before the Assembly by Euthydemos of Eleusis, the priest of Asklepios.[32] This inscription shows that change within the ritual administration of Attic sanctuaries was directly initiated by the cult's priesthood and the Assembly. *Epistatai*, overseers or attendants within the sanctuary, would then be responsible for sacrificing the προθύματα (*IG* II² 47. 28–30); these pre-sacrifices are described in detail on a second *lex sacra* (*IG* II² 4962), clearly related to *IG* II² 47 and discussed below.

The new sacrifices, sanctioned by and made on behalf of the Athenian *demos*, likely represent a reorganization of the sanctuary in accordance with its coming under state control.[33] The inscription even specifies the income by which these new sacrifices were funded: the sanctuary was collecting revenue from a quarry, presumably a cult-owned property that was rented or leased out for profit.[34] The proceeds from this sacred realty funded the upkeep of the cult, in this case, the preliminary sacrifices. Other revenue from the cult-owned quarry was used to construct τὴν οἰκοδομίαν τοῦ ἱεϱô, a nondescript building within the sanctuary; presumably if this money was earmarked for the construction of the temple, the decree would have specified "ναός." This was likely another structure within the precinct, separate from the temple, perhaps to be identified with Petritaki's new rectangular building. The mention of this building in the inscription suggests that the sanctuary was likely undergoing expansion at this time. Finally, *IG* II² 47 cites an unnamed festival of Asklepios based in the Piraeus, which culminated in a bull sacrifice; specifications were given for the precise order in which the meat was to be distributed, with the *prytaneis* receiving the meat from the ἡγεμόνος βοός. The participation in the festival of not only the *prytaneis* but also the nine Archons suggests that the cult was indeed state officiated – and highly celebrated – by this time.[35] The amount of official attention is striking, as are the financial statements about sacred revenues, and the

involvement of Athens' top office-holders in the sanctuary's otherwise unattested festival; perhaps this inscription captures the moment and process by which the cult came under the control of the *demos*.

The rite of incubation also played an important role in the cult's operations. By the simplest definition, incubation consisted of a ritualized sleep within the confines of the sanctuary; it afforded an encounter between the worshipper and divinity, in this case Asklepios. This intimate, personalized interaction is captured on votive reliefs from the sanctuary, presented to Asklepios by incubants themselves (Figure 5.6). The practice was preceded by an array of other rites that led up to and enhanced the experience of incubation within the sanctuary. Hedvig von Ehrenheim argues that devotees incubating within the Piraeus Asklepieion were required to dress in white clothing because of purity concerns.[36] Sacred laws from other Asklepieia stipulate similar, specific rules about pre-incubation procedures: at Pergamon, for example, sexual intercourse, goat meat, and goat cheese were forbidden for three days prior to incubating.[37] Whether similar prohibitions were in place at the Piraeus sanctuary is unknown, but such potential restrictions are helpful in reconstructing the experience of the incubating worshipper. Incubants also bathed in the sea before entering the Piraeus Asklepieion, purifying themselves with salt water before entering the sacred space (Ar. *Plout.* 656); bathing preceded incubation at the Asklepieia in Korinth, Gortys, and Epidauros, in addition to the sanctuary of Amphiaraos at Oropos (Xen. *Mem.* 3.13.3).[38] Worshippers looking to incubate within the Piraeus Asklepieion also had to offer particular preliminary sacrifices and libations to specific groups of divinities, a ritual described in detail below.

Such ritual procedures, outside quotidian routine, would have conditioned and shaped the devotees' expectations leading up to incubation. Combined with the very public accounts of Asklepios' prior cures – both inscribed and visual testimonies that were displayed within the sanctuary – participants must have had high hopes upon entering the dormitory; they were preconditioned for divine healing during the overnight incubation ritual. Incubation afforded specialized attention to an individual's health and well-being, and this distinct feature of healing cults seems to have been what propelled their popularity and expansion throughout the Greek world.

After these preliminary rites were completed and night had fallen, visitors to the Piraeus Asklepieion began the incubation process. Ritual incubation required the worshipper to sleep somewhere within the Piraeus sanctuary in order to obtain a dream or actual temple healing. Dreams received during incubation were understood to have been sent by Asklepios, and could contain provisions for regaining ones health, such as dietary or exercise regimes (Aelius Aristides' *Hieroi Logoi*, written in the 2nd century

*Figure 5.3 Copy of Reconstructed Telemachos Monument (IG II²
4960-1), South Slope Asklepieion; Photo J. Lamont*

*Figure 5.4 Votive Relief from Piraeus Asklepieion, ca. 420 BC.
Ny Carlsberg Glyptothek Inv. 1430. Photo O. Palagia, with kind
permission*

*Figure 5.5 Piraeus Asklepieion Lex Sacra, IG II² 4962, Sides A
& B. Piraeus Archaeological Museum Inv. 1622, Photographs
© Piraeus Museum, ΚΣΤ´ Εφορεία Προϊστορικών και Κλασικών
Αρχαιοτήτων, with kind permission.*

holy space, perhaps atop the fleeces of animals that had
been sacrificed earlier to Asklepios.[40]

Votive reliefs also attest the importance of incubation
within the Piraeus Asklepieion. Dedicated and displayed
within the sanctuary, they illustrate worshippers incubating
in the presence of Asklepios, revealing the centrality of the
ritual process within the workings of the cult. One such
votive, a wide rectangular relief dedicated to Asklepios, once
hung in the Piraeus Asklepieion where it was likely visible
to worshippers (Figure 5.6). The incubation experience is
related through a tripartite narrative: shown in small scale
on the left, a family group consisting of three adults and one
child approaches, their right hands reverently raised toward
the deity. At the center of the scene reclines the incubant, a
woman lying on her side on a bed. No more than a raised
platform, the bed is lined with linen and an outspread
animal skin. To the right of the incubant stand Asklepios
and a female figure, Hygieia; both are shown in profile.
Asklepios leans over the incubating woman and, extending
both arms, tends to her right shoulder. Asklepios and the
incubating worshipper form a visual unit: as the god's two
hands angle down toward the incubating woman's head,
the woman's left arm dips back behind the bed and grazes
Asklepios' right leg. Both god and worshipper are shown in

AD, offers the best examples). That actual healing took
place during the nighttime ritual is made clear by literary
sources. In Aristophanes' *Ploutos*, the main character
sleeps inside the temple and observes – in the dark of night
while all incubants are asleep – Asklepios and his crew of
personifications (including Iaso and Panakeia, as per Ar.
Plout. 701–2) milling their way through slumbering groups
of worshippers. The three divinities and their sacred temple
snakes healed the sick with the aid of a mortar, pestle,
medicine chest, ground-up poultices, linens, and wraps (Ar.
Plout. 711–732).[39] All incubants slept together within the

interaction, which was both the promise and appeal of the ritual. The reclining woman – placed at the very center of the relief – is clearly incubating; that she alone among the seven figures gazes outward and engages us, the viewers, activates the ritual and conveys Asklepios' potency as a divine *iatros* within the cult.

The Mechanisms of Cult Appropriation: the Attic Asklepios

How did this Piraeus sanctuary and its new healing deity attract such attention, from both individuals and the state, in such a short time? In part, this non-Attic incubation cult was integrated into the religious community through the rite of shared sacrifice. *IG* II² 4962, another early 4th century BC *lex sacra*, makes clear that Asklepios shared his Piraeus sanctuary with other deities, *sunnaoi theoi*.[41] This inscription must be a near contemporary of *IG* II² 47, discussed above, as it references the same preliminary offerings and priest responsible for proposing the προθύματα, Euthydemos of Eleusis. Erected in front of the sanctuary's altars, this inscription publishes the rules for pre-sacrificial ritual within the Piraeus Asklepieion (Figure 5.5a–b, *IG* II² 4962):

Figure 5.6 *Votive Relief from Piraeus Asklepieion: Ritual Incubation, ca. 350 BC. Piraeus Archaeological Museum Inv. 405, Photograph © Piraeus Museum, ΚΣΤ΄ Εφορεία Προϊστορικών και Κλασικών Αρχαιοτήτων, with kind permission.*

Face A (Front)
θεοί.
κατὰ τάδε προθύεσθα-
(3) ι· Μαλεάτηι πόπανα τρ-
ία· Ἀπόλλωνι πόπανα τ-
ρία· Ἑρμῆι πόπανα τρί-
(6) α· Ἰασοῖ πόπανα τρία· Ἀ-
κεσοῖ πόπανα τρία· Πα-
νακείαι πόπανα τρία·
(9) κυσὶν πόπανα τρία· κυνηγέταις πόπανα τρί<α>.

vac. 0.13

Εὐθύδημος
(12) Ἐλευσίνιος
ἱερεὺς Ἀσκληπιō
τὰς στήλας ἀνέθηκ[ε]
(15) τὰς πρὸς τοῖς βωμοῖς
ἐν αἷς τὰ πόπανα πρῶτος
ἐξηικάσατο, ἃ χρὴ πρ[ο]-
(18) θύεσθ[αι — —]

Face B:
Ἡλίωι
ἀρεστῆρ[α]
(3) κηρίον.
Μνημο-
σύνηι
(6) ἀρεσ[τῆ]-
ρα
κηρίον.
(9) νηφάλ[ι]-
οι τρεῖς
βωμοί.

Face C:

[νη]φάλιοι
τρεῖς
(3) βωμοί.

Face D:
νηφάλιοι.

Figure 5.7 *Votive Relief Depicting Machaon and Podaleirios with Dogs, from Epidauros, ca. 350 BC. Athens National Archaeological Museum Inv. 1426. Photo C. Gardner, with kind permission.*

The front face of this four-sided inscription states that "the preliminary sacrifices shall be made as follows"[42] (Side A, lines 2–3; Figure 5.5a). Visitors were then instructed to make bloodless preliminary offerings to a specified collectivity of deities, all of whom required ritual "pre-sacrifices" (προθύματα) within Asklepios' own *temenos*. Three *popana*, small sweet cakes, were to be offered to divinities closely associated with Asklepios in his role as a

healer: Maleatas, Apollo, Hermes, Iaso, Akeso, Panakeia, the Dogs, and the Hunters (lines 3–10).[43] The lower part of the main inscription – incised in a different and (perhaps) slightly later hand – states that Euthydemos of Eleusis, the priest of Asklepios, set up these *stelai* on which the rules for pre-sacrifice were copied.[44] Euthydemos' name is incised in very large letters, cut on a scale bigger than that used for the divine invocation and sacrificial regulations. Taken together with Euthydemos' appearance on *IG* II² 47, we may infer that he was a prominent (if somewhat egotistic) figure in the running of the cult.[45] The accusative plural τὰς στήλας alerts us to the existence of other *stelai* like this one, which were erected in front of the sanctuary's three altars on which the *prothumata* were to be sacrificed (Side A: line 15 πρὸς τοῖς βωμοῖς; Side B: lines 10–11 τρεῖς βωμοῖ; Side C: lines 2–3 τρεῖς βωμοῖ). Hence multiple altars to multiple gods existed within this single *temenos*. Side B specifies that additional pre-sacrifices came to be required within the Asklepieion, not just *popana* but another sort of cake, an *arester*, along with a honeycomb (*kerion*). On Sides B, C, and D, the *lex* also prescribes that *nephalioi*, 'sober' wine-free libations of milk and honey, were to be made "on the three altars." The *stele* thus captures a formative stage in the cult's development, with respect to both ritual and official sanctuary protocol.

The altars and sacrifices mentioned in this inscription mirror those described in the *Ploutos* of Aristophanes. Set within the Piraeus Asklepieion, the play calls for the sacrifice of cakes prior to incubation. As in the *lex sacra*, προθύματα were consecrated on an altar: here πόπανα were burnt together with another sort of pre-sacrifice, a liquid mixture of meal, honey, and oil called a πέλανος (Ar. *Plout.* 659–2).[46] More cakes and dried figs were then placed on a sacred offering table within the incubation hall, only to be eaten by the temple priests themselves. After consuming the cakes from the τράπεζα, Aristophanes' priests would then circle "all of the altars" to see whether any morsels remained there.[47] The *Ploutos* thus depicts the Piraeus Asklepieion as a sanctuary with multiple altars to multiple deities, closely linked to Asklepios through the rite of sacrifice.[48] The similarities in ritual procedure found in the *lex sacra* (*IG* II² 4962) and Aristophanes' contemporary *Ploutos* are striking, and show that the Piraeus Asklepieion was so prominent by this time that its ritual protocol was known both in the Athenian Assembly (*IG* II² 47 lines 23–30) and contemporary comedy. Bloodless offerings – required in groups of threes on several altars – clearly were a characteristic and significant part of sanctuary ritual, perhaps just as much as the animal victims. It was the rite of sacrifice, the reduplicated ritual act within a shared sacred space, that led the worshipper to associate these specialized deities with the newcomer Asklepios. The rituals initiated the sense of contact with the divine and – as they preceded incubation – helped shape the ultimate interaction with Asklepios.

The divinities who shared the space with Asklepios, and received prescribed offerings, lent salubrious, familiar associations to the primary god of the shrine, either as newly coined Attic personifications, or deities famous from the mother sanctuary at Epidauros. Asklepios was surrounded in space and ritual by his immediate mythological family. Apollo was the father of Asklepios, and Iaso, Akeso, and Panakeia came to be understood as his daughters. These latter three divinities were Attic personifications, whose names literally meant "Curer", "Healer", and "All-Heal"; they are associated with Asklepios quite early in the Piraeus cult. Hermes, as the bringer of dreams, was an important presence in the incubation process. The more puzzling figures receiving sacrifice, such as Maleatas, the dogs, and the hunters, probably serve to link the Piraeus cult

with the mother sanctuary at Epidauros. The presence of Maleatas as a single entity, here divorced from Apollo, is surprising; Maleatas at Epidauros was a shadowy figure, already fused with Apollo in the Archaic iteration of the *temenos* on Mount Kynortion.[49] Κυνηγέταις should refer to Asklepios' sons Machaon and Podalirios, who appear as heroic hunters accompanied by dogs on votive reliefs from Attica and beyond in the 4th century BC.[50] The dog was more generally tied to the aristocratic pursuit of the hunt and, like the horse protome so common to this type of votive relief, cues the trappings and pastimes of the hero.[51] In one relief from Epidauros, Machaon and Podaleirios are depicted with two dogs, and one of the sons wears hunting boots (Athens NM 1426, Figure 5.7); in another votive relief from the *astu* Asklepieion, the sons again appear as heroic nude figures accompanied by dogs (Athens NM 1372). That the sons of Asklepios were present in his sanctuary on the south slope of the Akropolis is evident from *IG* II² 4353, in which the names of both are inscribed on the dedication to Asklepios, their father. These heroes, the sons of Asklepios, were likely the κυνηγέταις named in the Piraeus inscription with cult regulations. They represent the cult's roots, and Asklepios' perceived origins at the sanctuary at Epidauros.[52]

On one narrow side of the stone, the inscription states that Helios and Mnemosyne, divinities linked to incubation through dreams and the process of seeing and recollecting, were to receive a cake and honeycomb (ἀρεστῆρα, κηρίον). That they too received "pre-sacrifices" suggests that these rites likely preceded incubation, the setting in which the worshipper most needed the faculties of vision and memory (for the seeing and recollecting of dreams).[53] These divinities, in addition to Hygieia – herself the personification of health – were so visible within the Piraeus cult that they became a defining part of Asklepios' own identity, surrounding him in cultic ritual such as sacrifice and the pouring of libations. By rooting these deities in sanctuary ritual, these deities reciprocally helped root Asklepios in Attica.

Several votive reliefs depict Asklepios alongside these other divinities, who colored the way in which worshippers understood the new healing god, and the health benefits that he offered. For example, the personification of gentleness and soothing, Epione, appears in the 5th century BC votive from the Piraeus Asklepieion alongside Asklepios, Hygieia, and a male figure identified as a son of Asklepios (Figure 5.4).[54] Though the identity of this latter figure is uncertain, his short-cropped hair, beardless face, and emphasized nudity correspond closely to the iconography of Asklepios' sons, Machaon and Podaleirios, as they appear in nineteen other votive reliefs.[55] In these reliefs, the beardless males are characterized by their short hair and so-called "heroic nudity," as seen in the votive from Epidauros (Figure 5.7); the *chlamys* draped around their shoulders serves to emphasize their nude bodies, rather than cloak them. Because of these close iconographic parallels, the nude male figure in the Piraeus votive relief is likely either Machaon or Podaleirios.[56] These votives were dedicated by the Athenians who visited and incubated within this shared sanctuary, and show that Asklepios was in fact seen in relation to these other deities – all of whom benefited the new cult and, accordingly, the Attic religious community.

Conclusion

I conclude with comparanda and some general observations. The phenomenon of shared sanctuaries and, in particular, shared altars was not unique to the cult of Asklepios in the Piraeus. Such arrangements existed in contemporary Attic healing cults, such as the cult of Asklepios on the south slope of the Akropolis, and also that of Amphiaraos at Oropos. In central Athens, Asklepios was first lodged in the city Eleusinion, alongside Demeter and Kore (*IG* II² 4960–61.10–12). These established, age-old deities not only lent the new non-Attic Asklepios a temporary *temenos*, but also an eponymous day within one of Attica's oldest festivals, the Greater Eleusinia. With such celebrated integration, Asklepios gained legitimacy in the Attic pantheon. The involvement of Eleusinian priests in early Attic Asklepieia is striking: Asklepios was lodged in the city Eleusinion (presumably run by a member of an Eleusinian *genos*), the Kerykes feature problematically in the Telemachos Monument (*IG* II² 4960–61, lines 21–23), and Euthydemos of Eleusis, the priest of Asklepios, appears throughout the earliest *leges sacrae* from the Piraeus Asklepieion. It seems that Eleusinian *gene*, the Eumolpidai and/or Kerykes, played a role in establishing the cult of Asklepios in Attica. Asklepios was worshipped alongside Demeter and Kore even after he received his own lodgings in the South Slope sanctuary, as evidenced by votive reliefs such as Athens NM 1332, and a festival day within the Mysteries.

Another contemporary instance of shared sanctuaries and cult absorption can be seen at Oropos; there the non-Attic Amphiaraos was eased into the religious community (again) through a collectivity of divinities, who shared his altar and received sacrifices and dedications.[57] While Amphiaraos was the main attraction at Oropos, archaeological and literary evidence show that other deities, many associated with health, were also brought into the sanctuary. As in the Piraeus Asklepieion, the altar of Amphiaraos at Oropos was shared: we encounter Apollo the Healer, Panakeia, Iaso, Hygieia, and Athena the Healer – deities associated with healing – in addition to those with long standing Attic cults, such as Pan, the Nymphs, and Herakles. The similarities in the working of the cult to the Piraeus Asklepieion are striking, and again illustrate the means by which non-Attic deities could be absorbed into the Attic pantheon.

Associations of deities, many specifically connected with health, were being worshipped alongside new healing gods in the late 5th century BC. These groups of divinities served to reinforce the identity of new Attic healing cults, and bolstered their appeal. Through shared altars and *temene*, non-Attic healing deities like Asklepios were comfortably eased into the local pantheon through sanctuary rites and ritual. The Piraeus Asklepieion, an important but understudied Classical sanctuary, provides an exemplary lens through which to examine this process of cultic absorption; it also demonstrates how ritual was utilized to shape the experience of individual worshippers. In an effort to approach the larger issue of religious innovation, and the ways in which new cults were integrated into the Attic community, this paper has attempted to resurrect the Piraeus Asklepieion – a sanctuary overlooked in much scholarship. An analysis of the elusive and patchy material evidence, combined with both literary and epigraphic sources, shows that this sanctuary was expansive, incorporating not only a temple, a possible open-air precinct, and additional buildings, but also several altars to multiple divinities. These divinities, sanctuary-mates of Asklepios, played an important role in the early workings of the cult, which might well have been the first Asklepieion founded on the Attic mainland. It seems to have been established between 422 BC and 419 BC, and also likely came under state control by the early 4th century BC, well before its sister sanctuary on the Akropolis. Through the interplay of the cult's administration and sanctuary ritual, this seaside Asklepieion offers a glimpse of practiced religion, and the ways in which it structured and shaped the behavior of its participants.

Acknowledgements

I thank Margie Miles and Alan Shapiro for their support and guidance, in addition to the anonymous reviewers for their helpful suggestions. This paper especially benefitted from the incisive comments and edits of Gil Renberg. Finally, I thank Georgia Boundouraki for her company on walks through Piraeus, and Jake Morton for reading an earlier version of this paper at the 2014 Chicago AIA, when inclement weather foiled my travel plans.

Notes

1   I use here both the terms "god" (*theos*) and "hero" (*heros*), because the ancient Athenians also saw elasticity in Asklepios' nature. Recent scholarship has been collapsing these once-polarized categories on the basis of epigraphic evidence, sanctuary architecture, and sacrificial ritual (Ekroth 2002). In Attica, sanctuaries of Asklepios contain elements that can be described as "chthonic," such as the *bothros* in the Asklepieion on the south slope of the Akropolis, and the undeniable iconographic similarities between the Telemachos Monument and so-called *Totenmahlreliefs* (Riethmüller 1999, pp. 123–43; Beschi 1967/68, 1982). Yet within the same sanctuary can be found a full altar and temple (Papaefthymiou 2009, pp. 67–90; Lefantzis and Jensen 2009, pp. 91–124); Asklepios

is also referred to as *theos* throughout Aristophanes' *Ploutos*, in addition to the Lykourgan "Accounts of the Treasurers of the Other Gods," *SEG* LIV 143.21, and other inscriptions.

2   At least four new healing cults were founded in Attica within less than ten years of each other: that of Asklepios in the Piraeus, Asklepios in the Eleusinion (C. Lawton, this volume), Asklepios on the Akropolis' south slope (*IG* II² 4960–1; Melfi 2007, pp. 313–432; Riethmüller 2005, I: 241–273), and the healing sanctuary of Amphiaraos at Oropos (Sineux 2007). The healing shrines of the *Heros Iatros,* located northeast of the Classical Agora, and Amynos, on the western slope of the Akropolis, also seem to have been founded or reorganized around this time, though their dates cannot be pinpointed with any certainty: Kutsch 1913, pp. 12–16; Gorrini 2001, pp. 304–6.

3   See: Wickkiser 2008; Melfi 2007, pp. 313–432; Riethmüller 2005, I, pp. 241–273; Aleshire 1989, 1991.

4   Odos T. Moutsopoulou, the modern road ringing Zea Harbor, was being constructed; this prompted the discovery of the snake-themed votive reliefs, some of which (e.g., Athens NM 1431, *IG* II² 4618) were dedicated to Zeus Meilichios. Many were uninscribed. See Riethmüller 2005, II:26–7; Milchhöfer 1881, p. 59.

5   Ionic column base: inscription unlisted in *IG*, found in the south of the Catholic church (Milchhöfer 1881, p. 60). Horos: *IG* I³ 1081; Judeich (1931, p. 441) and Milchhöfer (1891, p. 107) associate the *horos* with the Asklepieion, as does Riethmüller (2005, II, p. 27), but he notes that its mid 5th century date is problematic, and accordingly down-dates it to the late 5th century BC.

6   *Lex sacra:* found on the eastern shore of Zea Harbor, *IG* II² 4962, described in detail below. All finds securely from the Asklepieion, with current whereabouts unclear: Riethmüller 2005, II, pp. 27–28.

7   Additional pieces of the statue were found soon after, including the hand and a portion of the snake: Dragatsis 1888, p. 132, Athens NM 258. The statue has been dated to around 200 BC by Stewart on the basis of the twisting torso, along with the technique of construction, which was executed in separate pieces (Stewart 1979, pp. 48–51).

8   Dragatsis 1888, pp. 134–135; Riethmüller (2005, II, p. 29) notes that their current locations are unknown. Considering the striking presence of snakes in sanctuary architecture at the Piraeus Asklepieion, it is tempting to interpret the two snakes shown on the tympanum of the Telemachos Monument (from the south slope Asklepieion) as a faithful representation of the sanctuary's architectural adornment.

9   Dragatsis 1888, p. 132. The *peribolos* wall and temple foundations were confirmed by the autopsy of P. Wolters, to whom Dragatsis personally pointed out these *in situ* architectural remains a few years later: Wolters 1892, p. 10.

10   von Eickstedt 2001, p. 2, fig.1; Hoepfner-Schwandner 1986, p. 12; Judeich 1901 (map), 1931, p. 441.

11   Petritaki 2010, pp. 445–6.

12   Petritaki 2010, pp. 445–6, Figs. 3–4 (Figs.: dedication to Asklepios, statue of girl holding goose); *SEG* 57: 196.

13   Petritaki 2010, p. 446; Garland 1987, pp. 135–7, 159; Judeich 1931, p. 442.

14   e.g., Milchhöfer 1881, p. 59. The western Gaggera Hill at Selinous supports a similar cluster of chthonic cults. In this region of Zea, it is possible that Zeus Meilichios and the other divinities were associated with purification; the proximity of Phreatto, the offshore lawcourt in which homicide trials were held, may have created a need for handling concerns of *miasma* (Dem. 23.77–8; Arist. *Pol.* 1300 b 29; Paus. 1.28.11: "Phreattys" rather than "Phreatto"). Judeich (1931, p. 436) locates this open-air court, in which the defendant was tried on a ship at sea, on the eastern shore of Zea harbor.

15   The Serangeion existed by the year 422, when it was mentioned in Aristophanes' lost play the *Geôrgoi* (*CAF* I, fr. 122: Kock 1880–8, p. 421); Garland 1987, p. 159; Dragatsis 1925–6, pp. 1–8.

16   That the shrine was healthy and active at least in the 3rd century AD is attested by *IG* II² 2963 of 212/3 AD, an inscription by the *Paianistai* of "Mounichian Asklepios." For a useful but select list of inscriptions from this sanctuary, see Garland 1987, pp. 230–231. Pausanias does not mention the Zea Asklepieion when describing Piraeus.

17   Parker 1996, p. 175.

18   So too Aleshire 1989, p. 35; Garland 1987, p. 115; Sartori 1972/3, pp. 369–372; Burford 1969, pp. 25–6, 51. Against: Riethmüller 2005, I, pp. 241–250, II, p. 25. I write "mainland Attica" to discount the earlier Asklepieion on nearby Aigina, which would have come under Athenian control when Aigina became a kleruchy in 431 BC.

19   *SEG* 25: 226 (Beschi) = *SEG* 47: 232 (Clinton) = *IG* II² 4960–61; the texts of Beschi and Clinton are followed here. This sanctuary was located on the Akropolis' sunny south slope, and by the year 400 BC included an altar, *peribolos* wall, elevated *bothros*, *propylon*, temple, Ionic stoa, and landscaped greenery: *IG* II² 4960–61, with Lefantzis and Jensen 2009, pp. 91–124; Wickkiser 2008, pp. 67–76; Melfi 2007, pp. 313–331; Riethmüller 2005, I, pp. 242–278; Beschi 2002/3 pp. 13–42; Aleshire 1989, pp. 7–36; Beschi 1967–8.

20   See Parker 1996, p. 181, fn. 101.

21   For the most thorough discussion of the relief's iconography, see Beschi 1967–8, pp. 386–97. See also Riethmüller 2005, I, pp. 242–250; Wickkiser 2008, pp. 67–76.

22   It thus corresponds, almost as a doublet, to the visual cues used to represent the south slope sanctuary, which had its own group of horse protomes, sanctuary dogs, and incubation scene.

23   For the suggestion that the monument merely alludes to Asklepios' arrival at Zea, and not that any sanctuary existed there before the *astu* Asklepieia, see Riethmüller 2005, I, p. 249.

24   Wickkiser 2008.

25   Now in Copenhagen, the relief likely came from the Piraeus Asklepieion, as the provenance on its acquisition card states. During the excavations around the Tsocha Theater in the late 1880s, a number of votive reliefs were recovered; while some made their way to the Piraeus Museum, others surfaced on the art market or ended up in private hands. At least two votive reliefs were acquired by the Ny Carlsberg Glyptothek in Copenhagen several years after the excavations in Zea Harbor, including the Asklepios relief under discussion, and

a second votive relief dedicated to Zeus Philios (Ny Carlsberg Glyptothek 1558). While not certain, these two reliefs likely came from the same region of chthonic cults discussed above during excavations around the Tsocha Theater, acquired together from the Piraeus by the Copenhagen Glyptothek.

26 Lawton 2009, pp. 76–77, 84, fig. 21.

27 *IG* I³ 1081; Milchhöfer (1891, p. 107) and (Judeich 1931, p. 441) associate the *horos* with the Asklepieion, as does Riethmüller (2005, II, p. 27), but he notes that its mid 5th century date is problematic, and accordingly down-dates it to the late 5th century BC.

28 While all agree that Aristophanes' *Ploutos* was set in an Attic Asklepieion, there is debate over which Asklepieion was being referenced: that on the south slope of the Akropolis, or the Asklepieion at Zea. I agree with the majority (e.g., Aleshire 1989, p. 13; Garland 1987, p. 200; Judeich 1931, p. 441; Milchhöfer 1891, CXII Nr. 55, et al.) that the *Ploutos* was set at Zea in the Piraeus, reading lines 654–6: "Having arrived as quickly as possible near the sanctuary leading our man, then the most wretched, but now blessed – fortunate! – we first led him to the sea to bathe/purify him." The setting of the passage hinges upon reading "θάλατταν" naturally as "sea," and thus that the incubant was led to the sea for purification, where he would have bathed in seawater before entering Asklepios' *temenos*. Since the sanctuary at Zea stood on the shore of the harbor, the simplest reading should accept a setting in the Piraeus Asklepieion. Impeding this interpretation is a scholion (*Schol. Ar. Plout.* 621) that associates the *Ploutos* with the *astu* sanctuary; attempts have accordingly been made to read "θάλατταν" as "spring," a stretch at best (Girard 1881, pp. 70–71; see also Riethmüller 2005, I, pp. 250–1, II, p. 25). Following Aleshire in rejecting the scholion as "representing no more than an inference on the part of a rather clumsy scholiast" (Aleshire 1989, p. 13), I would add that the plot of the *Ploutos* corresponds closely with what we know of Zea sanctuary ritual from *IG* II² 4962, the *lex sacra* discussed above.

29 Sommerstein 2001, pp. 28–33.

30 Athens took an intensely active role in Aigina's cult affairs (after it became at kleruchy) as documented by a series of *horoi* that partitioned and rededicated Aiginitan *temene* to distinctly Athenian deities, even if only with respect to rented income (see Polinskaya 2009, pp. 231–267, 2013, pp. 263–5). That the Asklepieion was utilized by Athenians for incubation purposes by the year 422 is clear from Ar. *Vesp.* 122–3. The Aiginetan Asklepieion was likely the first place in which Athenians came into direct contact with Asklepios, as Epidauros was off-limits during the *Pentakontaetia*, when Athenian relations with most Peloponnesian *poleis* were icy at best. No archaeological remains from the Aigina sanctuary are extant, nor are its whereabouts known.

31 The Akropolis Asklepieion came under state control only around 360–340 BC: Aleshire 1989, pp. 14–15.

32 *IG* II² 47.23–26: περὶ ὧν ὁ ἱε|ρεὺς λέγει ὁ τοῦ Ἀσκληπιō Εὐθύδημος, ἐψηφίσθ|αι τῶι δήμωι· ὅπως ἂν τά τε προθύματα θύηται| ἃ ἐξηγεῖται Εὐθύ[δ]η[μ]ος ἱερεὺς τō Ἀσκληπιō. As in both sanctuaries of Asklepios in the *astu*, the involvement of an Eleusinian priest in the early Piraeus cult is striking.

33 The Asklepieion's "reorganization" may be seen in connection to the building activity and renovations going on in the Piraeus at this time: the Kononian-phase of the Long Walls was being built, and the attention being directed toward the navy would likely have meant renovating or patching up the ship sheds. To stretch the evidence even further, perhaps the Asklepieion's revenues were coming from the blocks of Piraeus limestone being used to rebuild the Long Walls, in part from the *lithotomeion* owned by the Asklepieion itself.

34 *IG* II² 47. 28–32: ἐψηφίσθαι τῶι δήμωι τοὺς ἐπιστάτας τοῦ Ἀσκ|ληπιείο θύεν τὰ προθύματα ἃ ἐξηγεῖται [Εὐ]θύδη|μος ἀπὸ τοῦ ἀργυρίο τō ἐκ τō λιθοτομε[ί]ο [....|.]ō ἐξαιρομένο, τὸ δὲ ἄλλο ἀργύριον [κα]τα[βά]λλ[ε]ν ἐς τὴν οἰκοδομίαν τοῦ ἱερō: "It was voted by the *demos* that the Asklepieion's *Epistatai* are to sacrifice the preliminary-offerings, which Euthydemos proposed, from the money taken from the quarry, and to set down the other money toward a building (τὴν οἰκοδομίαν) of the sanctuary." For the leasing of sacred realty, see Papazarkadas 2011.

35 In addition to other prominent cult officials, like the *Hieropoioi* and those heading the procession: *IG* II² 47 lines 35–38, νέμεν δὲ τὰ | [κρέ]α τὸ μὲν ἡγεμόνος βοὸς τοῖς πρυτάνεσιν | [καὶ τ]οῖς ἐννέ, ἄρχοσιν κα[ὶ] τ[οῖ]ς ἱ[ε]ροποιοῖς [κ]α̣ὶ | [τοῖς πο]μ[π]εῦσιν.

36 Based on later comparative evidence for white clothing being worn by incubants, and the translation of ὡς νομίζεται in Ar. *Plout.* 625 as "in the customary garb" (Sommerstein 2001, p. 179), von Ehrenheim 2011 argues that worshippers incubating within the Piraeus Asklepieion wore white (pp. 75–77).

37 *IvP* III 161 A, lines 11–14: ἁγνευέτω δὲ ὁ | [εἰσπορευ]όμενος εἰς τὸ ἐγκοιμητήριον ἀπό τε τῶν προειρημέ- | [νων πάν]των καὶ ἀφροδισίων καὶ αἰγείου κρέως καὶ τυροῦ κα[ὶ] | [.. c.7 .. .]ΙΑΜΙΔΟΣ τριταῖος. Dated by Wörrle to ca. 100 AD, upon a Hellenistic original (see von Ehrenheim 2011, p. 236; Lupu 2005, pp. 60–1; Habicht 1969, p. 187).

38 von Ehrenheim 2011, pp. 33–37; Melfi 2007, pp. 498–506.

39 Aside from Aristophanes' *Ploutos*, set in the Piraeus, other evidence suggests that worshippers received actual medical treatment during their nighttime incubation: metal doctor's tools, non-votive in character – cauterizing knives (Λ246, 331), scalpels (Λ69, 71, 280), cupping vessels (Λ349a, 381–3), forceps (Λ88, 91, 92, 332, 358), saws for cutting bone (Λ247), needles (Λ262a, 263), probes (Λ76, 77, 239, 241, 286, 287), and even vaginal dilators (Λ273) – have been found at both the Asklepieion at Epidauros (all the above "Λ" museum numbers) and the Amphiaraion at Oropos (images in Petrakos 1997). The so-called *iamata* from Epidauros, inscribed testimonies and public records of the divine cures worked by Asklepios, also suggest that a great deal of temple healing took place during overnight incubation (*IG* IV² 1, 121–24; LiDonnici 1995).

40 That incubants within healing sanctuaries slept on the skin of a sacrificed animal is suggested by several other contemporary votive reliefs from Athens, Rhamnous, and Oropos (see Petropoulou 1981 *passim*, along with Athens NM 1397, 2505, 2488; there is another now lost votive from the Piraeus Asklepieion depicting an incubating worshipper being healed by Asklepios: once in the Piraeus Museum with no inventory

number, location now unknown, see von Eickstedt 2001, p. 39, fig. 19). Pausanias (1.34) describes the rite of incubating on the skin of a sacrificed animal within the healing cult of Amphiaraos.

41 *IG* II² 4962= *LSCG* 21; Pentelic marble inscribed on four faces: on the front (Face A), left side (Face B), on the surface (Face C), and on the reverse (Face D). The dating is highly problematic. Sokolowski (*LSCG* 21), following Prott & Ziehen (*LGS* II 18), notes that the text was inscribed in several stages; the dates are thus not uniform: Side A, lines 1–10 (*stoichedon*) date to the beginning of the 4th century; lines 11–18, were added slightly later by the priest Euthydemos. It seems odd that there would be different dates for these two sections as they clearly relate to one another, with Euthydemos asserting his role in proposing the regulations; I suggest that all text on Face A was inscribed contemporarily, by different hands. Sokolowski vaguely notes that the inscriptions on the stele's other three sides are "more recent." Lupu 2005, p. 63 dates all four sides to the 4th century; see also Guarducci 1967–78, IV, p. 15.

42 Unclear is whether this "pre-" sacrifice preceded incubation or a more substantial animal sacrifice to the sanctuary's main deity, Asklepios: see von Ehrenheim 2011, p. 51; Lupu 2005, pp. 63–4. It is known from *IG* II² 47, the other *lex sacra,* in addition to votive reliefs from the sanctuary (Piraeus AM 1407) that Asklepios did in fact receive animal sacrifices, and on at least one occasion, bull sacrifice. In either case, it can be said with certainty that these bloodless sacrifices preceded incubation; the question is whether or how often there was an additional step of animal sacrifice in between.

43 For types of sacrificial cakes and *prothumata*: Kearns 1994, esp. pp. 67–69; Mikalson 1972, pp. 580–1.

44 For a prosopographical analysis of Euthydemos, see Aleshire 1991, pp. 244–246; Threpsiades 1939, pp.177–180. "Copied" for ἐξηικάσατο: Kearns, following Sokolowski (*LSCG* 21), translates ἐξηικάσατο quite literally (and incorrectly, in my opinion), as referring to actual *images* of the *popana*. She writes that Euthydemos "caused diagrams of the appropriate type of cake to be engraved," assuming then that the part of the *stele* containing this "illustration" was broken off (Kearns 1994, p. 68; Lupu 2005, pp. 63–4 assumes a similar understanding). While the empty space separating the two texts on Face A would certainly allow for a painted image (Figure 5.5a), ἐξηικάσατο is better understood here as "copied" or "represented;" we know that Euthydemos did indeed go before the Assembly with his proposal concerning *prothumata*, and that it was approved by vote (*IG* II² 47 lines 23–30). The phrase could thus refer to the act of representing or copying the required preliminary sacrifices (τὰ πόπανα) onto the *stelai* that Euthydemos erected before the altars. Rather than incising pictures of cakes, in other words, Euthydemos caused the rules for preliminary *popana* sacrifices to be represented on, or copied onto, *stelai* such as this one (Figure 5.5a–b). It is worth noting the rarity of the verb in question, ἐξηικάσατο; this inscription may be the only appearance of the verb in this form.

45 Here an Eleusinian, likely a member of the Kerykes or Eumolpidai, is involved in the early workings of another early Attic Asklepios cult (cf. the role of the *astu* Eleusinion,

and presumably the Kerykes, in lodging Asklepios before he was situated in the south slope sanctuary; also the reference to Kerykes in line 21 of *IG* II² 4960–1, the Telemachos Monument). See Lawton (this volume); Clinton 1994, pp. 17–34.

46 In translating πέλανος as a viscous liquid-mixture, rather than another sort of small wheat-flour cake (similar to a *popanon*), I follow von Ehrenheim 2011, p. 50. That the πόπανα and πέλανος together formed the προθύματα, see Mikalson 1972, p. 582.

47 That there was also a τράπεζα in the Zea Asklepieion, on which offerings were kept in the early 4th century, see *IG* II² 47.1. It was not uncommon for priests to receive the unburnt *trapeza* offerings as due portions from the sacrifice, so perhaps Aristophanes was again referencing an actual cultic practice: *LSAM* 24.23–25 (*IK* 2.205); *IG* V,1 1390.84–89; Gill 1991, pp. 15–19.

48 Several *leges sacrae* (*LSCG* 22–27) require cake offerings on small altars, but they cannot securely be shown to have originated in the Piraeus Asklepieion (Lupu 2005 p.64; Petropoulou 1991, pp. 27–9).

49 Apollo Maleatas and Asklepios at Epidauros: Lambrinoudakis 2002, pp. 213–224. For the possibility that the cult originated at Trikka, see Aston 2004, pp. 18–32. Apollo Maleatas received sacrifice before Asklepios at both Epidauros and Trikka (*IG* IV², 1 128.30–31; *Hymn of Isyllos*).

50 von Eickstedt 2001, p.13; von Ehrenheim adds that in Xenophon (*Cyn.* 1.1; 1.14), Machaon and Podaleirios are mentioned as being renowned for their hunting skills (2011, p. 56 fn. 246).

51 The dogs receiving *popana* in the sacred law were probably understood in connection to the κυνηγέταις; yet within the cult of Asklepios, the dog was a sacred and prominent animal in its own right. A tale in which a blind boy from Hermione had his eyes licked by a sacred temple dog, and left the sanctuary cured, suggests that dogs might have been involved in the incubation process at Epidauros, and were thought to have curative capabilities (*IG* IV² 1.121–23, 20). A later account by Aelian, set in an unspecified Attic Asklepieion, relates how a temple dog alerted the authorities to a robbery within the sanctuary: a thief had entered the temple during the night and stolen a number of offerings. The sanctuary dog pursued the thief, barking, until the man was caught and reprimanded; dogs could thus serve as guards within Asklepieia (Ael. *NA* 7.13). At Epidauros, furthermore, the chryselephantine cult statue of Asklepios sat holding his staff and a snake, with a dog lying by his side (Paus. 2.27.2). These accounts suggest that the dog was a physical presence and played a functional role in the cults of Asklepios, and perhaps on account of this received pre-sacrifices.

52 An alternative interpretation of κυσίν and κυνηγέταις relates their presence on the Attic sacrificial law to a myth first attested in the Hellenistic Period, in which the infant Asklepios was exposed by his mother near Epidauros, reared by a dog, and discovered by a group of "hunters with dogs" (Parker 1996, p. 182, with Apollodorus of Athens, *FGrH* 244 F 138, Paus. 2.26.3–5). The presence of dogs and hunters-with-dogs within the Piraeus cult would thus be a move toward establishing something of an Athenian Asklepios. It

is difficult to reconcile this theory with the obvious reference to Epidauros in the figure of Maleatas; it seems contradictory to push an Attic upbringing on Asklepios in one part of the *lex sacra*, only to acknowledge his origins in Epidauros six lines prior (via Maleatas). Furthermore, with the Epidauria festival, the Peloponnesian origin of Asklepios seems to have been recognized and even celebrated in Athens.

53 Helios is known for his seeing abilities in Hom. Hym *Dem.* 62, 70–4, where he is described as the watchman of gods and men, θεῶν σκοπὸν ἠδὲ καὶ ἀνδρῶν; his capacity for observation is tied to knowledge and understanding, as Helios was able to inform Demeter about the abduction of Persephone. In a second pre-incubation ritual, Mnemosyne received another sort of *popanon*, a round cake with nine buttons (πόπανον ἐννεόμφαλον), in a specific part of the Asklepieion at Pergamnon, ἔξω θυμέλην (*IvP* III 161 A.9–11, 28–29; von Ehrenheim 2011, p. 52). A fragmentary 4th century BC inscription from the Athenian Agora shows that Mnemosyne again received a cake and honeycomb (*arester kerion*) in a context likely unrelated to incubation (Meritt 1963, pp. 45–6, no. 62).

54 Lawton 2009, p. 77, 84; Comella 2002, p. 74, 220, fig. 66; Meyer 1987, pp. 213–24; Mitropoulou 1977, pp. 45–6, no. 67, fig.105.

55 After Meyer 1987, p. 217 fn.22, to which I add Athens NM 1330.

56 An obvious objection to this is the representation of only one rather than both sons of Asklepios; in most but not all of our other examples, they function as a paired unit. The frequent presence of Asklepios' family members in cultic ritual seems to outweigh this concern, so I follow the *communis opinio* in identifying this figure as one of the sons of Asklepios.

57 Pausanias 1.35.3 notes the following peculiarity: the altar was divided into parts, and dedicated to groups of heroes and gods. Pausanias' observations are corroborated by statuary, inscriptions, and votive reliefs from the 4th century BC and later, showing that these deities were indeed worshipped at Oropos alongside Amphiaraos. See Sineux 2007; Petrakos 1968, 1997.

References

Aleshire, S. 1989. *The Athenian Asklepieion: the People, their Dedications, and the Inventories,* Amsterdam.

Aleshire, S. 1991. *Asklepios at Athens: Epigraphic and Prosopographic Essays on the Athenian Healing Cults,* Amsterdam.

Aston, E. 2004. "Asclepius and the Legacy of Thessaly," *Classical Quarterly,* pp. 18–32.

Bell, C. 1992. *Ritual Theory, Ritual Practice,* Oxford.

Beschi, L. 1967–68. "Il monument di Telemachos, fondatore dell' Asklepieion Ateniese," *Annuario della Scuola archeologica di Atene e delle Missioni italiane in Oriente* 45–46, pp. 381–436.

Beschi, L. 1982. "Il rilievo di Telemachos ricompletato," *Athens Annals of Archaeology* 15, pp. 31–43.

Burford, A. 1969. *The Greek Temple Builders at Epidauros,* Liverpool.

Burkert, W. 1992. *The Orientalizing Revolution,* Cambridge MA.

Clinton, K. 1994. "The Epidauria and the Arrival of Asclepius in Athens," *Ancient Greek Cult Practice from the Epigraphical*

Evidence, Proceedings of the Second International Seminar on Ancient Greek Cult, ed. R. Hägg, Stockholm, pp. 17–34.

Comella, A. 2002. *I Rilievi Votivi Greci di Periodo Arcaico e Classico: Diffusione, Ideologia, Committenza,* Bari.

Dübner, F. 1877. *Scholia Graeca in Aristophanem,* Paris.

Dillon, M. 1994. "The Didactic Nature of the Epidaurian Iamata," *Zeitschrift für Papyrologie und Epigraphik* 101, pp. 239–260.

Dragatsis, I. 1884. "Ἀνασκαφαὶ ἐν Πειραιεῖ (Ἀσκληπιεῖον)," *Archaiologikon Deltion,* pp. 132–136.

Dragatsis, I. 1886. "Ἀνασκαφαὶ ἐν Πειραιει," *Praktika tes en Athenais Archaiologikes Etaireias,* pp. 82–4.

Dragatsis, I. 1888. "Ἀνασκαφαὶ," *Archaiologikon Deltion,* pp. 131–135.

Dragatsis, I. 1925–6. "Το εν Πειραιεί Σηράγγιον," *Archaiologike Ephemeris,* pp. 1–8.

Edelstein, E. J. and L. Edelstein. 1945. *Asclepius: A Collection and Interpretation of the Testimonies,* Baltimore.

Ekroth, G. 2002. *The Sacrificial Rituals of Greek Hero-Cults in the Archaic to the Early Hellenistic Periods* (Kernos Supplement 12), Liège.

Garland, R. 1987. *The Piraeus: From the Fifth to the First Centuries B.C.,* London.

Girard, P. 1881. *L'Asclépieion d'Athènes d'après de récentes découverts (Bibliothèque des Écoles françaises d'Athènes et de Rome 23),* Paris.

Graf, F. 1992. "Heiligtum und Ritual: das Beispiel der Greichisch-Römischen Asklepieia," in *Le Sanctuaire Grec: Entretiens sur l'Antiquité Classique. Fondation Hardt: Pour l'étude de l'antiquité Classique Tome XXXVII,* ed. B. Grange & O. Reverdin, Genève, pp. 159–200.

Graf, F. 1996. "Incubation," *Oxford Classical Dictionary,* pp. 753–4.

Hägg, R., ed. 1994. *Ancient Greek Cult Practice from the Epigraphical Evidence. Proceedings of the Third International Seminar on Ancient Greek Cult,* Stockholm.

Herzog, R. 1932. *Kos: Ergebnisse der deutschen Ausgrabungen und Forschungen,* Berlin.

Hoepfner, W. and E. Schwandner. 1986. *Haus und Stadt im klassischen Griechenland,* München.

Jensen, J. T., G. Hinge, P. Schultz, and B. Wickkiser, eds. 2009. *Aspects of Ancient Greek Cult: Context, Ritual and Iconography (Aarhus Studies in Mediterranean Antiquity, Vol. VIII),* Aarhus.

Judeich, W. 1905. *Topographie von Athen,* Munich.

Judeich, W. 1931. *Topographie von Athen,* Munich.

Kearns, E. 1989. *Heroes of Attica (Bulletin of the Institute of Classical Studies of the University of London Supp, 57),* London.

Kearns, E. 1994. "Cakes in Greek Sacrifice Regulations," in *Ancient Greek Cult Practice from the Epigraphical Evidence; Proceedings of the Second International Seminar on Ancient Greek Cult,* ed. R. Hägg, Stockholm, pp. 65–70.

Kutsch, F. 1913. *Attische Heilgötter und Heilheroen,* Giessen.

Lawton, C. 2009. "Attic Votive Reliefs and the Peloponnesian War," in *Art in Athens During the Peloponnesian War,* ed. O. Palagia, Cambridge, pp. 66–93.

Lefantzis, M. and J. T. Jensen. 2009. "The Athenian Asklepieion on the South Slope of the Akropolis: Early Development, ca. 420–360 B.C.," in *Aspects of Ancient Greek Cult: Context, Ritual and Iconography (Aarhus Studies in Mediterranean*

Antiquity, Vol. VIII), ed. J. T. Jensen, G. Hinge, P. Schultz, and B. Wickkiser, Aarhus, pp. 91–124.

LiDonnici, L. 1995. *The Epidaurian Miracle Inscriptions: Text, Translation and Commentary*, Atlanta.

Melfi, M. 2007. *I Santuari di Asclepio in Grecia* 1, Rome.

Meyer, M. 1987. "Ein frühes Weihrelief für Asklepios und Hygieia," *Mitteilungen des Deutschen Archäologischen Instituts, Athenische Abteilung* 102, pp. 213–24.

Mikalson, J, 1972. "Prothyma," *American Journal of Philology*, pp. 577–583.

Mikalson, J. 1984. "Religion and the Plague in Athens, 431–423 B.C.," in *Studies Presented to Sterling Dow (Greek, Roman and Byzantine Monographs 10)*, ed. K. J. Rigsby, pp. 217–25.

Milchhöfer, A. 1881. "Der Peiraieus," in *Karten von Attika*, ed. E. Curtius and J. Kaupert, Berlin, pp. 59–60.

Mitropoulou, E. 1977. *Corpus I: Attic Votive Reliefs of the 6th and 5th Centuries B.C.*, Athens.

Palagia, O., ed. 2009. *Art in Athens During the Peloponnesian War*, Cambridge.

Pancucci, D. 1980. "I *Temenoi* del santuario delle divinita ctonie ad Agrigento," in *Miscellanea di studi classici in onore di Eugenio Manni*, eds. M. Fontana, M. Piraino, F. Rizzo, Rome, pp. 1665–1676.

Papaefthymiou, V. 2009. "Der Altar des Asklepieions von Athen," in *Aspects of Ancient Greek Cult: Context, Ritual and Iconography (Aarhus Studies in Mediterranean Antiquity, Vol. VIII)*, ed. J. T. Jensen, G. Hinge, P. Schultz, and B. Wickkiser, Aarhus, pp. 67–90.

Papazarkadas, N. 2011. *Sacred and Public Land in Ancient Athens*, Oxford.

Parker, R. 1996. *Athenian Religion*, Oxford.

Patera, I. 2010. "Theoi sumbômoi et autels multiples," in *Kernos* 23, Liège, pp. 223–238.

Petrakos, B. 1968. *Ὁ Ὠρωπὸς καὶ τὸ Ἱερὸν τοῦ Ἀμφιαράου*, Athens.

Petrakos, B. 1997. *Οἱ Ἐπιγραφές του Ὠρωπού*, Athens.

Petropoulou, A. 1981. "The *Eparche* Documents and the Early Oracle at Oropos," *Greek, Roman and Byzantine Studies* 22, pp. 39–63.

Petropoulou, A. 1991. "Prothysis and Altar: A Case Study," in *L'Espace Sacrificiel dans les Civilisations Méditerranéennes de l'Antiquité*, ed. R. Étienne and M. Le Dinahet, Paris, pp. 25–31.

Polinskaya, I. 2009. "Fifth-Century Horoi on Aigina: A Reevaluation," *Hesperia* 78, pp. 231–267.

Polinskaya, I. 2013. *A Local History of Greek Polytheism: Gods, People and the Land of Aigina, 800–400 BCE*, Leiden.

Prott, J. and L. Ziehen. 1896–1906. *Leges Graecoorum Sacrae e Titulis Collectae*, Leipzig.

Reithmüller, J. 1999. "Bothros and Tetrastyle: The *Heroon* of Asclepius in Athens," in *Ancient Greek Hero Cult. Proceedings of the Fifth International Seminar of Ancient Greek Cult*, ed. R. Hägg, Stockholm, pp. 123–43.

Reithmüller, J. 2005. *Asklepios: Heiligtümer und Kulte*, 2 vols., Heidelberg.

Sartori, F. 1972–3. "Aristofane e il Culto Attico di Asclepio," *Atti e memorie dell'Accademia Patavina di Scienze, Lettere ed Arti* 85 (1972/3), pp. 369–372.

Sommerstein, A. 1983. *The Comedies of Aristophanes: Wasps*, Warminster.

Sommerstein, A. 2001. *The Comedies of Aristophanes: Volume 11, Wealth*, Warminster.

Stewart, A. 1979. *Attika: Studies in Athenian Sculpture of the Hellenistic Age*, London.

Threpsiades, J. 1939. "Decree in Honor of Euthydemos of Eleusis," *Hesperia* 8, pp. 177–180.

Tomlinson, R. 1983. *Epidauros*, London.

van Straten, F. T. 1995. *Hiera Kala. Images of Animal Sacrifice in Archaic and Classical Greece (Religions in the Graeco-Roman World 127)*, Leiden.

Verbanck-Piérard, A. 2000. "Les Héros Guérisseurs: des Dieux comme les Autres! À Propos des Cultes Médicaux dans l'Attique Classique," in *Héros et Héroïnes dans les Mythes et les Cultes Grecs*, ed. V. Pirenne-Delforge and E. Suárez de la Torre, Liège, pp. 281–332.

Vikela, E. 2006. "Healer Gods and Healing Sanctuaries in Attica. Similarities and Differences," *Archiv für Religionsgeschichte* 8, pp. 41–61.

von Ehrenheim, H. 2011. *Greek Incubation Rituals in Classical and Hellenistic Times*, Stockholm.

von Eickstedt, K. 2001. *Το Ασκληπιείον του Πειραιώς*, Athens.

Wickkiser, B. 2008. *Asklepios, Medicine, and the Politics of Healing in Fifth-Century Greece*, Baltimore.

Wolters, P. 1892. "Darstellungen des Asklepios," *Mitteilungen des Deutschen Archäologischen Instituts, Athenische Abteilung* 17, Athens, pp.1–10.

6

Sarapis as Healer in Roman Athens: Reconsidering the Identity of Agora S 1068

Brian A. Martens

This study revisits an under-life-size, Roman-period, marble statue of a draped male divinity from the excavations of the Athenian Agora (S 1068) and proposes a new identification for the image as a hybridized version of Asklepios and Sarapis. The statue's iconography illustrates the close connections between these cults in Roman Athens, particularly in their shared ability to perform cures. A contextual analysis of this statue presents an opportunity to examine the evidence for the Egyptian gods as healing deities in Hellenistic and Roman Greece, as well as the use of iconographic hybridity to integrate foreign gods with local ones.

Introduction

While studying statuary of Asklepios from the excavations of the Athenian Agora, I was urged to reconsider the identity of an unusual, draped male divinity found on the northern slope of the Areopagos[1] (Figures 6.1, 6.2, 6.3 and 6.4). Since its discovery over seventy-five years ago, the statue has been called Asklepios, owing to the serpent-entwined staff positioned at the figure's left side.[2] This identification, however, privileges an isolated aspect of the image – the healer's attribute – over its much more meaningful whole. Close examination of the statue's iconography and technical details provides evidence for a new identification for the figure as a hybridized version of Asklepios and Sarapis. I revisit this long-known sculpture, adding substantially to the scant archaeological evidence for the worship of the Egyptian gods in Roman Athens and further illuminating how Sarapis functioned within Athenian religion. Although the Egyptian gods were worshipped widely in the eastern Mediterranean basin as healing divinities – and indeed, some of the Athenian evidence hints at such a role – this statue is, to my knowledge, the first clear evidence of Sarapis' ability to grant cures in the city of Athens.[3]

Agora S 1068

Agora S 1068, a Pentelic marble statue of a draped male figure, about one-half life size,[4] was excavated in 1938 on the northern slope of the Areopagos in section Omega (Figure 6.5). The fragmentary statue is missing the head and neck, the right arm from above the elbow, the feet from above the ankles, and the lower portion of the snake and staff. The sculpture's surface is weathered throughout and is chipped along the ridges of the drapery folds. In addition, the upper portion of the serpent-entwined staff has been badly damaged. The figure's now-absent right arm, which probably projected outward, was attached separately, as evidenced by three dowel holes: one under the break at the arm and two at the side of the body. Tool marks, discussed at length below, are visible along the figure's right leg.

The figure stands on his left leg with his right leg relaxed. A heavy himation is draped over the figure's left shoulder and hangs freely down his side. An over-fold rests across the lower abdomen, extending just below the waist. Long diagonal folds rise from the lower right leg, emphasizing the projecting knee. Most critically for the re-identification that follows, the figure wears a short-sleeved chiton underneath the himation. Thin U-shaped folds in the chiton droop over the mid-chest. The figure's left hand emerges from the himation, lightly grasping the serpent-entwined staff, positioned low and close at the figure's side. The reverse drapery is heavy and block-like, having been treated only summarily. The statue is Roman on the basis of style,

Figure 6.1 Agora S 1068, front. Courtesy American School of Classical Studies at Athens: Agora Excavations.

Figure 6.2 Agora S 1068, back. Courtesy American School of Classical Studies at Athens: Agora Excavations.

possibly a work of the 3rd century AD. Its material indicates local production.

Towards a New Identification

The figure's dress is a critical component for understanding the statue's identity. In particular, the chiton-covered chest is unparalleled amongst the iconographic models known for Asklepios.[5] In Athens, as elsewhere, the favored model for depicting Asklepios was the Giustini image type.[6] In this image type, Asklepios stands with weight partially distributed on his left leg; the balance is placed on a serpent-entwined staff, positioned under his right arm. A himation is draped over his left shoulder, while the right shoulder and chest remain bare. The edge of the himation forms a curving band of drapery that extends from under the right armpit, across the upper abdomen, and ends at the projecting left elbow.

At least twenty statuettes and statuette fragments from the Agora follow the Giustini model to varying degrees – a comparatively high frequency that demonstrates the image type's popularity in the city.[7] These sculptures, mostly of the Roman imperial era, exemplify the god's brawny, bare-chested physique, covered only by the himation. A 2nd century AD small-scale statue from the Southwest Baths in the Agora, for instance, depicts the god in this manner[8] (Figure 6.6). The chiton-covered chest of Agora S 1068 is inconsistent with the repetitive iconographic models known for Asklepios – Giustini image type or otherwise – and moreover, is altogether rare imagery for Greek male divinities. The garment indicates that the figure is not Asklepios and thereby urges a reconsideration of the statue's identity.

While unusual for Greek male divinities, the layered costume is standard attire for Sarapis, an Egyptian deity who

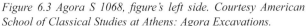

Figure 6.3 Agora S 1068, figure's left side. Courtesy American School of Classical Studies at Athens: Agora Excavations.

Figure 6.4 Agora S 1068, figure's right side. Courtesy American School of Classical Studies at Athens: Agora Excavations.

gained prominence under the patronage of the Ptolemies.[9] It is unlikely that, as has been argued, the Ptolemaic court supported the Sarapis cult as a means to negotiate, or to blend, Greek and Egyptian religious traditions.[10] Critically, Sarapis' archetypal image relied heavily on a Greek visual vocabulary and incorporated only a few Egyptian elements, as shown by surviving versions of the cult statue at Alexandria, a work attributed to the sculptor Bryaxis.[11] Sarapis is presented in the enthroned statue as mature, bearded with curly hair, and accompanied by Kerberos, the three-headed guardian of the underworld.[12] His himation and chiton, too, borrow from a Hellenic vocabulary, but when paired, the costume is unusual for the depiction of male gods in Greece. Andrew Stewart finds the combination entirely foreign, as Sarapis is "in barbarian fashion."[13] This combination of garments was worn by non-Greeks; Mausolos is an obvious example. Throughout the Hellenistic and Roman periods, however, the

himation with chiton was "standard Greek civilian dress," especially in the Greek cities of Asia Minor.[14] For Sarapis, the layered fashion was probably adopted to highlight the god's chthonic associations and link with Hades, who, too, occasionally wears the himation with chiton.[15] Standing representations of Sarapis, although varied in details, often feature drapery arrangements comparable to the Agora statue: loose, U-shaped sags in the chiton over the mid-chest and the occasional over-fold of the himation at the waist.[16] A 2nd century AD bust of Sarapis from the Agora, for example, exhibits the distinctive fashion (Figure 6.7).[17]

An examination of the sculpture's technical details suggests that the statue was originally part of a group composition that included another figure. There is a series of tool marks at the figure's lower right leg, along the drapery ridges that rise backward from the shin (Figure 6.8). These tool marks were not abraded during the final phases of the

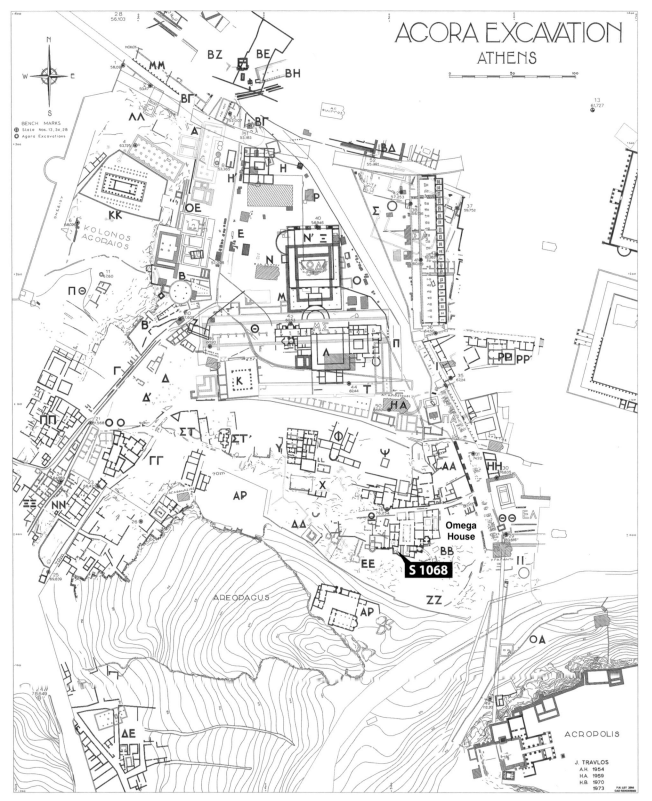

Figure 6.5 Plan of the Agora showing the Omega House and the find-spot of Agora S 1068. Courtesy American School of Classical Studies at Athens: Agora Excavations [with additions by B. Martens].

Figure 6.6 Small-scale statue of Asklepios (Agora S 1991). Courtesy American School of Classical Studies at Athens: Agora Excavations.

Figure 6.7 Bust of Sarapis (Agora S 355). Courtesy American School of Classical Studies at Athens: Agora Excavations.

sculpting process, or alternatively, were incurred during later damage to the statue. In either case – whether the sculptor neglected to smooth the surface because additional statuary obstructed his reach or blocked its sight, or whether the marks were caused during later removal of an adjacent figure – these marks imply the existence of another figure situated in this area. The location at the lower right leg is fitting for Sarapis' customary companion, Kerberos, who commonly sits at the right of his statues; there is no indication of, or need for, an adjoining tree-trunk support.

The presumed placement of the figure's now-absent arm further supports Kerberos' presence. The right forearm was attached separately, as evidenced by three dowel holes. The join was made at a point where the chiton sleeve is fastened – a deliberate break that argues for attachment at the time of manufacture. The figure's hand apparently projected outward, beyond the plane of the original marble block, thus necessitating the join. In compositions with Kerberos, Sarapis often extends his hand over his companion. The gesture is frequent in surviving statues, as well as in other media, including lamps and gemstones.[18] The

extended forearm excludes other possible companions, such as Asklepios' healing associate Telesphoros. In such compositions, Asklepios often places his hand on his hip with Telesphoros below, buttressed against his lower leg.[19]

The serpent-entwined staff, the canonical attribute of Asklepios, occasionally accompanies Sarapis, as known from previously overlooked parallels. Notable amongst these images is an over-life-size, early 3rd century AD statue of Sarapis, found outside of the cella of the Sarapieion at Leptis Magna (Figure 6.9).[20] Sarapis stands, holding a tall staff or scepter with a climbing serpent. The himation and chiton are worn together, and Kerberos sits at his right. There are, however, important differences between the two statues. For instance, the left arm of the statue from Leptis Magna is elevated, whereas the left arm of Agora S 1068 rests at its side grasping a much shorter staff. Even in images of Asklepios, the height and positioning of the staff varies. Agora S 1068 does not replicate the composition of the Leptis Magna statue; as a hybrid figure, it instead selectively adapts established iconographic elements.

Apart from this statue, there apparently is no evidence

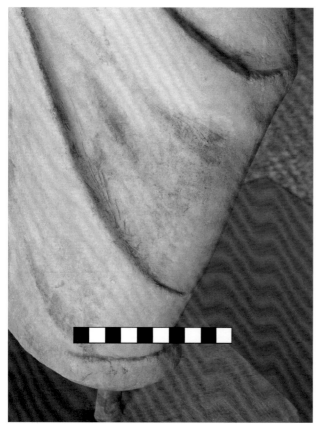

Figure 6.8 Agora S 1068, detail showing tool marks along right leg. Courtesy American School of Classical Studies at Athens: Agora Excavations.

Figure 6.9 Statue of Sarapis from Leptis Magna, inv. unknown. Drawing by Ed Chapman IV.

from Leptis Magna that indicates Sarapis functioned as a healing god there.[21] In Athens, though, where statuary and votive reliefs depicting Asklepios with the serpent-entwined staff survive in impressive numbers, ancient viewers must have associated the attribute foremost with Asklepios and, in turn, with healing.[22] This attribute, however, when fused with the distinctive dress and Kerberos, creates something new within its local Athenian context: not simply Asklepios or Sarapis, but a hybridized version of the two gods.[23] To avoid oversimplification or generalization, a single identification should be avoided for Agora S 1068, because ancient audiences likely interpreted the hybrid image variously. The statue possesses inherent flexibility in meaning, thus permitting individual religious perceptions. Viewers, for example, might have understood the statue to be Sarapis in the form of an Asklepios-like healer, Asklepios in an Egyptian form, or perhaps even Sarapis and Asklepios as a single god. The context of its primary use, which cannot be reconstructed due to its secondary deposition, would have additionally shaped ancient understandings. Nevertheless, it is abundantly clear that the statue reflects the close relationship between the two cults in Athens and, moreover,

that the presence of the ritually important snake and staff communicates healing powers that must also have been counted amongst the capacities of the Sarapis cult there.

The Agora statue can be contextualized within a long tradition of adapting visual elements to highlight ritual function. In Athens, Asklepian imagery was integrated with other divine iconographies as early as the late classical period. The Attic healing god Amphiaraos appears in an Asklepios-like form on a late 4th century BC document relief from the Athenian Agora; an inscription secures the identification.[24] Here, Amphiaraos could easily be mistaken for Asklepios, and even Hygieia stands alongside him, an indication that Amphiaraos also adopted figures from Asklepian cult. Additional examples can be cited, including the 4th century BC votive relief of Archinos, dedicated to Amphiaraos at Oropos.[25] From an early date, then, elements of Asklepian imagery were used in Athens and Attica as recognizable models to portray healing character.

The Egyptian Gods as Healers in Hellenistic and Roman Greece

Sarapis was closely aligned with the Egyptian underworld god Osiris, from whom he inherited his chthonic associations and his consort Isis. Indeed, the name Sarapis finds its origins in Osiris-Apis, the divinized bull Apis assimilated with Osiris in the Memphis region.[26] Sarapis, with ties to regeneration and rebirth, functioned as a healer in Egypt from the Hellenistic period. The god's celebrated sanctuary at Kanopos, just east of Alexandria, offered miraculous cures through incubation as early as the reign of Ptolemy I.[27] Demetrios of Phaleron, for instance, was famously cured of his blindness at Kanopos and composed hymns to the god in thanksgiving.[28] The sanctuary's healing capacity was also well known to Strabo (17.1.17), who described the role of ritual incubation there. Yet, incubation as a means for enacting cures seems to have been isolated to the Delta region where it was imported as a Greek tradition.[29]

Athens

The cults of the Egyptian gods spread into the Aegean during the Hellenistic period, arriving in Athens early, by the second half of the 4th century BC. A decree of 333/32 BC refers to an already founded sanctuary of Isis, probably in Piraeus.[30] Isis' consort, Sarapis, seems to have followed sometime thereafter. The earliest known material evidence for Sarapis in Athens is an inscription of 215/14 BC, which describes an established and active cult society, the Sarapiastai.[31] The Egyptian gods came to enjoy great popularity in Athens, due in part to their healing abilities.

Sarapis was well known as a healer in the eastern Mediterranean, but a medical role has remained elusive for his Athenian cult. The epigraphic record of a probable sanctuary of Isis on the southern slope of the Acropolis, though, hints at healing capacities.[32] A Hadrianic inscription concerning the sanctuary's monumentalization names its female donor as ὀνειροκρίτις or interpreter of dreams.[33] This Isiac office is attested on Delos and implies incubation, a ritual process during which the goddess appeared in a dream to attend to her worshippers' requests.[34] It is unclear, however, if incubation was practiced for therapeutic or oracular purposes, or both; a single 2nd century BC inscription from Delos references the office in connection with the delivery of a cure.[35] The ὀνειροκρίτις is altogether

unknown in the cult of Asklepios, which commonly used incubation for healing.

The Athenian inscription names cult officials who are known from another dedication. Eukarpos Philasios, son of Dionysos and an Athenian, was ζάκορός and ἁγιαφόρος in the cult of Isis. He dedicated an image of Asklepios on divine orders, κατ᾿ ἐπίταγμ[α], on behalf of himself and other male officials of Isis' cult, including the priest and stolist.[36] Although Eukarpos' offering does not specify a recipient deity, these named Isiac officials suggest provenance from the Iseion.[37] Again, there are Delian parallels: dedications to the Egyptian gods on the island were frequently erected after divine orders, κατὰ πρόσταγμα, following instructions received in a dream.[38] Three offerings from Sarapieion C on Delos make an explicit connection with the ὀνειροκρίτις: "...κατὰ πρόσταγμα διὰ ὀνειροκρίτου..."[39] Eukarpos' dedication of an image of Asklepios, most probably in the sanctuary of Isis, illustrates the Egyptian cult's close relationship with the neighboring Asklepieion, located some fifty meters at the east.[40] Moreover, parallel offices and similar dedicatory phrases show a Delian influence on the Acropolis cult.

Delos

The Athenians were familiar with Sarapis' ability to heal from their interactions with his cult on Delos.[41] Treasury inventories, recorded after Athens resumed management of the island in 167/6 BC, list votive body parts at the Sarapieion. Amongst the dedications in precious metals are 17 eyes or pairs of eyes, two ears, a foot, a throat, a breast, a womb, and genitalia.[42] Anatomical votives are characteristic of Greek healing divinities and many survive today in stone or terracotta from sites elsewhere.[43]

A contemporary 2nd century BC inventory from the Delian Asklepieion is substantially more modest.[44] Surprisingly, the inventory does not mention anatomical votives, but this does not preclude their existence on some of the sanctuary's many pinaxes or on objects of non-precious materials that were not recorded. A single anatomical votive sculpture of male genitalia survives from the Delian Asklepieion, confirming that the practice was not altogether unknown at the site.[45] Yet, anatomical votives were commonly dedicated to Asklepios elsewhere in Greece, so their infrequent appearance is notable.[46] Based in part on a comparison of these inventories, some have suggested that Sarapis' success in providing cures may have slowed the growth of the cult of Asklepios on the island.[47]

An interesting case of healing is recorded on two mid 2nd century BC bases from Sarapieion A. The dedicatory inscription from one of these bases proclaims the circumstances of its commemoration: "Nikaso, daughter of Hippokrates, a Delian, [dedicated these] as thank-offerings to the listening gods, Sarapis, Isis, Anoubis, and Harpokrates for delivering cures…"[48] Nikaso made a second dedication, this time in conjunction with her husband, for the healing of their son.[49] The offerings demonstrate that the Egyptian deities attended to pressing parental concerns, such as the health and wellbeing of offspring. So, too, children were placed under the protection of Asklepios at sanctuaries such as Epidauros.[50]

Offerings addressed to Asklepios and Hygieia have been found in Sarapieion C.[51] These dedications were appropriately sited in the precinct on account of the gods' shared ability to heal. One dedication is noteworthy for implying that Asklepios and his family even shared altars and temples with the Egyptian gods. The 2nd century BC dedication by an Athenian, who also dedicated a phiale in the temple of Anoubis, was found near Sarapieion C:[52]

> To Asklepios, Hygieia, Apollo, Leto, Artemis the huntress, and to all of the gods and goddesses who share the same altars and same temples, Damon, son of Patron, an Athenian, [dedicated this] on behalf of himself and his children and those who depend on him, in thanksgiving.

Philippe Bruneau argued that Damon's inclusion of θεοῖς συμβώμοις καὶ συννάοις refers to the named deities in Egyptian forms: Asklepios, Hygieia, and Apollo, as Sarapis, Isis, and Horus.[53] Diverse divinities, however, are invoked in Sarapieion C's dedications and, as such, it is difficult to disentangle fully the significance of Asklepios' and Hygieia's presence there.[54] The associations with Asklepian cult and healing are perhaps more clearly demonstrated by dedications addressed to Isis-Hygieia and to Sarapis in Kanopos, invocations which presuppose healing ritual.[55] We find, then, a healing character at the Delian Sarapieia during Athenian management of the island's religious affairs, and have instances of Athenians making dedications there.

Epidauros

At the Epidaurian Asklepieion, Pausanias (2.27.6) records a temple of Hygieia, Asklepios, and Apollo in their Egyptian forms amongst the sanctuary improvements sponsored by a Roman senator, Antoninus: "He made also a temple to Hygieia, Asklepios, and Apollo, the last two surnamed Egyptian."[56] The passage alludes to an integration with Isis, Sarapis, and perhaps, Harpokrates or Horus. Pausanias, however, is the monument's only source and its location in the archaeological record remains elusive. Milena Melfi has cautiously proposed its identification with a large 2nd century AD establishment at the northwestern corner of the precinct partly on the basis of construction tiles that bear the name of Antoninus.[57] Yet, according to Pausanias, the senator was responsible for several projects at the sanctuary.

The Egyptian gods received dedications in the Asklepieion at Epidauros. Two 2nd or 3rd century AD altars were given to Sarapis and Isis respectively by Epaphroditos, a priest.[58]

A third dedication, a statue, was offered to Isis Chrysallis, again by Epaphroditos, but who this time identifies himself as ἰατρός, commemorating his medical role.[59] Many divinities were presented with offerings at Epidauros, especially during the Roman period, but these dedications, coupled with the testimony of Pausanias, bear witness to the presence of the Egyptian gods at Epidauros for reasons of healing.

Argos

Nearby, at Argos, the resident deity of a 2nd century AD cult complex has been interpreted variously as Sarapis, Asklepios, or a hybridized form of these gods. In its first phase, the structure consisted of a vaulted cult chamber with an apse and a crypt below. The cult room was fronted by a porch and accessed by means of a monumental staircase, which ascended from a large, sunken peristyle court. In a second phase, the court was remodeled to incorporate bathing facilities.

Pierre Aupert proposed that the complex housed a cult of Sarapis, partly because he understood the technique of its brickwork to have originated in Egypt.[60] His interpretation, however, conflicts with Pausanias (2.21.1), who saw a temple of Asklepios near the Argive marketplace, presumably the same structure. To explain Pausanias, Aupert argued that the cult of Sarapis, which had a healing character, was syncretized with Asklepios during its second phase and by the time of Pausanias' visit.[61] Although Aupert's interpretation of the complex's building technique was recently disproven,[62] certain architectural features – namely, the sunken peristyle courtyard and the crypt below the cella apse that was possibly supplied with water – still argue for the presence of an Egyptian cult.[63] The complex's dedication during its first phase remains controversial on a lack of evidence, but certainly after its renovation, Asklepios had a pronounced presence on the site, as evidenced by the bath's sculptural program.[64]

Iconographic Hybridity and the Egyptian Gods

The identification of Agora S 1068 as a hybridized image fits within the religious culture of Roman Athens, and more broadly, of Roman Greece, where foreign gods routinely integrated aspects of the visual identities of their Greek counterparts.[65] For the Egyptian gods, who possessed greater iconographic fluidity, a varied visual vocabulary played a critical role in the success of the cult in Greece by communicating the multiple functions of the gods.

At Argos, for instance, Richard Veymiers has called attention to the iconographic hybridity of a Roman-period marble statuette of Harpokrates-Telesphoros.[66] The figure lifts his finger to his lips, a familiar and identifiable gesture for Harpokrates, but wears a full-body cloak that is unusual for the god.[67] The youthful deity, who, in Greece, is typically depicted nude, wears a costume strikingly similar to that of Telesphoros, a healing associate of Asklepios. A fragmentary hand on top of the statuette's head indicates that the figure was part of a group composition; he likely stood alongside Isis or Sarapis, or some similarly hybridized image, perhaps even of Sarapis and Asklepios.[68] The positioning of the hand is at an appropriate height for Telesphoros, who commonly stands low at Asklepios' side. The locally produced image further illustrates the connections between the Asklepian and Egyptian cults at Argos and is good evidence for the Egyptian gods as healers there.

To take but another example, from the sanctuary of the Egyptian gods at Brexisa near Marathon, two statues of Isis grasp attributes that, as Iphigeneia Dekoulakou has explained, reflect longstanding relationships with Greek counterparts.[69] In addition to iconographic and stylistic details, the identification of these images as representing a form of Isis is secured by find-spots in their contexts of primary use. The over-life-size statues flanked the complex's monumental Egyptianizing entrances, as indicated by their bases, which were found in situ. At the south propylon, Isis stood holding in each hand a sheath of grain, an object associated with Demeter.[70] Isis maintains a distinctly Egyptian character in her costume and rigid, frontal pose, and is thus differentiated from Demeter, but the sheaths of grain doubtless represent her role as a goddess of fertility and rebirth. At the west propylon, archaeologists recovered a statue of Isis holding roses, flowers closely associated with Aphrodite.[71] Similarly, the roses probably indicate Isis' role in the realm of sexuality.

A revealing passage in Aelius Aristides' *Sacred Tales* highlights the iconographic similarities between Asklepios and Sarapis. Aristides, a mid 2nd century AD sophist, suffered a long bout of various illnesses, which led him to spend extended periods at the Pergamene Asklepieion. Aristides describes how Sarapis and Asklepios appeared to him in a dream, during which Sarapis performed a medical procedure. Aristides (49.46) is astounded by their shared appearance: "Sarapis also appeared on the same night, both he himself and Asklepios. They were marvelous in their beauty and magnitude, and in some way like one another."[72] In Aristides' vision, the gods maintain distinct characters, but appear similar during a critical moment in healing ritual. Aristides' visions were shaped by his encounters with art, noting in another dream that Sarapis appeared "in the form of his seated statues" (49.47).[73]

It is clear that Aristides did not consider Sarapis and Asklepios to be a single deity, but fully syncretized forms are known from other sources. An exceptional late Roman inscription from the sanctuary of Asklepios at Lebena, Krete, records a dedication to an apparent syncretized version of Zeus, Sarapis, and Asklepios, as doctor: "Διὶ Σεράπιδι/ Ἀσκληπιῷ ἰα/τρῷ..."[74] Zeus, like Sarapis and Asklepios,

appears as a mature, bearded man. The three especially evoked one another in their enthroned cult states at Olympia, Alexandria, and Epidauros, respectively. The dedication's invocation to the physician leaves little doubt about the circumstances of the offering.

In Roman Athens, Sarapis could function as a healer, much as he did at Pergamon and Lebena. The capacity of Sarapis to offer cures accords with the general resurgence of healing cults in Athens during the Roman period. The City Asklepieion was refurbished in Augustan times and was again filled with votive dedications from the 1st century AD after a decrease in the preceding two centuries.[75] The sanctuary of Zeus Hypsistos flourished on the Pnyx with niches cut for votive plaques, many bearing representations of parts of the human body.[76] This renaissance occurs elsewhere in Greece; for instance, an increased number of votive offerings at the Epidaurian Asklepieion reference healing ritual during the Roman period.

Display Contexts and Abandonment

Agora S 1068 might have been commissioned as a votive offering in a sanctuary of Sarapis. The site of the Athenian Sarapieion is known only through a brief notice given by Pausanias (1.18.4), who saw the sanctuary after leaving the Prytaneion on the northern slope of the Acropolis: "As you descend from here to the lower part of the city, is a sanctuary of Sarapis, whose worship the Athenians introduced from Ptolemy."[77] Pausanias' passing mention is topographically unrevealing, not least because the Athenian Prytaneion is still unattested in the archaeological record.[78] Inscriptions related to the Egyptian cult have been found in the area of the Metropolitan Church and, for this reason, the sanctuary has been placed near the Roman marketplace.[79]

There is, however, a wide dispersal of finds related to the cult of Sarapis throughout the city, including objects from the excavations of the Agora: a 1st century BC dedicatory altar, a possible dipinto on a 1st century AD amphora, a statuette bust, some statuette fragments, and some lamps and terracottas.[80] In addition, a dedication to Isis and Sarapis, and perhaps, too, Anoubis, was found near an unnamed church on the northern slope of the Acropolis, presumably the Hypapante.[81] The location, not far from the find-spot of Agora S 1068, is south of the City Eleusinion on the northern slopes of the Acropolis, above the Agora. The inscription, dated around 200 BC, bears the name of an Athenian priest of Sarapis, which Sterling Dow took as evidence for the establishment of an official state cult by this time.[82] Yet another inscription related to the Egyptian cults, a 1st century AD dedication with better-recorded provenance, was found nearby the Church of the Hypapante, reused as building material in a modern wall. It was offered by οἱ θερα[πευταί] or, alternatively, οἱ θερα[πευθέντες].[83] The association of the θεραπευταί is well known in the cults of the Egyptian gods on Delos,[84] but it is also attested in the cult of Asklepios outside of Athens. The obscure term probably denotes those in ritual subservience to the deity, rather than involvement in healing.[85]

Still more finds related to the cults of Isis and the other Egyptian gods have been found during the excavations. A spatial distribution of the find-spots of these objects shows no specific concentration, but there is a general gathering south of the Agora, along the northern slopes of the Areopagos and the Acropolis. Although none of these finds are from contexts of primary use, they provide a general indication of the location of the Sarapieion – or another cult place belonging to the god – the topographical possibilities for which might be extended further west in the direction of the Agora.

In a secondary use, Agora S 1068 was possibly incorporated into a sculptural assemblage for display in a domestic space. The statue was excavated in 7th century AD destruction debris over the Omega House, a substantial, late antique, private establishment on the northern slope of the Areopagos[86] (Figure 6.5). The structure, controversially identified as one of the city's famous philosophical schools, was richly appointed with statuary.[87] On the basis of its find-spot, the statue has been associated with these sculptural collections. The Omega House's sculptural assemblage features diverse mythological and historical subjects that were brought together over an extended period of time. The sculptures vary in date and style, having been produced between the 4th century BC and the 3rd century AD. A healing god is not unusual amongst such a collection; images of Asklepios, for example, were common in the private spaces of Roman and late antique Athens.[88] Moreover, the Egyptian gods apparently held a degree of importance for the inhabitants of the Omega House. A Roman-period furniture support depicting the Egyptian god Khnum was excavated in destruction fill over its courtyard.[89] In a comparable late antique residence on the south slope of the Acropolis, the so-called House of Proklos, a fragment of a statue of Isis was found. The upper body and neck of the goddess, identifiable by her knotted mantle, was from an over-life-size marble image, which the home's inhabitants probably salvaged from the then-ruined Iseion, located on the terrace above.[90]

The discovery of Agora S 1068 in a late context suggests a long lifespan, perhaps available for use as late as the 7th century AD. At some point, the image fell victim to iconoclasm; there are scars at the base of the rear neck where an object was forcibly driven to remove the head. Kerberos, if still present, was removed entirely, and portions of the snake were deliberately chiseled away. As a source of the god's healing powers and as an identifying characteristic, the serpent-entwined staff required removal in order to negate the statue's religious potency. This selective defacing is a vivid reminder of the attribute's ritual significance.[91] Three other sculptures from the Omega House were also deliberately defaced, suggesting that Christians occupied the establishment in its final phase.[92]

The statue's connection with the Omega House, however, is not secure. Agora S 1068 was found in the immediate vicinity of a large kiln. Excavators found thin deposits of powdered lime along the kiln's walls and more at floor level, but emphasized that its function nevertheless remained uncertain. Further obscuring matters is the kiln's complicated chronology, which probably dates from later reuse of the building in the 7th century AD, but could be earlier. One wonders if the statue awaited burning and, if so, its journey there might warrant disassociation with the Omega House.

Conclusion

Agora S 1068, a hybridized image of Asklepios and Sarapis, shows that the Athenian cults of the Egyptian gods could, too, be invoked for cures, as attested by the ritually important snake and staff, which in its local Athenian context undoubtedly indicates healing ritual. The statue is the first clear indication known from Athens of Sarapis' healing function, a role that is well attested elsewhere in Greece during the Hellenistic and Roman periods. For the Egyptian gods, greater iconographic fluidity allowed their images to express the various functions of their cults. This new identification for the Agora image allows us to understand better how the Egyptian deities functioned within Athenian religion and, furthermore, puts scholars on notice to recognize the complex iconographic forms present in Roman Athens.

Notes

1   A version of this paper was presented at the 115th Annual Meeting of the Archaeological Institute of America on January 3, 2014, in Chicago. I am grateful to John Camp for allowing me to study these materials; to Erin Averett, Martha Habash, Carol Lawton, Julia Lenaghan, Milena Melfi, and Bert Smith for offering advice on specific points; to two anonymous reviewers for their helpful criticisms; to Craig Mauzy for the exceptional images; and to Sylvie Dumont for facilitating access to these materials. Translations are the author's own, except where noted.

2   Agora S 1068: Thompson 1976, p. 302; Frantz 1988, p. 41, pl. 39:d; Gawlinski 2014, p. 95.

3   For studies of the Egyptian gods in Athens, see Dow 1937; Dunand 1973, pp. 4–17, 132–153; Walker 1979; Walters 1988; Simms 1989; Muñiz Grijalvo 2009. For related inscriptions, including the Isiac funerary stelai, see *RICIS* 101/0201–0254. On the healing cults of Athens, see Kutsch 1913; Aleshire 1989, 1991; Forsén 1993; Vikela 1994; Verbanck-Piérard 2000; Gorrini 2001; Riethmüller 2005, vol. 1, pp. 241–278; vol. 2, pp. 10–22; Vikela 2006; Melfi 2007b, pp. 313–433; Lawton, Lamont in this volume.

4   H. 0.84; W. 0.37; D. 0.185 m.

5   *LIMC* II, 1984, pp. 863–897, s.v. Asklepios (B. Holtzmann).
6   The Giustini model was favored civically, found, for instance, on certain issues of the city's imperial period coinage (J. P. Shear 1936, p. 312, fig. 19; Kroll and Walker 1993, nos. 216, 217, 277, 367). The Giustini model's frequent appearance in Athens has given rise to its association with the now-lost cult statue in the City Asklepieion, although some dispute the connection. The Giustini type is favored elsewhere, as at Epidauros (Katakis 2002, pp. 207–219). For a history of scholarship of the type with bibliography, see Lattimore 1996, pp. 43–48, no. 90.
7   Compared to the frequency of other Asklepios image types present in the Agora collection. Giustini type: Agora S 710: T. L. Shear 1936, pp. 197–198, fig. 17; Meyer 1988, pp. 141–142, no. LE5, pl. 19:3. Agora S 875: Frantz 1988, p. 36, pl. 23:a; Sirano 1994, p. 207, figs. 8:a–b. Agora S 1991: Thompson 1958, p. 154, pl. 43:d; Meyer 1988, p. 121, no. G9. Other Giustini types, unpublished: Agora S 357, S 480, S 562, S 727, S 854, S 1262, S 1337, S 1633, S 1687, S 1807, S 2232, S 2754, S 2918, S 3160, S 3202, S 3331, S 3503. Few other Asklepios image types exist in the Agora collections. Albani type: Agora S 1589: Thompson 1953, pp. 54–55, pl. 19:c–d; *LIMC* II, 1984, p. 883, no. 258, s.v. Asklepios (B. Holtzmann). Eleusis type: Agora S 323: Hausmann 1954–1955, p. 146; *LIMC* II, 1984, p. 883, no. 241, s.v. Asklepios (B. Holtzmann). Velia type: Agora S 1805: unpublished. Others are too fragmentary to distinguish a type.
8   Agora S 1991: see n. 7.
9   *LIMC* VII, 1994, pp. 666–692, s.v. Sarapis (G. Clerc and J. Leclant).
10   Dunand 2007, pp. 259–261; Moyer 2011, pp. 144–153.
11   Clement of Alexandria (*Protrepicus* 4.43) attributes the statue to Bryaxis, see Stewart 1990, pp. 300–301, no. T149. Bryaxis' image evokes the cult statues of Asklepios at Epidauros and of Zeus at Olympia. The most notable Egyptian element is the *kalathos* or grain measure, a symbol of bounty and fertility.
12   *LIMC* VII, 1994, pp. 666–667, s.v. Sarapis (G. Clerc and J. Leclant).
13   Stewart 1990, p. 203.
14   Smith 1998, pp. 65–66; Smith 2006, pp. 37–38, 151–152.
15   *LIMC* IV, 1988, pp. 367–370, s.v. Hades (S.-C. Dahlinger). Tacitus (*Hist.* 4.83–84), for instance, comments that some identify Sarapis with Asklepios, Osiris, or Zeus, but most with Pluto "arguing from the attributes of the god that are seen on his statue or from their own conjectures" (trans. Moore 1931). On Sarapis' associations with Hades/Pluto, see Stambaugh 1972, pp. 27–35.
16   On standing images of Sarapis, see Tran Tam Tinh 1983.
17   Agora S 355: Shear 1935, pp. 397–398, fig. 24; Camp 1980, p. 20, fig. 40. Found with its base (not pictured).
18   E.g., Tran Tam Tinh 1983, pp. 93–94, nos. IA 9–10, figs. 12–13; p. 96, no. IA 16bis, fig. 17.
19   *LIMC* VII, 1994, pp. 870–878, s.v. Telesphoros (H. Rühfel).
20   Leptis Magna, inv. unknown: Tran Tam Tinh 1983, p. 91, no. IA 5, fig. 6.
21   On the Sarapieion at Leptis Magna and its inscriptions, see Brouquier-Reddé 1992, pp. 101–105; Di Vita et al. 2003; *RICIS* 702/0101–0118.
22   For examples of statuary, see n. 7. For the votive reliefs from

Athens, see Svoronos 1908–1937; Hausmann 1948; Comella 2002. Five votive reliefs with Asklepios and his snake have been found in the Agora excavations: Agora S 593, S 1258, S 2323, S 2505, S 2741.
23   For hybrid images in ancient art, see Counts 2008 with bibliography. On the connections between Asklepios and Sarapis, see Stambaugh 1972, pp. 75–78.
24   National Museum, Athens, inv. 1396: Lawton 1995, pp. 147–148, no. 153, pl. 81; Kaltsas 2002, p. 236, no. 496; Leventi 2003, p. 152, no. R 68, pl. 44. On the adoption of Asklepios' iconography with other examples, see Gorrini and Melfi 2002, pp. 249–251.
25   National Museum, Athens, inv. 3369: Kaltsas 2002, pp. 209–210, no. 425.
26   Moyer 2011, p. 147, with bibliography.
27   Stambaugh 1972, p. 76.
28   Diog. Laert. 5.5.76.
29   Alvar 2008, pp. 330–331.
30   *IG* II² 337 = *RICIS* 101/0101: Simms 1989.
31   *IG* II² 1292 = *RICIS* 101/0201: Dow 1937, pp. 188–197.
32   On the identification and history of the sanctuary, see Walker 1979. For the epigraphic evidence, see *RICIS* 101/0219–0223.
33   *IG* II² 4771 = *RICIS* 101/0221: Walker 1979, pp. 253–256.
34   E.g., *ID* 2071, 2073, 2105, 2106, 2110, 2120.
35   *ID* 2120 = *RICIS* 202/0245.
36   *IG* II² 4772: Walker 1979, pp. 254–256.
37   The dedication of an image of one deity in a sanctuary of another was commonplace in antiquity.
38   On the frequent use of this formula on Delos, where it is typical of Greek dedications to the Egyptian gods, see Moyer 2011, pp. 166–168.
39   *ID* 2105, 2106, 2110.
40   A small altar dedicated to Sarapis by a certain Gaius (*IG* II² 4815 = *RICIS* 101/0223) was found in the Asklepieion and is further evidence for the connection, although the altar may have traveled from the Iseion.
41   Dow 1937, pp. 202–207; Mikalson 1998, pp. 229–231. On the Delian Sarapieia, see Roussel 1915–1916; 1916, pp. 249–252; Bruneau 1970, pp. 457–466; Dunand 1973, pp. 83–115; Siard 2003, 2009.
42   Hamilton 2000, pp. 196–200, 223–240.
43   Van Straten 1981, pp. 105–151; Forsén 1996.
44   Hamilton 2000, pp. 190–191, 211–213. On the Delian Asklepieion, see Bruneau 1970, pp. 355–377; Riethmüller 2005, vol. 2, pp. 338–339; Melfi 2007b, pp. 456–479.
45   Delos, inv. A 4203: Forsén 1996, p. 95, no. 28.1, fig. 97. Here, Bruneau (1970, p. 371, no. 2) and Van Straten (1981, p. 127) also categorize a hand.
46   For anatomical votives offered to Asklepios in Greece, see Roebuck 1951; Aleshire 1989; Forsén 1996. Tzonou-Herbst (2014, pp. 245–246) has proposed down-dating some deposits of anatomical votives at Corinth to as late as the 2nd century BC.
47   Roussel 1916, pp. 239, 262; Mikalson 1998, p. 229; Contra Melfi 2007b, p. 468.
48   *ID* 2117 = *RICIS* 202/0198: Νικασὼ Ἱπποκράτου Δήλια Θεοῖς ἐπηκόοις ἰατρεῖα,/Σαράπιδι, Ἴσιδι, Ἀνούβιδι, Ἁρποχράτει χαριστήρι-/α...
49   *ID* 2116 = *RICIS* 202/0197: ...ὑπὲρ τοῦ υἱοῦ Ξενοφῶντος

62   *Brian A. Martens*

ἰατρεῖα θεοῖς ἐπηκόοις Σαρά-/πιδι, Ἴσιδι, Ἀνούβιδι, χαριστήριον...

50 On Asklepios and Hygieia as *kourotrophoi*, see Leventi 1999–2000.

51 *ID* 2384, 2386, 2387.

52 *ID* 2387 = *RICIS* 202/0414: Ἀ[σ]κληπιῶι καὶ Ὑγιείαι καὶ Ἀπ[ό]λλωνι καὶ Λητοῖ/καὶ Ἀρτέμιδι Ἀγροτέραι καὶ θεοῖς συμβώμοις/καὶ συννάοις πᾶσι καὶ πά[σ]αις, Δάμων Πάτρωνος/Ἀθηναῖος ὑπὲρ ἑαυτοῦ καὶ τῶν τέκνων καὶ ὑπαρ-/χόντων, χαριστήρια.

53 Bruneau 1970, p. 375.

54 Other deities present at Sarapieion C (Moyer 2011, p. 201, n. 191): Herakles Apallaxikakos, Demeter and Kore, Zeus Kynthios, Zeus Ktesios, Zeus Soter, Pluto, Hermes, Dionysos, Aphrodite, Artemis-Hekate, Artemis Hagia, Dioskouri, Athena, and Pan. Moreover, dedications to Asklepios have been found throughout the island, including in the sanctuary of the Syrian gods (*ID* 2224, 2248, 2261, 2264), see Bruneau 1970, pp. 374–375; Melfi 2007b, pp. 468–469.

55 Isis-Hygieia: *ID* 2060. Sarapis in Kanopos: *ID* 2129, 2176. Another Delian dedication references a priest of Sarapis in Kanopos: *ID* 2081. Pausanias (2.4.6) mentions two sanctuaries to Sarapis on the slopes of Akrokorinth, one of which was dedicated to Sarapis in Kanopos, see Smith 1977, pp. 210–212.

56 Trans. W. Jones (Loeb): ἐποίησε δὲ καὶ Ὑγείᾳ ναὸν καὶ Ἀσκληπιῷ καὶ Ἀπόλλωνι ἐπίκλησιν Αἰγυπτίοις. Pausanias (7.26.7) also mentions a statue of Asklepios alongside statues of Sarapis and Isis in the temple of Apollo at Aigeira.

57 Melfi 2007b, pp. 111–115.

58 *IG* IV² 534 = *RICIS* 102/0403. *IG* IV² 535 = *RICIS* 102/0402.

59 *IG* IV² 577 = *RICIS* 102/0404. For a 1st century AD statuette head of Isis from the sanctuary, see Katakis 2002, pp. 92–93, no. 90, pl. 104.

60 Aupert 1985; Aupert and Ginouvès 1989.

61 Aupert 1985, pp. 172–174.

62 Lancaster (2010, pp. 447–472) has convincingly re-dated the complex's building phases and has shown a Parthian, not Egyptian, influence in its building technique. For other arguments against the identification of the cult space with Sarapis, see Riethmüller 2005, vol. 2, pp. 73–83, no. 26.

63 Aupert 1985, pp. 162–171; 2001, p. 448. Aupert (2001, p. 446) also points to certain finds from the area with an Egyptian or oriental flavor. Wild (1981) explores the role of water in the cult of the Egyptian gods. On the Egyptian gods at Argos, including other possible cult spaces, see Veymiers 2011.

64 Excavators recovered two statues of Asklepios and one statue of Hygieia in the frigidarium at Argos. Asklepios: Marcadé 1980, pp. 135–138, figs. 3–5. Asklepios (youthful): Marcadé 1980, pp. 148–150, fig. 19. Hygieia: Marcadé 1980, pp. 138–140, fig. 6. Images of Asklepios and Hygieia were common in bathing contexts, as Lucian describes (*Hipp.*, 5).

65 For a look at recent scholarship on Egyptianizing art in Roman Greece, see Mazurek 2013.

66 Argos, inv. unknown: Veymiers 2011, pp. 115–117, fig. 8.

67 *LIMC* IV, 1988, pp. 415–445, s.v. Harpokrates (V. Tran Tam Tinh, B. Jaeger, and S. Poulin).

68 Compare a statuette in the Carthage Museum depicting Telesphoros alongside Asklepios with *kalathos*, see Kater-Sibbes 1973, p. 137, no. 739, pl. XXIV.

69 Dekoulakou 2010, pp. 112–113; 2011, pp. 28–29.

70 Dekoulakou 2010, pp. 111–112, figs. 2-5; 2011, pp. 28–29, fig. 3.

71 Dekoulakou 2010, pp. 112–113, figs. 6-9; 2011, p. 29, fig. 4.

72 Trans. Behr 1981: ἐφάνη δὲ καὶ ὁ Σάραπις τῆς αὐτῆς νυκτὸς, ἅμα αὐτός τε καὶ ὁ Ἀσκληπιὸς, θαυμαστοὶ τὸ κάλλος καὶ τὸ μέγεθος καί τινα τρόπον ἀλλήλοις ἐμφερεῖς. On Aristides and the Egyptian gods, see Behr (1978), who argues that the cults of Asklepios and Sarapis were in competition: "the two gods were waging for their convert" (p. 16).

73 Trans. Behr 1981.

74 *IC* I xvii 27 = *RICIS* 203/0301: Melfi 2007a, p. 194, no. 48.

75 Melfi 2007b, pp. 374–377.

76 Forsén 1993, p. 517.

77 Trans. Jones 1918 (Loeb): ἐντεῦθεν ἰοῦσιν ἐς τὰ κάτω τῆς πόλεως Σαράπιδός ἐστιν ἱερόν, ὃν Ἀθηναῖοι παρὰ Πτολεμαίου θεὸν ἐσηγάγοντο.

78 On the location of the Athenian Prytaneion, see Wycherley 1957, pp. 168–169, no. 553; Miller 1978, pp. 38–66; Camp 2001, p. 27. For the suggestion of its location near the Monument of Lysikrates, see Schmalz 2006.

79 Judeich 1931, p. 380; Dow 1937, p. 209; Wycherley 1963, pp. 161–162; Travlos 1971, p. 28; Dunand 1973, p. 134.

80 Dedicatory altar: Agora I 6627: Meritt 1963, p. 47, no. 68, pl. 16; Geagan 2011, p. 319, no. V609; *RICIS* 101/0211. Dipinto: Agora P 12471: Lang 1976, p. 77, no. He 11; *RICIS* 101/0212. Bust: Agora S 355: see n. 17. Some possible statuette fragments (likely from domestic spaces): Agora S 383: Stewart 2013, p. 618, no. 3, fig. 4; others unpublished: Agora S 448, S 561, S 630, S 1089, S 1267. Some lamps: Agora L 2695: Perlzweig 1961, p. 92, no. 240, pl. 7; Agora L 4274: Perlzweig 1961, pp. 121–122, no. 805, pl. 18. Some terracottas: Agora T 482: Grandjouan 1961, p. 51, no. 267, pl. 7. Agora T 2052: Grandjouan 1961, p. 51, no. 268. For a review of some of the evidence for the Egyptian cults found throughout the city, see Kater-Sibbes 1973, pp. 85–87; Trianti 2008, pp. 400–404.

81 *IG* II² 4692 (*IG* II 1612) = *RICIS* 101/0202: Dow 1937, pp. 198–201. On the identification of the inscription's find-spot with the church of Hypapante, see Shear 1935 (p. 398), who also notes a boundary stone of the Dioskouri found in this area.

82 Dow 1937, p. 200.

83 Agora I 5717 = *SEG* XXI 776: Meritt 1961, p. 273, no. 113, pl. 53; Aleshire 1991, p. 171; Geagan 2011, p. 56, no. C117.

84 E.g., *ID* 2077–2081.

85 Pleket 1981, pp. 159–161.

86 Frantz (1988, pl. 39:d) incorrectly places the statue in neighboring "House B." Compare with her previous statement (p. 41) which provides an accurate provenance.

87 On the identification as a philosophical school, see Frantz 1988, pp. 44–47; Camp 1986, pp. 202–211; 1989, pp. 50–55. Contra: Sodini 1984, pp. 348–349; Fowden 1990, pp. 495–496; Castrén 1994, p. 8.

88 Martens 2014.

89 Agora S 2353, joining with fragment Agora S 2432, found near the Library of Pantainos: unpublished.

90 Special inv. for marbles found south of the Akropolis, 1955 NAM 40: Walker 1979, pp. 252–253, 257; Walters 1988, p. 63; Karivieri 1994, pp. 131–132; Brouskari 2002, pp. 137–139, 195, figs. 139–140.

91 For a selective pattern of defacing at Aphrodisias, where scenes of cult were amongst the offensive aspects of images, see Smith 2012. On the selective destruction of specific body parts of pagan sculptures, see Kristensen 2013, pp. 89–106. Several statuettes from the Agora and votive reliefs from the City Asklepieion demonstrate a similar pattern of defacing, e.g., Agora S 710: see n. 7; Fitzwilliam Museum, Cambridge, inv. GR.14.1865: Hausmann 1948, p. 168, no. 28, pl. 20.

92 Agora S 2361, S 2337, I 7154: Lawton 2006, pp. 49–51, figs. 53–55.

References

Aleshire, S. B. 1989. *The Athenian Asklepieion: the People, their Dedications, and the Inventories*, Amsterdam.

Aleshire, S. B. 1991. *Asklepios at Athens: Epigraphic and Prosopographic Essays on the Athenian Healing Cults*, Amsterdam.

Alvar, J. 2008. *Romanising Oriental Gods: Myth, Salvation and Ethics in the Cults of Cybele, Isis and Mithras*, trans. R. Gordon, Leiden.

Aupert, P. 1985. "Un sérapieion argien?," *Comptes rendus des séances de l'Académie des inscriptions et belles-lettres (Paris)*, pp. 151–175.

Aupert, P. 2001. "Architecture et urbanisme à Argos au Ier siècle ap. J.-C.," in *Constructions publiques et programmes édilitaires en Grèce, entre le IIe siècle av. J.-C. et le Ier siècle ap. J.-C. (Bulletin de correspondance hellénique Suppl. 39)*, ed. J. Y. Marc and J. C. Moretti, Paris, pp. 439–454.

Aupert, P. and R. Ginouvès. 1989. "Une toiture revolutionnaire à Argos" in *The Greek Renaissance in the Roman Empire: Papers from the Tenth British Museum Classical Colloquium (Bulletin of the Institute of Classical Studies of the University of London Suppl. 55)*, ed. S. Walker and A. Cameron, London, pp. 151–155.

Behr, C. A. 1978. "Aristides and the Egyptian Gods" in *Hommages à Maarten J. Vermaseren 1*, ed. M. B. Boer and T. A. Edridge, Leiden, pp. 13–24.

Behr, C. A. 1981. *P. Aelius Aristides: The Complete Works*, 2 vols., Leiden.

Brouquier-Reddé, V. 1992. *Temples et cultes de Tripolitaine*, Paris.

Brouskari, M. S. 2002. "Οι ανασκαφές νοτίως της Ακροπόλεως – Τα γλυπτά," *Archaiologike Ephemeris* 141, pp. 1–204.

Bruneau, P. 1970. *Recherches sur les cultes de Délos a l'époque hellénistique et a l'époque impériale*, Paris.

Camp, J. McK. 1980. *Gods and Heroes in the Athenian Agora (Agora Picture Book 19)*, Princeton.

Camp, J. McK. 1986. *The Athenian Agora: Excavations in the Heart of Classical Athens*, London.

Camp, J. McK. 1989. "The Philosophical Schools of Roman Athens," in *The Greek Renaissance in the Roman Empire: Papers from the Tenth British Museum Classical Colloquium (Bulletin of the Institute of Classical Studies of the University of London Suppl. 55)*, ed. S. Walker and A. Cameron, London, pp. 50–55.

Camp, J. McK. 2001. *The Archaeology of Athens*, New Haven and London.

Castrén, P. 1994. "General Aspects of Life in Post-Herulian Athens" in *Post-Herulian Athens: Aspects of Life and Culture in Athens, A.D. 267–529*, ed. P. Castrén, Helsinki, pp. 1–14.

Comella, A. 2002. *I rilievi votivi greci di periodo arcaico e classico: diffusione, ideologia, committenza*, Bari.

Counts, D. B. 2008. "Master of the Lion: Representation and Hybridity in Cypriote Sanctuaries," *American Journal of Archaeology* 112, pp. 3–27.

Dekoulakou, I. 2010. "Statues of Isis from the Sanctuary of the Egyptian Gods at Marathon" in *Marathon the Battle and the Ancient Deme*, ed. K. Buraselis and K. Meidani, Athens, pp. 109–133.

Dekoulakou, I. 2011. "Le sanctuaire des dieux égyptiens à Marathon" in *Bibliotheca Isiaca II*, ed. L. Bricault and R. Veymiers, Bordeaux, pp. 23–46.

Di Vita, A., et al. 2003. "Il Serapeo di Leptis Magna: il tempio, le iscrizioni, i marmi," *Quaderni di Archeologia della Libya* 18, pp. 267–292.

Dow, S. 1937. "The Egyptian Cults in Athens," *Harvard Theological Review* 30, pp. 183–232.

Dunand, F. 1973. *Le culte d'Isis dans le bassin oriental de la Méditerranée 2*, Leiden.

Dunand, F. 2007. "The Religious System at Alexandria" in *A Companion to Greek Religion*, ed. D. Ogden, Oxford, pp. 253–263.

Forsén, B. 1993. "The Sanctuary of Zeus Hypsistos and the Assembly Place on the Pnyx," *Hesperia* 62, pp. 507–521.

Forsén, B. 1996. *Griechische Gliederweihungen: eine Untersuchung zu ihrer Typologie und ihrer religions- und sozialgeschichtlichen Bedeutung*, Helsinki.

Fowden, G. 1990. "The Athenian Agora and the Progress of Christianity," *Journal of Roman Archaeology* 3, pp. 494–501.

Frantz, A. 1988. *The Athenian Agora, XXIV. Late Antiquity: A.D. 267–700*, Princeton.

Gawlinski, L. 2014. *The Athenian Agora: Museum Guide*, 5th ed., Athens.

Geagan, D. J. 2011. *The Athenian Agora, XVIII. Inscriptions: The Dedicatory Monuments*, Princeton.

Gorrini, M. 2001. "Gli eroi salutari dell'Attica," *Annuario della Scuola archeologica di Atene e delle Missioni italiane in Oriente* 79, pp. 299–315.

Gorrini, M. and M. Melfi 2002. "L'archéologie des cultes guérisseurs: quelques observations," *Kernos* 15, pp. 247–265.

Grandjouan, C. 1961. *The Athenian Agora, VI. Terracottas and Plastic Lamps of the Roman Period*, Princeton.

Hamilton, R. 2000. *Treasure Map: A Guide to the Delian Inventories*, Ann Arbor.

Hausmann, U. 1948. *Kunst und Heiltum: Untersuchungen zu den griechischen Asklepiosreliefs*, Potsdam.

Hausmann, U. 1954-1955. "Οινοφοροι," *Mitteilungen des Deutschen Archäologischen Instituts, Athenische Abteilung* 69/70, pp. 125–146.

Judeich, W. 1931. *Topographie von Athen*, 2nd ed., Munich.

Kaltsas, N. 2002. *Sculpture in the National Archaeological Museum, Athens*, trans. D. Hardy, Los Angeles.

Karivieri, A. 1994. "The 'House of Proclus' on the Southern Slope of the Acropolis: a Contribution" in *Post-Herulian Athens: Aspects of Life and Culture in Athens, A.D. 267–529*, ed. P. Castrén, Helsinki, pp. 115–139.

Katakis, S. 2002. *Τα γλυπτά των ρωμαϊκών χρονών από το ιερό τού Απόλλωνος Μαλεάτα και του Ασκληπιού*, Athens.

Kater-Sibbes, G. J. F. 1973. *Preliminary Catalogue of Sarapis Monuments*, Leiden.

Kristensen, T. M. 2013. *Making and Breaking the Gods: Christian Responses to Pagan Sculpture in Late Antiquity* (*Aarhus Studies in Mediterranean Antiquity* 12), Aarhus.

Kroll, J. H. and A. S. Walker. 1993. *The Athenian Agora*, XXVI. *The Greek Coins*, Princeton.

Kutsch, F. 1913. *Attische Heilgötter und Heilheroen*, Giessen.

Lancaster, L. C. 2010. "Parthian Influence on Vaulting in Roman Greece? An Inquiry into Technological Exchange under Hadrian," *American Journal of Archaeology* 114, pp. 447–472.

Lang, M. 1976. *The Athenian Agora*, XXI. *Graffiti and Dipinti*, Princeton.

Lattimore, S. 1996. *Isthmia*, VI. *Sculpture, II: Marble Sculpture, 1967-1980*, Princeton.

Lawton, C. 1995. *Attic Document Reliefs: Art and Politics in Athens* (Oxford Monographs on Classical Archaeology), Oxford.

Lawton, C. 2006. *Marbleworkers in the Athenian Agora* (*Agora Picture Book* 27), Princeton.

Leventi, I. K. 1999–2000. "Οι θεότητες του κύκλου του Ασκληπίου ως κουροτρόφοι. Οι εικονογραφικές μαρτυρίες," *Archaiognosia* 10, pp. 87–102.

Leventi, I. K. 2003. *Hygieia in Classical Greek Art* (*Archaiognosia* Suppl. 2), Athens.

LIMC = *Lexicon Iconographicum Mythologiae Classicae*, Zurich and Munich.

Marcadé, J. 1980. "Sculptures argiennes (III)" in *Études argiennes* (*Bulletin de correspondence hellénique* Suppl. 6), Paris, pp. 133–184.

Martens, B. A. 2014. "Asklepios in the Domestic Spaces of Roman and Late Antique Greece," in *The Religious Life of Things, Archiv für Religionsgeschichte*, ed. I. Moyer and C. Schultz.

Mazurek, L. A. 2013. "Reconsidering the Role of Egyptianizing Material Culture in Hellenistic and Roman Greece," *Journal of Roman Archaeology* 26, pp. 503–512, (book review).

Melfi, M. 2007a. *Il Santuario di Asclepio a Lebena*, Athens.

Melfi, M. 2007b. *I Santuari di Asclepio in Grecia. I*, Rome.

Meritt, B. D. 1961. "Greek Inscriptions," *Hesperia* 30, pp. 205–292.

Meritt, B. D. 1963. "Greek Inscriptions," *Hesperia* 32, pp. 1–56.

Meyer, M. 1988. "Erfindung und wirkung: zum Asklepios Giustini," *Mitteilungen des Deutschen Archäologischen Instituts, Athenische Abteilung* 103, pp. 119–159.

Mikalson, J. D. 1998. *Religion in Hellenistic Athens* (*Hellenistic Culture and Society* 29), Berkeley.

Miller, S. G. 1978. *The Prytaneion: its Function and Architectural Form*, Berkeley and Los Angeles.

Moyer, I. 2011. *Egypt and the Limits of Hellenism*, Cambridge.

Muñiz Grijalvo, E. 2009. "The Cult of the Egyptian Gods in Roman Athens" in *Les religions orientales dans le monde grec et romain: Cent ans après Cumont (1906–2006)*, ed. C. Bonnet, et al., Brussels and Rome, pp. 325–341.

Perlzweig, J. 1961. *The Athenian Agora*, VII. *Lamps of the Roman Period: First to Seventh Century after Christ*, Princeton.

Pleket, H. W. 1981. "Religious History as the History of Mentality: the 'Believer' as Servant of the Deity in the Greek World" in *Faith Hope and Worship: Aspects of Religious Mentality in the Ancient World*, ed. H. S. Versnel, Leiden, pp. 152–192.

RICIS = Bricault, L. 2005. *Recueil des inscriptions concernant les cultes Isiaques*, 3 vols., Paris.

Riethmüller, J. 2005. *Asklepios: Heiligtümer und Kulte*, 2 vols., Heidelberg.

Roebuck, C. 1951. *Corinth*, XIV. *The Asklepieion and Lerna*, Princeton.

Roussel, P. 1915–1916. *Les cultes égyptiens à Délos du IIIᵉ au Iᵉʳ siècle av. J.-C.*, Paris and Nancy.

Roussel, P. 1916. *Delos colonie athénienne*, Athens and Rome.

Schmalz, G. C. R. 2006. "The Athenian Prytaneion Discovered?," *Hesperia* 75, pp. 33–81.

Shear, J. P. 1936. "Athenian Imperial Coinage," *Hesperia* 5, pp. 285–332.

Shear, T. L. 1935. "The Sculpture Found in 1933," *Hesperia* 4, pp. 371–420.

Shear, T. L. 1936. "The Current Excavations in the Athenian Agora," *American Journal of Archaeology* 40, pp. 188–203.

Siard, H. 2003. "Nouvelles recherches sur le Sarapieion C de Délos," *Revue archéologique*, pp. 193–197.

Siard, H. 2009. "Le Sarapieion C de Délos: Architecture et cultes," *Revue archéologique*, pp. 155–161.

Simms, R. R. 1989. "Isis in Classical Athens," *Classical Journal* 84, pp. 216–221.

Sirano, F. 1994. "Considerazioni sull'Asclepio 'Tipo Nea Paphos': Ipotesi su un gruppo di sculture di età imperiale," *Archeologia classica* 46, pp. 199–232.

Smith, D. E. 1977. "The Egyptian Cults at Corinth," *Harvard Theological Review* 70, pp. 201–231.

Smith, R. R. R. 1998. "Cultural Choice and Political Identity in Honorific Portrait Statues in the Greek East in the Second Century A.D.," *Journal of Roman Studies* 88, pp. 56–93.

Smith, R. R. R. 2006. *Aphrodisias*, II. *Roman Portrait Statuary from Aphrodisias*, Mainz am Rhein.

Smith, R. R. R. 2012. "Defacing the Gods at Aphrodisias" in *Historical and Religious Memory in the Ancient World*, ed. B. Dignas and R. R. R. Smith, Oxford, pp. 283–324.

Sodini, J.-P. 1984. "L'habitat urbain en Grèce à la veille des invasions" in *Villes et peuplement dans l'Illyricum protobyzantin*, Rome, pp. 341–397.

Stambaugh, J. E. 1972. *Sarapis Under the Early Ptolemies*, Leiden.

Stewart, A. 1990. *Greek Sculpture: An Exploration*, New Haven.

Stewart, A. 2013. "Sculptors' Sketches, Trial Pieces, Figure Studies, and Models in Poros Limestone from the Athenian Agora," *Hesperia* 82, pp. 615–650.

Svoronos, I. N. 1908–1937. *Das Athener Nationalmuseum*, 3 vols., Athens

Thompson, H. A. 1953. "Excavations in the Athenian Agora: 1952," *Hesperia* 22, pp. 25–56.

Thompson, H. A. 1958. "Activities in the Athenian Agora: 1957," *Hesperia* 27, pp. 145–160.

Thompson, H. A. 1976. *The Athenian Agora: a Guide to the Excavation and Museum*, 3rd ed., Athens.

Tran Tam Tinh, V. 1983. *Sérapis debout: corpus des monuments de Sérapis debout et étude iconographique*, Leiden.

Travlos, J. 1971. *Pictorial Dictionary of Ancient Athens*, London.

Trianti, I. 2008. "Ανατολικές Θεότητες στη Νότια Κλίτυ της Ακρόπολης" in *Η Αθήνα Κατά τη Ρωμαϊκή Εποχή*, ed. S. Vlizos, Athens, pp. 391–409.

Tzonou-Herbst, I. 2014. "The Use-Life of the Anatomical Votives from the Asklepieion at Corinth" in *Archaeological Institute of America 115th Annual Meeting Abstracts*, Boston, pp. 245–246 (abstract).

Van Straten, F. T. 1981. "Gifts for the Gods" in *Faith Hope and Worship: Aspects of Religious Mentality in the Ancient World*, ed. H. S. Versnel, Leiden, pp. 65–151.

Verbanck-Piérard, A. 2000. "Les héros guérisseurs: des dieux comme les autres! À propos des cultes médicaux dans l'attique classique" in *Héros et héroïnes dans les myths et les cultes grecs* (*Kernos* Suppl. 10), ed. V. Pirenne-Delforge and E. Suárez de la Torre, Liège, pp. 281–332.

Veymiers, R. 2011. "Les cultes isiaques à Argos. Du mythe à l'archéologie" in *Bibliotheca Isiaca II*, ed. L. Bricault and R. Veymiers, Bordeaux, pp. 111–129.

Vikela, E. 1994. *Die Weihreliefs aus dem Athener Pankrates-Heiligtum am Ilissos: religionsgeschichtliche Bedeutung und Typologie* (*Mitteilungen des Deutschen Archäologischen Instituts, Athenische Abteilung* Suppl. 16), Berlin.

Vikela, E. 2006. "Healer Gods and Healing Sanctuaries in Attica: Similarities and Differences," *Archiv für Religionsgeschichte* 8, pp. 41–62.

Walker, S. 1979. "A Sanctuary of Isis on the South Slope of the Athenian Acropolis," *Annual of the British School at Athens* 74, pp. 243–258.

Walters, E. J. 1988. *Attic Grave Reliefs That Represent Women in the Dress of Isis* (*Hesperia* Suppl. 22), Princeton.

Wild, R. A. 1981. *Water in the Cultic Worship of Isis and Sarapis*, Leiden.

Wycherley, R. E. 1957. *The Athenian Agora*, III. *Literary and Epigraphical Testimonia*, Princeton.

Wycherley, R. E. 1963. "Pausanias at Athens, II: A Commentary on Book I, Chapters 18–19," *Greek, Roman and Byzantine Studies* 4, pp. 157–175.

The Experience of Greek Sacrifice:
Investigating Fat-Wrapped Thighbones

Jacob Morton

In this paper I present research through experimental archaeology into what kind of fat was used to wrap the thighbones in Homeric and Classical sacrifice. The textual, iconographic, and archaeological sources clearly indicate that an important element of the ritual of sacrifice was the burning of thighbones twice wrapped in fat. Until now, the precise meaning of 'twice-wrapped fat' around these thighbones was not clearly understood. I burned 38 fat-wrapped thighbones in a reconstructed altar over 17 months to explore what fat was wrapped around the thighbone and why. The findings are then used to elucidate and clarify textual and iconographic sources.

Introduction

Animal sacrifice was the most important religious act in ancient Greece. While this act involved many separate components, the interaction between man and the gods took place at the altar. Much scholarly attention has been directed towards the meanings and origins of this divine interaction but less has been paid to the realities of what actually happened at the altar.

During ancient sacrifice, after slaughter, part of the victim was taken to the altar and part was taken for distribution to people as raw or cooked meat. After the victim was killed, the first step in the butchery process was to open up the chest cavity and take out the internal organs, including the *splánchna* (the heart, lungs, liver, spleen, and kidneys[1]) and the omentum (a sheet of fatty membrane that hangs down from the stomach). Then, the legs including the tail were removed. While the remainder of the carcass was distributed as food, the legs, tail, *splánchna*, and potentially the omentum were taken to the altar.

At the altar, sacrificial victims' thighbones wrapped in fat were burned, the tails were burned, and the *splánchna* were roasted. As the textual, iconographic, and archaeological evidence concerning these rites is limited, to better understand the rituals performed at the altar I conducted experiments attempting to recreate them. There have been

previous attempts to explore sacrifice from a practical perspective.[2] My project addresses new research questions and, most importantly, I designed it to build up a larger body of data through repetition. The broader goal of the project is to develop a methodology for better understanding Greek sacrificial ritual, demonstrating that experimental archaeology can clarify the ancient sources. The fat-wrapped thighbones are the focus here: I identify what fat was wrapped around the thighbone, and I establish why this choice was made through experimental archaeology.

I explored this problem from two perspectives: butchery and burning. Each week I went to Central Market in Athens and bought two lamb legs with tails attached from lambs between 8 and 18 months old. I removed the thighbones and tails from the legs and then wrapped the thighbones in omentum, or in the fat from the thigh itself, or left them bare; the choice depended on availability as well as experimental goals. For this I used my training in butchery, acquired during my 10 years working as a professional cook.

Then I studied how the differently wrapped thighbones burned. At the American School for Classical Studies at Athens, along with fellow Member Daniel Diffendale, I built an *eschára*, or ground level altar, for my experiments.[3] I burned 38 lamb thighbones over 22 events between December 8, 2012 and May 13, 2014.

The Textual and Iconographic Evidence

In Homer (*Il.* 1.460–1, 2.423–4; *Od.* 3.457–8, 12.361–2), burning thighbones wrapped in fat is an important element of sacrifice. Later authors, including Aeschylus (*PV* 496–499), Sophocles (*Ant.* 1005–1011), and Aristophanes (*Av.* 1230–3), attest that this practice continued in the Classical period.[4] Excavations of altars and sanctuaries confirm that thighbones were burned on altars.[5] Yet we know very little about the fat wrapped around these thighbones, a significant component of the sacrifice specifically mentioned by ancient authors.

Scholars have interpreted one fragment of Eubulus (the Middle Comic poet), and three red-figured vase images to indicate that the thighbones were wrapped in the layer of fat hanging below the stomach called the omentum in English, *epipólaion* or *epíploon* in ancient Greek, and *bólia* in modern Greek.[6] A closer examination of the evidence shows that this argument is not as firm as has been assumed.

In the fragment of Eubulus (fr. 94 Kassel-Austin[7]), Dionysus says:

πρῶτον μὲν ὅταν ἐμοί τι θύωσίν τινες,
† αἷμα, κύστιν, μὴ καρδίαν
μηδὲ ἐπιπόλαιον οὐκ ἐγὼ γὰρ ἐσθίω
κλυκείαν οὐδὲ μηρίαν †

First if they offer anything to me,
it is blood, bladder – not heart or omentum.

For I eat no sweet thing
nor thighbone.

Nothing in the passage says that the omentum is wrapped around the thighbones. Dionysus could be referring to the omentum as part of the *splánchna* along with the heart. Such a natural grouping of parts is suggested by the word order.[8] It also reflects the modern Greek practice of wrapping up the omentum together with the heart and other organs and roasting it as the traditional dish *kokorétsi*.

Three vases have been identified in the scholarship as depicting a thighbone wrapped in omentum:[9] an Attic red-figure bell-krater by the Painter of London in the British Museum depicts a fat-wrapped thighbone on the altar behind a tail (Figure 7.1),[10] and two Attic red-figure bell-kraters, one by the Hephaistos Painter in Frankfurt (Figure 7.2)[11] and one by the Pothos Painter in Paris,[12] depict a priest placing a fat-wrapped thighbone on an altar. We cannot tell from these images if the thighbones are wrapped in omentum or a different fat.

I propose to add a fourth vase to this corpus, the Attic red-figure calyx-krater by the Kleophon painter in St. Petersburg (Figure 7.3).[13] If we accept Gunnel Ekroth's proposal that the bell-krater by the Hephaistos Painter in Frankfurt (Figure 7.2) depicts a priest placing a fat-wrapped thighbone on an altar[14] (and I strongly believe she is correct), the scene on the krater by the Kleophon Painter in St. Petersburg (Figure 7.3)

Figure 7.1 Attic red-figure bell krater, ca. 450–425 BC, Painter of London E 494. London, British Museum E 494. Photo © Trustees of the British Museum.

Figure 7.2 Attic red-figure bell krater, ca. 450–440 BC, Hephaistos Painter. Frankfort β 413. Photo © Archaeological Museum Frankfurt.

Figure 7.3 Attic red-figure calyx-krater, ca. 440–420 BC, Kleophon Painter. The State Hermitage Museum, St. Petersburg B-1658. Photo © The State Hermitage Museum / photo by Vladimir Terebenin, Leonard Kheifets, Yuri Molodkovets.

should be also identified as a priest placing a fat-wrapped thighbone on an altar due to the similarity of the scene and the shape of the object in the priest's hand.[15] The textual and iconographic evidence can only help so much, and from here I investigated the issue through experimental archaeology.

Cutting Out the Thighbone

To extract the thighbone from a lamb leg is a fast and simple process for someone with experience, and we know from a passage in Plato that there were skilled butchers in Classical Athens. In the *Phaedrus* (265e 1–3), Socrates says that a good orator should be able to address a topic like an expert butcher,

> κατ᾽ ἄρθρα / ᾗ πέφυκεν, καὶ μὴ ἐπιχειρεῖν καταγνύναι μέρος μηδέν, κακοῦ / μαγείρου τρόπῳ χρώμενον
>
> according to its natural joints, and not try to break any part into pieces, like an inexpert butcher. (Trans. Rowe)

The first step is to remove the layer of fat from the outside of the thigh, and this fat comes off easily. One makes a small cut between the fat and the muscle at the proximal end of the thigh, and then the layer of fat peels off the leg (Figure 7.4). There is no need for a special tool; it could be done with any sharp knife. Once this layer of fat is removed, a seam between the muscles is exposed. This seam is such that you can pull the muscles on either side of it apart with your fingers with no cutting (Figure 7.5). The thighbone is at the bottom of the anterior side of the seam. A slide of the knife down the seam along the thighbone exposes it (Figure 7.6). Continue cutting out the thighbone by repeatedly sliding the knife along the bone freeing it from the surrounding muscle (Figure 7.7). Then, slice easily through the knee and you have extracted the thighbone (Figures 7.8 and 7.9). By this method, one can remove a thighbone in less than five minutes, and speed would have been important especially when dealing with the logistics of large sacrifice such as a hecatomb.

The remainder of the leg now looks like images from vases that have been identified as legs from sacrifices that have had their thighbone removed, and this verifies that the butchery technique described above is accurate[16] (Figures 7.10 and 7.11). Only by carefully cutting along the natural divisions of the leg, as Plato specifies an expert butcher does, will the leg form this distinctive shape after the thigh bone has been removed. This leg is often specified in sacred laws as the reserved special portion, the *géras*, for the priest or other honored person.[17]

This method of removing the thighbone is the easiest and fastest and results in a piece of fat being removed that could be wrapped around the thighbone. The leg thus appears to be a self-contained sacrificial unit comprising thighbone, fat for wrapping the thighbone, tail, and the reserved leg meat.

Wrapping the Thighbone

The next step is to wrap the thighbone in fat. No author specifies what fat was used, but Homer does say that the priests wrap the thighbone in fat making it *díptucha* (*Il.* 1.460–1, 2.423–4; *Od.* 12.360–1; *Od.* 3.457–8 has slight variation in the first half of line 457).

> μηρούς τ᾽ ἐξέταμον κατά τε κνίσῃ ἐκάλυψαν
> δίπτυχα ποιήσαντες, ἐπ᾽ αὐτῶν δ᾽ ὠμοθέτησαν
>
> They cut out the thighbones and wrapped them in fat, making them *díptucha* and laid shreds of raw meat on them. (Trans. Lattimore)

Scholars have understood *díptucha* to mean that the fat

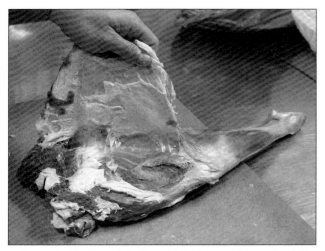

Figure 7.4 Peeling of the layer of fat. Photo Morgan Condell

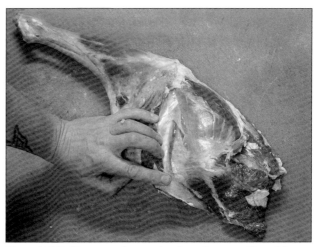

Figure 7.5 Pulling apart the muscles along the seam. Photo Morgan Condell

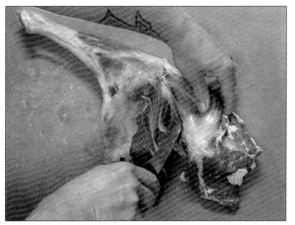

Figure 7.6 Sliding the knife down the seam along the thighbone. Photo Morgan Condell

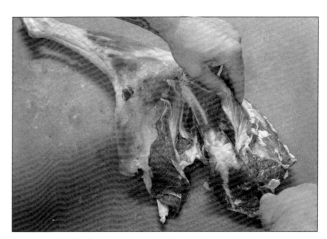

Figure 7.7 Extracting the thighbone. Photo Morgan Condell

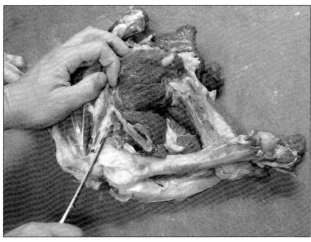

Figure 7.8 Slicing through the knee. Photo Morgan Condell

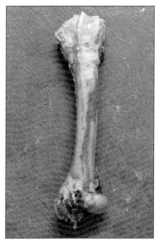

Figure 7.9 The fully extracted thighbone. Photo Morgan Condell

Figure 7.10 Left: Attic red-figure kylix, ca. 500–475 BC, Makron. Photo © Staatliche Antikensammlungen und Glyptothek München, photo by Renate Kühling. Right: Leg with bone extracted. Photo Morgan Condell.

Figure 7.11 Left: Attic red-figure kylix, ca. 500–475 BC, Makron. London, British Museum E 62. Photo © Trustees of the British Museum. Right: Leg with bone extracted. Photo Morgan Condell.

Figure 7.12 Top: Thighbone wrapped twice in thigh fat. Bottom: Thighbone wrapped twice in omentum. Photo Morgan Condell.

wraps around the thighbone twice.[18] The butchery process of removing the thighbone has just created a piece of fat which can wrap around the thighbone twice and this then looks like the images that are thought to be fat wrapped thighbones on vases (Figure 7.12). The amount of fat on a lamb leg is quite variable, due to many factors (e.g. diet, species, breed, rainfall, temperature, type of soil, amount of exercise, etc). A lamb or sheep could not be relied upon to always have enough fat on the thigh to sufficiently wrap the thighbone.[19]

Omentum also wraps around the thighbone twice and when wrapped also looks like the images that are thought to be fat wrapped thighbones on vases (Figure 7.12). The omentum is not part of the self-contained leg, but the omentum was removed from the carcass before the legs. Since one would then have the omentum in hand before the thighbone was removed, using the omentum would involve no time delay or extra step.

In a lamb younger than eight months, the omentum is not sufficiently developed enough to be usable. Instead of being a fatty, white, net-like substance that can entirely conceal the bone when covering it, the omentum of a young lamb has white fat around the edges but only transparent membrane in the middle and thus would be unable to conceal the bone, as well as having a low fat content which would not burn well. [20]

Thus, both kinds of fat could be used to wrap the thighbones twice, but both kinds of fat have potential availability issues; neither could always have sufficed.

Therefore, we need to find another type of evidence to determine what fat they were using.

Turning to the archaeological record cannot help us here. Excavated thighbones from sanctuaries and altars cannot tell us whether sufficient fat was originally on the lamb's thigh or tell us enough about the age of the animal to know if there was sufficient omentum.[21]

A relevant Homeric scholion may be brought into this discussion. Found in the T scholia,[22] the scholiast is explicating the word *knisé* at Iliad 21.363.

ὡς δὲ λέβης ζεῖ ἔνδον ἐπειγόμενος πυρὶ πολλῷ
κνίσην μελδόμενος ἀπαλοτρεφέος σιάλοιο
πάντοθεν ἀμβολάδην

As a pot seethes within, driven on by much fire
melting *knisé* of a well fed pig
bubbling up from every side (Trans. Lattimore)

Our scholiast defines three ways Homer uses the word *knisé*: as ἀναθυμίασις, rising vapor; as λίπος, fat; and importantly for us, as ἐπίπλοον, omentum. He says:

σημαίνει δὲ καὶ τὸν ἐπίπλουν, ὡς ὅταν λέγῃ "κατά τε κνίσῃ ἐκάλυψαν / δίπτυχα ποιήσαντες" (*Il.*1.460 – 1)· διπλᾶ γὰρ ποιήσαντες τὰ κνίση τοὺς
μηροὺς ἐκάλυψαν· "δίπτυχα" δὲ αὐτὰ τὰ κνίση "ποιήσαντες"· ἐπεὶ
γὰρ δύο οἱ μηροί, τὸν ἐπίπλουν εἰς δύο διελόντες ἑκάτερον τῶν μηρῶν
θατέρῳ μέρει τοῦ ἐπίπλου ἐκάλυπτον.

Knisé also means the omentum, as when he [Homer] says "and he covered it with *knisé* making it *díptucha*". (*Il.*1.460–1). For having made double the *knisé* he covered the thighs. "Making" this *knisé* "*díptucha*". Since indeed there are two thighs, dividing the omentum into two they used to cover each of the thighs with one half of the omentum.

This scholion says that the fat used to wrap thighbones in Homeric sacrifice is omentum. Furthermore, a scholion from the D scholia to *Il.*1.461 is a gloss that defines *knisé* as omentum and a scholion from the A scholia to *Il.* 2.424 says that the shreds of raw meat placed on the wrapped thigh were "placed into the omentum" (εἰς τὸν ἐπίπλουν ἐνθέντας), implying that the thighbones were wrapped in omentum at the time.

The T scholion also suggests a new meaning for *díptucha*, namely that the omentum itself is cut into two parts and each of these then enwrap one thighbone. Figure 7.13 shows the omentum from a one to one-and-a-half year old lamb cut in half and able to wrap twice around two lamb thighbones as described in the scholion.

Although the Homeric scholia are in agreement that omentum was being used, it is better to view this as indicating a preference because of the practical problems with relying on omentum with young lambs. Comparative anthropology, economic considerations, and the archaeological record compel us to understand that they were sacrificing young

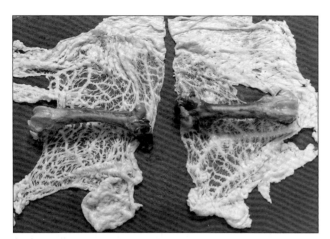

Figure 7.13 Omentum from a one to one-and-a-half year old lamb cut in half for wrapping twice. Photo Morgan Condell.

Figure 7.14 Burst of flame above altar as fat-wrapped bone catches fire. Photo Morgan Condell.

lambs at least some of the time.[23] Sheep birth in the spring and one can feed lambs through the summer on milk and in pasture at no expense. During the fall, with the return from pasture and weaning, feeding expenses increase. As a result scholars assume many young lambs were culled and sacrificed in the fall. These lambs would have been too young for people making sacrifice to rely on their omentum.

The archaeological record might confuse rather than clarify the issue, as my experiments have shown that thighbones of younger lambs are destroyed and disappear when burnt to a much greater degree than bones from older animals.[24] As a result, the archaeological record would under-represent the thighbones of animals too young to have sufficient omentum. The archaeological evidence would then skew our interpretation towards a higher percentage of older animals whose thighbones could have been more easily wrapped in omentum.

In sum, we see a preference for omentum fat for wrapping thighbones in the Homeric scholia as well as evidence from practical butchery that indicates the availability of thigh fat. Thighbones look essentially the same when wrapped in either fat, and both fats also have availability issues.

Burning the Thighbone

Can burning wrapped thighbones reveal a practical reason why these two fats could not be used interchangeably or even together? To compare how they behave on a burning altar, I burned thighbones wrapped in omentum, in thighfat, in both fats, and unwrapped. For contrast, I also burned fully fleshed thighbones wrapped in omentum.

At each event, I built a pyre imitating the ones pictured on Greek vases (e.g. Figures 7.1, 7.2 and 7.3).[25] When the fire was around 600 degrees Celsius, but putting off no impressive flames, I would place the thighbone on the pyre. Within seconds of placing the wrapped thighbone, flames

would begin to form around it, whether the thighbone was wrapped in thigh fat, omentum, or a combination of both. Within two minutes the flame would greatly increase, and in less than six minutes the flame would be high above the altar and have obscured the thighbone (Figure 7.14). Based on my experiments, a thighbone wrapped with at least 200 grams of fat will always cause this burst of flame. I found that the omentum from a one to one-and-a-half year old lamb consistently weighs 400–600 grams and thus this critical mass of 200 grams accords with half the omentum of a single animal (supporting the assertion of the aforementioned T scholion) as well as with the amount of fat often found on the thigh itself.

The only difference I have observed in behavior of the two fats is that sometimes the thigh fat would unwrap from the bone while on the pyre. The fat and the bone still burned in this case, but the bone being concealed by fat is an important element of the literary evidence.[26] I found that a light wrapping of omentum around a thigh fat wrapped bone keeps the thigh fat from unwrapping. The amount of omentum found in a young lamb suffices for this.

In direct contrast to the behavior of the wrapped thighbone, unwrapped bones, wrapped fleshed bones, bones with an insufficient wrapping of fat, as well as tails caused no burst of flame or any other kind of dramatic change to the pyre.

There is no way to tell from the archaeological evidence whether the bone was wrapped in fat or bare because my experiments have shown that an unwrapped bone and a fat-wrapped bone look the same after they have been burned. On the other hand, fully fleshed bones have a different pattern of breakage, but overall are more completely destroyed when burned and thus would be hard to identify in the archaeological record. Fully fleshed bones take a much larger quantity of fuel and a much longer time to burn than defleshed bones and, even when wrapped in 300 grams of omentum, a fully fleshed bone puts off no burst of flame.

Broader Implications

The evidence from these experiments concerns what may be considered only a small detail of the larger act of sacrifice – what fat wrapped around the thighbone – but this detail has larger implications. For instance, this information might help us understand certain vase imagery and a critical scene in Sophocles' *Antigone*.

There is only one extant image thought to portray a wrapped thighbone burning on an altar, the lump on the altar visible behind the tail depicted on the krater by the Painter of London in the British Museum (Figure 7.1). The distinct sideways-hourglass shape of the lump that could represent the bulbous ends of the thighbone is drawn recognizably. The fire portrayed here is leaping above the tail and wrapped thighbone as it does over the thighbones in my experiments. But the experiments have shown also that a burning tail alone makes no change in the fire. The fact that the wrapped thighbone produces a distinctive surge of flame every time, while the tail alone produces no such flame, urges us to view images of leaping flames over curling tails as indicating the implied presence of the wrapped thighbone next to the tail, even though the painter has not explicitly included it in the image.[27]

Understanding how a thighbone burns helps us to better understand the scene of failed sacrifice in Sophocles' *Antigone*. This scene is horrifying because of the contrast with expected behavior understood by the audience. At line 1005, Tiresias says:

Εὐθὺς δὲ δείσας ἐμπύρων ἐγευόμην
βωμοῖσι παμφλέκτοισιν· ἐκ δὲ θυμάτων
Ἥφαιστος οὐκ ἔλαμπεν, ἀλλ᾽ ἐπὶ σποδῷ
μυδῶσα κηκὶς μηρίων ἐτήκετο
κἄτυφε κἀνέπτυε, καὶ μετάρσιοι
χολαὶ διεσπείροντο, καὶ καταρρυεῖς
μηροὶ καλυπτῆς ἐξέκειντο πιμελῆς.

At once I was alarmed, and attempted
Burnt sacrifice at the altar where I kindled fire; but the fire
God raised no flame from my offerings. Over the ashes a
Dank slime oozed from the thighbones, smoked and sputtered;
The gall was sprayed high into the air and the thighs,
Streaming with liquid, lay bare of the fat that had concealed
them. (Trans. Lloyd-Jones)

From the description in the passage, the audience knows that the ritual has been set up correctly: they lit the fire, wrapped the thighbone in fat, and placed it on the altar. But the ritual did not work as it is supposed to, as everyone in the audience would have understood. Flames did not rise up from out of the sacrifice but instead liquid dripped down.[28] The contrast with the regular, expected behavior of a burning wrapped thighbone, as seen in my experiments, is what gives the passage its power.

Conclusions

Sacrificial ritual is designed to succeed; it is reliable and predictable. I have demonstrated through my experiments that a wood pyre built in the manner depicted on vases always burns at sufficient temperature to curl the tail and consume the thighbone and does not spill the tail and thigh as the wood is consumed. I have burned 38 tails and the tail always curls. A thighbone wrapped in 200 or more grams of fat always produces the desired surge of flame. The passage from Sophocles illustrates the deep anxiety about sacrifices not being accepted and my experiments have shown that these indicators of divine acceptance were designed to succeed every time.[29] As such, an over-reliance on a specific kind of fat, the supply of which could not be guaranteed, is implausible.

For the thighbone to give the anticipated response – approximately seven minutes of jumping flames – a minimum amount of fat needs to be wrapped around the bone. Since the goal was to have success every time, no impractical restrictions could be put on this fat. The scholia I discussed surely indicate a preference for omentum, but practical considerations must keep the thigh fat as a possibility as well.

For these rituals at the altar, every step is very fast: removal of thigh bone takes less than five minutes; thighbones throw up striking flame in four minutes and are burned out in ten minutes; tails curl in less than seven minutes. The burning is visually striking, it is engaging, and it is exciting. Burning the wrapped thighbone and the tail on the altar provide ten intense minutes in which all time seems to slow down and the quotidian merges with the divine.

Acknowledgements

I wish to thank Jeremy McInerney, Gunnel Ekroth, Nancy Bookidis, and Margaret M. Miles for their support, guidance, and inspiration. Special thanks go to Daniel Diffendale, with whom I conceived and began the larger project of which this is a part. Finally, I would like to thank Ray Risho for teaching me the practicalities of butchery so many years ago.

Notes

1   Arist. *Part. an.* 665 a28 – 672 b8 defines and discusses the *splánchna*.

2   Burning tails: Jameson 1966, Jameson 1983, pp. 60–61, Ekroth 2009, p. 149, Ekroth 2013b p. 20. Wrapping

thighbones in omentum: Forstenpointer 2003. Experimental butchery of forelegs: Ekroth 2013a. Comparing burned fleshed bones, defleshed 'green' bones, and defleshed dry bones: Buikstra and Swegele 1989. For an overview of the history and methodological problems of experimental archaeology related to cult, see Forstenpointer et al. 2013.

3   For discussion of the *eschára*, see Ekroth 2002 pp. 25–59, esp. pp. 58–59. For the image closest to the altar we built, see the Attic red-figure Panathenaic amphora by the Kleophon painter (440/420 BC), Darmstadt A 1969:4 (478), *ARV²* 1146/48.

4   See van Straten 1995, pp. 118–141.

5   Reese 1989, Forstenpointer 2003, Ekroth 2009. For bibliography of faunal remains from sanctuaries and altars, see Reese 2005, MacKinnon 2007a, pp. 490–491, MacKinnon 2007b, pp. 17–19.

6   Van Straten 1995, p. 125, Forstenpointer 2003, pp. 210–211, Forstenpointer 2013, pp. 237–238, Ekroth 2013b, pp. 20–21. Arist. *Part. an.* 677 b15, explains that *epíploon* is the omentum. Hesychios ε.5084 defines *epipólaion* as *epíploon*, with reference to the Eubulus fragment in question.

7   κλυκείαν cod: γλυκείαν Morelius, vid. Meineke IV p. 613sq.

8   Smyth 2163: copulative use of μηδέ.

9   Images identified by Ekroth 2013, p. 21. For a discussion of the use of vase imagery as testimony for how sacrifice is conducted, see van Straten 1995, pp. 5–9.

10 London BM E 494, *ARV²* 1408/1, ca. 450–425 BC.

11 Frankfurt ß 413, *ARV²* 1683/31, ca. 450–440 BC.

12 Paris Louvre G 496, *ARV²* 1190/24, ca. 425–400 BC. On this bell-krater (not pictured), Durand 1986, p. 137 called the item in the priest's hand a ritual cake, Jameson 1986, p. 65 n.15 a metal phiale, van Straten 1995, p. 144 a heart or bladder, but Ekroth 2013, p. 20 follows Forstenpointer 2003, pp. 200–201 interpreting it to be two thighbones wrapped together in omentum.

13 Saint Petersburg B-1658, *ARV²* 1144/14, ca. 440–420 BC.

14 Ekroth 2013, p. 21.

15 Jameson 1986 argued that the object in the priest's hand depicted a gall bladder; van Straten 1995, p. 128 questions this interpretation. Even if the vase depicts the failed sacrifice scene in Antigone, as Jameson asserts, it still probably depicts a wrapped thighbone in the priest's hand given the greater emphasis on the thighbone in the scene.

16 Durant 1984; Tsoukala 2009; Ekroth 2013b.

17 See Tsoukala 2009 for discussion.

18 Most influentially, Kirk 1985, p. 101.

19 The bibliography on factors influencing fat composition of ovicaprids in the field of meat science is large. Suffice it to say that the fat on lamb legs is variable. e.g. "It is well established that fat is the most variable tissue in the carcass." Mahgoup et al. 2004, p. 582. I have seen this in Central Market in Athens as well – lamb legs of different ages and sizes do not have consistent amounts of fat.

20 I have had extensive discussions about this with the butchers in Central Market in Athens and have seen these low-fat, low-weight transparent omenta from young lambs. For low weights of the omentum in ovicaprids, see Alvarez-Rodriguez et al. 2009; Gaili 1978; Purroy 1995. I warmly thank Dr. Barbara Grandstaff, University of Pennsylvania School of Veterinary Medicine, for answering questions about omentum.

21 On the issues with aging animals by means of epiphysial fusion of the femur: Silver 1970, pp. 284–289; Zeder 2006; David Reese, (pers. comm.); I thank Flint Dibble for extensive discussions on the topic.

22 This specific scholion derives either from Porphyry or a common source for Porphyry, either way giving the scholion a terminus ante quem of the mid 3rd century AD. Kirk 1985, pp. 38–43; Erbse 1969; MacPhail 2011; Richard Janko (pers. comm.).

23 For comparative anthropology, see Hesse 1982; Ryder 1983, pp. 679–681; Zeder 2001. For economic considerations, see Jameson 1988. For the archaeological record, see Reese 1989.

24 This accords with Lyman 1994, pp. 397–8 concerning why smaller bones appear to disappear from the fossil record at a higher rate than larger bones for numerous reasons, including their higher surface-to-volume ratio. See also Payne 1985.

25 This specific woodpile shape is depicted on 23 different 5th century Athenian vases pictured in van Straten 1995 and Gebauer 2002. The shape of the woodpile seems to be important and recognizable from its regular portrayal on these vases taken together with Ar. *Pax* 1026, in which Trygaeus rhetorically asks the audience if he is arranging the woodpile on the altar "like a mantis," implying that there is a recognizable shape for a woodpile on an altar.

26 e.g. the thighbone becoming exposed from its surrounding fat being the culmination of the failed sacrifice scene in Soph. *Ant.* 1005–1011, as discussed below.

27 e.g. van Straten figs. 123, 135, 142, 145, 153.

28 The scholiast to this passage says that the thighbone behaved this way because the components of the sacrifice were wet. I tested this by using wet wood and dunking the wrapped thighbone in water, however the thighbone burned the same as it does dry. I thank Nikos Manousakis of the University of Athens for pointing out this scholion to me.

29 For more on Greek anxieties about divine acceptance of sacrifice, see most recently Naiden 2013.

References

Alvarez-Rodriguez, J., Spanz, A., Joy, M., Carrasco, S., Ripoli, G., & Teixeira, A. 2009. "Development on organs and tissues in lambs raised on Spanish mountain grassland," *Canadian Journal of Animal Science* 89, pp. 37–45.

Berthiaume, G. 1982. *Les Roles du Mageiros* (*Mnemosyne* Suppl. 70), Leiden.

Berthiaume, G. 2005. "L'aile ou les *mêria*. Sur la nourriture carnéedes dieux grecs," in *La cuisine et l'autel: Les sacrifices en questions dans les sociétés de la Méditerranée ancienne* (*Bibliothèque de l'École des hautes études scienes religieuses* Vol. 124), ed. S. Georgoudi, R. Koch Piettre, and F. Schmidt, Paris, pp. 241–251.

Buikstra, J., & Swegle, M. 1989. "Bone Modification Due to Burning: Experimental Evidence," in *Bone Modification*, ed. R. Bonnichsen, & M. Sorg, Orono, ME: Center for the Study of the First Americans, pp. 247–258.

Durand, J.-L. 1979. "Betes grecques: Propositions pour une topologique des corps a manger," in *La Cuisine du Sacrifice*, ed. M. Detienne, & J.-P. Vernant, Paris, pp. 133–166.

Durand, J.-L. 1984. "Le faire et le dire. Vers une anthropologie des gestes iconiques," *History and anthropology* 1, pp. 29–48.

Ekroth, G. 2002. *The sacrificial rituals of Greek hero-cults in the Archaic to the early Hellenistic periods* (*Kernos* Suppl.12), Liege: Centre International d'Etude de la Religion Grecque Antique.

Ekroth, G. 2008. "Meat, man, and God: On the division of the animal victim at Greek sacrifices," in *ΜΙΚΡΟΣ ΙΕΡΟΜΝΗΜΩΝ*, ed. P. Matthaiou and I. Polinskaya, Athens, pp. 259–290.

Ekroth, G. 2009. "Thighs or Tails? The Osteological Evidence as Source for Greek Ritual Norms," in *La Norme en Matiere religieuse en grece ancienne,* ed. P. Brule, Liège: Centre International d'Etude de la Religion Greque Antique, pp. 125–152.

Ekroth, G. 2013a. "Forelegs in Greek Cult," in *Perspectives on ancient Greece: Papers presented in celebration of the 60th anniversary of the Swedish Institute at Athens*, ed. A. L. Schallin, Stockholm: Svenska Institutet i Athen, pp. 113–134.

Ekroth, G. 2013b. "What we would like the bones to tell us: a sacrificial wish list," in *Bones, behaviour and belief*, ed. G. Ekroth, and J. Wallensten, Stockholm, Sweden: Svenska Institutet i Athen, pp. 15–30.

Erbse, H. 1969. *Scholia Graeca in Homeri Iliadem (Scholia Vetera)*, Berlin.

Forstenpointer, G. 2003. "Promethean legacy: investigations into the ritual procedure of 'Olympian' sacrifice," in *Zooarchaeology in Greece: Recent Advances*, ed. E. Kotjabopoulou, Y. Hamilakis, P. Halstead, C. Gamble, and P. Elefanti, London, pp. 203–214.

Forstenpointer, G., A. Galik, and G. Weissengruber. 2013. "The zooarchaeology of cult: Perspectives and pitfalls of an experimental approach," in *Bones, behaviour and belief*, ed. G. Ekroth, and J. Wallensten, Stockholm: Svenska Institutet i Athen, pp. 233–242.

Gaili, E. 1978. "A comparison of the development of body components in Sudan desert sheep and goats," *Tropical Animal Health and Production* 10, pp. 103–108.

Gebauer, J. 2002. *Pompe und Thysia,* Münster.

Hesse, B. 1982. "Slaughter Patterns and Domestication: The Beginnings of Pastoralism in Western Iran," *Man* 17, pp. 403–417.

Hooker, E. 1950. "The Sanctuary and Altar of Chryse in Attic Red-Figure Vase-Paintings of the Late Fifth and Early Fourth Centuries B.C.," *Journal of Hellenic Studies* 70, pp. 35–41.

Jameson, M. 1966. "The Omen of the Oxtail," *Scientific American* 214, p. 54.

Jameson, M. 1986. "Sophocles, Antigone 1005–1022: an illustration," in *Greek Tragedy and its Legacy*, ed. M. Cropp, E. Fantham, and S. Scully, Calgary, pp. 59–66.

Jameson, M. 1988. "Sacrifice and animal husbandry in Classical Greece," in *Pastoral Economies in Classical Antiquity* (*Proceedings of the Cambridge Philological Society* Suppl. 14), ed. C. R. Whittaker, Cambridge, pp. 87–119.

Janko, R. 1992. *The Iliad: A Commentary books 13–16,* Cambridge.

Kirk, G. 1985. *The Iliad: A Commentary books 1–4,* Cambridge.

Lyman, R. L. 1994. *Vertebrate Taphonomy,* Cambridge.

MacKinnon, M. 2007a. "Osteological research in Classical archaeology," *American Journal of Archaeology* 111, pp. 473–504.

MacKinnon. 2007b. "Osteological research in Classical archaeology: Extended bibliography," *American Journal of Archaeology* 111, 1–40 (online).

MacPhail Jr, J. 2011. *Porphyry's Homeric Questions on the Iliad,* Berlin.

Mahgoub, O., I. Kadim, N. Al-Saqry, and R. Al-Busaidi. 2004."Effects of body weight and sex on carcass tissue distribution in goats," *Meat Science* 67, pp. 577–585.

McInerney, J. 2010. *The Cattle of the Sun: Cows and culture in the world of the ancient Greeks,* Princeton.

Meineke, A. 1841. *Fragmenta Poetarum Comoediae Novae,* Berlin.

Naiden, F. 2013. *Smoke Signals for the Gods,* Oxford.

Papageorgius, P. 1888. *Scholia in Sophoclis Tragoedias Vetera,* Leipzig.

Payne, S. 1985. "Zoo-Archaeology in Greece: A Reader's Guide," in *Contributions to Aegean Archaeology: Studies in Honor of William A. McDonald*, ed. N. C. Wilkie and W. D. E. Coulson, Minnesota: Center for Ancient Studies, University of Minnesota, pp. 211–244.

Peirce, S. 1993. "Death, Revelry, and *Thysia*," *Classical Antiquity* 12, pp. 219–266.

Purroy, A. E. 1995. "Size and number variation of adipocytes during the growth of Rasa Aragonesa Lambs," in *Body Condition of Sheep and Goats: Methodological Aspects and Applications*, ed. A. Purroy, Zaragosa, pp. 179–184.

Reese, D. 1989. "Faunal Remains from the Altar of Aphrodite Ourania, Athens," *Hesperia* 58, pp. 63–70.

Reese, D. 2005. "Faunal Remains from Greek Sanctuaries: A Survey," in *Greek Sacrificial Ritual, Olympian and Chthonian*, ed. R. Hagg and B. Alroth, Stockholm: Svenska Institutet i Athen, pp. 121–123.

Ryder, M. 1983. *Sheep and Man,* London.

Silver, I. 1970. "The Ageing of Domestic Animals," in *Science in Archaeology*, 2nd ed., ed. D. Brothwell and E. Higgs, New York, pp. 283–302.

Smith, C. 1888. "Two Vase-Pictures of Sacrifices," *Journal of Hellenic Studies* 9, pp. 1–10.

Topper, K. 2012. *The Imagery of the Athenian Symposium,* Cambridge.

Tsoukala, V. 2009. "Honorary shares of sacrificial meat in Attic vase painting: Visual signs of distinction and civic identity," *Hesperia* 78, pp. 1–40.

Van Straten, F. 1995. *Hiera Kala,* New York.

Zeder, M. 2001. "A Metrical Analysis of a Collection of Modern Goats (Capra hircus aegargus and C. h. hircus) from Iran and Iraq: Implications for the Study of Caprine Domestication," *Journal of Archaeological Science* 28, pp. 61–79.

Zeder, M. 2006. "Reconciling Rates of Long Bone Fusion and Tooth Eruption and Wear in Sheep (Ovis) and Goat (Capra)," in *Ageing and Sexing Animals from Archaeological Sites*, ed. D. Ruscillo, Oxford, pp. 87–118.

The Mutilation of the Herms:
Violence toward Images in the late 5th century BC

Rachel Kousser

The mutilation of the herms is among the best-documented and most notorious episodes of the Greeks' violence toward their own religious sculptures. This article draws on archaeological and artistic evidence to analyze how the Athenians responded to the mutilation of the herms. It identifies a range of visual strategies, from the retention of intact monuments to the repair of damaged ones and the ritual disposal of those too injured to restore, and also examines the creation of counter-monuments. Taken together, these works suggest a forceful yet nuanced response to the attack in its immediate aftermath, centered upon the maintenance of traditional religious sculptures and the erection of new monuments celebrating the power of the Athenian demos.

Introduction

This article concerns the mutilation of the herms, the best-documented and most notorious example of the Greeks' violence toward their own religious sculptures. Described by Thucydides in some detail (6.27), the incident has been examined for its political ramifications, particularly its impact on the Sicilian expedition, a major military initiative of the Peloponnesian war. So, too, it has been discussed in terms of its religious implications, given the herms' key role in popular ritual. But while the literary sources describing the affair have been extensively mined, scant attention has been paid to the archaeological evidence. And there has been little analysis of the incident from an art historical perspective, as an example of damage to statues and the responses it evoked in Classical Athens.[1]

This discussion draws on archaeological and artistic evidence to analyze how the Athenians responded to the mutilation of the herms. I begin with the normal functioning of these sculptures in the late 5th century, highlighting their ubiquitous, accessible character as demonstrated by comic writings and vase paintings. I then address the mutilation, identifying a range of visual strategies deployed by the Athenians to come to terms with it; these included the retention of intact monuments, the repair of damaged ones, and the ritual disposal of those too injured to restore. And I

conclude by examining the creation of counter-monuments, above all, the large-scale, prominently displayed stelai which detailed the auctioning of property from those convicted in the affair.[2] Taken together, these works suggest a forceful yet nuanced response to the attack in its immediate aftermath, centered upon the maintenance of traditional religious sculptures and the erection of new monuments celebrating the power of the Athenian demos.

The mutilation of the herms has significant implications for our understanding of the sculpted landscape of late 5th century Athens. In recent years, scholars have paid increased attention to such landscapes, highlighting for example the accumulation of honorific portraits in the Agora and the recycling of funerary monuments in the Kerameikos.[3] But these studies have been concentrated primarily on the Hellenistic era; so, too, they have been concerned above all with the creation of new monuments and the visual effects of accumulation and juxtaposition. This analysis focuses instead on the sculpted landscape of Classical Athens, and on its transformation through damage, removal, and the repair of injured statues. In this way, it serves as a useful reminder of the mutability of these seemingly permanent marble monuments and the power of absence, as well as presence, in Athenian visual culture.

The Herms

Before addressing the mutilation itself, it is useful to consider briefly the functions of herms under normal circumstances. To begin with, one should stress that these statues – which combined a bust-length sculpted head of a mature bearded man with a four-sided inscribed shaft and an erect phallus – were everywhere in Classical Athens. On the Acropolis, there are fragmentary remains of at least three herms of Late Archaic date, along with one inscribed shaft; an Early Classical head, most plausibly that of a herm, was also found nearby on the south slope. Herms also appeared in the Agora, the political and economic heart of the city. Three are clearly datable prior to 415 BC, while a fourth may be Early Classical or Archaistic; others are attested in the literary sources.[4] In addition to these high-profile locations in the city center, herms were also found on the road to every deme; these alone numbered about 130, according to the calculations of Johann Crome. And from literary sources and vase paintings, we know that herms also appeared at doorways and street corners throughout Athens.[5] By the late 5th century BC, herms thus permeated the Athenian civic landscape, modest yet significant traces of the divine visible everywhere in daily life.

Just as they were omnipresent, so, too, the herms were readily available. As vase paintings and the archaeological remains make clear, they tended to be set not behind closed doors or on high pedestals, but out in the open air, and at eye-level: typically they were raised at the most on short bases of one or two steps.[6]

Images of Herms

Perhaps for this reason, herms were also the divine sculptures that called forth the most frequently represented interaction from worshippers. On vase paintings, they not only received libations and food offerings, but were also touched – and by ordinary worshippers, not just priests.[7] On an Early Classical column krater, for example, an older man puts his hand to the herm's chin in a characteristic Greek gesture of supplication; this was a very direct and interactive manner of seeking help, appropriate to statues as well as human individuals.[8] So, too, on a red-figure cup from the same era, a young woman bends forward and grasps the "shoulders" of a herm in a heartfelt if awkward embrace.[9] One sees from this how much the sacred body of the herm was treated like an ordinary mortal body, despite its radical abbreviation of the human form and the consequent discomfort attendant upon interacting with it in this manner. In some paintings, the herm even seems to respond to the adoration of his worshippers; a black-figure oenochoe in Frankfurt, for instance, shows the statue turning his head toward the young woman bearing a sacrificial basket to him.[10]

One cannot of course take such images entirely at face value; as scholars of Greek vase painting have emphasized,

Figure 8.1 Marble herm, ca. 425 BC, deposited in Crossroads Enclosure ca. 415 BC. Athens, Agora Museum no. S 2452. Photo courtesy American School of Classical Studies at Athens: Agora Excavations.

these are sophisticated fictions, not straightforward depictions of everyday life.[11] While they do not provide incontrovertible evidence for actual ritual practice, the painted depictions of herms do allow us to reconstruct a range of interactions that was considered plausible, and worthy of depiction. To judge from the paintings, wreathing, conversing with, or even embracing a herm was *thinkable*; the purchaser of the vase might not have routinely done such things, but might nonetheless have appreciated their portrayal in one of the well-executed scenes of daily life popular in the Classical era. Furthermore, there are notable differences in vase painting between the representations of herms and those of other statues, where elevation and isolation from worshippers is more the rule.[12]

Literary Testimonia

The literary sources, when available, support the evidence provided by vase paintings for the Greeks' horizon of expectations regarding herms.[13] In Aristophanes' *Clouds*,

Figure 8.2 Reconstruction of the northwest corner of the Agora ca. 415 BC, with area of the herms and Crossroads Enclosure in which herm Agora S 2452 was deposited (lower center). Drawing courtesy American School of Classical Studies at Athens: Agora Excavations

for example, the herm by the protagonist's door plays a key role in the story, and is responsible for the play's dramatic dénouement.[14] So, too, we have a brief literary fragment from the contemporary playwright Phrynichos, which deals explicitly with the mutilation of the herms: a character tells Hermes to be careful and not fall over, so as to give an opportunity to a latter-day Diokleides with malicious intent; the reference is to one of the informers who gave evidence in the affair, subsequently discredited. In the play, Hermes replies that he does not want to give a reward to Teukros, a second informer, either.[15] As with Aristophanes, so, too, with Phrynichos, the herm is a down-to-earth and interactive character in the play; he is also quite well-informed about contemporary politics. Taken together, the evidence suggests that in Classical Athens, herms were distinguished by their combination of ubiquity, access, and close connection to their worshippers; in this way, they were the paradigmatic emblems of democratic popular religion.[16]

The Mutilation of the Herms

Due to the herms' popular and democratic nature, their

mutilation in 415 BC could not go unacknowledged by the Athenian populace. It was well-organized – taking place over the course of a single night – and also comprehensive; according to Thucydides (6.27), almost all the stone herms in the city were mutilated.[17] The mutilation was, furthermore, secretive both in its planning stages and also in its immediate aftermath.[18] The damage that night coincided not only with the preparations for the Sicilian expedition, soon to be launched, but also with the threat of a small Spartan military force marching north to the Isthmus of Corinth, some 50 miles from Athens. Although Thucydides is careful to state this was coincidental (6.61), at the time it surely only served to heighten the Athenians' anxiety further.

The mutilation of the herms thus shared key features – organization, secrecy, an apparent connection to external military affairs, and of course physical violence – with the oligarchic conspiracies so prevalent in late 5th century poleis, and greatly feared by the Athenians.[19] So it is perhaps unsurprising that it sparked a popular furor and engendered a strong response from Athenian officials. Thucydides notes, "[the] deed was taken rather seriously. For it seemed to be a [bad] omen for the expedition and to have been done on

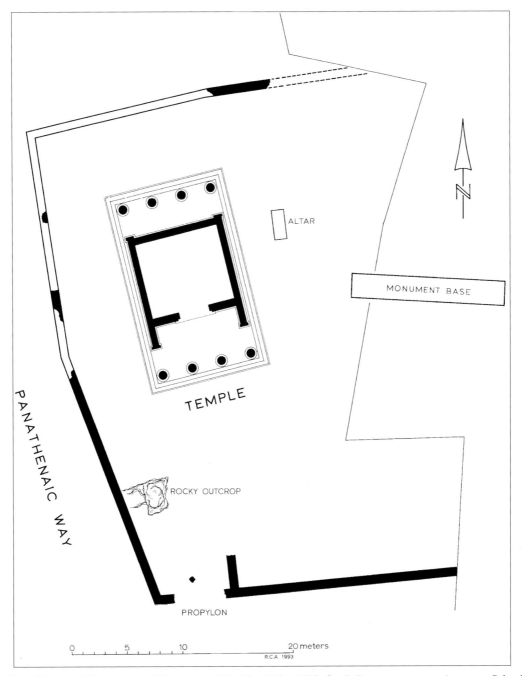

Figure 8.3. .Plan of the City Eleusinion, mid 5th century BC. After Miles 1998, fig. 8. Drawing courtesy American School of Classical Studies at Athens: Agora Excavations.

account of a conspiracy to bring about a revolution and the overthrow of the democracy" (6.27).[20] It engendered a political witch hunt and show trials, resulting in the exile or execution of at least 23 suspected herm mutilators, according to Andokides' later self-defense (1.34–35, 53). The related affair of the profanation of the Eleusinian Mysteries led to the conviction of 26 others, including Alcibiades, a leader of the expedition and one of the most influential politicians

in the city.[21] Those convicted had their property confiscated and sold, with the proceeds dedicated to Demeter and Kore by the polis; if the individuals preserved on the Attic Stelai are representative, this raised a very considerable sum, on the order of 500–1,000 talents, that is, roughly equivalent to the annual tribute of the Athenian empire.[22] When he learned that he had been condemned *in absentia*, Alcibiades abandoned the gathered Athenian forces on their

Figure 8.4. Marble herm, Agora, Athens, ca. 480–470 BC. Athens, Agora no. S 211. Photo courtesy American School of Classical Studies at Athens: Agora Excavations

way to Sicily, and fled to the state best able to protect him: Athens' chief enemy, Sparta.[23] In this way, what began as an act of symbolic violence toward ubiquitous sculptured images of Hermes took on far-reaching political, military, and economic repercussions for the Athenian demos.

After the Damage was Done

As noted above, the mutilation of the herms also had important implications for the sculptural landscape of Classical Athens. In 415 BC, the injured statues were conspicuous reminders of the presence within the polis of *asebountes*, impious individuals whose actions threatened

the gods – and also the state, given that the mutilation was interpreted as part of an oligarchic conspiracy. What to do with them? Some were apparently hidden: excavators in the Athenian Agora found a marble head dating to the third quarter of the 5th century in the Crossroads Enclosure, a small shrine at the northwest corner of the Agora just opposite the Stoa Basileos (Agora no. S 2452). The shrine consisted of a large outcropping of natural rock which was surrounded by an enclosure of poros blocks ca. 430.[24] To judge from the offerings, it was most popular in the late 5th century, but an analysis of the pottery suggests that gifts were brought from ca. 450 onward, thus even before the shrine was enclosed; it went out of use during the 4th century BC.[25] The shrine might thus have seemed an appropriate – and convenient – place of deposition for a desecrated herm, removing it from view, but at the same time retaining and indeed enhancing its association with the divine, as the herm became the very direct recipient of cult offerings.[26]

A second, Early Classical, herm from the Agora may show a different response to the mutilation (Agora no. S 211).[27] The sculpture is badly preserved, with heavy weathering of the surface as well as major breaks at the right temple and left chin, so that caution must be exercised in evaluating it. The herm bears evidence of clear traces of an ancient repair in the nose area: the broken surface was rubbed flat, then roughed with a point, and a 6 mm hole was bored in at what would have been the tip of the nose for a dowel to attach the new piece. The joint surface has the same patina as the rest of the herm, demonstrating that this was ancient. E. Harrison suggests that this was done in response to the mutilation of the herms, for a sculpture that had experienced only limited injury.[28] Whatever the reason for the repair, the intervention seems to have been successful, since the herm may have remained above ground in antiquity, as it was eventually built into the cellar of a modern house.[29]

Whether or not the Early Classical herm was damaged in 415, it is important to stress that it was not unique in its continued display after the late 5th century. Only eight Athenian herm sculptures from the sixth and 5th centuries are preserved.[30] Of these, the two discussed above seem plausibly injured during the mutilation, while three were found in Persian destruction levels on the Acropolis and thus likely unavailable to the herm-mutilators.[31] Of the rest, one has no recorded provenance, and for a second, the information is so limited that no clear deductions can be made.[32] The third, however, was found in the earliest Byzantine level of a house in the northwest Agora, suggesting that it remained above ground in antiquity.[33] We know from literary texts that some of the most famous Archaic and Classical herm monuments survived, for instance the one commemorating the Athenian victory at Eion – discussed in detail by fourth century and later sources[34] – and at least some of the dedications of Hipparchos, mentioned by Pseudo-Plato (*Hipparch.* 228b–c).[35] We should thus imagine the injured herms evaluated on a case by case basis, with some retained above ground (with repairs as necessary) and others buried in appropriate sacred locales.

New Monuments

In addition to the herms themselves, the events of 415 were also commemorated through the creation of new, very different monuments. Most notable among the preserved works were the Attic Stelai mentioned above, which detailed the actions taken against those condemned of *asebeia*.[36] The Attic Stelai were written texts, but also significant visual interventions in Athens' landscape, due to their scale and prominent location in the city center. Remains of an estimated ten stelai were found in fragments in the area of the City Eleusinion.[37] This highly visible location in the Athenian Agora linked the stelai to the divinities whose cult was most affected by the profanation of the mysteries, Demeter and Kore, and suggests that the actions inscribed on the monument functioned as a way to make amends to them in a concrete and public manner. The stelai's neat, precise letter-forms list in extraordinary detail the prices paid at auction for the property of those condemned in the profanation of the mysteries as well as that of the five individuals "guilty of both;" we should imagine a similar monumental inscription elsewhere in the city for those associated with the mutilation of the herms alone, perhaps on the Acropolis.[38] According to Athenaeus (11.476e), this is the location in which were set up stelai listing those whose property was confiscated for impiety. And an inscription of ca. 411/10 supports Athenaeus' claim, at least for the herm-mutilators, since it decreed that "the Tamiai of Athena are to erase what is written about Timanthes [one of the herm-mutilators] on the Acropolis from the stele."[39]

The Attic Stelai commemorated, in a visually innovative fashion, an unprecedented undertaking. Never before had Athens seen mass trials for *asebeia*, nor so many prominent individuals condemned at once on so serious a charge. Delays in the auctioning of property – the inscriptional evidence suggests a date in the early spring of 413 for the last sales – may be due to the challenges of creating an institutional mechanism for the large volume of sales, and for carrying so many of them out; 26 profaners and 23 mutilators likely had their property auctioned off.[40] And the sums of money raised by the sales were by Athenian standards enormous, over 100 talents for the 15 individuals named on the inscriptions that are preserved.[41] The stelai thus represented an unusual and visually striking assertion of the power of the democratic state against those believed to be undermining it, carried out in the most public manner possible. In this way, they were perhaps the most effective rejoinder to the mutilation of the herms as interpreted by the Athenians, that is, as the prelude to an oligarchic coup.

Conclusions

This investigation of the mutilation of the herms from an archaeological perspective has focused on the various strategies deployed by the Athenians to deal with the injured statues, including burial, repair, retention, and the creation of counter-monuments such as the Attic Stelai. The goal of all these interventions was in part to restore the sculptural landscape of Classical Athens to its original intact condition, obliterating the traces of a deeply upsetting and potentially dangerous politico-religious incident: this illustrates the social power of the sculptural landscape. At the same time, as the discussion of the Attic Stelai suggests, the Athenians also aimed to transform their visual environment; they did so through new works that demonstrated, in forceful, concrete terms, the power of the demos over conspirators who may have aimed to overthrow the democracy.[42] In this way, the archaeological evidence for responses to the mutilation of the herms in its immediate aftermath correlates well with the impression given by Thucydides' account of the incident: this episode of damage to sculptures was interpreted by contemporaries as an existential threat to Athenian democracy, and required a well-organized and equally violent rejoinder.

At the same time, it is important to stress that this interpretation of the herms episode soon changed, particularly following the Athenians' experiences of real oligarchic coups in 411 and 403 BC.[43] By the time the orator and suspected herm mutilator Andokides made his speech *On the Mysteries* ca. 400, it was possible to suggest that the incident was in no way the prelude to a coup; rather, it was the work of a few social deviants, concerned to create group solidarity within an aristocratic drinking club (Andoc. 1.61). This was a useful narrative for Andokides himself – it minimized his crime – and also a more comforting one for the Athenian populace. It stripped the mutilation of political and religious resonances and made it simply one more example of bad behavior by the Athenian *jeunesse dorée*. As such it was adopted with alacrity by other orators, for instance Lysias (14.42), and, later, Demosthenes (21.147) attacking Meidias. It has influenced modern interpretations of the episode, for instance that of Kenneth Dover.[44] The heuristic advantage in looking back at the archaeological evidence for the mutilation of the herms and the responses to it is that it helps us to recognize the danger inherent in symbolic violence toward sculptures, and aids us in understanding the actual violence it engendered. The mutilation of the herms and the aftermath illustrate the strong potency of sculpted images in Classical Athens.

Notes

1   On the political implications of the incident, see Furley 1996; Hornblower 2008. On the religious implications, see Graf

2000; Rubel 1999. For discussions of the incident which rely on the literary evidence alone, see, e.g., Aurenche 1974, pp. 165–171, 172–176, 193–228; Ostwald 1986, pp. 537–550. The most extensive discussions from an art historical perspective are those of Osborne 1985 and Quinn 2007, but both authors focus more on the Archaic origins of herms than on their mutilation in 415.

2 *IG* I³ 421–30, 431, 432(?). On the Stelai, see especially Amyx 1958a; Amyx 1958b; Pritchett 1953, 1956, 1961; Miles 1998, pp. 65–66, 203–205.

3 E.g., Ma 2013, 111–151; Houby-Nielsen 1998.

4 E.g., the Late Archaic herms of Hipparchos, on which see Pl. [*Hipparch.*] 228b–229b, and the Early Classical herms dedicated by victorious generals after the battle of Eion, described by Aeschines (*In Ctes.* 183–185).

5 From the Acropolis, the three herms of Late Archaic date are Athens, Acropolis Museum nos. 3694, 642 (possibly attaching to 170), and 530; the inscribed shaft of the early 5th century is *IG* I³ 750. A head of Early Classical date found on the Acropolis south slope (Athens, National Archaeological Museum no. 96) was identified by Wrede 1928 as a mask of Dionysos, but Harrison (1965, p. 143 n. 3) argues that the irregular breaks on the back of the head are more appropriate for a herm; the four-square look of the work, with elaborate detailing of the sides of the face, also fits a herm well, and the iconography is close to herms of the Early Classical era such as Agora no. S 211. The preserved herms dating prior to 415 include Agora nos. S 211, S 2452, and S 3347. Another Agora herm (no. S 159) may be Early Classical or Archaistic in date; its provenance is late (Harrison 1965, pp. 144–145 no. 158 pl. 141). For the herms on the road to every deme, see Pl. [*Hipparch.*] 228b–229b; for discussion, see Crome 1935/36, p. 306, and for a fragmentarily preserved shaft of one of these herms, Peek 1935. For the herms at doorways and street corners, see the texts collected in *LIMC* V, p. 306 no. 187.

6 For vase paintings, see Zanker 1965 and for the archaeological and epigraphic evidence, Rückert 1998, pp. 77–111.

7 An illustration of the herms as very direct recipients of offerings: an Attic red-figure bell krater fragment with a man pouring libations on a herm's phallus; the vase was found in Tarentum and dates ca. 430–20 BC (Amsterdam, Allard Pierson Museum 2477). Other statues too could be physically interacted with – for example the statue of Athena at Argos, ritually brought down to the river to bathe, as described by Kallimachos (*Hymn* 5.1–32, 49–55). What sets the herms apart is the frequency and comparative informality of such interactions, and their accessibility to everyday devotees rather than religious specialists. I thank Jessica Paga for her comments on this issue.

8 Bologna, Museo Civico no. 203.

9 Berlin, Staatliche Museen no. F 2525.

10 Frankfurt, Museum für Vor- und Fruhgeschichte no. VF 307.

11 Oenbrink 1997; McNiven 2009.

12 As discussed by McNiven 2009.

13 For the horizon of expectations, see Jauss 1982.

14 Ar. *Nub.* 422–26, 1483–85.

15 Phrynichos frg. 61A quoted in Plut. *Alc.* 20.7.

16 Although the Peisistratid tyrant Hipparchos set up many herms within Athens, later dedications have a more democratic

character. For Hipparchos' herms, see Plato (*Hipparch.*) 228b–c; for democratic ones, above all the Eion dedication, Aeschines (*In Ctes.* 183–185). For further discussion of the democratic connotations of herms in late fifth century Athens, see Kousser forthcoming.

17 Thucydides specifies that these were stone herms (*lithinoi*); presumably wooden ones also existed, on which see Jameson 1992, p. 228. Concerning the whereabouts of the mutilated herms, Kratippos (date unknown) is quoted in Pseudo-Plutarch's life of Andokides (834D) as saying that the focus was on the herms by the Agora; since the Agora likely held the largest concentration of herms in Athens, this may come to the same thing.

18 Thuc. 6.27.2. On the secretive nature of the conspiracy as described by Thucydides, see Hornblower 2008, pp. 375–376.

19 See the descriptions in Thucydides 3.60–62 (Corcyra, followed by an equally bloody democratic counter-revolution), 5.81 (Argos). On the subsequent oligarchic coups in Athens, see Shear 2011.

20 Trans. C. F. Smith, Cambridge, Mass., 1927.

21 See the useful chart in Dover 1970, pp. 277–280.

22 On the Stelai, see above, n. 2, and for the sum raised, see Lewis 1966, p. 188.

23 Thuc. 6.61.

24 Shear 1973, p. 364.

25 Shear 1973, 360–369; Camp 1986, 79–82.

26 Shear 1973, pp. 164–165.

27 Agora no. S 211. Shear 1933, pp. 514–516, figs. 511, 512; Harrison 1965, pp. 142–144 no. 156, pl. 140.

28 Harrison 1965, p. 144, 1990.

29 Harrison 1965, p. 142.

30 Agora nos. S 211, S 2452, S 3347; Acropolis nos. 170, 530, 642, 3694; National Archaeological Museum no. 96. As mentioned above, n. 7, it is possible that Agora no. S 159 is Early Classical in date, although it could also be a later archaizing work, on which see Harrison 1965, p. 145. There is also a herm from the Cincinnati Art Museum (1962.390) said to be from Attica, although this provenance is not secure (Crome 1935/36, p. 301, pl. 102).

31 Acropolis nos. 170, 530, 642; on these see Schrader 1928.

32 Acropolis no. 3694 has no recorded provenance (Schrader 1939, p. 248 no. 327, fig. 276); National Archaeological Museum no. 96 was found in 1876 on excavations on the south slope of the Acropolis, but no further information is available (Wrede 1928, p. 78 fig. 22.73–23.71; Harrison 1965, p. 143, pl. 165b; Karusu 1969, p. 41).

33 Agora no. S 3347: Shear 1984, pp. 42–43 (for herm), 42 n. 79 and 50–51 (for findspot), pl. 10.

34 E.g., Aeschin. *In Ctes.* 183–185.

35 On the dating of this dialogue within the fourth century, see Friedländer 1964, pp. 127–128.

36 *IG* I³ 421–30, 431, 432(?). On the Stelai, see especially Amyx 1958a; Amyx 1958b; Pritchett 1953, 1956, 1961; Miles 1998, pp. 65–66, 203–205.

37 For the findspots, see Miles 1998, pp. 65–66; Pritchett 1953, pp. 234–235.

38 Furley 1996, pp. 45–48.

39 *IG* I³ 106.21–23. Timanthes was mentioned as one of those accused and convicted in the mutilation in Andocides 3.34–35.

40 For dating, see Pritchett 1953, pp. 232–234, with the comments of Lewis 1966, p. 181. The count is based on the lists in Andocides 1.
41 Lewis 1966, p. 188.
42 Although the goal of the conspirators remains uncertain, it is clear from the narratives of Thucydides and Andokides that they were seen by the Athenians in 415 BC as intending to establish an oligarchy. Thucydides (6.27) described how the demos saw the mutilation as a conspiracy and a threat to their democracy; Andokides, by contrast, aimed to persuade the Athenians that the mutilation was not an oligarchic conspiracy. He did however discuss at length the narrative of the informer Diokleides – which put forward an oligarchic explanation for the herms, and was initially accepted by the Athenians (Andokides 1.38–42) – before offering his own, very different story, which was subsequently believed. Diokleides' story is relayed in Andokides 1.38–42, and Andokides' own account of the mutilation in Andokides 1.61–67.
43 On these coups and Athenian responses to them, see Shear 2011.
44 Dover 1970, p. 286.

References

Amyx, D. A. 1958a. "The Attic Stelai, Part III." *Hesperia* 27.3, pp. 164–252.

Amyx, D. A. 1958b. "The Attic Stelai, Part III." *Hesperia* 27.4, pp. 255–310.

Aurenche, O. 1974. *Les Groupes d'Alcibiade, de Léogoras et de Teucros: Remarques sur la Vie Politique Athénienne en 415 avant. J.C.*, Paris.

Camp, J. 1986. *The Athenian Agora: Excavations in the heart of Classical Athens.* London: Thames and Hudson.

Crome, J. 1935/36. "Hipparcheio Hermai." *Mitteilungen des Deutschen Archäologischen Instituts, Athenische Abteilung* 60/61, pp. 300–313.

Dover, K. J. 1970. *A Historical Commentary on Thucydides* 4, Oxford.

Friedländer, P. 1964. *Plato*, New York.

Furley, W. D. 1996. *Andokides and the Herms. (Bulletin of the Institute for Classical Studies Supplement* 65), London.

Graf, F. 2000. "Die Mysterienprozess." in *Grosse Prozesse im antiken Athen*, eds. L. Buckhardt and J. v. Ungern-Sternberg, Munich, pp. 114–127.

Harrison, E. 1965. *The Athenian Agora*, XI. *Archaic and Archaistic Sculpture*, Princeton.

Harrison, E. 1990. "Repair, Reuse, and Reworking of Ancient Greek Sculpture." in *Art Historical and Scientific Perspectives on Ancient Sculpture*, eds. M. True and J. Podany, Los Angeles, pp. 163–184.

Hornblower, Simon. 2008. *A Commentary on Thucydides*, Vol. 3, Oxford.

Houby-Neilsen, S. 1998. "Revival of archaic funerary practices in the Hellenistic and Roman Kerameikos," *Proceedings of the Danish Institute of Archaeology* 2, pp. 127–45.

Jameson, M. 1992. "L'espace Privé dans la Cité Grecque," in *La Cité Grecque d'Homère à Alexandre*, eds. O. Murray and S. Price, Paris, pp. 201–229.

Jauss, H. R. 1982. *Toward an aesthetic of reception*, trans. Timothy Bahti, Minneapolis.

Karusu, S. 1969. *Archäologisches Nationalmuseum: Antike Sculpturen*, Athens.

Kousser, R. forthcoming. *The afterlives of monumental sculptures in Classical and Hellenistic Greece: Interaction, transformation, destruction.* Cambridge.

Lewis, D. M. 1966. "After the Profanation of the Mysteries," in *Ancient Society and Institutions: Studies Presented to Victor Ehrenberg on his 75th Birthday*, Oxford, pp. 177–191.

LIMC = Lexicon Iconographicum Mythologiae Classicae, Zurich and Munich.

Ma, J. 2013. *Statues and cities: Honorific portraits and civic identity in the Hellenistic world*, Oxford.

McNiven, T. 2009. "'Things to Which We Give Service': Interactions with Sacred Images on Athenian Pottery," in *An Archaeology of Representations: Ancient Greek Vase-painting and Contemporary Methodologies*, ed. D. Yatromanolakis, Athens, pp. 298–324.

Miles, M. M. 1998. *The Athenian Agora*, XXXI. *The City Eleusinion*, Princeton.

Murray, O. 1990. "The Affair of the Mysteries: Democracy and the Drinking Group," in *Sympotica: A Symposium on the Symposion*, ed. O. Murray, Oxford, pp. 149–161.

Oenbrink, W. 1997. *Das Bild im Bilde: Zur Darstellung von Götterstatuen und Kultbildern auf griechischen Vasen.* Frankfurt.

Osborne, R. 1985. "The Erection and Mutilation of the *hermai*," *Proceedings of the Cambridge Philological Society* 31, pp. 47–73.

Ostwald, M. 1986. *From Popular Sovereignty to the Sovereignty of Law: Law, Society, and Politics in 5th-Century Athens.* Berkeley.

Peek, W. 1935. "Eine Herme des Hipparch," *Hermes* 70.4, pp. 461–463.

Pritchett, W. K. 1953. "The Attic Stelai, Part I," *Hesperia* 22.4, pp. 225–299.

Pritchett, W. K. 1956. "The Attic Stelai, Part II," *Hesperia* 25.3, pp. 178–328.

Pritchett, W. K. 1961. "Five New Fragments of the Attic Stelai," *Hesperia* 30.1, pp. 23–29.

Quinn, J. C. 2007. "Herms, Kouroi, and the Political Anatomy of Athens," *Greece and Rome* 54.1, pp. 82–105.

Rubel, A. 1999. *Stadt in Angst: Religion und Politik in Athen während des Peloponnesischen Krieges*, Darmstadt.

Rückert, B. 1998. *Die Herme im öffentlichen und privaten Leben der Griechen*, Regensburg.

Schrader, H. 1928. "Hermen aus dem Perserschutt," *Antike Plastik: Walther Amelung zum sechzigsten Geburtstag*, Berlin, pp. 227–232.

Schrader, H., ed. 1939. *Die Archaischen Marmorbildwerke der Akropolis*, 2 vols., Frankfurt.

Shear, T. L., Jr. 1973. "The Athenian Agora: Excavations of 1971," *Hesperia* 42.1, pp. 121–179.

Shear, T. L., Jr. 1973. "The Athenian Agora: Excavations of 1972," *Hesperia* 42.4, pp. 359–407.

Shear, T. L., Jr. 1984. "The Athenian Agora: Excavations of 1980–1982," *Hesperia* 53.1, pp. 1–57.

Shear, J. 2011. *Polis and Revolution: Responding to Oligarchy in Classical Athens*, Cambridge.

Shear, T. L. 1933. "The American Excavations in the Athenian Agora: Second Report (1933): The sculpture," *Hesperia* 2.4, pp. 514–541.

Wrede, W. 1928. "Der Maskengott," *Mitteilungen des Deutschen Archäologischen Instituts, Athenische Abteilung* 53, pp. 66–95.

Wycherley, R. F. 1957. *The Athenian Agora*, III. *Literary and Epigraphical Testimonia*, Princeton.

Zanker, Paul. 1965. *Wandel der Hermesgestalt in der attischen Vasenmalerei*, Bonn.

9. Funerals for Statues?
The Case of Phrasikleia and her "Brother"

Angele Rosenberg-Dimitracopoulou

The significance of the kore of Phrasikleia to the study of Archaic funerary monuments has eclipsed the material context and thereby obscured the statues' history. In this article I revisit four neglected black-figured lekythoi that were excavated near the statues (see cat. 1–4). These have never been published or directly incorporated into a study of the statues. Yet, as I argue, they are crucial for both the dating of the burial of Phrasikleia and her "brother" and the circumstances under which this occurred. This new evidence should help shape how we interpret the function of these statues.

The 1972 excavations at Merenda

In May 1972, the kore of Phrasikleia and a kouros dubbed her "brother" were discovered in remarkably good condition in Merenda, Attica (the ancient deme of Myrrhinous) (Figures 9.1 and 9.2).[1] Well before the kore of Phrasikleia was discovered the statue's base was known and published. The base of Phrasikleia's kore was reused as the capital of an engaged column in an early Byzantine church of the Panaghia in Merenda and had already been identified in the 18th century.[2] An epigram on the front of the base announces the statue's function,

σ εῖμ α Φρασικλείας| κόρε κεκλέσομαι | αἰεί
ἀντὶ γάμο| παρὰ θεὸν τοῦτο | λαχõσ' ὄνομα

The *sêma* of Phrasikleia. I shall always be called a kore, having received this name from the gods instead of marriage.[3]

While the surface of the stone has suffered considerable damage,[4] the neat arrangement of the letters into columns and rows is still visible.[5] The sculptor's signature on the left side of the base is in much better condition,

Ἀριστίον Πάρι[ός μ' ἐπ]ο[ίε]σε.[6]

The base of the kouros remains to be found.[7]

The kore of Phrasikleia and the kouros were found approximately 200 m north of the church of the Panaghia.[8] The excavator quickly joined the kore with the inscribed base in the nearby church to form the only complete female funerary monument from this period in Attica. A lead ring found next to the kore's feet in the same pit joined the statue to the base, leaving little doubt that they were from the same monument.[9] On the basis of the carving style of the statue, the letter-forms, and the relative chronology of Aristion of Paros, scholars have agreed that the kore was probably carved between 550 and 540 BC.[10] The kouros was probably made between 540 and 530 BC given its sculptural style, but its lack of an inscription or of an attribution to an artist makes this date more tentative.[11]

The statues were buried side by side in a single pit in the cemetery of Myrrhinous, now situated along the modern road to Markopoulos just south of the Olympic Equestrian Center.[12] The kouros was detached from its plinth just above the ankles and both of the arms were broken off. The right arm was neatly placed above the head and the left arm was found below the statue. The kore was in much better condition. Still attached to the plinth, only the left hand was broken at the wrist. Vibrant colors preserved on the chiton are important to the study of polychromy in archaic sculpture.[13] The pit itself cut into debris from older graves, as proto-attic sherds found beneath the statues attest.[14]

Approximately three meters west of the pit were the remains of a pyre (see Π11 in Figure 9.3). In July 2013, I was able to examine its unpublished contents, which had

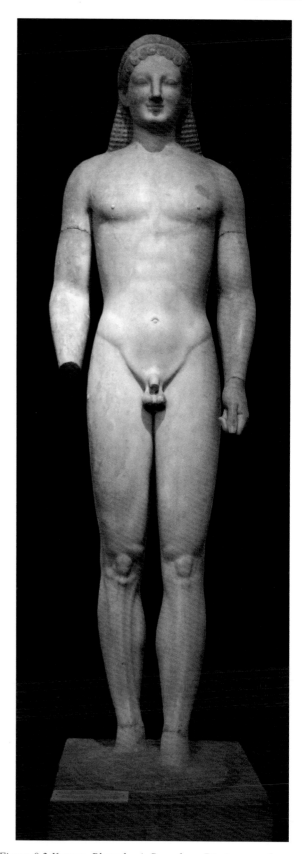

Figure 9.1 Sema of Phrasikleia. Photo by A. Rosenberg-Dimitracopoulou

Figure 9.2 Kouros. Photo by A. Rosenberg-Dimitracopoulou

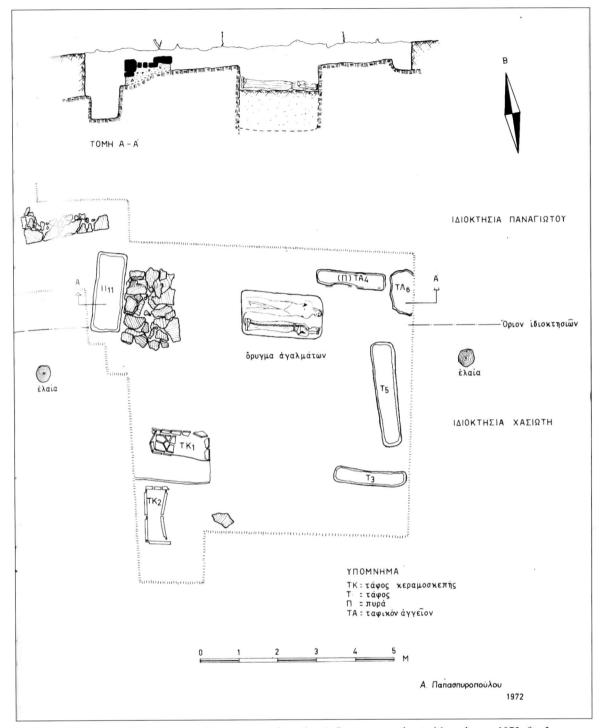

ΤΟΜΗ Α – Ά

Β

ΙΔΙΟΚΤΗΣΙΑ ΠΑΝΑΓΙΩΤΟΥ

(Π) ΤΑ4
ΤΑ₆

Ά

Όριον ίδιοκτησιῶν

όρυγμα άγαλμάτων

έλαία

έλαία

ΙΔΙΟΚΤΗΣΙΑ ΧΑΣΙΩΤΗ

Τ₅

ΤΚ₁

Τ₃

ΤΚ₂

ΥΠΟΜΝΗΜΑ
ΤΚ = τάφος κεραμοσκεπὴς
Τ· = τάφος
Π = πυρά
ΤΑ = ταφικόν ἀγγεῖον

0   1   2   3   4   5
                               Μ

Α. Παπασπυροπούλου
1972

*Figure 9.3 Plan of 1972 excavation. Drawing by author after A. **Papaspyropoulou** in Mastrokostas 1972, fig. 2.*

been collected in 1972.[15] These consisted of charred earth, burned and unburned fragments of ceramic vessels, chunks of charcoal, pieces of ceramic tile, and four black-figured lekythoi (treated in detail in the next section). There were no bones – human or animal – included in the debris. The excavator did not indicate how the edges of the pyre were

defined but the tiles suggest that its walls might have been lined with them.[16] Although most of the shapes of the broken vessels were undistinguishable, there were fragments of at least two black-glazed lekythoi in the group, without decoration. The rest of the smashed vessels ranged in size and were mostly coarse ware with some examples of finer clay. The clay was largely consistent with Attic types, save for one fragment that resembled either Corinthian or Boiotian fabric. The sherds were unglazed, coated in a solid black glaze, or decorated with simple decorative patterns in black glaze. The discernible patterns included rays, bands, and one body sherd with a lozenge pattern on it.[17]

Two fragments of stone bases that do not join to each other were found between the pit with the statues and the pyre described above. A circular cutting on one may indicate that it supported a kore. The other piece is more fragmentary but three letters of an inscription – NTO – are preserved on it.[18] The excavator suggested that this base belonged to the "brother" because it has the appropriate dimensions and the style of the letter-forms agree with the statue's style.[19] The association between the two blocks is not conclusive because the fragmentary base may not have supported a kouros statue and more grave markers were damaged in the immediate area. Beside the fragmentary bases and also between the pyre and the pit was a pile of stones arranged in a rectangle.[20] These stones, since reburied, may be the fragments of destroyed plinths and bases that once supported grave markers.

Burials in the rest of the cemetery began during the Geometric period and continued without significant breaks through the Roman period.[21] The precise limits of the cemetery have not been identified but four human burials in the vicinity indicate that the statues were buried within its boundaries (Figure 9.3). Although the ceramic finds from these human burials await full publication, autopsy suggests that the burials date to the Geometric and Classical periods.[22] Furthermore, their form confirms the approximate chronology of the interred materials.[23] Two simple shaft graves common to the Geometric period lay to the east and southeast. Tile graves of the Classical period were found with inhumed skeletons to the southwest. It is unlikely that any of these were the graves that the kore and kouros originally marked, since they either predate or postdate the proposed dates for the statues.

Four black-figured lekythoi from the pyre

The four black-figured lekythoi that prompted this review of the 1972 excavations at Merenda were found along the northern edge of the pyre (cat. nos. 1–4).[24] These vessels are comparatively well preserved in contrast to the rest of the ceramic material in the pyre, and they do not appear to have been burned.[25] Briefly mentioned in the initial publication, these lekythoi were misplaced after the excavation and disregarded in subsequent treatments of the pair of statues. This omission is an oversight given that the lekythoi can provide a *terminus post quem* of ca. 480–460 BC for the statues' burial, assuming that the pyre should be associated with the pit.

The mass production of small black-figured lekythoi occupied several workshops in Athens during the 5th century

BC.[26] They first appear in the Athens 581 and Diosphos workshops.[27] Lekythoi from the Athens 581 workshop that were probably made and sold together as a group were found in the Marathon tumulus and the so-called Douris grave on Stadiou Street in Athens.[28] The Haimon workshop and the Beldam workshop took over the production of these smaller, mass-produced black-figured lekythoi from the Athens 581 workshop at the end of the first quarter of the 5th century BC.[29]

Two of the lekythoi from Merenda (MEP 1891 Figures 9.4, 9.5, 9.6 and MEP 1892 Figures 9.7, 9.8, 9.9) are chimney lekythoi, named after the distinctive mouth. This shape was made in the Beldam workshop and scholars have attributed chimney lekythoi to the hands of the Beldam Painter, the Emporion Painter and the Haimon Painters.[30] The sloping shoulders and the curve of the body as it meets the foot suggest that the two examples from Merenda may fall later in the series. The chimney lekythos was probably introduced in the workshop of the Emporion painter where it has a flat shoulder, is curved at the point where the body meets the foot and has a foot in two degrees.[31] In the work of the Beldam workshop, the shoulders have a greater slope, the walls of the body are tapered and the foot is now painted in two degrees.[32] The Haimon Painter's style evolved, beginning with the Emporion Painter's shape and then incorporating the Beldam Painter's shape.[33] Based on a comparison of their shape as well as their decoration, the two lekythoi from Merenda were probably made between 480 and 460 BC.

MEP 1893 (Figures 9.10, 9.11, 9.12) is a pattern lekythos decorated with an ivy-berry motif.[34] Although the top half of the neck and the mouth are missing, it probably had a calyx mouth.[35] Widely exported throughout the 5th century BC, pattern lekythoi were used as grave offerings as well as normal vessels of daily life.[36] Many pattern lekythoi with the ivy-berry motif have been found in the course of the Kerameikos excavations. An early example with similar checkered patterns framing the rounded leaves of the ivy comes from a grave dating between 470 and 450.[37] Comparable examples come from graves in the Kerameikos, which date to as late as 430/420 BC. It appears then that the ivy-berry lekythos in Merenda was part of a series that was mass-produced over a considerable time-period. Consequently, it is not particularly helpful for dating the pyre with any more precision.

MEP 1894 (Figures 9.13, 9.14, 9.15) is a hybrid lekythos with an inward curve of the body at the join that is characteristic of the Beldam Painter's type (BEL) but smaller and without the false interior.[38] Most of the shoulders as well as the neck and mouth are missing. It is not possible to reconstruct the shape of the mouth with any certainty, as bodies with a similar outline have either chimney or calyx mouths.[39] The painted subject of Herakles wrestling the Nemean lion is helpful for the present chronological purposes. The subject matter was favored for the decoration of small black-figured lekythoi in the workshops of the Class of Athens 581 ii and of the Haimon Painter.[40] Based on the activity of these workshops, the lekythos with Herakles wrestling the lion from Merenda was probably made between around 480 and 460 BC.[41]

Although early 5th century ceramic chronology is problematic, closed deposits from elsewhere in Attica broadly confirm the stylistically derived chronology of the lekythoi found in Myrrhinous. The pottery excavated from the tumulus at Marathon includes lekythoi attributed to the Class of Athens 581 ii Painter as well as lekythoi decorated in the manner of the Haimon Painter.[42] The Persian destruction wells in the Agora of Athens also contained significant amounts of lekythoi attributed to the Class of Athens 581 as well as lekythoi and skyphoi attributed to the Haimon workshop.[43] John K. Papadopoulos has suggested that these wells are better understood as "agora creation" deposits, filled with debris from the Persian destruction in order to prepare the area for the new Classical agora.[44] Papadopoulos makes the convincing argument that the agora was relocated to the location north of the akropolis because it was better suited both for the new port at the Piraeus and for stronger hegemony to be exerted over Eleusis.[45] As he argues, the "agora creation" deposits must have been made after, but probably not long after, the Persian wars.[46]

The closed deposits of the Marathon tumulus and the agora wells support the dating of the lekythoi from Merenda to ca. 490–460 BC.[47] The chronology of these late black-figured lekythoi provides a date for the pyre. Although it is possible that the pyre was burned as early as 490, it is much more likely that it occurred after 480 given the chronologies of the workshops of the Class of Athens 581 ii, the Haimon Painter, and the Beldam Painter. The ivy-berry pattern lekythos could be as late as 430/20 BC, but its earliest production begins at a time more contemporary to the other pieces. It is more plausible that the Merenda example is from the beginning of the series rather than the alternative explanation that the other three lekythoi remained above ground for thirty to sixty years. Thus, it appears that the ritual during which the pyre was burned took place between 480 and 460 BC.[48]

Pyre Π11: an offering ditch for Phrasikleia's kore and the kouros

The study of pyres found in cemeteries has relied primarily on the finds from the excavations of the Kerameikos cemetery in Athens.[49] Relevant evidence from graveside pyres in other cemeteries in Athens as well as in Vari, Vourva and Marathon has supplemented the finds from the Kerameikos. These pyres, usually collections of offerings with traces of burning, have largely been found next to burials dating from the late 8th century BC to the early 6th

century BC. Graves from the 5th century rarely have pyres next to them. The practice reappears, albeit in a different form, in the 4th century BC.

The German excavators of the Kerameikos have identified four types of grave pyres:[50] *Opferrinnen, Opfergruben, Opferplätze,* and *Opferstellen.*[51] *Opferrinnen* or *Opfergruben* refer to long ditches that are dug into the ground in which offerings are burned. Sometimes they are lined with mudbrick (*Opferrinnen*), although not always (*Opfergruben*). In addition to ash, excavators have found broken vessels, animal bones, eggshells, and the pits or seeds of local vegetables and fruits such as olives. *Opferplätze* and *Opferstellen* refer to burned areas near graves that are found either on the earth's surface or dug into a shallow pit. These burned areas are more characteristic of burials of the fourth century. Ash, broken pottery, and animal bones have been found in them as well.[52] The difference in form between those pyres dug into the ground and those burned on its surface may correspond to different graveside rituals. The pyres that were dug into the ground (*Opferrinnen* and *Opfergruben*) were probably burned at the time of the burial whereas the areas of burning on the surface (*Opferplätze* and *Opferstellen*) were most likely part of a ritual that took place after the funeral.[53]

Like the collections of burned offerings found during the excavations of the Kerameikos, the graveside pyre at Merenda was burned during a funerary ritual. The fact that the pyre was found in a cemetery and that it contains charcoal, ash, sherds with and without traces of burning, and intact vessels supports this interpretation. Although offering ditches frequently contain animal bones and other bits of consumed food, such traces of ritual feasting are not always evident.[54] The pyre at Merenda is closest to the *Opfergruben* or the simple ditches dug into the ground without the addition of mudbrick along the sides.

Pyre Π11 can be associated with the pit in which the kore of Phrasikleia and the kouros were buried despite the fact that they were approximately three meters apart. As the excavations in 1972 revealed, this part of the cemetery of Merenda was not densely occupied (Figure 9.3). Unlike the cemeteries in the Kerameikos, there is space between the graves. Thus, the relatively sparse layout of the Merenda cemetery makes the relationships between features clearer.

Pyre Π11 was most probably burned as part of a ritual for the burial of the statues because the pyre and the pit align with one another in a similar fashion to offering ditches and their associated graves in other Attic cemeteries. The closest parallels to the form and placement of the Merenda pyre come from sixth century graves in the Kerameikos. While some graveside pyres have been found directly next to the grave,[55] those that are separated from the grave are still in alignment with it.[56] Even though only a section of this part of the Merenda cemetery has been investigated, the pyre does not align with any another excavated graves.

Figure 9.4 MEP1891. Photo by A. Rosenberg-Dimitracopoulou

Figure 9.5 MEP1891. Photo by A. Rosenberg-Dimitracopoulou

Figure 9.6 MEP1891. Photo by A. Rosenberg-Dimitracopoulou

Figure 9.7 MEP1892. Photo by A. Rosenberg-Dimitracopoulou

Furthermore, pyre Π11 was found 8 mm above the statues' pit.[57] Examples of this also exist in the Kerameikos where graveside pyres were either burned at similar depths as the graves with which they were associated (*Opferrinnen* and *Opfergrube*) or above them (*Opferplätze* and *Opferstellen*).

Two pyres excavated from the Marathon tumulus provide good contemporary parallels to the Merenda example.[58] Both pyres were lined with mudbrick and filled with animal bones, fragments of vessels as well as ash. One (labeled Γ by the excavators) was inside the tumulus whereas the other one (labeled E) was just outside of it. The ditch outside of the tumulus was disturbed and its precise dimensions could not be determined. The pyre inside the tumulus was almost 10 m long and approximately 1 m wide.[59] The example from Merenda was slightly smaller at 2 m long, 0.71 m wide and between 0.50 and 1 m deep.[60]

Another five offering ditches with material from the 5th century have been excavated in the area of the Kerameikos.[61] All of these are dated to after ca. 450 BC and they were filled with similar items to those of the previous century.[62] Smaller than the ditches at Marathon, these later 5th century pyres are only slightly larger than the example from Merenda.[63] Despite this, the pyre of ash, charcoal and burned pottery must have been an offering ditch given the nature of its contents as well as its location in cemetery.

The pile of fragmentary plinths and bases also aligns with the pyre and pit on either side of it.[64] This alignment suggests that it may have been part of the same deposition.

It is difficult to conclude with any certainty how the three features are related without a more precise indication of the depth at which the bottom edge of this pile was found. Despite this limitation, the proximity and alignment of the features suggest a certain narrative. Like the break at the "brother's" ankles, this pile is evidence of the forcible destruction of grave markers at the same cemetery. It appears then that a whole cohort of markers was destroyed and the debris subsequently collected into a pile alongside the buried statues; a wooden pyre was then constructed for a ceremony that involved the lekythoi. Further investigations of the area may locate more damaged grave markers and supplement this reconstruction. Despite the present gaps in the archaeological evidence, the relative placement of the three features within the spacious cemetery at Merenda suggests that the construction of the pyre, the pile of stones, and the pit with the buried statues all belong to the same contemporaneous event.

The Persian destruction at Merenda

The *terminus post quem* of ca. 480–460 BC provided by the four black-figured lekythoi is specifically relevant to an ongoing debate about when the statues were buried and

Figure 9.10 MEP1893. Photo by A. Rosenberg-Dimitracopoulou

Figure 9.11 MEP1893. Photo by A. Rosenberg-Dimitracopoulou

Figure 9.8 MEP1892. Photo by A. Rosenberg-Dimitracopoulou

Figure 9.9 MEP1892. Photo by A. Rosenberg-Dimitracopoulou

why.[65] Since their discovery, scholars have proposed two separate historical events as the context in which they were buried. It has been argued that the statues were implicated in a feud mentioned by Isokrates between the Peisistratid and Alkmaionid families of the late 6th century BC that involved desecrating tombs (Isok. 16.26). One scholar identifies the buried markers as belonging to the Alkmaionid family while others associate them with the Peisistratids.[66] Others have argued that the statues were damaged during the Persian invasion of Attica of 480 BC and then buried.[67] There is further disagreement about whether the statues were buried in anticipation of a destructive event or after the damage was inflicted. Opposing conclusions rest in part on differing assessments about the level of damage that the statues have sustained: do they look like they were buried as a protective measure or were they damaged prior to their burial?[68]

The dates of the associated lekythoi (ca. 480–460 BC) challenge the interpretation that places the burial in the context of the power struggles between the Alkmaionid and Peisistratid families in the late 6th century BC. Instead, they support the conclusion that the statues were damaged in the course of the Persian invasion. Herodotos reports that after the battle of Thermopylai in 480 BC, "the barbarians

had reached Attica and were destroying all of it by fire" (Hdt. 8.50).[69] Myrrhinous was situated a little less than five kilometers east from the shoreline and along the road between Athens and Steiria, an important port connecting the polis to the Cyclades.[70] The Persian invaders may have sacked the deme on their way to Steiria while they occupied Attica between 480 and 479 BC.

Other statues that were likely vandalized by the Persians and subsequently buried have been found elsewhere in Attica.[71] Examples from sanctuaries include the famous korai pit on the acropolis in Athens as well as the deposits of votives found in the sanctuaries of Athena and Poseidon at Sounion.[72] The funerary kouros of Aristodikos is another possibility. Damage concentrated on the statue's face has suggested to some that the statue was deliberately vandalized.[73] This kind of vandalism, however, diverges from the kinds of destruction visible at the sanctuaries in Athens and Sounion and may be the result of local Greeks rather than the Persian invaders.[74]

The traces of a ritual ceremony accompanying the burial of the statues in Myrrhinous do not seem to have any direct parallels in the Attic material.[75] The closest example of the deferential treatment of a statue may be the famous Berlin kore, a statue that is often compared to the kore of Phrasikleia on stylistic grounds.[76] Rumor has it that the statue was found wrapped in lead. Unfortunately, there are no more details of this tantalizing discovery.[77]

Towards an interpretation of the statues' burial

One implication for Archaic sculpture of the pyre burned for the buried statues at Merenda is in its relationship to Jean-Pierre Vernant's theory on the ontological status of statues in early Greek thought. Vernant argued in various essays that a fundamental distinction between Archaic and Classical images was the means by which they signified.[78] He suggested that Archaic statues were substitutes for their real world referents. More specifically, in the instance of funerary statuary, korai and kouroi were stand-ins for the deceased. He went on to argue that a significant ontological shift occurred during the Classical period. Images came to designate the absent bodies of gods and of the deceased by looking like them, rather than by standing in for them. Mimesis replaced substitution as the mechanism by which images related to the world.

In his essay on *kolossoi*, Vernant explicitly looked at cenotaphs where objects were used instead of corpses in order to examine the mechanisms of substitution during the Archaic period.[79] Most of his discussion rests on literary testimonia[80] and Pausanias' testimony of tombs at Phlius and Leibadeia.[81] The examples from the material record include a 13th century BC cenotaph at Midea and a collection of upright markers (the *cippi* in the Campo di Stele) in Selinunte that Vernant interprets as analogous to wooden and wax *kolossoi* mentioned in two inscriptions from Cyrene. The cenotaph from Midea significantly predates the literary evidence and the upright markers are more likely related to local cult activity.[82] The absence of a contemporary example from the material record undermines Vernant's theory positing that *kolossoi* could act as substitutes for corpses. The statues that were buried in Merenda with a pyre and grave offerings provide such an example. In lieu of bodies, the people of ancient Myrrhinous treated the statues as though they were corpses.

This consideration of the material context of the kore of Phrasikleia suggests a more direct connection between the statue and the deceased than the word *sema* in the inscription has previously indicated.[83] More than just a sign or marker, the kore is Phrasikleia's double, or as Vernant explains, it is "an external reality…whose peculiar character, in its very appearance, sets it in opposition to familiar objects and to the ordinary surroundings of life. It exists simultaneously on two contrasting planes: just when it shows itself to be present, it also reveals itself as not of this world and as belonging to some other, inaccessible sphere."[84] To a certain degree, it was due to their status as doubles of the deceased that the kore of Phrasikleia and her "brother" were buried in Merenda according to a ritual customary for corpses.

Catalogue

1 Figures 9.4, 9.5, and 9.6   MEP 1891
SHAPE AND ORNAMENT   Chimney mouth, flat on top. Neck offset from mouth and shoulder, white. Handle oval in section from neck to shoulder. Slightly sloped shoulder. Body cylindrical with slight curve inward at the join with the shoulder and sharp curve towards foot. Disk foot, narrower at top than at bottom. Exterior and interior of mouth black. Top of mouth white. Neck, shoulder and underside of handle white. Tongue pattern above inverted rays on shoulder. On front of body at join with neck simple meander running right. Two black lines circle body below meander. Side and underside of foot reserved.

SUBJECT   Chariot facing to the right with two women mounting the chariot. One women holds a lyre (?). Woman seated on folding stool in front of quadriga.

ATTRIBUTION AND DATE   Unattributed. Ca. 480–460 BC (475–450 based on Leiden comparisons).

DIMENSIONS AND CONDITION   H. 0.135; diam. 0.041.

Intact. Much of surface is pitted.

TECHNICAL FEATURES   Added white on top of mouth, neck, shoulder, interior of handle, top of body at join with shoulder, faces and arms of women, lyre (?), and reins (?) of horse. White drip from top of body to the right of seated woman. Incised lines detailing folds on drapery of all three figures, legs of horses (?), and heads of horses (?). Pair of incised lines below picture (break in the top line on front of body).

BIBLIOGRAPHY   Unpublished

COMPARANDA Compare with chimney lekythoi attributed to Manner of the Haimon Painter *CVA* Leiden 2 pl. 95.10–12, pl. 96.7–9. See also *CVA* Palermo, Coll. Mormino 1, III H pl. 16, 1–2. Scene and overall shape of lekythos are similar except that the details are more precise and the vessel has a foot in two degrees. On the quadriga scene with three women attributed to the Manner of the Haimon Painter see *ABV* 539–542.

2 Figures 9.7, 9.8, and 9.9   MEP 1892
SHAPE AND ORNAMENT   Chimney mouth, curved on top. Neck offset from mouth and shoulder. Handle oval in section from neck to shoulder. Slightly sloped shoulder. Body cylindrical, sharply curves towards foot. Disk foot. Tongue pattern above inverted rays on shoulder. On front of body at join with neck vertical tongues framed by one black line above and two black lines below. Two reserved lines below picture circle body. Neck, shoulder, underside of handle, and side and underside of foot reserved.

SUBJECT   Symposium. Seated draped

woman, facing right, on folding stool; draped woman to right with lyre seated at the foot of the line; reclining draped male. Draped woman seated on folding stool facing left.

ATTRIBUTION AND DATE   Unattributed. Ca. 480–460 BC.

DIMENSIONS AND CONDITION   H. 0.125; diam. 0.038.

Intact. Much of surface is worn and pitted. Calcific deposits on mouth.

TECHNICAL FEATURES   Added white on bits of neck and shoulder, on faces and arms of women, on stools at far and far right, and on lyre. Incised lines detailing folds on drapery of four seated figures.

Misfired to red-brown on exterior, top, and interior of mouth and exterior of handle. Glazed applied thinly at figures on the far left and far right, lower part of body and top of foot.

BIBLIOGRAPHY   Unpublished

COMPARANDA Symposium scenes on chimney lekythoi attributed to Manner of the Haimon Painter *CVA* Aberdeen, pl. 19.6–7; *CVA* Leiden 2, pl. 97 nos. 1–7; *CVA* Karlsruhe Badisches Landesmuseum 1, pl. 14.10–1. Symposium group was a common theme amongst the painters in the Haimon Group, see *ABV* pp. 551–533. The Merenda example is not as carefully executed as the vessels attributed to this group and it omits the ivy tendrils that are often in the background. See *CVA* Prague 1, pl. 44.4–6 and *CVA* Amsterdam 3, pl. 172.1–3 for a symposium scene without the ivy tendril and without the added white on a small secondary shape.

3 Figures 9.10, 9.11, and 9.12   MEP 1893
SHAPE AND ORNAMENT   Secondary shape. Neck offset from shoulder. Sloping shoulder. Hybrid: the inward curve of the body at the join with the shoulder characteristic of BELs but smaller. Handle oval in section from neck to shoulder. Disk foot, wider at top than at bottom. Tongue pattern above inverted rays on shoulder. Two black lines at join with neck. Body white. On front of body below two black lines, checkered band, four horizontal lines; then one black line. Another black line and checkered band, two horizontal lines below picture. One line and another pair of lines in white on black lower body. Side and underside of foot reserved.

SUBJECT   Ivy branch with berries. Ivy leaves are rounded as they near the stem. Berries are rosettes made up of seven dots.

ATTRIBUTION AND DATE   Unattributed. Ca. 470–460, although could be as late as 430 BC.

DIMENSIONS AND CONDITION   H. (as preserved) 0.163; diam. 0.061.

Put together from three fragments. Top of neck and all of mouth are missing. Much of the surface is worn and pitted.

TECHNICAL FEATURES   Stems connecting leaves to branch are misfired to red-brown.

BIBLIOGRAPHY   Unpublished

COMPARANDA For the rounded shape of the leaves and somewhat haphazardly executed and spaced out checkered pattern see Zurich University 2496 (*CVA* 28–29, pl. 20.19–20); Winterthur, Archaölogische Sammlung 292 (*CVA* 26, pl. 18.15); Leiden, Rijskmuseum van Oudheden ROII53 (*CVA* 11–12, pl. 12.14); Leiden, Rijskmuseum van Oudheden GNV113 (*CVA* 11–12, pl. 112.11); Paris, Musée August Rodin (*CVA* 28, pl. 9.8); Poznan, Musée Wielkopolski (*CVA* 54, pl. 3.11); Reading, University 25.IX.4 (*CVA* 21, pl. 12.8); Braunschweig, Herzog Anton Ulrich Museum 365 (*CVA* 21, pl. 11.15); *Kerameikos* VII.2, pl. 88 1.1, 4.8. For the ivy-berry motif, see *Corinth* XIII, pp. 164–5. For the use of white lines, see *Kerameikos* VII.2, pl. 55. 282,11.1.12.

4 Figures 9.13, 9.14, and 9.15   MEP 1894
SHAPE AND ORNAMENT   Neck offset from shoulder. Sloping shoulder. Hybrid: the inward curve of the body at the join with the shoulder characteristic of BELs but smaller. Handle oval in section from neck to shoulder. Foot in two degrees. Tongue pattern above inverted rays on shoulder. Black line circles body at join with shoulder. On front of body at join with neck simple meander running right framed below by two black lines that circle body. One reserved line circles body below picture. Another pair of reserved lines below that. Two black lines mark the lower degree of the foot. Shoulder, interior of handle, side and underside of foot are reserved.

SUBJECT   Herakles and the Nemean lion. Athena stands at left, in profile to the right, wearing helmet, aegis, chiton, himation, and holding two spears in her right hand. Her left hand stretches out over Herakles' back. At center a bearded Herakles wrestles the lion who lifts its left hindleg to Herakles' head in a standard pose for this scene. Bow, cloth, and quiver are suspended in the ivy above them. Mid-sized dots fill the space between the ivy branches. A figure, likely Iolaos, stands at left, his body in profile to left, his head in profile to right, holding a club in his left land. A himation hangs over his right extended arm.

ATTRIBUTION AND DATE   Unattributed. Ca. 480–460 BC.

DIMENSIONS AND CONDITION   H. (as preserved) 0.198; diam. 0.09.

Put together from three fragments. Most of shoulder, neck, and mouth are missing. Much of surface is pitted and worn.

TECHNICAL FEATURES   Incision for

Figure 9.12 MEP1893. Photo by A. Rosenberg-Dimitracopoulou   *Figure 9.13 MEP1894. Photo by A. Rosenberg-Dimitracopoulou*   *Figure 9.14 MEP1894. Photo by A. Rosenberg-Dimitracopoulou*   *Figure 9.15 MEP1894. Photo by A. Rosenberg-Dimitracopoulou*

details on Athena, Herakles, lion, suspended cloth, bow, and quiver, and Iolaos. Added red on Athena's himation and chiton, on Iolaos' hair, beard, and himation. Red drip across right side of Iolaos' chest.

Pair of black lines below meander misfired to red-brown.

BIBLIOGRAPHY   Unpublished.

COMPARANDA   Herakles wrestling the Nemean lion (with or without Athena and Iolaos) was popular in both the workshops of the Class of Athens 581 ii and of the Haimon Painter. For the Class of Athens 581 ii see *ABV* 491, 499 and *Para* 232; for the Haimon Painter see *ABV* 548. Like the Merenda example, these workshops placed ivy in the background with Herakles' bow, quiver and cloak suspended in the branches. For the secondary ornament see Parlama and Stampolidis 2000, p. 309 n. 310 (authors compare to a lekythos attributed to the Workshop of the Haimon Painter) and *Kerameikos* IX p. 92 no. 26.2 (Haimonian lekythos by Class of Athens 581 ii). The Diosphos Painter and the painters in the workshop of the Haimon Painter added red onto drapery as well as incision. See Parlama and Stampolidis 2000, p. 304 no. 304 (authors compare lekythos to vessels attributed to both workshops). For the relationship between the Diosphos Painter, the Class of Athens 581 workshop, and the Haimon workshop see Kurtz 1975, pp. 147–153.

Notes

1   Both statues are now in the National Archaeological Museum in Athens (NM 4889 and NM 4890). I thank those working at the 2nd Ephoreia of Classical Antiquities for granting me access to the relevant materials as well as the staff at the Archaeological Museum at Brauron for facilitating my study of finds from Mastrokostas' 1972 excavations in Merenda. Vicky Skaraki at the 2nd Ephoreia and Euaggelos Vivliodetis at the National Archaeological Museum, Athens were particularly generous with their time and knowledge. The work presented here was supported by an Edward L. Ryerson Travel Fellowship in Archaeology awarded by the University of Chicago and a Samuel H. Kress Fellowship in art and architecture awarded by the American School of Classical Studies at Athens. It is my pleasure to thank friends and colleagues Margaret Miles, Richard T. Neer, Jaś Elsner, Verity Platt, Ann Patnaude, Alan Shapiro, Julia Shear, Jim Wright, Ioanna Damanaki, Joe Day, Simon Oswald, Heather Graybehl, Sara Franck, and Lakshmi Ramgopal. I also thank the anonymous reviewers for their productive feedback as well as the participants of a seminar on Greek sculpture that I took with Richard T. Neer in the winter of 2007 for their comments on the class presentation that sparked this project. Early versions of this paper were given in Athens (2013) and at the annual AIA meeting in Chicago (2014). Any remaining errors are my own.

2   *IG* I³ 1261 (= *CEG* 24) and now on display with the statue in the National Archaeological Museum in Athens. See also Austin 1938, pp. 10–13; Jeffery 1962, pp. 138–139 no. 46 (provides description of the base *in situ* and suggests a

connection with her no. 2); Jeffery 1990, no. 29; Kontoleon 1970, p. 90. For a discussion of the epigram after the statue was discovered, see Immerwahr 1990, no.460; Svenbro 1993, pp. 8–25; Martini 2008; Kissas 2000, no. 14.

3 Translation adapted from Stieber 2004, p. 146.

4 Jeffery suggests that the letters were scratched out in order to prepare the surface for the plaster when the block was reused in the church, see Jeffery 1963, p. 139. It is equally possible that this damage is part of the natural deterioration of the limestone surface. Unlike the kore statue, the base was not buried and was available as building material in the thirteenth century. Further study of the weathering of the base might clarify its history. Thanks are due to Simon Oswald and Joe Day for discussing the state of the base with me.

5 Austin and Jeffery identify the inscription as stoichedon (see footnote 2). For a recent challenge to this identification, see Keesling 2003a, p. 47. I am grateful to Reader A for this reference.

6 Scholars agree that this inscription can be restored as the signature of Aristion of Paros.

7 Mastrokostas tentatively identifies one of two fragmentary statue bases excavated nearby as that of the kouros given its comparable dimensions and the style of the letter-forms. As will be seen, there is evidence of extensive destruction at the cemetery and, as a result, this association remains uncertain. See Mastrokostas 1972, fig. 23, p. 310.

8 The discovery was first reported in Greek and in French, see Mastrokostas 1972. For another version of the events in 1972, see Euaggelos Ch. Kakoyiannis' narrative in Valavanis 2007, pp. 332–337.

9 On the join between statue and base, see Mastrokostas 1972, pp. 304–308, figs. 7–8 and 16.

10 See Kaltsas 2002b, pp. 16–26 for a recent discussion of the statue's chronology including references to previous treatments.

11 For an analysis of the kouros' stylistic chronology as well as for earlier bibliography, see Kaltsas 2002b, pp. 32–37.

12 For the topography of the deme, see Kakovogiannis in Vasilopoulou and Katsarou-Tseleveki 2009, pp. 47–78 and Vivliodetis 2007, pp. 94–116.

13 Mastrokostas 1972, p. 314 (autopsy); Karakasi 2001, pp. 121–126 (autopsy); Kaltsas 2002b (microscopic analysis of pigments); Brinkmann, Koch-Brinkmann and Piening 2010 (UV-VIS absorption spectroscopy and X-ray fluorescence analysis).

14 Mastrokostas 1972, pp. 314.

15 I did not receive permission to photograph, measure, or draw anything. The description of the contents is based on my notes taken while in the storeroom at the Archaeological Museum at Brauron. Although the burned earth has been collected, it has not been water-sieved for food residue and it was not possible to do so in 2013. Cf. Mastrokostas 1972, pp. 308, 310.

16 As will be discussed in the following section, graveside pyres from the 6th century BC were sometimes lined with mudbrick. The tiles in the pyre at Merenda may have been lining the walls in a similar fashion.

17 A very small fragment with green glaze, presumably much later in date, was also included in the bags of the excavated pyre. This fragment is most likely a contamination given that the rest of the ceramic material is ancient.

18 For the base with the circular cutting, see Mastrokostas 1972, p. 310, fig. 3 and p. 321, fig. 22. For the inscribed base, see Mastrokostas 1972, pp. 310, fig. 3 and p. 322, fig. 23.

19 Mastrokostas 1972, pp. 310–314.

20 For the excavator's description of the pile of stones, see Mastrokostas 1972, p. 308.

21 For a history of the excavations in the cemetery between 1960 and 1972, see Vivliodetis 2007, pp. 165–171.

22 For the ceramics of graves excavated in other campaigns investigating other parts of the cemetery, see Vivliodetis 2008.

23 For an overview of grave types, see Kurtz and Boardman 1971, pp. 54–55 and 64–67; *Kerameikos* VI.1 and Houby-Nielsen 1996.

24 Mastrokostas 1972, p. 308.

25 Thanks are due to Heather Graybehl for looking at the pictures of the lekythoi as well as for discussing the effects of fire on ceramics with me.

26 Sparkes and Talcott 1970, pp. 46–47.

27 Kurtz 1975, pp. 147–150. On the Class of Athens 581, see *ABV,* pp. 489–506 and *Para,* pp. 222–246.

28 For the lekythoi from the Marathon tumulus, see Staïs 1893. For those from Stadiou Street see Papaspyridi and Kyprassi 1927–1928. See also Kurtz 1975, p. 147–8.

29 Kurtz 1975, pp. 148, 150–155. For the problems of distinguishing between the pattern lekythoi produced in the Haimon and Beldam workshops, see Kurtz 1975, pp. 152–3. On the relationship between painters in the Haimon workshop and the Diosphos workshop, see Jubier-Galinier 2003. For a recent discussion of the Haimon Group, see *CVA* Netherlands 8, pp. 43–44.

30 See Kurtz 1975, p.87.

31 Vienna, Kunsthistorisches Museum 5247 *ABL* pl. 48.4a–4b, Athens, National Museum 1062 *ABL* pl. 48 3, Athens, National Museum 609 *ABL* pl. 48.5. See *ABL,* p. 165 for a description of the chimney lekythoi made in the Emporion painter's workshop.

32 Athens, National Museum 491 *ABL* pl. 53.4, Athens, National Museum 599 *ABL* pl. 53.5a–5b, Athens, National Museum 610 *ABL* pl. 53.6. See *ABL,* p. 138 for the developments of the Beldam painter.

33 Kurtz 1975, p. 87. See also *ABL* p. 138 where she identifies the Pholos Group's chimney lekythoi as a later phase of the Haimon painter.

34 For the workshops that produced pattern lekythoi, see Kurtz 1975, pp. 143–155. See also *CVA* Netherlands 8, pp. 54–55.

35 The ivy-berry motif is much more common on secondary shape pattern lekythoi with calyx mouths. I was not able to find an example with a chimney mouth.

36 Kurtz 1975, p. 131.

37 *Kerameikos* VII.2, pp. 130–131, pl. 88(4.8).

38 Kurtz 1975, pp. 84–87; *ARV* 675.

39 For a calyx mouth, see *ABL,* pl. 50.3. For a chimney mouth, see *ABL,* pl.53.4–6.

40 For the Class of Athens 581 ii see *ABV* 491, 499 and *Para* 232; for the Haimon Painter see *ABV* 548.

41 Cf. W.D.J. van de Put's recent attributions to the Class of Athens 581 ii, see *CVA* Netherlands 8, pp. 29–31, 55. For recent attributions to the Haimon Painter and his Group, see *CVA* Netherlands 8, pp. 44–45, 47–49.

42 See Shear 1993, pp. 408–409.

43 Ibid, pp. 395, 413–415.

44 Papadopoulos 2003, p. 297.

45 Ibid, p. 280–297.

46 For some of the ramifications of the down-dating of the chronology of Attic vase-painting in the late Archaic period, see Neer 2002, pp. 185–205. See also Lynch 2009, pp. 69–76 for a brief introduction to some of the issues at stake in dating the material in the Persian destruction wells at the Agora.

47 The lekythos with Herakles and the Nemean lion could have been made as early as 490 BC given its affinities to work attributed to the Class of Athens 581 ii Painter.

48 Small black-figured lekythoi continued to be produced between 460 and 400. Their chronology has yet to receive a precise treatment. Both Donna Kurtz in 1975 and W.D.J. van de Put in 2006 state that later pattern lekythoi are often attributed to the Beldam workshop when they probably should not be, see Kurtz 1975, p. 153; *CVA* Netherlands 8, p. 55.

49 Rotroff 2013, pp. 68–70 provides a recent overview of the evidence from the Kerameikos as well as references to parallels from elsewhere in Attica. Houby-Nielsen 1996 also provides a helpful synthesis of the material from Kerameikos. She adds that although these features are mostly found in Attica, there are some instances in Thera, see Pfuhl 1903.

50 For the sake of clarity I have adopted Rotroff's term, "graveside pyre", because it refers to all types of pyres near graves rather than a single one, see Rotroff 2013.

51 Ibid, p. 68–69; *Kerameikos* VII.1, pp. 187–188.

52 Ibid, p. 70 and Appendix III, nos. 1–15, 17, 20–28, 30, 31, 34–35, 40–42.

53 Ibid, p. 69.

54 For a slightly later parallel from the late 5th century BC, see Rotroff 2013, p. 196 no. 19.

55 For example see the following graves in *Kerameikos* VII.1: shaft grave 1 and offering place α, shaft grave 4 and offering place β and shaft grave 242 and offering place γ.

56 See shaft grave 613 from ca. 550 with offering place ε *Kerameikos* VII.1, p. 169. For the grave goods and the date see *Kerameikos* VII.3, pp. 149–150. For an exception to this tendency see graves 465 and grave 466 which do not align with offering trench δ. *Kerameikos* VII.1, pp. 138–9.

57 The pyre was found at a depth of 0.50 m and the pit was found at a depth of 0.58 m. See Mastrokostas 1972, 308 and 298. A section drawing done by A. Papaspyropoulou on p. 307 shows the statues above the pyre but the dimensions provided in the text clearly contradict the drawing.

58 Staïs 1893, pp. 53–55.

59 Ibid, figure on p. 49. Pyre E was disturbed and its precise dimensions could not be determined. The dimensions for pyre Γ are not provided and the scale on the sketch of the tumulus is not very precise. Judging from the drawing on p. 49, pyre Γ was almost 10 m long and about 1 m wide.

60 Mastrokostas 1972, p. 308.

61 In chronological order: Knigge 1966, p. 26 no. 40 (490/80 BC); Parlama and Stampolidis 2000, pp. 271, 338–343 (included terracottas from ca. 450 BC, pottery is unpublished); Knigge 1966, p. 36 no. 66 (ca. 440 BC); Rotroff 2013, p. 198 no. 32 (430–420 BC); Rotroff 2013, p. 198 no. 33 (430–420 BC); Knigge 1996, p. 44 no. 89 (420/10 BC?); Rotroff 2013, p. 196 no. 19 (late 5th century BC); Knigge 1966, pp. 47–48 no. 94 (end of the 5th century BC). The ones that have been associated with graves include: Knigge 1966, nos. 89, 94 and Rotroff 2013, no. 19.

62 The offering ditch found during the excavations for Kerameikos metro stop also had a group of terracotta figurines (mostly females) that showed traces of fire, see Parlama and Stampolidis 2000, pp. 338–343. The offering ditch found in Hügel K and possibly associated with Grave 242 did not include any pottery or offerings, only ash and burned small animal bones.

63 Rotroff 2013, p. 198 no. 32 was 5.00 × 0.80 m; Rotroff 2013, p. 198 no. 33 was 2.50 × 1.80 m; the offering ditch excavated in the Kerameikos metro stop excavations was 2.5 m long.

64 Mastrokostas 1972, pp. 308–9 suggests that the three features are related but he does not clarify the chronological relationships.

65 Cf. Vivliodetis 2007, p. 189 who references the debate in his article on the history of Myrrhinous.

66 Svenbro 1993, pp. 12–13 argues that these statues marked graves of the Alkmaionid family and that they were buried during the Peisistratid tyranny between ca. 546 and ca. 510 BC. More recently, Brinkmann, Koch-Brinkmann, and Piening 2010, pp. 189–191 have argued that the statues marked the graves of the Peisistratid family and that they were buried at the end of the tyranny in ca. 510 BC.

67 Kaltsas advocates this hypothesis in a recent article that discusses both statues from Myrrhinous, see Kaltsas 2002b, p. 7 and n. 2.

68 Mastrokostas 1972, pp. 314 argued that they were buried as a preventive measure. Svenbro 1993, pp. 12–13 disagreed, arguing that they were buried after they had sustained damages. See also Keesling 1999, p. 513 who points out the differences between how the kouros and the kore of Phraskleia have been treated.

69 ἥκειν τὸν βάρβαρον ἐς τὴν Ἀττικὴν καὶ πᾶσαν αὐτὴν πυρπολέεσθαι, translated by A.D. Godley. See also Shear 1993, pp. 415–417 for Herodotos' and Thucydides' accounts of the Persian invasion.

70 For the road from Athens to Steiria within the system of roads through the Mesogeia and Laureotic regions see Kakavogiannis in Korres 2009, pp. 182–197. For the evidence of the coastal deme's location see Traill 1986, p. 129. The road from Athens to the coastal deme is mentioned in [Pl.] *Hipparch.* 228ab.

71 For a recent review of the evidence of Persian destruction in Attica, see Miles 2014, pp. 123–26. I am grateful to Margie for letting me see a copy of this article before its final publication.

72 For the different deposits on the Akropolis and their relation to the *Perserschutt* see Lindenlauf 1997, Stewart 2008a. For discussions of the archaic korai from the northern side of the citadel see Karakasi 2001, pp. 130–131; Keesling 2003b, pp. 49–50. For the deposits at Sounion see Staïs 1914, p. 89; Papathanosopoulos 1983, pp. 40–43; Ridgway 1993, pp. 69–70; Goette 2000, pp. 19–20.

73 Karouzos 1961.

74 Holloway 2000, pp. 80–81.

75 Other statues that may have been buried based on their good state of preservation include the Volomandra kouros (EAM 1906) and the Anavyssos kouros (EAM 3851). Precise records of their excavation were not kept, however, and so it is impossible to determine whether there was either a pyre or grave goods around them. For the circumstances of discovery of the Volomandra kouros see Kavvadias 1902. For a comprehensive discussion of the events around the Anavyssos kouros' discovery in the 1930s see Neer 2010, pp. 24–28.

76 For the Berlin kore see Richter 1968, pp. 39–40 no. 42.

77 Another example of a statue that received special attention is an archaic bronze head that was set into a rectangular stone found near Herodou Attiki during the course of digging for the Athens metro. The head, dated stylistically to ca. 480 BC, was found in the fill of a Roman building complex. See Parlama and Stampolidis 2000, no. 181 pp. 198–203. Thanks are due to Julia Shear for bringing this example to my attention. Cf. Houser 1985 who raises the question of who was responsible for decapitating bronze heads.

78 Vernant 1983, pp. 305–20; Vernant 1990, pp. 17–82 and Vernant 1991, pp. 151–192. Many scholars have responded to Vernant's ideas: for example see Steiner 2001, pp. 3–78; Neer 2010, pp. 14–19.

79 Vernant 2006.

80 For example Aeschylus' *Agamemnon,* Euripides' *Alcestis,* and Euripides' *Protesilaus,* see Vernant 2006, pp. 326–327.

81 Ibid, pp. 323–324.

82 For a more recent interpretation of the upright markers and further bibliography, see Gaifman 2012, pp. 197–206.

83 See Steiner 2001, pp. 258–259.

84 Vernant 2006, p. 325.

References

ABL = Haspels, C. H. E. 1936. *Attic Black-Figured Lekythoi,* Paris.

ABV = Beazley, J. D. 1956. *Attic Black-Figure Vase-Painters,* Oxford.

ARV² = Beazley, J. D. 1963. *Attic Red-Figure Vase Painters, second edition,* Oxford.

Austin, R. P. 1938. *The Stoichedon Style in Greek Inscriptions,* London.

Boardman, J. 1978. *Greek Sculpture: the Archaic Period,* London and New York.

Brinkmann, V., U. Koch-Brinkmann and H. Piening. 2010. "The Funerary Monument to Phrasikleia," in *Circumlitio. The Polychromy of Antique and Mediaeval Sculpture,* edited by V. Brinkmann, O. Primaversi and M. Hollein, Munich, pp. 189–217.

Burn, A. R. 1984. *Persia and the Greeks. The Defense of the West, c. 546–478 BC,* Second edition with a postscript by D.M. Lewis, Stanford.

Catling, H. 1972–3. "Archaeology in Greece," *Archaeological Reports,* pp. 3–32.

Clairmont, C. W. 1974. "Gravestone and Epigram," *Archäologischer Anzeiger,* pp. 219–238.

CVA = *Corpus vasorum antiquorum* (Paris 1923–).

Daux, G. 1962. "Chronique des Fouilles et Découvertes Archéologiques en Grèce en 1961," *Bulletin de correspondance hellénique* 86, 629–975.

Daux, G. 1973. "Les Ambiguïtés du Grec Κορὴ," *Comptes rendus des séances de l'Académie des inscriptions et belles-lettres (Paris),* pp. 382–393.

D'Onofrio, A. M. 1982. "Korai e Kouroi Funerari Attici," *Annali del Seminario di Studi del Mondo Classico,* pp. 135–168.

D'Onofrio, A. M. 1985. "Kouroi e Stele: Iconografica e Ideologia del Monumento Funerario Arcaico in Attica," *Annali dell'Istituto Universitario Orientali di Napoli* 8, pp. 175–193.

D'Onofrio, A. M. 1988. "Aspetti e Problemi del Monumento Funerario Attico Archaico," *Annali dell'Istituto Universitario Orientali di Napoli* 10, pp. 83–96.

Eliot, M. and C. W. J. 1968. "The Lechaion Cemetery near Corinth," *American Journal of Archaeology* 37, pp. 345–367.

Gaifman, M. 2012. *Aniconism in Greek Antiquity,* Oxford.

Goette, H. R. 2000. *Ο Αξιόλογος Δήμος Σούνιον: landeskundliche Studien in Sudost-Attika,* Rahden/Westfalen.

Godley, A. D, trans. 1960–1963. *Herodotus,* Cambridge, Mass.

Floren, J. 1987. *Die Griechische Plastik I,* Munich.

Frel, J. 1973. "The Sculptor of the Kouros from Myrrhinous," 6: 367–369.

Frel, J. 1982. "Ancient Repairs of Archaic Sculpture." *Athens Annals of Archaeology* 15, pp. 202–214.

Frel, J. 1984. "Ancient Repairs to Classical Sculptures at Malibu," *Getty Museum Journal* 12, pp. 73–92.

Harrison, E. B. 1990. "Repair, Reuse, and Reworking of Ancient Greek Sculpture," in *Marble. Art Historical and Scientific Perspectives on Ancient Sculpture. Papers of the Symposium Malibu April 28–30, 1988,* Malibu, pp. 163–184.

Houby-Nielsen, S. 1996. "The Archaeology of Ideology in the Kerameikos: New Interpretations of the 'Opferrinnen'," in *The Role of Religion in the Early Greek Polis: Proceedings of the Third International Seminar on Ancient Greek Cult, organized by the Swedish Institute at Athens, 16–18 October 1992,* ed. R. Hägg, Stockholm, pp. 41–54.

Holloway, R. 2000. "The Mutilation of Statuary in Classical Greece," in *Miscellanea Mediterranea,* ed. R, Holloway, Providence, pp. 77–82.

Houser, C. 1985. "Slain Statues: Classical Murder Mysteries," Πρακτικά του XII διεθνούς συνεδρίου κλασικής αρχαιολογίας III, Athens, pp. 112–115.

Hurwit, J. M. 1989. "The Kritios Boy. Discovery, Reconstruction, and Date," *American Journal of Archaeology* 93, pp. 41–80.

Immerwahr, H. B. 1990. *Attic Script: A Survey.* Oxford and New York.

Jeffery, L. H. 1962. "The Inscribed Gravestones of Archaic Attica," *Annual of the British School at Athens* 57, pp. 115–153.

Jeffery, L. H. 1990. *The Local Scripts of Archaic Greece: a Study of the Origin of the Greek Alphabet and its Development from the Eighth to the Fifth Centuries B.C.,* Rev. ed. with a supplement by A. W. Johnston, Oxford.

Jubier-Galinier, C. 2003. "L'atelier des Peintres de Diosphos et de Haimon." *Le Vase Grec et ses Destins.* Ed. P. Rouillard and A. Verbanck-Piérard, Munich.

Kaltsas, N. 2002a. *Sculpture in the National Archaeological Museum, Athens,* translated by D. Hardy, Malibu.

Kaltsas, N. 2002b. "Die Kore und der Kouros aus Myrrhinous," *Antike Plastik* 28, pp. 7–39.

Karakasi E. 1997. " Die prachtvolle Erscheinung der Phrasikleia. Zur Polychromie der Korenstatue. Ein Rekonstruktionsversuch," *Antike Welt* 28, pp. 509–517.

Karakasi, K. 2001. *Archaische Koren*, Munich.

Karouzos, C. 1961. *Aristodikos. Zur Geschichte der spätarchaisch-attischen Plastik und der Grabstatue*, Stuttgart.

Kavvadias, P. 1902. "Ἀρχαικόν Ἄγαλμα ἐξ Ἀττικῆς," *Archaiologike Ephemeris*, pp. 43–50.

Keesling, C. M. 1999. "Endoios' Painting from the Themistoklean Wall: a Reconstruction," *Hesperia* 68.4, pp. 509–548.

Keesling, C. M. 2003a. "Rereading the Acropolis Dedications," in *Lettered Attica. A Day of Attic Epigraphy (Publications of the Canadian Archaeological Institute no. 3)*, ed. D. Jordan and J. Traill, Toronto, pp. 41–54.

Keesling, C. M. 2003b. *The Votive Statues of the Athenian Akropolis*, Cambridge.

Kerameikos = Kerameikos: Ergebnisse der Ausgrabungen.

Kissas, K. 2000. *Die attischen Statuen-und Stelenbasen archaischer Zeit*, Bonn.

Knigge, U. 1966. "Eridanos-Nekroploe", *AM* 81, pp. 1–135.

Kontoleon, N. 1970. *Aspects de la Grèce préclassique*, Paris.

Kontoleon, N. 1974. "Περί το σῆμα τῆς Φρασίκλειας," *Archaiologike Ephemeris*, pp. 1–12.

Korres, M. 2009. Ἀττικῆς Ὁδοί: Ἀρχαίοι Δρόμοι της Ἀττικῆς, Athens.

Kostoglou-Despoini, A. 1979. "Προβλήματα τῆς Παριανης πλαστικης τού 5ου αιονα π.Χ." (diss., Aristotelion Panepistimion Thessalonikes).

Kurtz, D. C. and J. Boardman. 1971. *Greek Burial Customs*, Ithaca, NY.

Kurtz, D. C. 1975. *Athenian White Lekythoi: Patterns and Painters*, Oxford.

Lindenlauf, A. 1997. "Der Perserschutt der Athener Akropolis," in *Kult und Kultbauten auf der Akropolis, Symposium Berlin 1995,* ed. W. Hoepfner, Berlin, pp. 46–115.

Lynch, K. M. 2009. "The Persian Destruction Deposits and the Development of Pottery Research at the Agora Excavations," in *The Athenian Agora: New Perspectives on an Ancient Site,* ed. J. McK. Camp II and C. A. Mauzy, Princeton, pp. 69–76.

Mannack, T. 2006. *Haspels Addenda: Additional References to C.H.E. Haspels, Attic Black-Figured Lekythoi*, Oxford.

Martini, W. 2008. "Zu den Epigrammen von Kroisos aus Anavyssos und Phrasikleia aus Merenda," in *Le Due Patrie Acquisite. Studi di Archeologia Dedicati a Walter Trillmich*, ed. E. La Rocca, P. Léon, and C. Parisi Presicce, Rome, pp. 268–276.

Mastrokostas, E. 1972. "Ἡ Κόρη Φρασίκλεια Ἀριστίωνος τοῦ Παρίου καὶ Κοῦρος μαρμάρινος ἀνεκαλύφθησαν ἐν Μυρρινοῦντι," *Athens Annals of Archaeology,* pp. 298–314.

MEP = Merenda.

Miles, M. M. 2014. "Burnt Temples in the Landscape of the Past," in C. Pieper and J. Kers, eds., *Valuing the Past in the Greco-Roman World*, Leiden, pp. 111–145.

Neer, R.T. 2002. *Style and Politics in Athenian Vase-Painting: the Craft of Democracy ca. 530–460 BC*, Cambridge and New York.

Neer, R. T. 2010. *The Emergence of the Classical Style in Greek Sculpture*, Chicago.

Palagia, O., ed. 2006. *Greek Sculpture: Function, Materials, and Techniques in the Archaic and Classical Periods*, Cambridge and New York.

Papadopoulos, J. K. 2003. *Ceramicus Redivivus: The Early Iron Age Potters' Field in the Area of the Classical Athenian Agora. Hesperia, Supplement 31*, Princeton.

Papaspyridi, S. and N. Kyprassi. 1927–1928. "Νέα Λήκυθος τοῦ Δούριδος," *Archaiologikon Deltion* 11, pp. 91–110.

Papathanasopoulos, G. 1983. *"Σούνιον Ιρόν": Συμβολή στην Εξέταση των Κούρων του Ιερού και στη Διεύρυνση του Προβλήματος της Παλαιότερης Υπαίθριας Λατρείας στο Σούνιο*, Athens.

Para = Beazley, J. D. 1971. *Paralipomena*, Oxford.

Parlama, L. and N. Stampolidis. 2000. *The City Beneath the City: Antiquities from the Metropolitan Railway Excavations*, Athens.

Pedley, J. G. 1976. *Greek Sculpture of the Archaic Period: the Island Workshops*, Mainz.

Pfuhl, E. 1903. "Der archaische Friedhof am Stadtberge von Thera," *Mitteilungen des Deutschen Archäologischen Instituts, Athenische Abteilung* 28, pp. 1–288.

Platt, V. 2011. *Facing the Gods: Epiphany and Representation in Graeco-Roman Art, Literature and Religion,* Cambridge.

Ridgway, B. 1993. *The Archaic Style in Greek Sculpture*, Chicago.

Richter, G. M. A. 1968. *Korai: Archaic Greek Maidens. A Study of the Development of the Kore Type in Greek Sculpture*, New York.

Richter, G. M. A. and M. J. Milne. 1935. *Shapes and Names of Athenian Vases*, New York.

Rolley, C. 1994. *La Sculpture Grecque: Des origins au milieu du Ve siècle,* Paris..

Rotroff, S. I. 2013. *Industrial Religion: the Saucer Pyres of the Athenian Agora, Hesperia, Supplement 47*, Princeton.

Schlörb-Vierneisel, B. 1966. "Eridanos-Nekropole, 1. Gräber und Opferstellen," *Mitteilungen des Deutschen Archäologischen Instituts, Athenische Abteilung* 81, pp. 4–111.

Shear, T. L., Jr. 1993. "The Persian Destruction of Athens: Evidence from Agora Deposits," *Hesperia* 62.4, pp. 383–482.

Sparkes, B. and L. Talcott. 1970. *The Athenian Agora*, XII. *Black and Plain Pottery of the 6th, 5th, and 4th centuries B.C.*, Princeton.

Staïs, B. 1893. "Ο ἐν Μαραθῶνι τύμβος." *Mitteilungen des Deutschen Archäologischen Instituts, Athenische Abteilung* 18, pp. 46–63.

Steiner, D. T. 2001. *Images in Mind: Statues in Archaic and Classical Greek Literature and Thought*, Princeton.

Stewart, A. F. 1977. "Aristion" *Athens Annals of Archaeology* 9, pp. 257–266.

Stewart, A. F. 2008a. "The Persian Invasions of Greece and the Beginning of the Classical Style: Part 1, The Stratigraphy, Chronology, and Significance of the Acropolis Deposits," *American Journal of Archaeology* 112, pp. 377–412.

Stewart, A. F. 2008b. "The Persian and Carthaginian Invasions of 480 B.C.E. and the Beginning of the Classical Style, Part 2, The Finds from Athens, Attic and Elsewhere in Greece, and on Sicily, Part 3, The Severe Style: Motivations and Meaning," *American Journal of Archaeology* 112, pp. 581–615.

Stieber, M. 1996. "Phrasikleia's Lotuses," *Boreas* 19, pp. 69–99.

Stieber, M. 2004. *The Poetics of Appearance in the Attic Korai*, Austin.

Svenbro, J. 1993. *Phrasikleia: an Anthropology of Reading in Ancient Greece*, translated by J. Lloyd, Ithaca, NY.

Traill, J. S. 1986. *Demos and Trittys: Epigraphical and Topographical Studies in the Organization of Attica*, Toronto.

Valavanis, P., ed. 2007. *Great Moments in Greek Archaeology*, translated by D. Hardy, Los Angeles.

Vasilopoulou, V. and Katsarou-Tzeleveki, S. eds. 2009. *Από τα Μεσόγεια στον Αργοσαρωνικό: Β' Εφορεία Προϊστορικών και Κλασικών Αρχαιοτήτων. Το έργο μιας δεκαετίας, 1994–2003. Πρακτικά συνεδρίου Αθήνα, 18–20 Δεκεμβρίου 2003*, Markopoulo.

Vernant, J. P. 1983. *Myth and Thought among the Greeks*, Boston.

Vernant, J. P. 1990. *Figures, Idoles, Masques*, Paris.

Vernant, J. P. 1991. *Mortals and Immortals: Collected Essays*, translated by F. Zeitlin, Princeton.

Vernant, J. P. 2006. *Myth and Thought among the Greeks*, translated by J. Lloyd with J. Fort. Brooklyn.

Vivliodetis, E. 2007. "*Ο Δήμος του Μυρρινούντος : η Οργάνωση και η Ιστορία του*," *Archaiologike Ephemeris* 144, pp. 9–235.

Vivliodetis, E. 2008. "Η Κεραμική από το Νεκροταφείο του Δήμου Μυρρινούντος," *Archaiologike Ephemeris* 146, pp. 79–129.

Roadside Assistance: Religious Spaces and Personal Experience in Athens

Johanna Best

The elusive phenomenon of personal or day-to-day religious experience may be accessed through the study of roadside religious spaces. This paper presents three examples of roadside religious sites in Athens: the Shrine of Nymphe, the naiskos at Poulopoulou 29, and the Altar of Zeus Herkeios, Hermes, and Akamas. The archaeological evidence, in combination with the literary and epigraphical sources, provides a more complete picture of Athenian religious topography and allows exploration of both incidental and organized worship outside major sanctuaries.

Roadside Religious Sites

Travel could be difficult and full of danger in antiquity, whether within or outside urban centers, and every crossroads presented the possibility of a wrong turn, both literally and metaphorically. While attending to business, getting water, socializing, or performing political activities, individuals used roads throughout their daily lives and interacted with roadside religious spaces for both incidental and organized worship. Roads are primarily associated with the divinities Hermes, Hekate, and Apollo Ἀγυιεύς (*Agyieus*), and religious spaces along roads flourished throughout both urban and rural areas of Attica.[1]

Multiple levels of religious participation (by individuals, by small groups, or by large groups as part of public festivals) are made evident in the archaeological remains of roadside religious sites in three main ways: the spaces available for the performance of rituals, the kinds of offerings that were dedicated, and the level of accessibility and visibility of the site from the road.[2] This framework provides the background, and the literary and epigraphical evidence, when available, combine to create a more complete picture of the elusive phenomena of day-to-day religious experience outside major sanctuaries.

The archaeological evidence from more than 20 roadside religious sites in Athens and the Kerameikos (Figure 10.1)

and an additional 24 sites in Attica provide the background for three Athenian examples, selected to show the variety of forms of roadside religious spaces found in urban areas. These examples, in combination with the literary and epigraphical evidence, present a tantalizing picture of the ubiquity and importance of such spaces.

Shrine of Nymphe: Worship by Hopeful Brides

The Shrine of Nymphe is located on the lower south slope of the Athenian Acropolis (Figure 10.1.1).[3] This shrine was part of a residential community that stretched along a north-south road, which led from the South Gate, through the area where the Odeion of Herodes Atticus was later built, and along a series of steps toward the bastion of the Temple of Athena Nike.[4] Archaic houses have been excavated to the northwest of the shrine, and Classical houses and a water channel were discovered immediately next to the shrine (Figure 10.2).[5] In the beginning of the Hellenistic period, the house of the shrine was torn down and the space became a *plateia*, which would have served the needs of the surrounding residential district.[6]

In the Archaic period, the shrine appears to have been an unwalled, open-air precinct containing an altar made of polygonal blocks. Finds dated to the Archaic period have

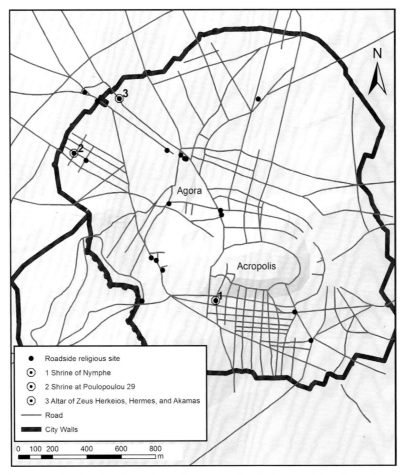

Figure 10.1 Plan of Athenian roads, the Themistoclean city walls, and the diateichisma with locations of roadside religious sites. Map J. Best, after Ficuciello 2008, map 1 and Theocharaki 2011, fig. 1

been found outside the (later) peribolos walls in layers approximately 2 m thick. These deposits may correspond to the refurbishment of the shrine in the Classical period.

In the second phase of the shrine, a peribolos wall made of limestone and mudbrick was constructed in an oval shape (est. 12.5 × 10.5 m). Entrances to the enclosure were located on the southern and western sides, with the western entranceway opening directly onto the road.[7] While the space did remain primarily open to the sky, an apsidal structure was built around the altar. Pottery deposits, found in layers approximately 1 m deep within the peribolos wall, date to the fifth century BC and later.[8] The shrine continued to be used until the second or first century BC, when it may have lost importance gradually or may have been destroyed during the sack of Sulla.[9] The destruction of the shrine was complete when the mudbrick superstructure of the temenos wall collapsed and, later, when a Roman-period house was constructed upon the remains of the shrine.

Finds in the enclosure included pottery, bases for stelai, masks and figurines, and a dedication to Zeus Meilichios.[10] The site produced thousands of potsherds from a variety of

black- and red- figure vessels, including *aryballoi, skyphoi, kotyles,* and *lekythoi,* but the great majority of pottery fragments comes from *loutrophoroi.*[11] Some loutrophoroi from this shrine depict scenes that may be associated with weddings, such as nuptial processions of men and women and the Judgment of Paris.[12] Loutrophoroi handles with the graffiti IEPA NYMΦHΣ, found at the site, and a horos of the fifth century BC (*IG* I[3] 1064, Figure 10.3), discovered to the north of the peribolos in a later wall, indicate that the shrine was sacred to Nymphe, meaning "maiden" or "bride."

Doorways on at least the western and southern sides of the shrine would have provided entranceways to access the interior, and the large number of dedications confirms that it was a space used frequently for offerings. The exterior of the shrine would have been highly visible from the nearby road, though the height of the walls (H. min. 1.1 m) would have likely made it difficult to see into the interior.

The archaeological evidence indicates that the Shrine of Nymphe was located within a residential district and that it was a site for the dedication of vessels associated with marriage ceremonies for at least six centuries. The position

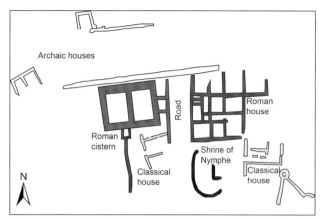

Figure 10.2 Plan of the Shrine of Nymphe and surrounding area. Drawing J. Best, after Brouskari 2002, fig. 27 and Greco 2010, fig. 107

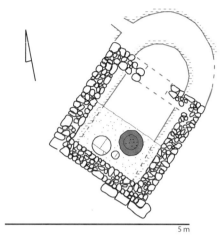

Figure 10.4 Plan of the naiskos at Poulopoulou 29. Drawing J. Best, after Karagiorga-Stathakopoulou 1978, fig. 2, Third Ephorate of Prehistoric and Classical Antiquities © Hellenic Ministry of Culture and Sports / Archaeological Receipts Fund

Figure 10.3 Boundary stone from the Shrine of Nymphe (IG I³ 1064). Photo Archives of the Acropolis Museum, Athens, First Ephorate of Prehistoric and Classical Antiquities © Hellenic Ministry of Culture and Sports / Archaeological Receipts Fund

used for prenuptial ritual bathing. She argues that this undiscovered, early water source close to the shrine dried up and forced women to collect water for their nuptial rituals at fountains near the Ilissos River.[13] The presence of nearby water sources, the Klepsydra and a spring close to the Sanctuary of Asklepios, may have brought women from the settlement areas surrounding the shrine frequently into contact with the highly visible boundary walls.[14] The dedications of loutrophoroi at this site confirm that it was associated with festivities linked with weddings, and the size of the enclosure could accommodate a group.[15] Such a site would have served the interests of the *polis* (through the celebration of the creation of citizen children through marriage), but also could address the family and personal concerns of residents of the surrounding community.

A Naiskos at Poulopoulou 29: Crossed by the Persians?

An Archaic naiskos now at Poulopoulou 29 was excavated west of the Agora at the junction of two ancient roads: one leading towards the Peiraic Gate and a second running northeast-southwest roughly parallel to the later Themistoclean city wall (Figure 10.1.2).[16] This area of Athens, likely called the Heptachalkon in antiquity, is best known today for the small Temple of Artemis Aristoboule, famously dedicated by Themistocles and found by excavators in the 1960s at Herakleion 1.[17] While the area primarily has yielded remains dating to the Hellenistic period, earlier buildings, including the sanctuary dedicated to Artemis Aristoboule and another shrine at Vasilis 18–20, follow the orientation of the Hellenistic street plan and suggest that Archaic and Classical streets took similar routes.[18]

of the site – on a main street to the Acropolis and as part of an extensively inhabited neighborhood – creates the possibility that the religious site could have been accessible to a variety of participants.

M. Brouskari writes that the Shrine of Nymphe may have been placed specifically to allow easy access to an Archaic spring, the water from which would have been

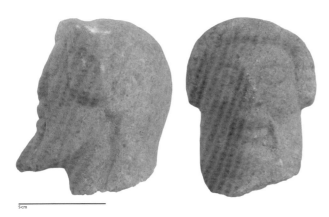

Figure 10.5 The herm head from the shrine at Poulopoulou 29. Photo J. Best

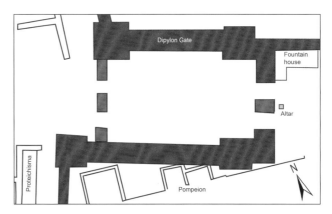

Figure 10.6 Plan of the Dipylon Gate and the Altar of Zeus Herkeios, Hermes, and Akamas. Drawing J. Best, after Knigge 1991, fig. 62

Figure 10.7 Altar of Zeus Herkeios, Hermes, and Akamas. Photo J. Best

Figure 10.8 Detail of the Altar of Zeus Herkeios, Hermes, and Akamas (IG II² 4983). Photo J. Best

From the analysis of the figurines and pottery found at the site, the excavators date the naiskos to the end of the sixth century or the beginning of the fifth century BC.[19] The 3.2 × 3 m naiskos (Figure 10.4) was constructed on top of a deposit of rubble and refuse from a terracotta workshop, including fragments of figurines, moulds, pottery, pigments, and other debris. The naiskos had a limestone- and clay- socle (W. est. 0.4 m) that probably supported a mudbrick superstructure. The floor of the cella was made of compressed clay. As a simple one-room naiskos with an entrance toward the northeast, the form of the building is quite similar to that of the Archaic shrine at the site of the fourth century BC

lesche near the Pnyx and the roadside shrine to the south of the Sanctuary of Dionysos.[20]

Opposite the entrance and in situ on the floor of the shrine, the excavators discovered two circular slabs (slab 1: polished stone, diam. 50 cm; slab 2: terracotta, diam. 20 cm) and the cut-off base of an amphora that was set upright in a layer of small stones and clay.[21] Offerings found under the smaller clay disk included a skyphos and a lekythos, a lamp, and an amphora containing the bones of small animals.[22] Other offerings, including an enthroned female figurine, animal figurines, black-figure vases, and loom weights, were found in the corners of the building and on either side of the entrance.

A sculpted head from a herm (H. 6.5 cm), made of white island marble and partly broken, was found lying on its right side over a pit containing material from the early fifth century BC (Figure 10.5).[23] The sculpture dates to about 500 BC and appears unfinished; the head is broken at the neck and the surfaces show signs of burning. F. Paxugianni-Kaloudi argues that the small herm, along with the seated female figurine, served as the focal points of the naiskos.[24] Because of the small size of the herm head, Paxugianni-Kaloudi further suggests that the head is part of a *hermidion*, a miniature image of Hermes mentioned in literary sources that served a similar function as the traditional, larger herm.[25]

The naiskos and its contents appear to have been consumed by fire, likely during the Persian destruction of Athens, a hypothesis supported by the deposit of ash, charcoal, and broken finds both inside and in front of the building.[26] The evidence from this shrine further supports the claims of Herodotus – and bolsters the archaeological evidence from the city – that the walls, the houses, and the temples of Athens were burned during the Persian sack (9.13.2).[27]

The naiskos at Poulopoulou 29 is situated within the Athenian road network at a location that – in later periods – provided access to both the inner and outer ring roads of the city. The finds excavated opposite the doorway suggest that votive practice on a small scale was taking place within the building when the site was burned. The naiskos, measuring approximately 2.8 × 2.6 m internally, could not have accommodated groups, but the presence of an outdoor courtyard remains a possibility as a gathering place. The visibility of the shrine would have been affected by the presence or lack of temenos walls, which are not indicated in the preliminary publication.

Paxugianni-Kaloudi suggests that the naiskos at Poulopoulou 29 accommodated the worship of a deity that might be especially important to an association of craftsmen, such as Athena Ergane or Hermes.[28] In other areas of Greece, and in later periods, such professional guilds that sponsored religious monuments and rituals are attested.[29] Here, however, there is no specific evidence (such as an inscription) that would allow us to make such a link. Alternatively, L. Ficuciello posits that this structure may be the *heroon* of Chalkodon, mentioned in Plutarch's *Life of Theseus* 27.3, which recounts that the Athenians fought the Amazons along the street that led to a gate by the shrine of Chalkodon.[30] This hero was from the family of Erechtheus and was associated especially with the protection of gates.[31] While these suggestions are plausible, without further evidence and publication of the finds, the site could just as easily be linked with any local hero or divinity that was particularly revered at this location.

At the Outer Edge of the City: Altar of Zeus Herkeios, Hermes, and Akamas

Just inside the Dipylon Gate on the Panathenaic Way, the Altar of Zeus Herkeios, Hermes, and Akamas reminded travelers that they were crossing an important boundary of

the city at its most famous gateway (Figure 10.1.3). Located physically in the road (Figure 10.6), the altar could be approached easily by those entering or leaving the city along the highly traveled route of the Panathenaic Way. The marble altar is circular, measuring approximately 1 m in diameter (Figure 10.7), and sits upon two rectangular curbstones, which likely helped to keep wheeled traffic at bay. The use of curbstones was not entirely effective, as both the stones and the altar itself show signs of wear from wheels.[32]

An inscription naming Zeus Herkeios, Hermes, and Akamas (*IG* II² 4983) is carved on its southeastern side (Figure 10.8).[33] While the square curbstones are dated to the second quarter of the fifth century BC or later because of their position on the Themistoclean street level, the letter-forms of the inscription may date the altar to the Hellenistic period.[34]

The deities and hero invoked on the altar are especially appropriate for this particular border of the city. Zeus Herkeios was the god of the fence or the peribolos, making the altar's placement before the city walls and the Dipylon Gate especially fitting.[35] Zeus Herkeios was also associated with courtyards, and the form of the Dipylon Gate during the Hellenistic period included a large courtyard on the western side and a smaller one on the eastern side. Hermes had strong links with travel, through his role of messenger and guide. Akamas, a son of Theseus and Phaedra, was the hero of the tribe Akamantis, to which the deme Kerameis belonged.[36]

The placement of the Altar of Zeus Herkeios, Hermes, and Akamas, so close to the Dipylon Gate and literally in the center of the road, made it a site that could not be ignored by passers-by. The altar was integral to the route of the Panathenaia, as the participants in this major public festival would gather at the Dipylon Gate, quite close to the altar. Citizen groups, too, may have identified this monument as particularly important to them, since Akamas was the eponymous hero of the tribe Akamantis. While E. Kearns suggests that demesmen living farther from the city might not have had the same attachment to their eponymous hero as those living close to the urban center, she does acknowledge that members of the same tribe would have felt some affiliation to one another (and to their tribe's eponymous hero) because they performed civic and military duties together.[37] Given its location right at the Dipylon Gate, the altar also must have been used by individuals of any tribe departing the relative safety of the city or by those arriving who might wish to celebrate a journey now complete.

Roadside Religious Spaces: Evidence for Personal Experience

The central Shrine of Nymphe, the naiskos in northwestern Athens, and the altar by the Dipylon Gate illustrate the limitations that are common to the study of the archaeological evidence of roadside religious sites and also offer a glimpse of what might be learned from additional investigation. Some such sites have been excavated and thoroughly published, but many more have only been summarily described and await more extensive publication. Significant work has been accomplished by L. Costaki and L. Ficuciello to understand the Athenian road network, but new excavations are always changing our understanding of its outlines.[38] As the literary evidence corroborates, many roadside religious sites (and the offerings and furnishings within them) were made of perishable materials, so our record is necessarily incomplete.

Such circumstances plague all students of the material culture of Greek religion, yet the archaeological evidence does provide a glimpse of the rich, ongoing religious life outside major sanctuaries. Once we can map their locations, their scope and levels of accessibility, and possibly the range of devotees who used them, roadside shrines provide a new framework for addressing multiple levels of religious participation in Athens. A combination of literary, epigraphical, and archaeological sources gives a more complete and dynamic picture of Athenian religious topography, beyond the major temples on the Acropolis, in the Agora, and out in the demes of Attica. The roadside shrines illustrate the many and varied opportunities for religious practice available to Athenians.

The Attic epigraphical evidence for roadside religious spaces is limited so far to a few boundary stones, lease documents, and some dedications, but the literary testimonia is much more abundant, with over 120 references to religious practices and spaces associated with roads. The literary sources document above all that these sites provided places for individual sacrifice, libation, prayer, and dedication.

While descriptions of sacrifice are brief, and generally sacrificial offerings go unspecified, ancient authors do note the various animals – such as goats, cattle, sheep, and dogs – offered to the gods at roadside shrines. In a fragment of Aristophanes, for example, we learn that dogs were sacrificed to Hekate, because the goddess sometimes looks like one: "Hekate's images, or bitches, for these are sacrificed to her / they say, and she is also portrayed as having a bitch's face."[39] We have a vivid picture of another intended offering in the fourth epigram of Theocritus: the lovelorn speaker is depicted as planning a lavish sacrifice and instructs a goatherd to pray to a roughly crafted image of Priapos at a roadside shrine. If Priapos makes the speaker's love for Daphnis dissipate, the speaker will give the god one sacrificial animal; but, in this bargain, if Priapos causes Daphnis to fall in love with the speaker, then the speaker promises to sacrifice a cow, a goat, and a sheep.

Libation at roadside religious spaces is described in literary accounts and is depicted on vases that show herms receiving liquid offerings. An Athenian black-figure amphora from the sixth century BC, attributed to the Edinburgh Painter, shows a man pouring a libation on a flaming altar.[40] Directly behind the altar stands a herm garlanded with ivy. On the other side of the vessel, a man pours a libation from a *phiale* onto a smoking altar, which again stands before a herm. Similarly, on a fragment of an Athenian red-figure krater of the fifth century BC, there is a depiction of a libation before a herm and altar.[41] Although the image on the fragment does not preserve the head of the herm, his rectangular body with a distinctive erect phallus indicates the presence of the image. From the Hellenistic period, a red figure *olpe* shows a woman pouring a libation on an altar with her right hand.[42] Her left hand is raised, palm down, before the face of a herm.

Among the literary evidence of libation, Theophrastus's *Superstitious Man* responds with characteristic enthusiasm when he falls to his knees in worship and pours a libation at a sacred space at a crossroads: "On passing one of the shining stones, which stand at the crossroads, [the Superstitious Man] pours a libation of oil from his flask and drops to his knees in worship before proceeding."[43] In a fable by Babrius, such libations become even more humorous – a dog passes by a herm and wishes to "anoint" it in his own manner and to lick off the oil already left there by previous worshippers:

> By the roadside stood a square-hewn statue of Hermes, with a heap of stones under it. A dog came up to this and said, "Greetings, Hermes, first of all, but more than that, I wish to anoint you. I could not think of passing by a god like you, especially since you are the athlete's god." "I shall be grateful to you," said Hermes, "if you do not lick off such olive oil as I already have, and do not pee on me. Beyond that, pay me no respect."[44]

Dedications at roadside shrines, like sacrifice, were made according to the needs and resources of the individual at a given moment; offerings such as fish, cakes, and fruit could be given to the gods. Fish are particularly associated with the monthly food offerings (δεῖπνον) that were left for the goddess Hekate at the crossroads.[45] In an especially detailed example from an epigram, a speaker offers "a portion of this great bunch of grapes…for you, Hermes Enodios, and a lump of rich cake from the oven, and a black fig, and soft olives and a bit of a wheel of cheese, and Cretan meal,…and an after-dinner drink of wine."[46] Even stones could be given to the gods of the roads: another epigram suggests that rocks were acceptable, if not prized, offerings to Hermes: "Men who pass by me have heaped up a pile of stones sacred to Hermes, and I, in return for their small kindness, give them no great thanks, but only say that there are seven stadia more to Goat Fountain."[47] The prayers offered at roadside religious spaces that might accompany these offerings reflect a broad range, from the short and casual greetings that a god might expect from a passerby to heartfelt pleas regarding love or stolen goods (e.g., Agora IL 493).

These examples of personal religious practice, what J.

Kindt terms "individual engagement with the supernatural about private concerns," likely served to form a sense of connection with the gods and heroes that were omnipresent in the Attic landscape.[48] Kindt's broad definition of personal religious practice accounts for the possibility that an individual may have felt drawn to different deities at different times because of life circumstances, may have found it spiritually or financially advantageous to engage in religious activities, or may have carried on familial or neighborhood traditions. In such situations, personal religious practice was not meant to override state religious activities, but rather to supplement them.

Students of Greek religion are moving towards a paradigm that recognizes the fluidity, interconnectedness, and variety of Greek religious participation. The evidence from roadside religious sites in Athens offers an opportunity to explore different spheres of engagement with divinities. The study of the material evidence for roadside religious sites in Athens – including their size and location, the kinds of dedications they attracted, and their accessibility – in combination with the evidence from literary sources demonstrates how such informal religious practices flourished. As significant parts of the fabric of urban Greek religion, the ubiquitous shrines along roads served Athenians as individuals.

Notes

1   I would like to acknowledge the help of A. A. Donohue, M. M. Miles, J. Paga, K. Sagstetter, and two anonymous reviewers for commenting on this paper, which was presented in its original form at the 2014 Archaeological Institute of America meeting in Chicago, IL. The paper was given under the title "Roadside Religious Spaces and Personal Religious Experience: Three Athenian Case Studies."

2   Roadside religious spaces were not categorized as such in antiquity. For this study, the religious space must be part of an active road network (i.e., the road upon which the site is located cannot only lead to the site) and must be either physically or visibly accessible from the roadway.

3   The Greek Archaeological Society excavated the Shrine of Nymphe in 1955–1960. See Brouskari 2002, pp. 33–37, 195–196.

4   Ficuciello 2008, p. 92; Korres 2009, p. 84.

5   Greco 2010, p. 202.

6   Wycherley 1978, p. 200.

7   Brouskari 2002, p. 34. The cuttings on the southern threshold indicate that the doors opened inwards.

8   Brouskari 2002, p. 31.

9   Brouskari 2002, p. 190.

10   1957 ΝΑΓ 89. While an offering to Zeus Meilichios at this location may seem to make sense because of Zeus Meilichios's associations with purification, fertility, abundance, and overall wellbeing, G. V. Lalonde notes that the stele was not found in situ and originally may have been dedicated in one of the two known sanctuaries of the god that are nearby. See Lalonde 2006, pp. 40, 63, 107. A fragmentary draped leg of a female

statue, which likely fell into the area from the Acropolis, was also found within the shrine. See Brouskari 2002, pp. 195–196.

11   Greco 2010, p. 200.

12   This and the other finds presented here are discussed in Papadopoulou-Kanellopoulou 1997, pp. 215, 220–221.

13   Brouskari 2002, pp. 36–37. As described by J. Oakley, prenuptial ritual bathing would purify both the bride and groom before the wedding. The bride would fetch her water for the bath in a loutrophoros, a process depicted on Athenian vases showing women processing between the fountain house and the home (Oakley and Sinos 1993, pp. 15–16).

14   Nevett 2013, p. 93.

15   Oakley and Sinos 1993, p. 42.

16   The Greek Archaeological Service excavated the naiskos at Poulopoulou 29 in 1978. For primary publications, see Karagiorga-Stathakopoulou 1978, pp. 10–12 and Paxugianni-Kaloudi 1984, pp. 342–353.

17   Costaki 2006, p. 132. The designation Heptachalkon is known from Plutarch's *Sulla* 14.1–3. The term describes the area of the city between the Peiraic and the Sacred Gates, which Sulla found most easy to attack. For the sanctuary of Artemis Aristoboule at Herakleion 1, see Amandry 1967–1968 and Threpsiades and Vanderpool 1964.

18   Costaki 2006, pp. VII.7, I.1, I.2; Ficuciello 2008, p. 125. For the shrine at Vasilis 18–20, see Spathari 1987.

19   The finds from the naiskos at Poulopoulou 29 are discussed in Karagiorga-Stathakopoulou 1978, pp. 10, 12.

20   For the shrine at the site of the fourth century BC *lesche*, see Costaki 2006, p. 346, Greco 2010, pp. 255–256, Judeich 1931, pp. 290, 299, Lalonde, Langdon and Walbank 1991, H2, Travlos 1971, pp. 275, fig. 202, Wycherley 1970, p. 291, and Wycherley 1978, p. 194. For the shrine to the south of the Sanctuary of Dionysos, see Costaki 2008, p. 158, Ficuciello 2008, pp. 87–88, Greco 2010, p. 166, Kalligas 1965, p. 16, Parlama 1992–1998, pp. 32–33, and Travlos 1971, pp. figs. 202, 678.

21   Karagiorga-Stathakopoulou 1978, p. 12.

22   Karagiorga-Stathakopoulou 1978, p. 12; Paxugianni-Kaloudi 1984, p. 342.

23   Paxugianni-Kaloudi 1984, p. 342.

24   Paxugianni-Kaloudi 1984, p. 349.

25   The term *hermidion*, a diminutive of Hermes, is mentioned in Ar. *Pax,* 924. Paxugianni-Kaloudi argues that hermidia would have been "ithyphallic Hermaic stelai in miniature particularly popular with the lower classes" (1984, p. 352).

26   Karagiorga-Stathakopoulou 1978, p. 12.

27   When the finds from this site are fully published, it will be worthwhile to compare the destruction debris to the material explored by T. L. Shear in his article on the evidence of Persian destruction from the nearby Agora. See Shear 1993.

28   Paxugianni-Kaloudi 1984, p. 349.

29   For a discussion of epigraphical sources related to professional (and other) religious organizations, see Ascough, Harland, and Kloppenborg 2012.

30   Ficuciello 2008, p. 121; Paxugianni-Kaloudi 1984, p. 349.

31   Kearns 1989, pp. 206, 254.

32   Knigge 1991, p. 73; Costaki 2006, pp. 456–457.

33 Costaki 2006, pp. 456–257; Knigge 1991, p. 71. The Greek Archaeological Society excavated the altar in 1873–1874. See Koumanoudis 1874, p. 12, Costaki 2006, pp. 456–257, and Knigge 1991, pp. 71–73.
34 Knigge 1991, p. 73; Koumanoudis 1874, p. 12. The monument has been dated by the letter-forms of the inscription to the Hellenistic period (third century BC), though such a method of dating is admittedly risky. If finds that might help with dating were encountered during the excavation of the altar, they are not mentioned in the publications.
35 Bikela 2011, p. 181. As comparanda, Zeus and Hermes are shown together in an Archaic relief on the Gate of Zeus and Hera, Thasos.
36 Knigge 1991, p. 73. See also Kearns 1989, p. 143.
37 Kearns 1989, p. 86.
38 Costaki 2006; Costaki 2009; Ficuciello 2008.
39 Ar. frag. 608 ap. Eustathius 1467.36, adapted from J. Henderson, Cambridge, Mass., 2007. Another fragment from an unknown play by Euripides (Eur. *TrGF* frag. 968 ap. Plut. *De Is.* 379E) suggests that "a dog would be a gift for light-bearing Hekate."
40 British Museum WT220, BAPD 467. *CVA*, London, British Museum 3, pl. 45.6a–6b.
41 Bonn Akademisches Kunstmuseum 1216.41–42, BAPD 12332. *CVA*, Bonn, Akademisches Kunstmuseum 1, pl. 34.13.
42 Frankfurt Museum für Vor- und Frühgeschichte B414, BAPD 12567. *CVA*, Frankfurt, Frankfurt am Main 2, pl. 79.5–6.
43 Theoph. *Char.* 16.5, adapted from J. Rusten and I. C. Cunningham, Cambridge, Mass., 2002.
44 Babrius 48, adapted from B. E. Perry, Cambridge, Mass., 1965.
45 For fish offerings see, see Ath. 7.325a and Antiphanes *Bout.* frag. 69, ap. Ath. 7.313b–c. For "meals" for Hekate see, Dem. 54.39, Ar. *Plut.* 595–598, Soph. frag. 734 ap. Pollux *Vocabulary* 6.83, and Plut. *Quaest. conv.* 708F–709A,
46 *Anth. Pal.* VI.299, adapted from W. R. Paton, London, 1916.
47 *Anth. Pal.* XVI.254, adapted from W. R. Paton, London, 1918.
48 Kindt 2012, pp. 1–2. The concept of a landscape infused with layers of interwoven meaning (human, natural, and imagined/mythological) is derived from the work of Cole 2004, p. 7.

References

Amandry, P. 1967–1968. "Thémistocle a Mélite," in *Χαριστήριον εις Αναστάσιον Κ. Ορλάνδον*, Athens, pp. 265–279.
Ascough, R. S., P. A. Harland, and J. S. Kloppenborg. 2012. *Associations in the Greco-Roman World: A Sourcebook*, Berlin.
Bikela, E. 2011. "Τὰ μικρὰ ἱερὰ τῆς Ἀθήνας." *Archaiologike Ephemeris* 150, pp. 133–195.
Brouskari, M. S. 2002. "Οι ανασκαφές νοτίως της Ακροπόλεως: Τα γλυπτά,» *Archaiologike Ephemeris* 141, pp. 1–204.
Cole, S. G. 2004. *Landscapes, Gender, and Ritual Space: The Ancient Greek Experience*, Berkeley.
Costaki, L. 2006. "The Intra Muros Road System of Ancient Athens" (diss. University of Toronto).
Costaki, L. 2008. "Πάντα πλήρη θεῶν εἶναι: Παρόδια ἱερὰ στήν

ἀρχαία Ἀθήνα," in *Μικρός ιερομνήμων μελέτες εις μνήμην Michael H. Jameson*, Athens, ed. A. P. Matthaiou and I. Polinskaya, pp. 145–166.
Costaki, L. 2009. "Οδικό δίκτυο των Αθηνών," in M. Korres, ed., *Αττικής οδοί: Αρχαίοι δρόμοι της Αττικής*. Athens, pp. 96–111.
Daux, G. 1958. "Chronique de fouilles," *Bulletin de correspondance hellénique* 82, pp. 644–830.
Ficuciello, L. 2008. *La strade di Atene*, Athens.
Greco, E. 2010. *Topografia di Atene: Sviluppo urbano e monumenti dalle origini al III secolo d.C.* 1, Athens.
Judeich, W. 1931. *Topographie von Athen*, Munich.
Kalligas, P. G. 1965. «Ἐργασίαι τακτοποιήσεως καὶ διαμορφώσεως τοῦ ἱεροῦ Διονύσου Ἐλευθερέως τῆς νοτίου κλιτύος Ἀκροπόλεως,» *Archaiologikon Deltion* 18, pp. 12–18.
Karagiorga-Stathakopoulou, T. 1978. «Ὁδός Πουλοπούλου 29,» *Archaiologikon Deltion* 33.B1, pp. 10–12.
Kearns, E. 1989. *The Heroes of Attica*, London.
Kindt, J. 2012. *Rethinking Greek Religion*, Cambridge.
Knigge, U. 1991. *The Athenian Kerameikos: History, Monuments, Excavations*, Athens.
Korres, M. 2009. «Ὁδικό δίκτυο γύρω ἀπό την Ἀκρόπολη,» in *Αττικής οδοί: Αρχαίοι δρόμοι της Αττικής*, ed. M. Korres, Athens, pp. 74–94.
Koumanoudis, S. A. 1874. *Praktika tes en Athenais Archaiologikes Etaireias* 1874, p. 12.
Lalonde, G. V. 2006. *Horos Dios: an Athenian Shrine and Cult of Zeus*, Leiden.
Lalonde, G. V., M. K. Langdon, and M. B. Walbank. 1991. *The Athenian Agora*, XIX. *Inscriptions: Horoi, Poletai Records, Leases of Public Lands*, Princeton.
Nevett, L. 2013. "Towards a Female Topography of the Ancient Greek City: Case Studies from Late Archaic and Early Classical Athens (c. 520–400 BCE)," in *Gender and the City Before Modernity*, ed. L. Foxhall and G. Neher, Hoboken, pp. 86–106.
Oakley, J. H., and R. H. Sinos. 1993. *The Wedding in Ancient Athens*, Madison.
Papadopoulou-Kanellopoulou, C. 1997. *Ιερό της νύμφης: μελανόμορφες λουτροφόροι*, Athens.
Parlama, L. M. 1992–1998. «'Αθήνα 1993–1995 από τις ανασκαφές του Μητροπολιτικού Σιδηροδρόμου,» *Horos* 10–12, pp. 521–544.
Paxugianni-Kaloudi, F. 1984. «Κεφάλι Ερμιδίου,» *Archaiologikon Deltion* 33, pp. 342–353.
Shear, T. L. 1993. "The Persian Destruction of Athens: Evidence from Agora Deposits." *Hesperia* 62, pp. 383–482.
Spathari, E. 1987. «Οδός Βασίλης 18–20,» *Archaiologikon Deltion* 34, pp. 26–27.
Theocharaki, A. M. 2011. "Ancient Circuit Wall of Athens: Its Changing Course and the Phases of Construction," *Hesperia* 80, pp. 71–156.
Threpsiades, J., and E. Vanderpool. 1964. "Themistokles' Sanctuary of Artemis Aristoboule," *Archaiologikon Deltion* 19, pp. 26–36.
Travlos, J. N. 1971. *Pictorial Dictionary of Ancient Athens*, New York.
Wycherley, R. E. 1970. "Minor Shrines in Ancient Athens," *Phoenix* 24, pp. 283–295.
Wycherley, R. E. 1978. *The Stones of Athens*, Princeton.

The Monumental Definition of Attica
in the Early Democratic Period

Jessica Paga

This essay explores how the large geographic territory of Attica was defined and delineated during the period between the Cleisthenic reforms of 508/7 BC and the Persian Wars of 490–480/79 BC. An examination of monumental construction projects at Eleusis, Rhamnous, and Sounion demonstrates how the Athenians attempted to define their borders during this period of socio-political upheaval, transition, and military uncertainty. The temples, theatral areas, and fortifications that appear during these years indicate an interest in the delineation of Athenian territory and demonstrate efforts to make the socio-political and military power of the nascent democracy visible and monumental.

Introduction

In the roughly 25 years between the passage of the Cleisthenic reforms in 508/7 BC and the end of the Persian Wars in 479/8 BC, the conception of what it meant to be an Athenian was radically redefined.[1] This period was fundamentally a transformative or transitional one, as the Athenians attempted to implement these new reforms across the vast geographic space of the polis, and also to determine how this new political system would not only work, but succeed. The movement from tyranny and stasis to what would become democracy was not a process that could happen overnight, nor was the success of the new political system guaranteed. This period saw tremendous innovation, adaptation, and experimentation. In the process, the Athenians would come to redefine who they were.[2]

This creative process of identity formation can been understood in the context of the administrative and bureaucratic changes that occurred with the passage of the reforms, and has been previously analyzed from the perspective of textual primary sources, such as Herodotos and the *Athenaion Politeia*, as well as epigraphic evidence.[3] Votive statues from the Acropolis, in combination with their dedicatory inscriptions, have been adduced as evidence for the changes in identity under the democracy.[4] Ceramic evidence, particularly the iconographic analysis of painted pottery, has also allowed scholars to consider the question of shifting Athenian identities.[5] The statues, pottery, and inscriptions might be considered stronger, or at least more contemporary, sources for the period under consideration, as both Herodotos and the author of the *Athenaion Politeia* wrote at some distance from the events in 508/7, yet challenges to the strength of many so-called "fixed points" in Athenian archaeology complicate the connections between the archaeological record and historical events.[6] These primary sources of evidence – literary, epigraphic, sculptural, ceramic – are often problematic in the pre-Persian period, and do not always provide sufficient traction on the slippery nature of collective identity formation and definition.[7] Another type of primary evidence, sometimes overlooked, provides a further lens through which to view the issue of identity: the built environment.[8]

The physical expression of a new sense of what it meant to be an Athenian can be seen in monumental forms throughout Attica. In total, it is possible to identify at least a dozen large-scale architectural structures in or near nine different demes during the 29-year period between 508/7 and 480/79[9] (Figure 11.1). Many of these structures have not been previously considered to belong to this period, either because of outdated chronologies, older dating criteria that have not been updated, general oversight, or

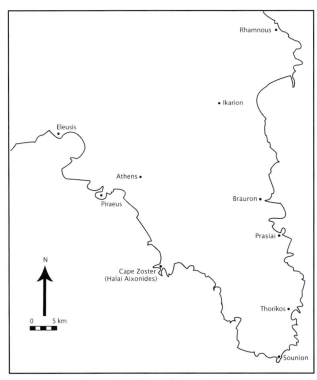

Figure 11.1 Map of Attica. J. Paga

time period, soon after the reforms of 508/7. When mapped, these structures reveal an additional connection: they are almost exclusively located on the coastal and land borders of Attica, effectively delineating the territory of the Athenian polis[12] (Figure 11.1).

Three Coastal Demes: Eleusis, Rhamnous, and Sounion

I begin with construction in three particular demes to illustrate what I believe is an organized effort to define Attica, and thereby to define part of what it now meant to be a democratic Athenian citizen. The three demes – Eleusis, Rhamnous, and Sounion – have been selected because they all preserve monumental structures still in situ (to varying degrees), have complicated chronologies in need of revision or clarification, and anchor three principle coastal edges of Attica. These three demes form a triangle, enclosing all of the territory that was officially incorporated into the Athenian state through the Cleisthenic reforms. All three demes also served defensive or military purposes and stood on borders with Athens' most hostile neighbors: Eleusis on the southwest, facing Megara and the Peloponnese, Rhamnous on the northeast, facing Euboia and Boiotia, and Sounion on the south, facing the sea, with a clear view of Aegina and any passing ship. The synchronicity of the building projects at these three demes is more than mere chance or coincidence. All three sites received costly elaborations or additions to their sanctuary spaces, which would have in turn sparked greater attention to the spaces and structures themselves, creating a reciprocal relationship between renown, prestige, and embellishment. The monumentalization, particularly of sacred spaces, at these three sites is a demonstration of the importance of their location on the edges of Attic territory and is indicative of the attempts by the nascent democracy to integrate and define the parameters of the Athenian polis.

Eleusis

Eleusis, in the southwest corner of Attica, approximately 21 km. from the city center of Athens, lies within the Thriasian plain, which forms part of the western extent of Attica, stretching between the Bay of Eleusis to the south and Mt. Parnes to the north. The area of the Thriasian plain acted as the border with the territory of Megara and several of the features at Eleusis betray this dual function of cult center and border guard.[13] Two structures deserve special consideration here: the fortifications around the sanctuary and the late Archaic Telesterion (Figures 11.2–11.3). Long considered indications of Peisistratid interest in the area, these two architectural elements are both better dated to ca. 500, or the early 5th century.

Little survives of the Late Archaic fortifications, but their masonry style shares similarities with the Telesterion, and

lack of publication. These structures, however, when their dates have been recalibrated and their locations mapped, provide a contemporary lens through which we can evaluate anew this transitional period of Athenian history. Taken as a whole, these structures indicate a spurt of building activity in the demes during the decades immediately following the Cleisthenic reforms. This concentrated effort in building is particularly noticeable when compared to the previous century, in which few large-scale structures are known – either archaeologically or textually – in the Attic countryside.[10]

These structures can be classified as "monumental" according to several categories, first, their materials: they are built primarily of stone, including limestone and, notably, marble, particularly from Mt. Pentele, which was not quarried extensively before this time, and their size: they are all, generally, large-scale.[11] Their placement is distinctive, in prominent locations within the topography of the deme and with maximum visibility. Many of the structures are sanctuary features, such as temples, and others served as infrastructure or had utilitarian functions, such as fortification walls and multi-purpose theatral areas. The permanent materials and large size of the structures speak to an important difference from previous buildings, as well as from contemporary residential and more ephemeral structures. By all accounts, these structures represent a distinct group of buildings, all constructed within a discrete

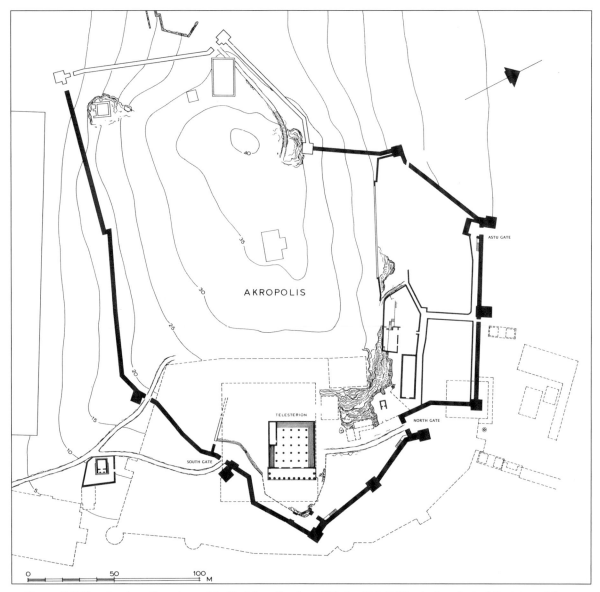

Figure 11.2 Eleusis, plan of sanctuary. Modified from Travlos 1988, fig. 136. © The Archaeological Society at Athens

they were built prior to the Persian destruction of Eleusis in 480, as is clear from their continued use in the 5th century despite indications of damage.[14] The Late Archaic walls encircled the sanctuary and a portion of the deme site; they thus protected the sacred rites as well as some of the inhabitants of Eleusis. The walls were constructed in three parts: foundations of roughly hewn limestone blocks, socles of polygonal Eleusinian stone, and superstructures of mudbrick.[15] The wall had a variable thickness of between 2.80 to 3.10 m., a further indication that it was not a mere peribolos defining the temenos of the sanctuary.[16] Several gates provided access, and three in particular stand out for their size and orientation: the South Gate, North Gate, and Astu Gate[17] (Figure 11.2). The presence of these gates

with their accompanying towers and the overall extent and careful construction of the wall indicate the overwhelmingly defensive purpose it served.

The remains of the Late Archaic Telesterion include the entire length of the south foundations and portions of the euthynteria, some of the eastern portico, and bedrock cuttings to receive the western wall (Figure 11.3); altogether they indicate a structure that measured 25.30 × 27.10 m., not including the porch, which would add an additional 4.55 m. to the east–west length (resulting in overall dimensions of 29.85 × 27.10 m.).[18] The nearly square interior space was supported by 22 columns, perhaps of the Ionic order, arranged in five rows of five or four columns each.[19] The entire structure was fronted by a porch of nine or ten Doric columns, with one or three doors to permit access to the inner naos. The dimensions and plan can thus be favorably compared to the Old Bouleuterion in the Agora.[20] The two structures differ only in the number of internal columns and both stand among the earliest incarnations of the hypostyle hall plan in Greece.[21] The foundations of the Telesterion are Kara limestone, while the wall blocks, set in ashlar courses, and the entablature are of a slightly softer limestone, and Parian marble was used for the sima and roof tiles, a material monumentalization of the building that far surpassed any earlier cult building on the site.[22] Along the full length of the north wall, as well as parts of the south and west walls, tiers of nine steps were built.[23] The steps were partially cut into the bedrock on the north side but otherwise built

up from carefully worked limestone blocks. These steps were too narrow to function as seats, so it is likely that the initiates stood to observe the rites of the Mysteries, which presumably took place in the center of the space.[24]

The foundations for the interior columns were cut into the bedrock in the western half of the building but were supported by built foundations of hard, irregularly worked limestone blocks sunk into fill on the eastern half. The stones used for these eastern foundations included reused blocks, three of which were inscribed and belong to a single dedication, dated to the first half of the 6th century (ca. 550). They provide a *terminus post quem* for the construction of the building.[25] The re-used inscription, the use of polygonal masonry for the foundations and walls, the use of different types of materials, the reconstructed slope of the roof, and – most importantly – the Parian marble ram's head finial and anthemion sima from the corner of the Telesterion, have all been adduced as evidence that this phase was "Peisistratid."[26] In general, the Late Archaic Telesterion was dated on comparison with the Old Athena Temple in Athens, from which an almost identical ram's head finial survives, and whose anthemion sima also bears similarities to the Eleusis example.[27] Noack also adduced the use of Ionic columns for the interior of the Telesterion as a "Peisistratid" feature, comparing it to the use of the Ionic order for the unfinished Olympieion, although it has now been shown that the columns for the Olympieion were originally Doric.[28]

This original association of the Telesterion with Peisistratos has, however, been challenged. T. Leslie Shear, Jr., for instance, ascribes the Telesterion and fortification walls to the sons of Peisistratos, placing the construction

Figure 11.3 Eleusis, view of the corner of Early Archaic Telesterion, to northwest. Photo J. Paga

Figure 11.4 Rhamnous, view of Classical Temple of Nemesis and Temple of Themis, view to west. Photo J. Paga

in the early part of the fourth quarter of the 6th century.[29] Several scholars have arrived at a conclusion that divorces the structure entirely from the tyrants: they argue that the Late Archaic Telesterion should be understood as a product of the early democracy.[30]

The Old Athena Temple on the Acropolis is now dated by most scholars to the last few years of the 6th century, or ca. 500.[31] Any comparison between the Telesterion and this building, therefore, such as the nearly identical ram's head finial, requires a recalibration of the Telesterion's date to ca. 500. Moreover, the slope of the roof, as reconstructed by Orlandos, bears comparison with other Late Archaic roofs, in particular with the Temple of Aphaia on Aegina, which should suggest a date significantly later than ca. 525.[32] The use of different types of materials can be seen in Archaic structures, such as the Dörpfeld foundations on the Acropolis and the Olympieion, but this practice continued well into the 5th century. The Old Parthenon, for example, employed Kara limestone for its bottom step, while the other two were of Pentelic marble; the outer foundations for the Old Bouleuterion were of Kara limestone, with a softer limestone used for the internal foundations; and the foundations of the Temple of Dionysos were built of both Kara and Acropolis limestone.[33] In addition, I would also point to the use of Z-clamps in the geison blocks of the Telesterion, as well as possibly in the foundations for the porch.[34] The earliest Athenian monuments that employ the Z-clamp can all be dated to ca. 500, or within the last decade of the 6th and first two decades of the 5th century.[35] All of the evidence provided by Noack for a "Peisistratid" date for the Late Archaic Telesterion can be comfortably placed in the late 6th and early 5th century. There is no stratigraphic evidence for a date of ca. 525 for the Telesterion and fortification walls, and instead, stylistic analysis of the sculptural and architectural elements supports a date of ca. 500. We should consider the Late Archaic Telesterion and fortification walls at Eleusis, then, to be firmly within the sphere of the building program of the early democracy.

The combination of the enlarged and monumental Telesterion with the extensive fortification walls indicates that Eleusis was a site of concerted architectural development in the decades immediately following the Cleisthenic reforms. The result of the building activity here is an elaborate sanctuary space that proclaims visually the wealth and prestige of the cult while simultaneously emphasizing the protection of Attic borderlands. Eleusis likely was considered part of Athenian territory since at least the late 7th century, and the monumentalization of the sanctuary in the years immediately following 508 demonstrates a continued commitment to the cult and perhaps its expanded popularity.[36] The larger size of the Telesterion also testifies to the growth of the Mysteries and should indicate increased attendance at the initiations after the reforms.[37] In addition to the symbolic import of the new temple, the walls, while

highlighting the level of secrecy necessary to the Mysteries, also point to this crucial area – close to the sea, within the fertile Thriasian plain, and bordering Megarian territory – as one pivotal to Athenian security. The highly visible fortifications concretely express these two important aspects of the deme of Eleusis: its place in the sacred landscape of Attica, and its role in defense.

Rhamnous

The deme of Rhamnous lies in the northeast corner of Attica, approximately 53 km. from the city center, and is well situated, elevated high above the coast, with a view north over the gulf to Euboia and south towards Marathon. These natural advantages led to the fortification of the deme in the Classical period, when it was used as a garrison.[38] In the Late Archaic and Early Classical periods, although the deme lacked walls, it still would have served an important look-out spot for detecting approaching enemies from the north. The deme was home to two important cults, for Nemesis and Themis. While the residential and civic area of the site provides little evidence for this period, the sanctuary material is indicative of a thriving cult with resources for multiple structures and topographic interventions (Figure 11.4). The sanctuary was located outside of the deme center, approximately 500 m. to the south, and was approached via a long processional way lined with tombs and funerary monuments[39] (Figure 11.5). Evidence of votive offerings from the area of the sanctuary indicates cult activity from at least the beginning of the 6th century.[40] The first half of the 6th century saw the construction of the first temple within the sanctuary, probably dedicated to Nemesis. The evidence for this Archaic structure is admittedly scant, consisting of fragments of Laconian roof tiles, one stamped with a lion, discovered below the Classical temple, as well as part of a brightly painted sphinx head, possibly used as an akroterion.[41] In addition, pottery from within the fill of the terrace that supported the hypothetical temple indicates that topographic modification occurred in this area within the first half of the 6th century.[42] While the size, form, and precise location of this early temple remain unknown, it was possibly a small distyle *in antis* structure, constructed from local limestone, with a terracotta roof.

At the close of the 6th century, a new limestone temple was built, possibly as a replacement for the earlier structure, or possibly as an additional elaboration of the sanctuary.[43] A large number of fragments from the temple survive, principally in drawings made by John Peter Gandy, a member of the Society of Dilettanti, who excavated the site in 1813. Other fragments have been recovered in the more recent excavations by Basileios Petrakos.[44] Petrakos reconstructs the building as a distyle *in antis* temple of the Doric order with a narrow pronaos and rear cella.[45] The stone for this temple almost certainly derived from

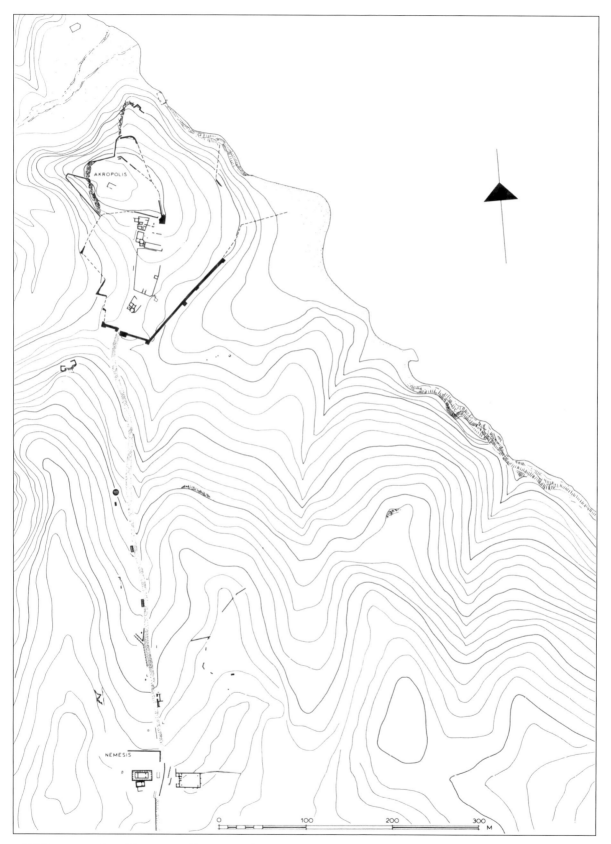

Figure 11.5 Rhamnous, plan of deme site and Sanctuary of Nemesis and Themis. Modified from Travlos 1988, fig. 512. © The Archaeological Society at Athens

Figure 11.6 Rhamnous, view of exterior polygonal wall face of Temple of Themis, view to southwest. Photo J. Paga

nearby limestone quarries, such as those near Marathon.[46] This temple was probably destroyed or damaged by the Persians in 480, and may have stood on the north side of the sanctuary, underneath the Classical Temple of Nemesis.[47]

Further support for the hypothesis that the Late Archaic temple may have served as a predecessor for the later Temple of Nemesis, and was thus originally located on the northern part of the terrace, can be found in the physical relationship between the Classical temple and the small shrine immediately to the south. In the early 5th century, a small temple-like structure was erected on the southern part of the terrace. This building was relatively diminutive, measuring approximately 9.90 × 6.15 m. (at the level of the krepidoma), and had no columns[48] (Figure 11.4, structure on the left). Like the limestone temple, the interior space of this structure was divided into a narrow pronaos and a rear chamber. The exterior wall faces were constructed in polygonal Lesbian masonry and the interior walls were formed with irregular courses of small stacked stones (Figure 11.6). The building has been dated to the early decades of the 5th century on the basis of its masonry and the pottery discovered from within and immediately outside of it.[49]

The relationship between this small polygonal structure and the later, Classical Temple of Nemesis is peculiar. The two structures are built so close together that they are separated by mere centimeters at their eastern corners[50] (Figures 11.4, 11.6). This unique siting is possibly explained by the existence of a predecessor to the Nemesis temple – a precise sacred topographical location from which the cult could not be moved.[51] The Late Archaic temple may have stood in this exact location, although its dimensions were significantly smaller, and, if so, the two buildings (the Late Archaic temple on the north and the polygonal structure to the south) would not have appeared as close together as they do now. After the Late Archaic temple was destroyed or damaged by the Persians and its replacement built in ca. 430–420, the increased size of the Temple of Nemesis resulted in its near overlap with the smaller structure to the south.[52] What was the function of the small polygonal building, then?

The polygonal structure has frequently been described as a Temple of Themis, based in part on the discovery of a statue of Themis, dedicated by a certain Megakles, son of Megakles, of Rhamnous.[53] Several other dedications were found within the polygonal building, dating from the 5th

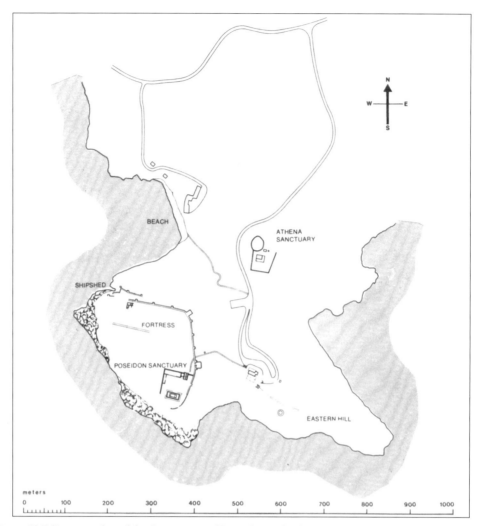

Figure 11.7 Sounion, plan of the Sanctuaries of Poseidon and Athena. Modified after W.B. Dinsmoor 1971

Figure 11.8 Sounion, Temple of Poseidon, view to northeast. Photo J. Paga

century through the Roman period. In the porch, flanking the central doorway, two marble thrones were found in situ, one dedicated to Nemesis and the other to Themis.[54] In addition, inscriptions from Rhamnous refer to the simultaneous worship of Nemesis and Themis, both of whom dealt with matters of divine justice, order, rightful retribution, and lawful distribution.[55] These factors all suggest that the small polygonal building should be considered a Temple to Themis.[56]

In the first two decades of the 5th century, then, two small temples stood within the sanctuary at Rhamnous. One, distyle *in antis*, was probably located on the northern part of the terrace, below the later Temple of Nemesis, and was dedicated to that goddess. The other, constructed of polygonal masonry in the Lesbian style, was located just to the south, and was dedicated to the goddess Themis. The construction of two temples, albeit relatively small in size, within the span of two or three decades may speak to the increasing wealth and resources of Rhamnous, and may also speak to the overall prominence of the deme within the broader Athenian polis. The use of locally quarried stone for these structures demonstrates the Rhamnousians' access to important material resources and further emphasizes the site specificity of the goddesses with the deme itself.[57]

Nemesis was reported to have assisted the Greeks during the battle of Marathon and their victory in 490 elevated the status of the deity throughout the polis and emphasized her important role within Attica.[58] We might imagine that this victory resulted in further elaboration of the sanctuary, perhaps in the form of a temple to her divine helper, Themis, in the decade after this battle; if so, the polygonal Temple of Themis would compare favorably with the Temple of Poseidon at Sounion and the Old Parthenon, all dedicated as thank offerings after Marathon.[59] The proximity of Rhamnous to Marathon would have further ensured the continued prosperity of the deme after 490, both due to the prominence of the plain of Marathon, as well as the nearby bay that facilitated trade in the region of northern Attica. That the deme prospered in the aftermath of the Persian Wars is further apparent by inscriptions that detail the financial resources of the treasury of Nemesis.[60] As with Eleusis, this deme sanctuary is neither wholly local nor wholly polis-wide: it retained a role of central importance to both the Rhamnousians and the Athenians.[61]

In the years around 500, the deme of Rhamnous was wealthy enough to expand its sanctuary to Nemesis and Themis.[62] This architectural elaboration highlights the prominent position of the sanctuary within the deme and was one of the ways in which the residents of Rhamnous chose to represent themselves visually within the landscape of Attica. The increasingly large and prosperous sanctuary aided in the formation of a deme-specific identity for the Rhamnousians, one that was centered on the cults of Nemesis and Themis and articulated in the construction of

two new monumental temples, and which complimented the new sense of being an Athenian, connected to the territory of Attica and recent military victories. These buildings would have been prominent landmarks in the northeast corner of Attica and they visually expressed the important role that Rhamnous played in this border area.

Although we lack clear evidence for the Archaic and Early Classical occupation of the deme site itself, some of its infrastructure, such as the theatral area, was likely already in place[63] (Figure 11.5). The remaining stone blocks have been dated to the late 4th century on the basis of epigraphic evidence, but an earlier phase may have existed in the Late Archaic and Early Classical period, given the form of the theater and structural similarities with theatral areas at Thorikos and Ikarion, which both had their first phases ca. 500.[64] A delineated theatral area used as a civic center would demonstrate that the residents of Rhamnous were rapidly able to incorporate some of the new provisions in the Cleisthenic reforms, such as deme Assembly meetings and deme-specific elections and lotteries. The space would also serve as a focal point for the citizens of Rhamnous, providing them with a centralized meeting or gathering area.

The deme of Rhamnous could boast of potentially three new monumental structures in the years immediately following the reforms of 508. These structures were all smaller than the Telesterion at Eleusis and the Temple of Poseidon at Sounion, but nonetheless express an interest in the elaboration of sanctuary space as well as an interest in administrative and/or multipurpose entertainment spaces. The attention lavished on this deme, in the far northeast corner of Attica, demonstrates that even geographically isolated demes were being transformed, physically and administratively, during this period.

Sounion

The deme of Sounion, in the southernmost part of Attica, is most famous for its sanctuaries of Athena and Poseidon, located on a narrow promontory of land that juts into the sea.[65] This geographic position emphasizes the important role the deme could – and did – play for the Athenian polis: from Sounion and its adjacent sanctuaries, most ships approaching Attica could be seen. This strategic location made Sounion a border deme, similar to Eleusis and Rhamnous. Unlike those two demes, however, there may not be a single residential center at Sounion, but rather isolated nuclei and individual residential dwellings associated with the nearby quarries, mines, or farmlands.[66] What is certain, though, is that the prominent sanctuaries indicate significant cult activity from the second half of the 7th century, if not earlier[67] (Figure 11.7). At that time, monumental stone *kouroi* were dedicated in large numbers at the sanctuary, along with other objects, such as bronze weapons, vases, and terracotta figurines.[68] It is possible that an ephemeral shrine or naïskos was also erected, but no traces of such a structure are currently known.[69] The size and material of the *kouroi* dedications indicate that Sounion was an influential site already in the Early Archaic period, the Poseidon sanctuary possibly serving as a repository for aristocratic and expensive votives. Some scholars have attempted to associate the Alkmaionidai with the area of southern Attica.[70] Although this family may have had strong links with nearby Anaphlystos or Aigilia and it is known that Themistocles was from the deme of Phrearrhioi (which was in the same trittys of phyle IV, Leontis, as Sounion), there is, unfortunately, no positive evidence for associating either the Alkmaeonidai or Themistocles with Sounion or the growth of the sanctuary of Poseidon in the 6th century.[71] If the sanctuary was a receptacle for elite dedications, however, it was not yet important enough to warrant any sort of permanent construction.

The earliest built cult structure that can be identified with certainty is the Late Archaic limestone predecessor to the Classical marble Temple of Poseidon, several reused blocks of which are visible in Figure 11.8. The marble temple both masks and incorporates remnants of the earlier temple, which succumbed to the Persians in 480. This earlier temple, although unfinished at the time of its destruction, had nearly identical measurements (ca. 13.06 × 30.20 m.) and plan (6 × 13) as the later 5th century temple, and it was constructed of limestone, possibly with marble metopes inserted between the triglyphs. In both material and size, not to mention its highly visible siting within the landscape, this can truly be considered a monumental edifice. The date of this earlier temple should be placed within the first two decades of the 5th century, on the basis of its architectural style and details; it was unfinished when it was destroyed.[72] It should be considered part of the building projects that occurred in the *astu* and countryside after the Battle of Marathon, like the polygonal Temple of Themis at Rhamnous.

This temple was the first monumental peripteral temple to be constructed outside of the *astu* and its prominent location – on the tip of the projecting cliff, thrust out towards the sea – guaranteed that it was highly visible. This temple served as a beacon, not just for the demesmen of Sounion, but for any ships (foreign and domestic) approaching Attica. Although it is clear from dedications that the sanctuary was in use throughout the Archaic period, the decision to construct a large-scale, expensive temple here in the early years of the 5th century is a deliberate one and should be considered evidence of an interest in the elaboration of sanctuary space and the visual monumentalization of this specific area.

Conclusion

What these three abbreviated case studies signal is an overarching attention to the fringes of Attic territory during a specific period. The construction of monumental buildings in

these three demes, alongside the structures in the additional six demes listed in the Appendix, indicates an effort to define physically the perimeter of Attica through monumental stone architecture, a visual articulation of borders that did not exist previously. I offer a few suggestions as to why this was such an important undertaking during the first decades of the new political system.

In 506/5, only a few years after the passage of the Cleisthenic reforms, the Athenians faced a quadripartite attack. The Boiotians and Chalkidians attacked from the north, while the Spartans and Corinthians crossed the Isthmus and marched on the southwest border of Attic territory. Herodotos reports that the Spartans and Corinthians established their base at Eleusis, seizing and occupying the sanctuary (5.74). The Athenians decided to face this challenge first, but before the battle began, the Corinthians withdrew and the Spartans, divided by the lack of communication between the kings, also left Eleusis and returned to the Peloponnese (Hdt. 5.75).

The Athenians then wheeled north to confront the Boiotians and Chalkidians, who had already seized the outlying demes of Oinoe and Hysiae.[73] According to Herodotos, it was here that the Athenians achieved their first victory under the new system of *isegoria* (political equality) instituted by the Cleisthenic reforms (5.77). They captured and ransomed 700 Boiotians and as many Chalkidians, authoritatively defending their territory and expressing their new military power. What the two-pronged attack revealed is the vulnerability of the western land border of Attica. Despite their successes, the simultaneous convergence of enemies at the southwest and northwest corners must have worried the Athenians. Although it is not possible to claim that all of the building activity at Eleusis and Rhamnous was entirely centrally motivated or funded, it is undeniable that serious construction did occur at precisely these two corners of Attica in the years immediately following the attacks. The fortifications at Eleusis kept the uninitiated out, but they also protected this strategic deme.[74] The temples and civic center at Rhamnous, on the other hand, are indicative of increased revenues and attention to this deme, poised at a crucial border of Athenian territory and somewhat distant from the *astu*.

The land borders were not the only vulnerable areas of Attica territory, however. Herodotos records multiple attacks by the nearby island of Aegina on the shoreline of Attica during the Archaic and early Classical periods, culminating in devastating raids at Phalcron and other southwestern coastal areas in the last decade of the 6th century, just prior to the embassy of Aristagoras and Ionian Revolution (5.79–90, 6.49–50, 6.87–94, 7.145). Herodotos also describes how the Aeginetans attacked the Athenians around Cape Sounion during a quadrennial festival held in the first decade of the 5th century (6.87–88).[75] From these accounts, it is evident that the Aeginetans posed a considerable threat to the Athenians throughout the period under consideration; the coastal borders, particularly those to the south, facing Aegina, were also weak areas in need of protection.

In the closing years of the 6th century, then, the Athenians faced challenges to their borders on all sides, by multiple enemies. The focused architectural attention in the border demes, both land and coastal, should be viewed as a response to these very real threats. The construction of large-scale structures in permanent materials and in highly visible locations broadcast the wealth and resources of those demes – and by extension, the polis – to those who would invade its borders. The heavy fortification walls at Eleusis and the new walls designed by Themistokles and begun in the Piraeus prior to 480 are indisputable evidence of a desire to protect and intimidate.[76] Although not defensive in design or outlook, the temples that lined the coastal and inland borders also aided in the propagation of a new understanding of Athenian power, mobility, and overall resources. They are a physical manifestation of the surging Athenian dominance in the Aegean, begun with the victories in 506/5, continued with the Athenian response to the Ionian Revolution, and solidified with the victory at Marathon in 490. Taken as a whole, these monumental structures helped to solidify the border areas of Attica and proclaim a new sense of Athenian power.

Part of this proclamation of Athenian power entails forging a one-to-one correlation between power or military might and Athenian-ness, in effect, making the two ideas synonymous. In this sense, we can view these structures as physical markers of both concepts, power and Athenian identity; they reflect the new military prowess of the Athenians, but they also help to generate this new sense of what it means to be an Athenian through their very monumentality and visibility in the landscape of Attica. We might compare this monumental creation of identity to the switch from the patronymic to demotic. The visible change from patronymic to demotic, as seen in the Acropolis dedications, illustrates one of the key components of the Cleisthenic reforms: the new emphasis on *belonging* to a deme.[77] The author of the *Athenaion Politeia* remarks that through these reforms, Cleisthenes "made the inhabitants of each deme fellow demesmen, so that they would not call attention to the new citizens by calling people according to their patronymic, but they would be designated according to deme."[78] The process of deme registration, which was now the first step to citizenship (*AthPol* 42), is literally written into the new identifying moniker.[79] To be an Athenian now meant, first and foremost, to be a member of a deme. The use of the demotic represents one of the ways the Cleisthenic reforms attempted to integrate the demes into the polis and how the notion of a new democratic Athenian identity permeated, and depended on, Attica.

This insistence on place of origin, on geography and landscape, is a key component of the new sense of Athenian-ness: one's Athenian citizenship status was now fundamentally tied to the land itself. After 508/7, the demes, as evidenced in the shift to the demotic, took on a newfound importance as the defining components of Athenian society. By delineating the area of Attica, the architectural monuments highlighted herein further endowed this new sense of belonging – this new focus on location – with a physical significance that had previously been lacking. These structures effectively created the geographic entity of Attica – they gave shape to the abstract policy of the Cleisthenic reforms by indicating, in monumental architectural form, what *is* Attica, and what is *not*, what is inside and included, and what is outside and excluded. They visually expressed the recently victorious defensive capabilities of the polis while simultaneously contributing to the very definition of what it meant to be an Athenian after 508/7.

Notes

1   I thank Margaret M. Miles for inviting me to contribute to this volume, and for her insightful comments. Thanks are also due to the three anonymous reviewers for their helpful comments on an earlier draft. A version of this paper was presented at the Archaeological Institute of America annual meeting in Seattle, W.A. in 2013, and I thank Danielle Kellogg and members of the audience there for their suggestions and critiques. All dates are BC unless otherwise specified; all translations are my own.

2   For previous work on ancient identity formation, particularly with respect to ethnicity, see Hall 1997, 2002; the collected essays in Malkin 2001 should also be consulted, particularly those by McInerney and Morgan; see further below for individual studies specifically related to Athenian democracy.

3   Loraux 1986 (primarily concerning the Classical period); Manville 1990; Boegehold and Scafuro 1994; Anderson 2003. Raubitschek's catalogue of dedications from the Athenian Acropolis (1949) is one place where we can see shifts in self-identification (the replacement of the patronymic by the demotic) in the years following the Cleisthenic reforms.

4   Keesling 2003, pp. 36–62.

5   Taylor 1991 (vase painting and sculpture); Hölscher 1998 (particularly with reference to the figure of Theseus); Shapiro 1998 (concerning the issue of autochthony), 2012 (also with an emphasis on Theseus, as well as Menestheus). These and other iconographical studies more commonly focus on the later 5th century.

6   Stewart (2008a and 2008b) demonstrates that many of the statues from the Acropolis that have been used as fixed points for understanding the development of the Early Classical style (the Severe Style) have a more ambiguous place in the chronological record than previously believed. It is also important to bear in mind the warning, articulated by Snodgrass and Elsner, that such "positivist" understandings of the archaeological evidence, namely that archaeological data can be directly – and without complications – mapped onto historical events, can often obfuscate both the physical evidence and our understanding of history (Snodgrass 1983, pp. 142, 145–146; Elsner 2012, pp. 6–13).

7 Other studies concerning identity formation deal with dress (B. Cohen 2001 and M. Miller 1997, pp. 153–187, 2011, 2013, the latter particularly regarding the role of Persian dress). All of these approaches have enriched our overall understanding of the formation of Athenian identity.

8 Previous studies that use the built environment as a means of understanding the new democratic Athenian identity include Shear 1994 (the Agora), 1995 (contra. S. G. Miller 1995, both regarding the Old Bouleuterion); Castriota 1998 (largely concerning the Tyrannicides); Hölscher 1998 (primarily concerning the Tyrannicides and later buildings in the Agora), all with a focus on the *astu* of Athens. Osborne (1985) is one of the few attempts to analyze the Attic countryside and its relationship to the democracy. He does not, however, focus on the particular moment of democratic transition, but the Classical period more generally.

9 See Appendix for demes and structures, with select bibliography.

10 Outside of the city center, Eleusis represents one of the only areas with clear evidence for monumental construction in the 6th century (see below for more details). Rhamnous and Ikarion also show some evidence for large-scale construction in the earlier Archaic period (for Rhamnous, see below; for Ikarion, see Biers and Boyd 1982, with further bibliography).

11 The scale of these structures is considered "large" in comparison to previous buildings of similar purpose (the Late Archaic Telesterion, for example, is larger than its predecessor), and in comparison to contemporary residential structures. The earliest significant use of Pentelic marble is the Old Parthenon, begun soon after 490. For these quarries more generally, see Korres 1995, especially pp. 94–100.

12 The theatral area at Ikarion – which may have had its first phase around 500 – is the only structure on the list located in an inland deme. For the dating and evidence for the deme theater and its uses at Ikarion, see Paga 2010, pp. 357–360.

13 The relationship between Athens and Megara, particularly in the post-Persian War period, should effect how we understand the continued role of fortifications at Eleusis. For a brief summary of the political history of Megara, see Robinson 2011, pp. 44–47.

14 These walls are often referred to as "peribolos" walls, but their construction details and extent can be favorably compared with other fortification walls. Lang (1996, pp. 22–24) classifies these walls as fortifications (Lang's "Type 4"); the point is also emphasized by Clinton 1994, p. 162. For evidence of destruction, see Noack 1927, pp. 30–32, 90–92; Mylonas 1961, pp. 93, 107–108 (attributed to the Persians). Additional burned debris recovered in pits similar to those on the Acropolis (the so-called *Perserschutt*) are detailed in Noack 1927, p. 93. See also Shear 1982, p. 133 (with n. 20 for additional bibliography). The most recent treatment of the Persian destruction of Athens and Attica, including evidence from Eleusis, Rhamnous, and Sounion, is Miles 2014.

15 For a description of the walls and gates, see Mylonas 1961, pp. 91–96.

16 Lang 1996, p. 23.

17 The South Gate measures ca. 4 m. wide and includes a square tower, parts of which are still visible near the southeast corner

of the Classical Telesterion; it would have provided access to the sanctuary and deme from the sea (Mylonas 1961, p. 92 (near his H38)). The North Gate served as the primary gate for the sanctuary, through which the Sacred Way passed, and was also furnished with a square tower (Mylonas 1961, p. 93 (his H18)). The Astu Gate shares similar dimensions with the South Gate, but was arranged with a large enclosed interior space, creating a double gate layout with a dog-leg, an undeniably militaristic arrangement of space (Mylonas 1961, pp. 94–95 (his H10)).

18 The north wall was subsumed into the Classical Telesterion, making the north–south measurements approximate.

19 No physical traces of these columns remain; the use of the Ionic order is adduced from the reference to σπεῖραι in *IG* I³ 386/387. For discussion of the number of columns and their order on both the façade and interior, see Mylonas 1961, pp. 80–83; Lippolis 2006, pp. 172–179.

20 Old Bouleuterion: 23.30 × 23.80 m. with a hipped roof supported by five internal columns, fronted by a pentastyle *in antis* porch with one or three doors into the interior chamber, built ca. 500 (for the date, see Shear 1993, pp. 419–422, with a full pottery catalogue, pp. 472–473, 1994, p. 236).

21 The use of five internal columns in the Old Bouleuterion demonstrates that the Telesterion could have employed a similar number, so the use of 22 columns must be read as a deliberate choice, probably to reflect and enhance the obfuscating nature of the rites that occurred within the structure, where visibility, revelation, and concealment were of great significance.

22 For further description of the building, see Noack 1927, pp. 48–70; Mylonas 1961, pp. 78–91; Lippolis 2006, pp. 172–180, 2007, pp. 589–590. For the so-called Solonian Telesterion of the late 7th or early 6th century, see Noack 1927, pp. 16–48; Travlos 1950–51, pp. 10–11; Mylonas 1961, pp. 63–76; Travlos 1988, pp. 92–93; also note Miles 1998, p. 28, where the date of this earlier structure is adjusted to the first half of the 6th century, a date more in line with similar embellishments in the City Eleusinion sanctuary.

23 For the number of steps and details of their construction, see Mylonas 1961, p. 88.

24 Hollinshead 2012 details the significance of monumental staircases, both those used for sitting and standing, and while she does not include the Telesterion as one of her examples, it fits into her category of stairs as viewing platforms.

25 Clinton (2005, vol. 1A, no. 2) collects the five total fragments and partially restores the inscription, dating it to around the middle of the 6th century. The fragments are restored in a slightly different order as *IG* I³ 990, dated ca. 550. The letter forms of this inscription are similar to those of the Patrokledes Altar, dedicated to Athena Nike (*IG* I³ 596), and dated to the mid-6th century on the basis of letter forms (Mark 1993, p. 33).

26 See especially Noack 1927, pp. 69–70, with contribution by Orlandos, pp. 63–68. Noack saw similarities between the Telesterion and the Old Athena Temple so strong that he suggested the two buildings were constructed by the same workshop, the Telesterion begun as soon as the Old Athena Temple was completed (p. 69).

27 Orlandos (in Noack 1927, pp. 64–67) remains the most detailed discussion of the ram's head finial and sima, but see also Hayashi 1992, pp. 20–29. For the ram's head finial from the Old Athena Temple, see Wiegand 1904, pp. 125–126.

28 Noack 1927, pp. 60–61. He relates the use of the Ionic order for these structures with what he calls the "Ionicizing tendencies" of the Peisistratidai. For the Peisistratid Olympieion, see Tölle-Kastenbein 1994, pp. 75–97, 136–142.

29 Shear 1982, p. 131.

30 Clinton (1994, p. 162) remarks that the Late Archaic Telesterion is "certainly [dated] after the third quarter of the sixth century, possibly even as late as the end of the century." Hayashi (1992, pp. 20–29), relying primarily on the ram's head finial, shows that the Peisistratid date for the building must be discarded. Miles (1988, pp. 27–28) highlights the lack of ancient testimonia associating the Peisistratidai with the Mysteries and argues that both the Telesterion and fortification walls should be considered products of the new democracy. Lippolis (2006, pp. 163–164, 177–180) also gives this dating (cf. Lippolis, et al. 2007, pp. 197–198, where this phase of the Telesterion is attributed to the Peisistratidai). A Peisistratid date is affirmed by Goette (1993, p. 274) and Camp (2001, p. 38).

31 Childs 1994.

32 Orlandos (in Noack 1927), p. 65. For the roof of the Temple of Aphaia on Aegina, see Ohnesorg 1993, pp. 28–29. The date of the Temple of Aphaia on Aegina is contested, but all accounts place it in the first quarter or early second quarter of the 5th century (500–480: Bankel 1993, pp. 169–170; Indergaard 2011; post-480: Stewart 2008a and 2008b; Hedreen 2011; Polinskaya 2013).

33 In general, Kara limestone was used throughout the 6th and early 5th century, but only sparingly in the Classical and Hellenistic periods (see Wycherley 1974, p. 58).

34 Noack (1927, p. 54) notes a cutting for a Z-clamp in a sima block, although he seems to be referring to one of the geison blocks that were built into the later peribolos wall. A further Z-clamp is indicated on the state plan at the southeast corner of the porch, although this could be a mistake of the draughtsman (plan 3). The most common clamp employed elsewhere in the porch foundations is the double-T.

35 The earliest secure uses of this clamp in Athenian buildings are the forecourt of the Old Propylon on the Acropolis, the Southeast Fountain House and Stoa Basileios in the Agora, the Temple of Dionysos, and the Temple of Poseidon at Sounion, none of which can be dated before ca. 500 (for the Z-clamp and dating of the Southeast Fountain House, see Paga forthcoming, 2015).

36 Eschatological or mysteric cult activity occurred at Eleusis since at least the Geometric period and the site was inhabited throughout the Proto-Geometric and Geometric periods (Mylonas 1961, p. 55). There are also Bronze Age remains (Cosmopoulos 2003, including review of prior scholarship).

37 It is possible that initiation for adult male citizens was actively encouraged under the democracy. The evidence for this may be adduced from Andokides, when the court is cleared of the uninitiated, implying that if one wanted to serve as a juror, initiation is a welcome factor that could have expanded the number of cases you could serve on (And., *On the Mysteries* 28); in addition, the Boule met in the City Eleusinion following the Mysteries, which would mean that all 500 *bouleutai* would have to be initiated (for the meeting of the Boule after the Mysteries, see Clinton 1993, p. 119). Thus, in order to participate in two important democratic institutions – the Boule and the law courts – initiation was probably highly encouraged, if not required.

38 For the later garrison, see Pouilloux 1954, pp. 23–92; Petrakos 1999, vol. 1, pp. 51–184.

39 The cemeteries along the road from the deme center to the sanctuary date from the 5th century through the Roman period (A.N. Dinsmoor 1972, p. 1).

40 Petrakos 1983, p. 7. There is also evidence for occupation during the Bronze Age.

41 Petrakos 1982, p. 136, 1999, vol. 1, p. 192.

42 Petrakos 1999, vol. 1, pp. 192–193. This terrace was expanded in the second half of the 5th century, but some amount of leveling would have been necessary during the Archaic period for the erection of the earlier temples. A short length of rubble wall running east–west, a few meters to the south of the Classical retaining wall, may indicate earlier terracing of the site (A.N. Dinsmoor 1972, p. 5; Petrakos 1983, p. 10, 1999, vol. 1, p. 213).

43 Petrakos (1999, vol. 1, p. 194) dates this temple to the very end of the 6th century on the basis of its architectural fragments.

44 See Petrakos 1999, vol. 1, p. 195, fig. 111, for drawings of a triglyph block, an anta capital with a handsome hawks beak moulding, and a Doric capital. Petrakos' excavations of 1975 brought to light several new fragments of the limestone temple and allowed for a more accurate reconstruction than that offered by Gandy (Petrakos 1999, vol. 1, p. 195; see also p. 194, fig. 110, for Petrakos' reconstruction). The initial discussion of the finds and evidence is presented in Petrakos 1982, pp. 136–142.

45 Petrakos 1999, vol. 1, p. 195. The distyle *in antis* façade is secure due to the survival of parts of Doric columns as well as anta blocks.

46 Petrakos 1999, vol. 1, p. 194. For the use of local stone in deme building projects more generally, see Osborne 1985, pp. 93–110.

47 Bergquist 1967, pp. 42–43. Petrakos has suggested that this temple replaced the earlier 6th century temple, and that both stood as precursors to the Classical temple (1983, p. 11, 1999, vol. 1, p. 194).

48 The small building had previously been reconstructed with a distyle *in antis* façade (A.N. Dinsmoor 1972, p. 19; Petrakos 1983, p. 11). Petrakos subsequently divorced the columnar façade from this building and assigned it to the Late Archaic temple instead (1999, vol. 1, p. 199).

49 Bergquist 1967, pp. 42–43; A.N. Dinsmoor 1972, p. 19; Petrakos 1983, p. 11. Cf. Petrakos 1999, vol. 1, pp. 198–199, where he prefers a post-480 date for the small polygonal temple. He does not detail any specific evidence to support this later date, and the only pottery mentioned dates to the first quarter of the 5th century, indicating that the structure must date between 500 and 475 at the latest (for the ceramic evidence, see p. 217).

50 Miles (1989, pp. 150–153, n. 34) discusses the closeness of the two buildings and describes how the south krepidoma of the later Temple of Nemesis takes the smaller building into account.

51 Miles also emphasizes the importance of site specificity and the continued sanctity of cult spaces in the sanctuary; she suggests that the foundations for the late 6th century Temple of Nemesis may have been reused by its Classical successor (1989, p. 153, n. 34).

52 Bergquist posits a similar relationship between the location of the earlier temples and the later Classical successor (1967, pp. 42–43). For the Classical Temple of Nemesis, see Miles 1989.

53 Temple of Themis: Bergquist 1967, pp. 42–43; Boersma 1970, pp. 77–78, 143; A.N. Dinsmoor 1972, pp. 19–22 (although she believes it is more likely an older temple to Nemesis, p. 19); Miles 1989, p. 139; Goette 1993, p. 248; Camp 2001, p. 301. The occasion of the statue's dedication was the awarding of a crown: *IG* II² 2109 (= Petrakos 1999, vol. 2, no. 120). The statue is over life-size and was carved of Pentelic marble by the sculptor Chaerestratos, son of Chaeredemos, also of Rhamnous; note that both the dedicator and sculptor use their demotic as a form of identification. The statue has been dated to the second half of the 4th century and did not serve as a cult statue (A.N. Dinsmoor 1972, pp. 21–22; Petrakos 1999, vol. 2, p. 99). Cf. Camp 2001, p. 301, who dates the statue to the 3rd century.

54 Petrakos 1999, vol. 2, nos. 121–122, both dated to the second half of the 4th century.

55 Wilhelm 1940, pp. 200–209; Miles 1989, p. 139, n. 7, with additional bibliography.

56 Another possibility, favored by Petrakos (1983 p. 12, 1999, vol. 1, pp. 200–203), is that the building originally served as a temple to Themis but later functioned as a treasury, perhaps having been converted for this purpose during the Classical period after the larger Temple of Nemesis was built.

57 The site specificity of the goddess of retribution with Rhamnous is further illuminated through the dedication of a helmet to Nemesis in her sanctuary by the "Rhamnousians on Lemnos" (*IG* I³522bis, dated ca. 475–450; cf. *SEG* 35.24, dated ca. 499). I thank one of the anonymous readers for drawing this dedication and its implications to my attention.

58 The cult statue of Nemesis that stood in the Classical temple was said to have been carved from a stone brought to Marathon by the Persians, concretizing the connection between the goddess and the Athenian victory in 490 (Paus. 1.33.2–3, cf. Pliny, *NH* 36.4). The epigram detailing this reuse of the stone is attributed to Parmenion and is dated to the 1st century (see Miles 1989, pp. 137–138 for the epigram, translation, and previous bibliography).

59 For the important connections between Marathon and temples, see Krentz 2007.

60 *IG* I³ 248 (= EM 12863, M&L 53, Pouilloux 35, Petrakos 1999, vol. 2, no. 182). The inscription encompasses five entries, apparently made annually; it is dated to ca. 450–440, prior to the construction of the marble Temple of Nemesis.

61 Rhamnous falls into the "grey area" identified by Parker, namely demes with sanctuaries that have both local and broader, polis-wide significance, local and central funding, and/or local and Athenian-wide festivals and rites; the same circumstances apply to Sounion (2005, pp. 58–62).

62 The funding for the construction of the two new temples was probably made in part by the deme of Rhamnous itself, along with private contributions, and in part by the state treasury, particularly given the connection between Nemesis and the battle of Marathon.

63 For the theatral area at Rhamnous see Pouilloux 1954, pp. 73–78; Petrakos 1999, vol. 1, pp. 89–94; Paga 2010, pp. 361–363.

64 All three theatral areas are rectilinear and the dimensions of those at Rhamnous and Ikarion are comparable; the theatral area at Thorikos is larger than both, but retains the same form (Paga 2010, pp. 355–363). Dilke (1950, p. 30) also suggests that an earlier theatral area likely existed at Rhamnous.

65 The deme of Sounion was not located on the promontory, but nearby, likely to the north of the Cape (Young 1941, pp. 165–166; Eliot 1962, pp. 90–92, esp. n. 58; Traill 1975, p. 45, with further bibliography, 1986, p. 131).

66 At present, only small sections within the late 5th and 4th century fortification walls near the sanctuary of Poseidon have been systematically excavated. It has been assumed that the dwellings uncovered probably housed a garrison of the Classical and Hellenistic period (Dinsmoor, Jr. 1971, p. 37). For non-centralized habitation during the Archaic period, see Salliora-Oikonomakou 2004, especially pp. 37–39.

67 Dinsmoor, Jr. 1971, pp. 2–4. The earliest literary reference to Sounion occurs in Homer, *Od.* 3.276: Σούνιον ἱρὸν. Sounion is also identified as the place where Phrontis, one of Menelaus' sailors, was buried. There is not yet any positive physical evidence, however, for a heroön or worship of Phrontis within the known deme site (contra. Sinn 1992, pp. 176–177).

68 Dinsmoor, Jr. (1971, pp. 2–5) discusses the evidence for early cult activity in the sanctuary of Poseidon. For additional comments on the early votive finds, see Staïs 1917, pp. 189–213; Salliora-Oikonomakou 2004, pp. 116–118; Theodoropoulou-Polychroniadis 2014. Dinsmoor, Jr. compares the *kouroi* finds to the pits of Persian destruction debris from Athens (1971, p. 11). For Persian debris pits on the Acropolis, see Lindenlauf 1997; Stewart 2008a; for Persian debris pits in the Agora, see Shear 1993; for the ramifications of the destroyed and damaged temples on Athenian identity and memory, see Miles 2014.

69 Contra. Salliora-Oikonomakou (2004, pp. 36–37), who argues that the limestone Temple of Poseidon was constructed well before ca. 500 (or that an earlier temple existed in the second half of the 6th century) and assigns a peribolos wall and possible early fortification wall to this phase. For the dating of the limestone temple, see Paga and Miles (2011) and discussion below.

70 For the connections between the Alkmaeonidai and Anaphlystos and, by topographical association, Sounion, see Camp 1994, pp. 8–9; Anderson 2000, pp. 388–393, with earlier bibliography. Eliot (1967) associates the Alkmaionidai with the district of Anavyssos and suggests a "home deme" of Aigilia during the 6th century. See also Stanton 1994, where the trittyes divisions are analyzed in terms of strengthening

and weakening traditional aristocratic families in Attica (esp. pp. 218–219).

71 The Alkmaionidai have stronger links with Alopeke, a city deme of phyle X, than with any other deme in Attica: *AthPol* 22.5: καὶ ὠστρακίσθη Μεγακλῆς Ἱπποκράτους Ἀλωπεκῆθεν. "Megakles, son of Hippokrates, from the deme Alopeke was ostracized." The demotic for members of the Alkmaeonidai is also attested in numerous ostraka, for which see Lang 1990, nos. 628–639 (pp. 93–95); Peek 1941, p. 83; Scheibler 1976, p. 23, no. 53, p. 153, nos. 2a–2c.

72 For the date and historical circumstances surrounding the construction of the Archaic Temple, see Paga and Miles 2011.

73 The newly discovered *kioniskos* from Thebes presents a challenge to the traditional Herodotean treatment of these events: the inscription on the votive column describes how the Thebans seized Oinoe and Phyle, but makes no mention (as preserved) of Hysiae, nor does Herodotos mention Phyle (Aravantinos 2006).

74 Clinton (1994, p. 162) arrives at a similar conclusion regarding the role of the fortifications at Eleusis and their connection with the events of 506/5.

75 Herodotos does not say whether the festival was held in honor of Poseidon or Athena.

76 For walls at Piraeus prior to 480, see Boersma 1970, p. 37; Garland 1987, pp. 163–165; Eickstedt 1991, pp. 23–24; Steinhauer 2000, pp. 42–45; Conwell 2008. Several additional elements support a pre-Persian build-up of the Piraeus: the theater at Mounychia (Garland 1987, pp. 161, 221; Travlos 1988, pp. 342–343; Paga 2010, pp. 360–361); sanctuary of Artemis Mounychia (Garland 1987, p. 14; Travlos 1988, p. 115); quarry activity, particularly for the massive podium of the Old Parthenon (Langdon 2000); cult of Zeus Soter, possibly founded around 480 (Steinhauer 2000, p. 115); ship sheds (Lovén 2012, pp. 1–14, 167–169).

77 Catalogued by Raubitschek 1949. In total, 26 dedications dated within a generation of the Cleisthenic reforms employ the demotic and not the patronymic, as compared with 49 that use the patronymic but not the demotic (p. 474). The demotic is also attested in numerous ostraka, for which, see Lang 1990, nos. 628–639 (pp. 93–95); and Peek 1941, p. 83; Scheibler 1976, p. 23, no. 53, p. 153, nos. 2a–2c. We can also highlight inscriptions from various demes, such as Sounion (*IG* I^3 1024A, dated to the end of the 6th century by Raubitschek [p. 472, *IG* I^2 830b]) and Eleusis (*IG* I^3 995 dated soon after 500), as indications that the demotic was present outside of the city center.

78 *AthPol* 21.4: καὶ δημότας ἐποίησεν ἀλλήλων τοὺς οἰκοῦντας ἐν ἑκάστῳ τῶν δήμων, ἵνα μὴ πατρόθεν προσαγορεύοντες ἐξελέγχωσιν τοὺς νεοπολίτες, ἀλλὰ τῶν δήμων ἀναγορεύωσιν

79 Haussoullier 1883, pp. 4–93; Hopper 1957; Whitehead 1986, pp. 86–129; Ober 1989, p. 70; for deme rituals and sacred calendars, see Whitehead 1986, pp. 176–222.

References

Alavanou, A. 1972. *Brauron and Halai Araphenides*, Athens.

Anderson, G. 2000. "Alkmeonid 'Homelands,' Political Exile, and the Unification of Attica," *Historia* 49, pp. 387–412.

Anderson, G. 2003. *The Athenian Experiment: Building an Imagined Political Community in Ancient Attica: 508–490 BC*, Ann Arbor.

Andreou, I. 1994. " Ὁ δῆμος των Ἀιξωνίδων Ἀλῶν," in *The Archaeology of Athens and Attica under the Democracy*, eds. W. D. E. Coulson, et al., Oxford, pp. 191–209.

Apostolopoulou-Kakovoianni, O. 1986. "Δυο Νεα Μνημεια Υστεροαρχαικης Πλαστικης απο τις Πρασιες," in *Archaische und Klassische Griechische Plastik*, vol. 1, ed. H. Kyrieleis, Mainz am Rhein, pp. 171–175.

Aravantinos, V. 2006. "A New Inscribed *Kioniskos* from Thebes," *Annual of the British School in Athens* 101, pp. 369–377.

Bankel, H. 1993. *Der Spätarchaische Tempel der Aphaia auf Aegina*, Berlin and New York.

Bergquist, B. 1967. *The Archaic Greek Temenos*, Lund.

Biers, W. R. and T. D. Boyd. 1982. "Ikarion in Attica: 1888–1981," *Hesperia* 51, pp. 1–18.

Boegehold, A. L. and A. C. Scafuro, eds. 1994. *Athenian Identity and Civic Ideology*, Baltimore.

Boersma, J. S. 1970. *Athenian Building Policy from 561/0 to 405/4 B.C*, Groningen.

Buck, C. D. 1888. "Discoveries in the Attic Deme of Ikaria, 1888," *American Journal of Archaeology* 4, pp. 44–46, 421–426.

Camp, J. 2001. *The Archaeology of Athens*, New Haven.

Camp, J. 1994. "Before Democracy: Alkmaionidai and Peisistratidai," in *The Archaeology of Athens and Attica under the Democracy*, eds. W. D. E. Coulson, et al., Oxford, pp. 7–12.

Castriota, D. 1998. "Democracy and Art in Late Sixth- and Fifth-Century BC Athens," in *Democracy 2500?*, eds. K.A. Raaflaub and I. Morris, Dubuque, I.A., pp. 197–216.

Childs, W. 1994. "The Date of the Old Temple of Athena on the Athenian Acropolis," in *The Archaeology of Athens and Attica under the Democracy*, eds. Coulson, et.al., Oxford, pp. 1–6.

Clinton, K. 1993. "The sanctuary of Demeter and Kore at Eleusis," in *Greek Sanctuaries: New approaches*, eds. N. Marinatos and R. Hägg, London, pp. 110–124.

Clinton, K. 1994. "The Eleusinian Mysteries and Panhellenism in Democratic Athens," in *The Archaeology of Athens and Attica Under the Democracy*, eds. W. D. E. Coulson, et al., Oxford, pp. 161–172.

Clinton, K. 2005. *Eleusis: The Inscriptions on Stone: Documents of the Sanctuary of the Two Goddesses and Public Documents of the Deme*, 2 vols., Athens.

Cohen, B. 2001. "Ethnic Identity in Democratic Athens and the Visual Vocabulary of Male Costume," in *Ancient Perceptions of Greek Ethnicity*, ed. I. Malkin, Cambridge, Mass., pp. 235–274.

Conwell, D. H. 2008. *Connecting a City to the Sea: The History of the Athenian Long Walls*, *Mnemosyne* Supplement 293.

Cosmopoulos, M. B. 2003. "Mycenaean Religion at Eleusis: The architecture and stratigraphy of Megaron B," in *Greek Mysteries: The Archaeology and Ritual of Ancient Greek Secret Cults*, ed. M. Cosmopoulos, Routledge, pp. 1–24.

Coulson, W. D. E., O. Palagia, T. L. Shear, Jr., H. A. Shapiro, and F. J. Frost., eds. 1994. *The Archaeology of Athens and Attica under the Democracy*, Oxford.

Despinis, G. 2007. "Neues zu der spätarchaische Statue des Dionysos aus Ikaria," *Mitteilungen des Deutschen Archäologischen Instituts, Athenische Abteilung* 122, pp. 103–137.

Dilke, O. A. W. 1950. "Details and Chronology of Greek Theatre Cavea," *Annual of the British School in Athens* 45, pp. 25–31.

Dinsmoor, A. N. 1972. *Rhamnous*, Athens.

Dinsmoor, W. B., Jr. 1971. *Sounion*, Athens.

Eickstedt, K. V. von. 1991. *Beiträge zur Topographie des antiken Piräus*, Athens.

Eliot, C. W. J. 1962. *Coastal Demes of Attika: A Study of the Policy of Kleisthenes*, *Phoenix* Supplement V, Toronto.

Eliot, C. W. J. 1967. "Where did the Alkmaionidai live?" *Historia* 16, pp. 279–286.

Elsner, J. 2012. "Material Culture and Ritual: State of the Question," in *Architecture of the Sacred: Space, Ritual, and Experience from Classical Greece to Byzantium*, eds. B. D. Wescoat and R. G. Ousterhout, Cambridge, pp. 1–26.

Fearn, D., ed. 2011. *Aegina: Contexts for Choral Lyric Poetry*, Oxford.

Garland, R. 1987. *The Piraeus: from the fifth to the first century BC*, London.

Gebhard, E. 1974. "The Form of the Orchestra in the Early Greek Theater," *Hesperia* 43, pp. 429–432.

Goette, H. 1993. *Athen-Attika-Megaris: Reiseführer zu den Kunstschätzen und Kulturdenkmälern im Zentrum Griechenlands*, Berlin.

Hackens, T. 1965 [1967]. "Le théâtre," in *Thorikos III*, eds. H. F. Mussche, J. Bingen, et al., Brussel, pp. 75–96.

Hall, J. M. 1997. *Ethnic identity in Greek antiquity*, Cambridge.

Hall, J. M. 2002. *Hellenicity: Between Ethnicity and Culture*, Chicago.

Haussoullier, B. 1884. *La vie municipale en Attique: essai sur l'organisation des dèmes au quatrème siècle*, Paris.

Hayashi, T. 1992. *Bedeutung und Wandel des Triptolemosbildes vom 6.–4. Jh. v. Chr.: Religionshistorische und typologische Untersuchungen*, Würzburg.

Hedreen, G. 2011. "The Trojan War, Theoxenia, and Aegina in Pindar's *Paean* 6 and the Aphaia Sculptures," in *Aegina: Contexts for Choral Lyric Poetry*, ed. D. Fearn, Oxford, pp. 323–369.

Hollinshead, M. B. 2012. "Monumental Steps and the Shaping of Ceremony," in *Architecture of the Sacred: Space, Ritual, and Experience from Classical Greece to Byzantium*, eds. B. D. Wescoat and R. G. Ousterhout, Cambridge, pp. 27–65.

Hölscher, T. 1998. "Images and Political Identity: The Case of Athens," in *Democracy, Empire, and the Arts*, eds. D. Boedeker and K. A. Raaflaub, Cambridge, Mass., pp. 153–183.

Hopper, R. J. 1957. *The Basis of the Athenian Democracy*, University of Sheffield, Inaugural Lecture, 30 January.

Indergaard, H. 2011. "Thebes, Aegina, and the Temple of Aphaia: A Reading of Pindar's *Isthmian* 6," in *Aegina: Contexts for Choral Lyric Poetry*, ed. D. Fearn, Oxford, pp. 294–322.

Keesling, C. M. 2003. *The Votive Statues of the Athenian Acropolis*, Cambridge.

Korres, M. 1995. *From Pentelicon to Parthenon: Exhibition Catalogue*, Athens.

Kourouniotes, K. 1927–28. "Τὸ Ἱερὸν τοῦ Ἀπόλλωνος τοῦ Ζωστῆρος," *Archaiologikon Deltion* 11, pp. 9–53.

Krentz, P. M. 2007. "The Oath of Marathon, Not Plataia?" *Hesperia* 76, pp. 731–742.

Lang, F. 1996. *Archaische Siedlungen in Griechenland: Struktur und Entwicklung*, Berlin.

Lang, M. L. 1990. *The Athenian Agora XXV: The Ostraka*, Princeton.

Langdon, M. K. 2000. "The Quarries of Peiraieus," *Archaiologikon Deltion* 55, A', pp. 235–250.

Lindenlauf, A. 1997. "Der Perserschutt der Athener Akropolis," in *Kult und Kultbauten auf der Akropolis. Internationales Symposium vom 7. bis 9. Juli 1995 in Berlin*, ed. W. Höpfner, Berlin, pp. 46–115.

Lippolis, E. 2006. *Mysteria: archeologia e culto del santuario di Demetra a Eleusi*, Milan.

Lippolis, E., M. Livadiotti, and G. Rocco, eds. 2007. *Architettura Greca: storia e monumenti del mondo della polis dale orgini al V secolo*, Milan.

Loraux, N. 1986. *The Invention of Athens: The Funeral Oration in the Classical City*, trans. A. Sheridan, Cambridge, Mass.

Lovén, B. 2012. *The Ancient Harbours of the Piraeus*, 2 vol., Athens.

Malkin, I. 2001. *Ancient Perceptions of Greek Ethnicity*, Cambridge, Mass.

Manville, P. B. 1990. *The Origins of Citizenship in Ancient Athens*, Princeton.

Mark, I. 1993. *The Sanctuary of Athena Nike in Athens: Architectural Stages and Chronology*, *Hesperia* Supplement 26, Princeton.

Meiggs, R. and D. Lewis, eds. 1969. *A Selection of Greek Historical Inscriptions to the end of the Fifth Century BC*, rev. ed., Oxford.

Miles, M. M. 1989. "A reconstruction of the Temple of Nemesis at Rhamnous," *Hesperia* 58, pp. 133–249.

Miles, M. M. 1998. *The Athenian Agora XXXI: The City Eleusinion*, Princeton.

Miles, M. M. 2014. "Burnt Temples in the Landscape of the Past," in *Valuing the Past in the Greco-Roman World: Proceedings from the Penn-Leiden Colloquia on Ancient Values VII*, eds. J. Ker and C. Pieper, Leiden, pp. 111–145.

Miller, M. 1997. *Athens and Persia in the fifth century BC: A study in cultural receptivity*, Cambridge.

Miller, M. 2011. "Imaging Persians in the Age of Herodotos," in *Herodot und das Persische Weltreich / Herodotus and the Persian Empire*, eds R. von Rollinger, B. Truschnegg, and R. Bichler, Wiesbaden, pp. 123–157.

Miller, M. 2013. "Clothes and Identity: The Case of the Greeks in Ionia c. 400 BC," *Antichthon* 47, pp. 18–38.

Miller, S. G. 1995. "Architecture as Evidence for the Identity of the Early *Polis*," in *Sources for the Ancient Greek City-State*, ed. M.H. Hansen, Copenhagen, pp. 201–244.

Mussche, H. F. 1975. "Thorikos in Archaic and Classical Times," in *Thorikos and the Laurion in Archaic and Classical Times*, eds. H. F. Mussche, P. Spitaels, and F. Goemaere-De Poerck, Ghent, pp. 45–61.

Mussche, H. F. 1990. "Das Theatre von Thorikos. Einige Betrachtungen," *Opes Atticae, Miscellanea philologica et historica*, ed. M. Geerard, The Hague, pp. 309–314.

Mussche, H. F. 1994. "Thorikos During the Last Years of the Sixth Century BC," in *The Archaeology of Athens and Attica under the Democracy*, eds. W. D. E. Coulson, et al., Oxford, pp. 211–215.

Mussche, H. F. 1998. *Thorikos: A Mining Town in Ancient Attika*, Gent.

Mylonas, G. E. 1961. *Eleusis and the Eleusinian Mysteries*, Princeton.

Noack, F. 1927. *Eleusis: Die Baugeschichtliche Entwicklung des Heiligtums*, Berlin.

Ober, J. 1989. *Mass and Elite in Democratic Athens: Rhetoric, Ideology, and the Power of the People*, Princeton.

Ohnesorg, A. 1993. *Inselionische Marmordächer*, Berlin.

Osborne, R. 1985. *Demos: The Discovery of Classical Attika*, Cambridge.

Paga, J. 2010. "Deme Theaters in Attica and the Trittys System," *Hesperia* 79, pp. 351–384.

Paga, J. 2012. *Architectural Agency and the Construction of Athenian Democracy* (PhD diss., Princeton University).

Paga, J. (forthcoming, 2015). "The Southeast Fountain House in the Athenian Agora: A Reappraisal of its Date and Historical Context," *Hesperia* 84.

Paga, J. and M. M. Miles. 2011. "The Archaic Temple of Poseidon at Sounion: New Discoveries," in *Archaeological Institute of America, 112th Annual Meeting Abstracts*, vol. 34, p. 98.

Papadimitriou, J. 1963. "The Sanctuary of Artemis at Brauron," *Scientific American* 208, pp. 110–120.

Parker, R. 2005. *Polytheism and Society at Athens*, Oxford.

Peek, W. 1941. *Kerameikos III: Inschriften, Ostraka, Fluchtafeln*, Berlin.

Petrakos, B. 1982. "Ἀνασκαφὴ Ραμνοῦντος," *Praktika tes en Athenais Archaiologikes Etaireias*, pp. 127–162.

Petrakos, B. 1983. *Rhamnous*, XII International Congress of Classical Archaeology, Athens.

Petrakos, B. 1999. Ο δῆμος του Ραμνοῦντος, 2 vol., Athens.

Polinskaya, I. 2013. *A Local History of Greek Polytheism. Gods, People, and the Land of Aegina, 800–400 BCE. Religions in the Greco-Roman World* 178, Leiden.

Pouilloux, J. 1954. *La forteresse de Rhamnonte: etude de topographie et d'histoire*, Paris.

Raubitschek, A. E. 1949. *Dedications from the Athenian Akropolis*, Cambridge.

Robinson, E. W. 2011. *Democracy Beyond Athens: Popular Government in the Greek Classical Age*, Cambridge.

Romano, I. B. 1980. *Early Greek Cult Images* (diss. University of Pennsylvania).

Romano, I. B. 1982. "The Archaic Statue of Dionysos from Ikarion," *Hesperia* 51, pp. 398–409.

Salliora-Oikonomakou, M. 2004. Ο Αρχαιος Δημος του Σουνιου: Ιστορικη και Τοπογραφικη Επισκοπηση, Koropi.

Scheibler, I. 1976. *Kerameikos XI: Griechische Lampen*, Berlin.

Shapiro, H. A. 1998. "Autochthony and the Visual Arts in Fifth-Century Athens," in *Democracy, Empire, and the Arts in Fifth-Century Athens*, eds. D. Boedeker and K. A. Raaflaub, Cambridge, Mass, pp. 127–151.

Shapiro, H. A. 2012. "Attic Heroes and the Construction of the Athenian Past in the Fifth Century." in *Greek Notions of the Past in the Archaic and Classical Eras: History without Historians* (Edinburgh Leventis Studies 6), eds. J. Marincola, L. Llewellyn-Jones, and C. Maciver, Edinburgh, pp. 160–182.

Shear, T. L., Jr. 1982. "The Demolished Temple at Eleusis," in *Studies in Athenian Architecture, Sculpture, and Topography Presented to Homer A. Thompson, Hesperia* Supplement 20, Princeton, pp. 128–140.

Shear, T.L., Jr. 1993. "The Persian Destruction of Athens: Evidence from Agora Deposits," *Hesperia* 62, pp. 383–482.

Shear, T.L., Jr. 1994. "Ἰσονόμους τἈθήνας ἐποιησάτην: The Agora and the Democracy." In *The Archaeology of Athens and Attica under the Democracy*, eds. W. D. W. Coulson, et al., Oxford, pp. 225–248.

Shear, T.L., Jr. 1995. "Bouleuterion, Metroon, and the Archives at Athens," in *Studies in the Ancient Greek Polis*, ed. M. Hansen, Copenhagen, pp. 157–190.

Sinn, U. 1992. "Sunion. Das befestigte Heiligtum der Athena und des Poseidon an der 'Heiligen Landspitze Attikas'," *Antike Welt* 23, pp. 175–190.

Snodgrass, A. 1983. "Archaeology," in *Sources for Ancient History*, ed. M. Crawford, Cambridge, pp. 137–184.

Staïs, B. 1917. "Σουνίου ἀνασκαφαί," *Archaiologike Ephemeris*, pp. 168–213.

Stanton, G. R. 1994. "The Rural Demes and Athenian Politics." In *The Archaeology of Athens and Attica under the Democracy*, eds. W. D. E. Coulson, et al., Oxford, pp. 217–224.

Steinhauer, G. A., M. G. Malikouti, and B. Tsokopoulos, eds. 2000. *Piraeus: Centre of Shipping and Culture*, Athens.

Stewart, A. 2008a. "The Persian and Carthaginian Invasions of 480 BCE. and the Beginning of the Classical Style: Part 1, The Stratigraphy, Chronology, and Significance of the Acropolis Deposits," *American Journal of Archaeology* 112, pp. 377–412.

Stewart, A. 2008b. "The Persian and Carthaginian Invasions of 480 BCE. and the Beginning of the Classical Style: Part 2, The Finds from Other Sites in Athens, Attica, Elsewhere in Greece, and on Sicily; Part 3, The Severe Style: Motivations and Meaning," *American Journal of Archaeology* 112, pp. 581–615.

Taylor, M. 1991. *The Tyrant Slayers: The Heroic Image in Fifth Century BC Athenian Art and Politics*, Salem.

Themelis, P. G. 1971. *Brauron*, Athens.

Themelis, P.G. 2002. "Contribution to the Topography of the Sanctuary at Brauron," in *Le orse di Brauron*, eds. B. Gentili and F. Perusino, Pisa, pp. 103–116.

Theodoropoulou-Polychroniadis, Z. 2014. "Terracotta Offerings from the Sanctuaries of Poseidon and of Athena at Sounion," *Newsletter of the Association for Coroplastic Studies* 11, pp. 5–7.

Tölle-Kastenbein, R. 1994. *Das Olympieion in Athen*, Cologne.

Traill, J. S. 1975. *The Political Organization of Attica, Hesperia* Supplement XIV, Princeton.

Traill, J. S. 1986. *Demos and Trittys: Epigraphical and Topographical Studies in the Organization of Attica*, Toronto.

Travlos, J. 1950–1951. "Τὸ Ἀνάκτορον τῆς Ἐλευσῖνος," *Archaiologike Ephemeris*, pp. 1–16.

Travlos, J. 1988. *Bildlexicon zur Topographie des antiken Attika*, Tübingen.

Whitehead, D. 1986. *The Demes of Attica, 508/7–ca. 250 BC*, Princeton.

Wilhelm, A. 1940. "Themis und Nemesis in Rhamnous," *Jahreshefte des Österreichischen Archäologischen Institutes in Wien* 32, pp. 200–209.

Wiegand, T. 1904. *Die archaische Porosarchitektur der Akropolis zu Athen*, Cassel und Leipzig.

Wycherley, R. E. 1974. "The Stones of Athens," *Greece & Rome*, 2nd ser., 21, pp. 54–67.

Young, J. H. 1941. "Studies in South Attica: The Salaminioi at Porthmos," *Hesperia* 10, pp. 163–191.

Appendix: Monumental Structures in Attica, ca. 508/7–480/79 BC

Deme	Structure	Date	Comments
Eleusis	Telesterion	ca. 500 (after 506/5)	previously attributed to the Peisistratidai
Eleusis	Fortification walls	ca. 500 (after 506/5)	contemporary with Telesterion; previously attributed to the Peisistratidai
Rhamnous	Poros Temple	late 6th or early 5th century	probably dedicated to Nemesis and located on north side of sanctuary, below Classical Temple of Nemesis
Rhamnous	Polygonal Temple	1st 1/4 5th century	probably dedicated to Themis, located on south side of sanctuary
Rhamnous	Theatral area	possible early phase in late 6th or early 5th century	also used as assembly area or agora (Paga 2010, pp. 361–363)
Ikarion	Theatral area	probable early phase in late 6th or early 5th century	also used as assembly area or agora (Paga 2010, pp. 357–360); cult of Dionysos attested by *IG* I³ 1015 and statue of Dionysos (Buck 1889, pp. 461–467; Romano 1980, pp. 316-334; Romano 1982; Despinis 2007)
Ikarion	Temple of Pythian Apollo	late 6th or early 5th century	cult attested by *IG* I³ 1015, dated to the last quarter of the 6th century, which may imply the existence of a cult building by this time (Biers and Boyd 1982, pp. 17–18; Paga 2012, p. 523)
Brauron	Temple of Artemis	ca. 500	temple structure, as well as retaining walls for platform (Papadimitriou 1968, pp. 113–115; Themelis 1971, p. 15; Travlos 1988, p. 55; Camp 2001, p. 278; Themelis 2002, p. 104)
Brauron	Bridge; cave structures	possibly ca. 500	Themelis (2002, p. 108) suggests that the bridge across the Sacred Spring, as well as the structures inside the cave, should be dated to the late Archaic or early 5th century building phase of the sanctuary, contemporary with the Temple of Artemis (note also Alvanou 1972, p. 17, detailing the pre-Persian finds recovered from the Sacred Spring); Papadimitriou (1986, p. 120, and plan of sanctuary, p. 114), Travlos (1988, p. 55) and Camp (2001, p. 279) place the bridge closer to the middle of the 5th century
Prasiai	Temple of Apollo?	ca. 500	cult attested by Pausanias (1.31.2); statue base (*IG* I³ 1018[3]), dated ca. 500 (*SEG* XXXVII.47, cf. Raubtischek 1949, nos. 10, 90); marble head, possibly from cult statue of Apollo, dated ca. 500–490 (Apostolopoulou-Kakavoianni 1986; Camp 2001, p. 281); no physical remains of cult building yet identified
Thorikos	Theatral area	ca. 500	also used as assembly area or agora (Paga 2010, pp. 355–356); details of construction and dating (Hackens 1965, pp. 80–84; Gebhard 1974, pp. 429–432; Mussche 1975, pp. 46–47, 52; 1990; 1994, pp. 213–214; 1998, pp. 29–31)
Sounion	Temple of Poseidon	ca. 490–480	unfinished at time of Persian destruction (Paga and Miles 2011)
Cape Zoster	Temple of Apollo, Artemis, and Leto	ca. 500	sanctuary probably under the jurisdiction of Halai Aixonides, rather than Aixone or Anagyrous (Eliot 1962, pp. 25, 32–33; Travlos 1988, p. 467; Andreou 1994, p. 191); temple (Kourouniotes 1927–28; Travlos 1988, pp. 467–468; Andreou 1994, pp. 191, 202; Camp 2001, pp. 316–317)
Piraeus	Mounychia theater	possible early phase in 1st 1/4 5th century	also used as assembly area or agora (Paga 2010, pp. 360–361); details of construction (Garland 1987, pp. 161, 221; Travlos 1988, pp. 342–343)
Piraeus	Fortification walls	1st 1/4 5th century	part of Themostoklean build-up of the Pireaus (Boersma 1970, p. 37; Garland 1987, pp. 163–165; Eickstedt 1991, pp. 23–24; Steinhauer 2000, pp. 42–45)

12. Triremes on Land:
First-fruits for the Battle of Salamis

Kristian Lorenzo

To commemorate their victory in the Battle of Salamis, according to Herodotus (8.121–22), the allied Greeks dedicated three captured enemy warships as thank offerings, one each at Isthmia, Sounion, and Salamis. Earlier scholars have proposed in very general terms either seaside locations or intra-sanctuary settings. In this paper, I argue for both the feasibility of over-land transport, and I offer specific intra-sanctuary locations for the dedicated Phoenician warships by considering the relevant topographical, archaeological, epigraphic and literary evidence. I also offer a new interpretation for some puzzling remains just south of the Temple of Poseidon at Sounion. Once dedicated, the warships both became the sacred property of the resident divinity as they assumed the aspect of monumental wooden sculpture. These triremes are salient examples of votive offerings that could only achieve their full symbolic meaning by prominent positions in the sanctuaries at Isthmia, Sounion and Salamis.

Introduction

With the March 2014 release of 300: Rise of an Empire, the movie version of Frank Miller's graphic novel *Xerxes* about the Battle of Salamis, modern popular knowledge of this pivotal naval battle reached new heights. The victory of the allied Greeks at Salamis against more than two-to-one odds literally turned the tide of the Persian wars and halted the seemingly inexorable advance of the Persian war machine.[1] In 479 BC, according to Herodotus (8.121–22),

> First of all they (the Greeks) chose for the gods, among other first fruits, three Phoenician triremes, the first was to be dedicated at the Isthmus, where it was till my time, the second at Sounion, and the third for Ajax at Salamis where they were.

Herodotus evidently saw one of the dedicated ships himself. Scholars have suggested either seaside locations for the dedications or vague sanctuary settings, but no one has yet studied the feasibility of sanctuary settings or put forth specific intra-sanctuary locations.[2] In this paper, I reconstruct the likely settings for the dedicated Persian warships, and suggest specific intra-sanctuary locations for them. I determine this on the basis of a thorough examination of the topographical and archaeological data for the sanctuaries at

Sounion and Isthmia, as well as the epigraphic and literary evidence for the sanctuary of Ajax on Salamis. As we shall see, given the salient physical features of Phoenician triremes, the ship-handling skills of the period, and the literary and physical evidence for dedicated ships in general, the allied Greek victors invested considerable effort to set these warships within the proposed intra-sanctuary settings as thank-offerings to the gods.

Phoenician Triremes

A Phoenician trireme, or primarily oar-driven wooden warship, is believed to have had three superimposed files of oarsmen on each side, unlike the Greek trireme that was equipped with an outrigger to help house the uppermost file of oarsmen.[3] The lowest level of Phoenician oarsmen worked their oars through oar ports in the hull, while the two upper levels of oarsmen manipulated theirs through open courses. Above the uppermost level of oarsmen, a raised fighting deck extended from gunwale to gunwale; along this deck there was usually a line of shields to form a *pavesade*;[4] a relatively-light cutwater sheathed in relatively-thin metal without heavy wales ended the prow.[5] Either a figurehead or a tutelary statue adorned the prow. Herodotus notes this custom when he relates that "the Phoenicians carry around on the prows of their triremes" likenesses of their dwarf-sized deities called *pataikoi* (3.37). Aeschylus describes the Persian triremes at Salamis as linen-winged and dark-eyed, so they probably had either apotropaic eyes made of carved stone or painted on the upper portion of their prows (*Pers.* 559).[6] The sternpost ends in the traditional Phoenician horse's head. Always carried near the stern, the ship's *stylis* consisted of a staff, or scepter, bearing a globe and crescent, the emblem of the goddess Astarte.

The dimensions of a Greek trireme were 39.6 × 5.6 × 5 (at deck) to 7 m (at end of the aphlaston), and such a warship weighed 20–25 tons, with all the oars, masts, sails and other paraphernalia removed.[7] A Phoenician trireme was the same length (39.6) as a Greek trireme, but may have been wider, perhaps 6.5–7 m, and taller, perhaps 6 m (at deck level).[8] It probably weighed ca. 21–26 tons empty. Both the structural differences and the multifarious eastern decorations, even with eyes (that Greek triremes had as well) adorning the captured Phoenician triremes, guaranteed that these warships would proclaim their otherness when set within the Greek sanctuaries at Isthmia, Sounion, and Salamis. As a monumental wooden sculpture, the warship within the sanctuary at Isthmia was truly fitting recompense both for the god's part in the battle and for his hosting of the congress of Greek city-states of 481, wherein the Greeks achieved the political unity they so desperately needed to repulse the Persians.[9] At Sounion, the captured trireme would rest amidst the destruction wrought by the Persians during their advance through Attica, a symbol of the fate of would-be barbarian oppressors and the renewed hope kindled in the hearts of Greeks after their victory at Salamis. The trireme dedicated in Ajax's cult site, which was near to the seashore on Salamis itself, honored the hero for his help during the battle. A festival *Aianteia* would much later during the late Hellenistic and early Imperial periods, celebrate such aid.[10]

Ship Handling Skills

Two hundred men in total made up the maximum crew size of a fifth-century Greek trireme: one hundred and seventy rowers, ten hoplites, four archers and about sixteen other crewmembers to sail the ship.[11] The size of the crew of a typical Phoenician trireme would have been comparable. Triremes usually did not remain at sea for very long periods of time since crews regularly went ashore at midday, as well as at night, to stretch their limbs, obtain food and water, and rest or sleep.[12] Crews did not draw their ships up onto the beach every time they needed to go ashore. Usually they moored the ship by securing the stern to the shore with ropes and dropping a bow anchor or what is commonly referred to as the "Mediterranean Moor."[13] This type of mooring

allowed easy access to the shore while making efficient use of the very limited living space aboard the trireme, but such mooring posed significant dangers to the fabric of the ship if a trireme was left in the warm Mediterranean water in such a static position too long or too often.

Crews often hauled their triremes out onto the beach. These shallow-drafted vessels could be beached and carried rollers to help move them onto the shore. Wooden keel supports provided maximum stability once they were there.[14] These haul-outs could occur as needed for protective or defensive purposes, to escape a storm, prevent destruction by an onshore gale or flee from a superior fleet.[15] Haul-outs also had to be performed so that the crews could make necessary repairs and complete vital preventive maintenance.[16] According to Lipke, "of all the potential weaknesses of the trireme as an expensive, high-tech warship...none would have been as hard to control, or full of risk to those involved, as its liability to shipworm (*Teredo navalis*) attack."[17] Shipworm damage typically cannot be patched or caulked; damaged planking had to be replaced. In the Aegean, infestation can occur rapidly in any season and at any time a ship is more or less stationary, such as when moored. Traditional coatings, such as the tar and pitch used by ancient shipwrights, were frequently reapplied to remain effective.[18] Under ideal conditions (i.e., an uninfested trireme during peacetime at a naval base with ship sheds) a trireme should have been hauled out the water and had its protective coating touched-up every few days to kill off any shipworms.[19] Regular haul-outs also allowed triremes to "dry-out." A dry ship was faster, lighter and less likely to rot than a waterlogged one.[20] On a regular basis the crews of triremes, whether Greek or Phoenician, were called upon to demonstrate a high level of ship-handling skill both in the water and on land. These land-based skills would then have been employed at seaside locations nearest to the sanctuaries at Isthmia, Sounion and Salamis to haul the triremes stern-first out of the water onto a prepared slipway so that they could dry out. Once dry, the crews could employ their knowledge of ship maintenance to begin prepping the ship for overland transport.

Beyond frequent moorings and the less frequent but even more vital regular hauling-outs, it was sometimes necessary for triremes to be dragged for a distance over land. The earliest author to mention this as a possible course of action is Herodotus (7.22–4), in his account of Xerxes' excavation of a canal across the Athos Isthmus on the eve of invading Greece.[21] The great Persian king spent three years and accrued the guilt of hubris during this endeavor, since, as Herodotus (7.24) notes, Xerxes just as easily could have had the ships carried over the isthmus. Thucydides (3.81.1) recounts how the Spartans executed such a feat when they dragged fifty-three of their ships across the Isthmus of Leukas, a distance of ca. 431 m, in 428 BC and then another fleet of sixty in 425 BC.[22] The Spartans' successful overland transit of a large number of warships, whether with commandeered draft animals or without (Thucydides is silent on the matter), provided good evidence that such a daunting enterprise was a feasible accomplishment.

Dedicated Ships: the Evidence

Herodotus provides the first written evidence for the dedication of whole ships in antiquity. He states that the Greeks in 479 dedicated three captured enemy warships as commemorative thank offerings, one to Poseidon at Isthmia, another at Sounion, and the third to Ajax at Salamis (8.121). The Greeks set aside these captured Phoenician triremes as sacred dedications a few months after their victory in the Battle of Salamis in 480 and Xerxes' hasty return to Asia Minor. Thucydides does not refer to the earlier dedicated Phoenician triremes when he relates how, in 429 first the Athenians (2.84.4) then the Peloponnesians (2.92.4–5) each set up a captured trireme in seaside locations on opposing sides of the mouth of the Corinthian Gulf after the events of the hard-fought sea battle near Naupaktos, the next attested example of dedicated ships. These triremes were not stand-alone monuments, as each one was paired with a traditional battlefield trophy comprised of an upright and crossbeam decorated with a panoply. The Athenians had been vastly outnumbered, but Phormio's brilliance led to overwhelming victory at the end; the Peloponnesians felt impelled nonetheless to mark their initial success.

Several later authors relate instances of whole dedicated ships. Plutarch in Theseus (23.1) says that the Athenians preserved the thirty-oared galley of Theseus down to ca. 307 BC by replacing its old timbers one at a time, and putting new and sound ones in their places (thus creating the model for a well-known conundrum about the nature of originality in form and material). Pausanius (1.29.1) refers to a ship on Delos, and knows of no ship that ever "conquered" the enneres or "Nine". Athenaeus (5.209e), reports that the Macedonian king, Antigonus Gonatas, dedicated a sacred 'trireme' to Apollo, but he does not include its location. In the realm of dedications of 'legendary' ships like Theseus', pseudo-Apollodorus in his Bibliotheca (1.9.27), a 2nd century AD compendium of myths and heroic legends drawn from earlier tragedies and epics, relates that Jason dedicated the Argo to Poseidon at Isthmia. Around the same time, the philosopher Favorinus (not Dio Chrysostom) relates in his Corinthian Oration (37.15) that Jason dedicated the Argo to Poseidon at Isthmia complete with a dedicatory epigram by Orpheus,

> I am the good ship Argo, to the god by Jason devoted,
> Victor in the Isthmian Games, crowned with Nemean pine.

Procopius, writing in the AD 550s, mentions one whole ship set in a building: the Romans enshrined the "ship of Aeneas" as a relic of their mythical Trojan founder's journey in its own purpose-built neorion, or ship shed, in the middle of the city on one of the Tiber's banks (*Goth.* 8.22.5–16).[23] In the same text, Procopius mentions other dedicatory ships: on the shore of Corfu, a merchant dedicated a marble boat inscribed to Zeus Kasios, although some believed that it was the boat Odysseus sailed from Phaeacia to Ithaca (8.23–26). At Porto Castri on Euboia an inscribed stone boat made by Tynnichus and dedicated to Artemis Bolosia (i.e. Eileithuia) playfully declared that Agamemnon set it up as a perpetual sign of the Greeks sailing to Troy, but the inscription was incomplete (8.27–29).

No physical evidence remains for the dedicated Phoenician triremes of 479 noted by Herodotus or the dedicated Greek triremes of 429 mentioned by Thucydides (but as always, absence of evidence is not proof of absence, especially given the perishable nature of wooden artifacts left in exposed locations). Archaeological evidence for a dedicated ship is preserved, however, at Samos, in the sanctuary of Hera. In the late seventh century a ship was set up 20 m south of the altar within the sanctuary.[24] Located approximately 170 m north of the modern shoreline, the length of the Samian ship's nine individual, regularly spaced, parallel stone foundations is ca. 23.33 m with a width of 3.22 m. The foundations could have supported a ship with maximum dimensions of ca. 30 m long and ca. 4 m wide, weighing ca. 15 tons.[25] Based on these maximum ship dimensions the Samian dedicated ship might have been a pentecontor, that is, a bi-level, multipurpose galley used in war, long-distance trade, and colonial expeditions, but it did not survive long. Its foundations were built over by a rectangular structure in the 6th century.[26] Since Samos became wealthy and prominent in the early Archaic period because of extended Mediterranean contacts, such a dedication is not surprising.

Elsewhere in Greece, and also in the setting of sanctuaries, the next physical evidence for Greeks dedicating whole ships comes from early in the Hellenistic period, more precisely ca. 306–286. In the southeast area of the sanctuary of Apollo on Delos a victorious king, most likely Demetrius Poliorcetes, set a dedicated warship, probably a penteres or Five, within its own purpose-built structure where the Five "floated" in a marble basin.[27] The neorion on Delos (also known as the Monument of the Bulls) is approximately 150 m from the modern shoreline. On the northern Aegean Island of Samothrace an unknown monarch dedicated a ca. 27 × 4 m long ship in a purpose-built rectangular building set on the slope of the Western Hill at the northwest corner of the Sanctuary of the Great Gods, located ca. 460 m uphill from the modern shoreline.[28] The Samothracian neorion is dated to the first half of the 3rd century BC, based on pottery recovered during excavations. The ship in this neorion was cradled on seven marble supports set on top of seven individual, regularly spaced, parallel stone foundations similar to the nine foundations used to help support the Samian ship.[29] The marble props have concave resting surfaces and become taller and narrower toward the end of the room. In addition to those from Samos, Delos and Samothrace, we also have as physical evidence for a dedicated ship keel supports made of schist, found southwest of the harbor of the main city of Thasos.[30] The excavators found the Thasian keel supports not far from a platform they interpret as intended for hauling ships out of the water. They associate the supports with the nearby temple of Thea Soteira, worshipped by sailors.

The literary and physical evidence for the dedication of whole ships is substantial and varied, and provides a compelling picture of an important Greek dedicatory practice, which may have lasted in one form or another for as long as a millennium. The archaeological evidence begins well before the dedicated Phoenician triremes of 479, and ends several hundred years later, providing ample testimony to the clear desire on the part of some Greeks to commemorate their naval victories with warships set in intra-sanctuary settings. The surprise and glamour of an actual ship set up as a monument on land, quite out of context but a vivid reminder of the perils of seafaring and naval battles, must have been balanced by its intrinsically ephemeral nature: thus such monuments were highly memorable.

Overland Transport

From the 7th century BC to the 4th century AD in Greece, stones weighing several tons were transported 10–25 miles.[31] Individual column drums and monoliths weighed a couple of tons and needed a team of several pairs of oxen. Column drums found at Eleusis, which weigh 8–10 tons might have needed 20–30 pairs of oxen.[32] Transports such as these were ordinary – even if they required tremendous labor and resources – and occurred sporadically during construction projects including those of the monumental temples at Delphi, Eleusis, Epidaurus and Didyma. The forty columns of the temple of Apollo at Corinth, built from 550–525, were 26-ton monoliths 7.21 m long each with a diameter greater than 1.3 m.[33] Raepsaet notes rare instances of building material as heavy as 50–70 tons.[34] By 479 the Greeks had much practical experience in successfully moving very heavy loads across distances up to 25 kilometers.

Indirect archaeological evidence for the overland transport of a warship, measuring ca. 30 × 4 m and weighing approximately 15 tons, partitioned into sections is provided by the evidence for the ship dedicated in the Sanctuary of Hera on Samos noted above, dated to the late seventh century. A more compelling but later example also noted above is the penteres, measuring ca. 45 × 6.4 m and weighing approximately 52 tons, that had been set within the neorion on Delos in ca. 306–286.[35] Although no 5th century BC or earlier literary evidence exists for such partitioning and overland transport, Arrian (*Anab.* 7.19.3),

Quintus Curtius Rufus (10.1.19), Strabo (16.1.11), and Plutarch (*Vit. Alex.* 68.1) recount how Alexander the Great had a fleet that was built in Phoenicia disassembled and transported for seven days across land, to be reassembled for operations on the Euphrates River. However, this fleet was probably composed of riverboats built using a form of construction such as laced mortise-and-tenon joinery that would allow them to be disassembled. These riverboats also probably lacked rams since such weapons need a more rigid type of joinery and the Euphrates is simply not big enough for vessels to maneuver effectively to use them.[36] As will be discussed below, the technique of pegged mortise-and-tenon joinery negates the possibility that disassembly was used for the Phoenician triremes.

If we re-imagine the Phoenician triremes not as warships per se, but as 25-ton payloads with the approximate dimensions of 39.6 × 6.5 × ca. 6 m destined for overland transport, then we can attempt to reconstruct the manner in which such transport occurred. Trireme crews hauled their ships out of the water using manpower and ropes, guiding them along fat-slicked rollers, carried for this express purpose, often setting their ships on wooden supports for maintenance and drying out. Using these skills and supplies, but with augmented numbers of personnel, a prepared route, and the necessary pairs of oxen, the Greeks could have moved partitioned triremes into intra-sanctuary settings from nearby shoreline locations.[37]

In my opinion, partitioning the triremes was an unfortunate operational necessity. Disassembly was not an option. The triremes were constructed with pegged mortise-and-tenon joinery in which transverse pegs locked the tenons in their mortises.[38] Most often hammered into the outer surface of the hull the ends of the pegs were adzed to be flush with their surrounding planks.[39] Any attempt to remove the pegs would have effectively destroyed the ships. Nor could these triremes be transported whole into the sanctuaries.[40] The 25 tons of one of the 39.6 m triremes plus a multi-ton wheeled undercarriage would have needed approximately 60 pairs of oxen. Each pair of oxen would be about 4 m long for a total of 240 m. Even if the oxen were divided into 4 teams of 60 m each, it would not have solved the underlying logistical problems. The 100 m length of the whole set up plus the width of the 4 teams would have produced an incredibly unwieldy solution that could not have physically maneuvered any of the triremes into the physical confines of any of the sanctuaries under discussion. There is no doubt that partitioning the triremes would have fatally disrupted their structural integrity, but these ships were never meant to sail again. The sections could have been nailed back together again with the addition of new internal frames, their hulls painted with pitch to help seal and hide the seams, and their wooden supports both designed and positioned to provide extra support in compromised areas and cover up a good portion of the seams.

Isthmia: The Sanctuary of Poseidon

The Sanctuary of Poseidon at Isthmia is located approximately 1380 m from the nearest shore of the Saronic Gulf. Hauling a ship over such a long land journey is technically possible, but it would have been extremely difficult, time-consuming, and very costly to attempt to move a partitioned trireme along the local road networks. In the case of this sanctuary, a second, much better route exists.

The *diolkos* was a paved limestone portage road built perhaps as early as the early sixth century BC across the narrowest part of the Isthmus of Corinth. Heavy building materials (e.g. timber, tiles), local Isthmian products (e.g., olive oil, quarried stone), pedestrian traffic and, at least in a few instances, ships could travel on wheeled trolleys from the Saronic gulf to the Corinthian gulf and vice versa on the *diolkos*.[41] Sites such as the Pan-Hellenic sanctuary at Isthmia located around a kilometer from the portage road received some of the carried goods.[42] The *diolkos* could have served the sanctuary by creating a means of supplying sometimes multi-ton loads of construction materials from both gulfs. It also functioned as the principal pedestrian and carriageway to Isthmia especially for those arriving at Poseidonia on the Corinthian Gulf or cutting south from the coastal road east of Lechaion, Corinth's northern port. Due to the depredations of time and man, the exact course of the *diolkos* and its precise distance from Isthmia is not known. Three possibilities have been suggested, with very approximate distances of ca. 1075 (Raepsaet), 600 (Pettegrew), and 300 m (Werner) between the pathway and the sanctuary[43] (Figure 12.1). In its proximity to the Pan-

Hellenic sanctuary, the *diolkos* was always the main road to Isthmia from either gulf. Once partitioned into smaller, but still multi-ton, payloads, the trireme could have traveled northwards on the *diolkos* from its Saronic gulf entrance, and then from there passed onto the shortest and most navigable pre-scouted and prepared overland route to the sanctuary, perhaps the road coming from Athens.

Although both textual and epigraphic evidence exists for whole warships portaging the Isthmus via the *diolkos*, it is the second overland, road-based portion of the Phoenician trireme's journey to the sanctuary that would, for practical reasons, necessitate partitioning.[44] A partitioned trireme could be set onto the *diolkos* in manageable portions and then transferred from the *diolkos* onto the road from Athens just like other carried materials. On the other hand, a complete warship would be bulky, unwieldy, and a danger to its handlers, as well as being at risk for great structural damage, if anything were to go wrong.

Thus I argue that the long experience Greeks gained from the 7th to 5th centuries BC with multi-ton overland transports, the ship-handling skills of a trireme crew, the presence of the *diolkos* and the skills necessary to transport safely multi-ton loads along its 6–7 km length over adjoining roads would have facilitated a partitioned Phoenician trireme in reaching the sanctuary of Poseidon at Isthmia.

Excavations have uncovered the major components of the late archaic sanctuary of Poseidon at Isthmia, allowing us to recreate its layout during this period (Figure 12.2). Oriented precisely facing east, the archaic Temple of Poseidon was the architectural centerpiece of the sanctuary until it was destroyed by fire in 470.[45] Directly to the east of the temple was its long rectangular altar, while to the southeast lay the stadium. The sanctuary was entered through two propylaea; the first one was situated ca. 25 m to the east of the altar and ca. 15 m northeast of the stadium's seating embankment; the second one lay ca. 35 m to the north of temple where it followed a northeast/southwest orientation and allowed access to the sanctuary through the temenos wall.[46] Most of the structures of the late archaic sanctuary were clustered on its eastern and southeastern sides, with only part of the temenos wall and a propylon on its northern side.

The prominence and Pan-Hellenic status of Isthmia were owed in part to its geographical position at the eastern edge of the Isthmus of Corinth, directly on the road from Attica and northern Greece to the Peloponnese. Ancient travelers from Attica approached the sanctuary from the northeast, while those from Corinth from the northwest (Figure 12.3). Given the layout of the archaic sanctuary and the routes visitors took when entering the sanctuary, I would place the Phoenician trireme in its northeast section. In this gently sloping area there would not only have been sufficient room for the trireme, but also the greatest visibility[47] (Figure 12.4). At ca. 39.6 m in length and 6.5 m in width the trireme is shorter and much narrower than Poseidon's archaic temple

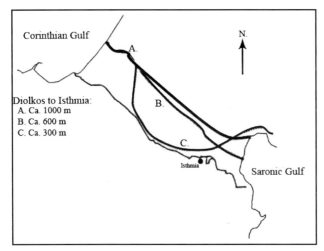

Figure 12.1 Three proposed paths of the diolkos: A. Raepset's more direct route; B. Pettegrew's reconstruction of a slightly different route; C. Werner's easier but longer route. The path of the Hexamilion Wall to the west and closest to Isthmia is included for context (after Pettegrew 2011). Courtesy David Pettegrew

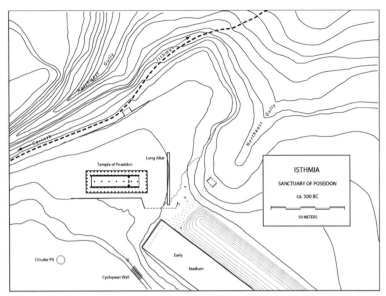

Figure 12.2 Contour plan of Isthmia, ca. 500 BC, by architect Frederick Hemans. Courtesy Elizabeth R. Gebhard, director of the University of Chicago Excavations at Isthmia

(ca. 40.0 m × ca. 14.0 m). The northeast section of the sanctuary lay between the two propylaea and close to the temple and altar, the focal point for the god's worship.

The dedication of a Phoenician trireme as a naval victory monument at Isthmia in 479 was a particularly fitting gesture. It was at this sanctuary in 481 that the congress of thirty-one Greek cities was held to deal with the second Persian invasion under Xerxes (Hdt. 7.145). Within easy visual range of the sanctuary's entrances and cult structures, the trireme must have been a continual reminder of the unexpected, yet resounding, victory of the allied Greek navy over the much larger Persian fleet.

Sounion: For Athena or Poseidon?

The promontory of Sounion is located 31 nautical miles southeast of Athens' port of Piraeus and was always an integral part of ancient Attica, as one of the demes of ancient Attica, belonging originally to the tribe of Leontis. Excavations conducted in the late nineteenth and early twentieth centuries brought to light the lifespans of the sacred sites on the promontory.[48] Of the two sanctuaries present, the one of Athena Sounias was mainly of local importance; that of Poseidon Sounios was closely connected with the power of Athens and was an important religious center from at least the eighth century. Homer implies that Sounion was a sanctuary, and narrates how Menelaos' helmsman, Phrontis, both died and was buried there (*Od.* 3.278–83). Excavations have shown that both sanctuaries developed in tandem down to the Persian sack, first with buildings and cult statues of impermanent materials; by the beginning of the sixth century each precinct saw the

dedication of monumental marble kouroi, standing young fit nude males. Herodotus does not specify which sanctuary at Sounion the Phoenician trireme was placed in (8.121–122).

Using the ship-handling skills and overland transport method discussed earlier, the captured Phoenician trireme likely came ashore in Sounion's broad western harbor. Coates outlines the following essentials for hauling out a ship onto a beach: excavation of a slipway of a max gradient of 1 in 10; use of greased timbers to allow a drag coefficient of 0.2; some form of bolster to provide a guide for the keel; portable shores to provide lateral support; spare *hypozomata* (ropes) of ca. 40 mm for dragging by at least 140 men and, if available, oxen.[49] After being hauled out, the ship would have been allowed to dry out, and then partitioned. Each of the five 5-ton divisions would be transferred into carts or onto wheeled undercarriages, and then the personnel and anywhere from 6–12 pairs of oxen (1 pair per ton or 1 pair per 1/2 ton) per wheeled conveyance would then pull the first division of the trireme up the promontory.[50] The closest sanctuary to the western bay is that of Athena.

Before the Battle of Salamis, the Persians devastated the sanctuary of Athena at Sounion, destroying temples and dedications alike (Hdt. 8.50, 9.13). The goddess' sanctuary is located approximately 200 m east of Sounion's broad western bay at an elevation of 37.95 MASL (Figure 12.5). It is 500 m northeast of Poseidon's temenos and the peribolos is large enough to have housed a trireme. The sanctuary's classical trapezoidal peribolos wall encloses ca. 350 m², but only the western portion of the sanctuary was level enough to receive the trireme in 479, since the sanctuary is on a hilltop.[51] The reduced space means that the trireme could only have been oriented north to south or vice versa.

The northwest section of the peribolos wall is covered by an earlier, roughly oval sanctuary, or heroön, possibly belonging to Phrontis.[52] No new monumental building took place in this sanctuary for approximately twenty years after the Persian invasion.

About 460, the eastern part of the hill was filled in to provide a level surface for the construction of the classical Temple of Athena Sounias.[53] The small prostyle temple to the north is either contemporaneous with the new marble temple or slightly later. These two temples could not have interfered with or dictated the trireme's placement, since they were not yet built. Due to its more northerly, inland setting and lower elevation, the sanctuary of Athena's best view is of the summit of the promontory and the sanctuary of Poseidon, not out to sea. In 479 only the western part of the hill was available for the dedicated trireme, a significant reduction in available space in which the warship would have overwhelmingly dominated the whole sanctuary. If the trireme had been placed in Athena's sanctuary, it would have been most visible to all those coming over land and to those sailing from the east. The view of the warship would have then been blocked by the promontory only to reappear at a great distance to those continuing to sail westward, and not anchoring in Sounion's broad harbor.

Before the Battle of Salamis, the Persians also laid waste to the sanctuary of Poseidon at Sounion, destroying sacred structures and kouroi alike. Poseidon Sounios was always closely linked with the power of Athens itself, and his sanctuary served as an important religious center from at least the eighth century. Soon after the Battle of Marathon (490 BC), construction began on a monumental temple to Poseidon made of poros stone that was still under scaffolding when the Persians arrived. The new, classical marble Temple of Poseidon was constructed over the earlier foundations in the 440s. It measures 31.12 × 13.47 m and replaced the slightly smaller 30.20 × 13.06 m, still unfinished archaic poros temple.[54] The propylaea, stoas, and *temenos* walls of the sanctuary belong to this same period. During the period after the Persian damage and before the construction of the marble temple, the Phoenician trireme must have rested among the ruins of Poseidon's sanctuary. The trireme measuring ca. 39.6 × 6.5 × 6 m could have fit easily within the 60 × 80 m enclosed by this sanctuary's peribolos wall.[55] In fact, an artificial terrace on the south side of the temple may have provided a prominent setting.

Up on the height of Poseidon's sanctuary, the trireme would have been visible 360° on the cliff rising from the sea. Before the Persian destruction, monumental kouroi and the incomplete archaic temple were visible from far out at sea. A captured Phoenician trireme placed in Poseidon's sanctuary just south of the ruins of the archaic temple at 73.36 m MASL would have made a very memorable and emphatic statement about the triumph of Greeks over impious barbarians[56] (Figure 12.6). In contrast to limited

visibility afforded to a trireme in Athena's sanctuary, such a ship set in Poseidon's sanctuary would have been visible to all coming over land and all sailing by, as well as even to those far out at sea. The god was recognized as the protecting deity of the Battle of Salamis, unlike the more local importance of Athena Sounias.[57]

A placement just south of the ruins of Poseidon's archaic temple would also help explain some puzzling remains in that area. A partial structure of rubble walls strengthened by poros column drums from the ruined archaic temple of Poseidon still exists immediately south of and very close to the western end of the remains of the classical marble temple (Figure 12.7). Previous interpretations have included an improvised shrine constructed between 479 and 449, or a chapel built in the Byzantine or Ottoman period.[58] No compelling evidence exists for either interpretation. I offer a third possible explanation. The partial structure of rubble walls strengthened by reused poros column drums could have been built to provide support for a terraced area and for the reception of wooden supports for the stern of the Phoenician trireme. The terrain here slopes down to the west; a declivity this partial structure – restored with at least one more upper course of rubble to complete the walls and packed with rubble and earth – would have corrected. Simultaneously, the terrace would have provided a firm bedding for the supports meant to keep the rear part of the warship stable and in position. Furthermore, this explanation helps provide a *raison d'être* for the southern extension of the partial structure's curving western wall. It could easily have functioned as a retaining wall, once restored with one or more upper courses and the space between it and the southern wall of the partial structure packed with rubble and earth.

A potential challenge to my proposed location for the trireme dedicated to Poseidon is the topography of the promontory itself. Between the shore and Athena's sanctuary the ground rises to 37.95 MASL over a distance of 200 m for a gradient of 18%, well over the optimal 10%. Another 28.99 m rise over a distance of about 420 m for a gradient of 7% exists between the goddess' sanctuary and the future site of the propylaea of the sanctuary of Poseidon. A steep incline of 6.42 m over about 60 m for a gradient of 11% separates the future site of the propylaea from the stylobate of the temple of Poseidon. Only the first gradient of 18% would necessitate extra muscle power, but it would probably not be prohibitive since the multi-ton architectural members of both the archaic poros temple and its classical marble successor all reached the summit of the promontory (perhaps in smaller load sizes with more trips). Thus it was feasible to bring the Phoenician ship into the Sanctuary of Poseidon and set it up in a very prominent location, south of the temple site and overlooking the sea (Figure 12.8). In this location the ship was vulnerable to Sounion's winds and weather, but it could have lasted some forty years or so, until the marble temple was built.[59]

Salamis: for Ajax

Modern Salamis is very much inhabited, and for this and
certain environmental reasons few or no remains of ancient
Salamis are visible. Therefore, my discussion of this site
begins with recovered inscriptions and the text of Pausanias.
Ephebic inscriptions of the second and first centuries
(127/6–45/4 BC) mention sacrifices to Zeus Tropaios at the
trophy of Salamis on the island of Salamis, home island of
Ajax in the course of the festival *Aianteia*.[60] During this
celebration, the ephebes rowed to the town of Salamis
where they sacrificed to Ajax at an unspecified location.
The people of Salamis honored them and, then, after the
ephebes sailed to the trophy at the tip of the promontory of
Cynosura, they offered sacrifice to Zeus Tropaios.[61] A boat
race or *hamilla ploion* and procession often accompanied
this sacrifice, while the ephebes also competed in foot races
with the youths of Salamis.[62] Celebrated in close conjunction
with the *Aianteia* was another festival, the *Mounichia*, in
which the ephebes raced sacred vessels from the great
harbor around the peninsula of Piraeus to the Temple of
Artemis Mounichia.[63] In these festivals the Athenians
honored primarily Ajax and Artemis for their help during
the Battle of Salamis, as well as Zeus Tropaios, whom they
also associated with this pivotal confrontation.

An Athenian inscription of the late 1st century BC sets
out provisions "concerning the temples and precincts [of
Attica], in order that they might be restored to the gods and
the heroes to whom they originally belonged" (*IG* II² 1035,
line 4). The inscription goes on to mention the "precinct
of Ajax" ([*temen*]*os Aiantos*) on Salamis, at the same
time as "Themistocles'" trophy over the Persians and "the
polyandrion of those who died in the battle [of Salamis]"
(*IG* II² 1035, lines 32–34). Therefore, during the same
period when there is evidence for annual commemorative
sacrifices being offered to Ajax on Salamis for his help
during the Battle of Salamis, there is also evidence for
the restoration of the hero's shrine. It could be that this
shrine was built in the second half of the 2nd century BC
to provide a ritual locus for the *Aianteia*, and then suffered
neglect or damage due to the political vicissitudes of the
1st century. Conversely, it could have been a 2nd century
rebuild of a much earlier shrine to Ajax whose connection
to the island Homer includes in the Catalogue of Ships (*Il.*
2.557–58) where he puts the Salaminian contingent, under
Ajax, next to the Athenian. Later on in the epic (*Il.* 7.198),
Ajax links himself to Salamis when, after his lot is chosen
for single combat with a Trojan, he says that he is one born
and brought up in Salamis.

In the 2nd century AD when Pausanias (1.35.2–36.2)
visited the island of Salamis, he saw the ruins of the agora
of the city of Salamis and next to this a temple of Ajax
(*naos Aiantos*) with an ebony statue (*agalma*) of the hero.
He also relates in the very next sentence "even at the present

day the Athenians pay honors to Ajax himself." All these
sources (the Ephebic inscriptions, *IG* II² 1035, Pausanias,
etc.) are much later than the 5th century. It is difficult, if not
impossible, to know when to date either Ajax's *temenos* or
his temple and statue mentioned by Pausanias, or even the
rites associated with them.

Due to further depredations of time and man, and a rise
in sea level (or a sinking of the land) of ca. 2.7 m, modern
visitors to Salamis see only the scattered remains of ancient
stones along the shore and in the waters of Ambelaki Bay.[64]
The ancient city of Salamis faced this body of water giving
its agora and sanctuary of Ajax relatively close seaside
locations. Since the other two Phoenician triremes can be
placed in sanctuary settings, the trireme dedicated at Salamis
for Ajax likely also was set up within the sacred precinct of
the hero. The only currently known candidate for such an
area would be that of the *temenos* of Ajax in the Athenian
inscription concerning the restoration of shrines in Attica.[65]
The temple and statue of Ajax noted by Pausanias, which he
mentions right after the ruins of Salamis' agora, help fill in a
few of the *temenos*' physical details. To *temenos*, *naos* and
agalma we should also add an altar (*bomos*), the focal point
for the rituals and cultic activity mentioned in the Ephebic
inscriptions and Pausanias. This would be in keeping with
the much earlier dedicated ship at the Heraion on Samos.
The Phoenician trireme dedicated to Ajax was a symbol of
defeated barbarian naval power and a conspicuous victory
monument honoring both the local hero of the place where
the Battle of Salamis was won, and the Greeks who fought
so valiantly in defense of their freedom.

Because there is not yet any evidence for the exact size,
location or layout of Ajax's temenos, the position of the
dedicated Phoenician trireme can only be hypothetical. The
temenos of the hero located next to an agora seems to have
been fully integrated within ancient Salamis' urban network.
To what extent the components of thentown would have
interfered with or prohibited an intra-sanctuary setting is,
currently, impossible to know. Considering the parallels of
those at Isthmia and Sounion, and the seaside location of
the ancient city of Salamis, and barring the *temenos* of the
hero being too small to accommodate a warship, I think
it most likely that the Greeks set the captured Phoenician
trireme inside the sanctuary of Ajax.

Conclusions

The unexpected and much needed victory in the Battle of
Salamis stopped the seemingly unstoppable advance of the
Persian war machine and reignited the hopes of the Greeks.
The value of victory at Salamis for reinvigorating the
Greek martial spirit not only to fight, but also to go on the
offensive, cannot be underestimated, especially since it came
so soon after the valiant self-sacrificial delaying actions
at Thermopylae and Artemisium. The outcomes of these

Figure 12.3 "Birds-eye" view of Isthmia, ca. 500 BC, from the northeast by Peggy Sanders. Courtesy Elizabeth R. Gebhard, director of the University of Chicago Excavations at Isthmia

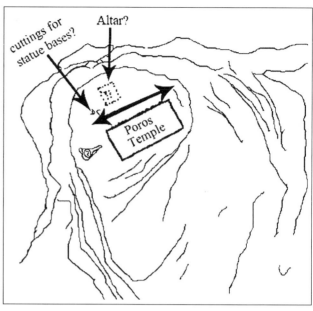

Figure 12.6 Contour plan of the Sanctuary of Poseidon Sounios, ca. 6th-century BC, by Courtney Bloom (after Herda 1995)

Figure 12.4 View of the area just north of the Temple of Poseidon at Isthmia, from the northwest. Photo K. L. Lorenzo

Figure 12.7 View of poros column drum "shrine," from the southeast. Photo K. L. Lorenzo

Figure 12.5 View of the broad western bay at Sounion and the Sanctuary of Athena Sounias, from the south. Photo K. L. Lorenzo

Figure 12.8 View of Temple of Poseidon Sounios, from the south. Photo K. L. Lorenzo

last two battles, while immensely symbolic, also served to reinforce the impression of inevitable Persian conquest. To commemorate the miraculous victory achieved at Salamis, the Greeks dedicated votive offerings to the divine powers credited with facilitating the victory, as was their customary practice for almost any type of victory, whether related to war, athletics, or another successful endeavor. Once an object became a votive offering, it also became the sacred property of the receiving deity and was, if at all possible, set within an area or a structure sacred to the divinity. This physical transferal was at the heart of such offerings. Instead of being beached in the manner of a carcass, we should think of the Phoenician warships mounted on wooden keel supports such as those they carried for normal day-to-day operations when on campaign. Herodotus' own testimony at 8.121 that "the first was to be dedicated at the Isthmus, where it was till my time," implies autopsy and for at least that ship destined for Isthmia, also a relatively sheltered intra-sanctuary setting far from the more destructive environmental conditions of the shoreline.

Once inside the deity's temenos the transaction inherent to votive offerings was complete; ordinary material transitioned into sacred property, the removal of which was a crime. In the case of Salamis, the Greeks honored Ajax, Poseidon, Artemis, and Zeus Tropaios, among others. The three captured Phoenician triremes mentioned by Herodotus are salient examples of just such votive offerings, and their full symbolic meaning was achieved by prominent positions in the sanctuaries at Isthmia, Sounion and Salamis.

Notes

1   I am grateful to the Associated Colleges of the Midwest, the Mellon Foundation, and Monmouth College for support for this research, and to N. Kontakis, M. Miles, C. Myers, R. Pitt, T. Sienkewicz, L. Vidličková, and R. Wright. All dates are BC unless specified otherwise. All translations are the author's own.

2   Rouse 1902, p. 105; West 1965, 91–2; Gauer 1968, 71–3; Murray 1989, 115; Rice 1993, 244; Morrison 2000, 36–7, 41 n 12, 180; Blackman 2001, 207–12; Wescoat 2005, 154 n 3.

3   Basch 1969, p. 140, pp. 160–162; Casson 1971, pp. 94–95; Tzahos, E. E. 2002, pp. 775–779; Mark 2008, pp. 268–270.

4   Gunwale: the uppermost course of planking on a ship's side; *pavesade*: a screen of canvas or another material extended along the side of a vessel in a naval engagement, to conceal from the enemy the operations on board. For these and other nautical definitions see Steffy 1994, pp. 266–298.

5   For the best discussion of the ancient evidence for cutwaters as opposed to rams, see Mark 2008, pp. 253–272 but especially pp. 267–270 for 5th century Phoenician triremes.

6   For preserved marble eyes from Greek ships, see Carlson 2009.

7   Coates and Shaw 1993, p. 88; Morrison et al. 2000, pp. 268–273. I have chosen to use these dimensions in agreement with Bjørn Lovén (2011, 161) that, "[a]lthough the 39.6 m

length of Coates' Mark II trireme is a rough estimate by scientific ship-reconstruction standards, it remains to date the only qualified guess." For the latest discussion of ancient warship dimensions, see Blackman and Rankov (2013, pp. 76–101) who give a length range of ca. 36–41 m.

8   The relative size of Phoenician and Greek triremes is disputed, and any disparity could have changed even within decades. The word "heavier" (*baruteras*) in texts may refer to water-sodden ships as opposed to "dried out" ships; this condition made the ships more difficult to maneuver. For discussion, see Casson and Linder 1991, pp. 67–71; Wallinga 1993, p. 170; Cawkwell 2005, pp. 258–259; Rankov 2012, p. 229, with earlier bibliography. Macan's remarks (1908, ad loc.) are still useful.

9   Hdt. 7.145; see also Brunt 1953, pp. 135–163.

10 Pritchett 1979, pp. 175–77.

11 Wallinga 1993, pp. 169–185; Morrison and Coates 1996, p. 349; Strassler 1996, p. 610; Morrison et al. 2000, pp.107–108.

12 Xen. *Hell.* 6.2.29–30; for the unusual, remaining at sea, Thuc. 3.49.

13 Whitehead 1993, pp. 95–98.

14 Strassler 1996, p. 610 (cf. Plut. *Them.* 14.3) Coates (2012, pp. 139–141) discusses the following essentials for beaching/hauling out a ship: excavation of slipway of a max gradient of 1 in 10; use of greased timbers to allow a drag coefficient of 0.2; some form of bolster to provide a guide for the keel; portable shores to provide lateral support; spare *hypozomata* (ropes) of ca. 40 mm for dragging by at least 140 men and, if available, oxen.

15 Hdt. 7.188 (storm and gale), 9.96 and Xen. *Hell.*1.6.17 (superior fleet).

16 Thuc. 7.12.3–5; Xen. *Hell.* 1.5.10, 8.44.4.

17 Lipke 2012, p. 203.

18 For the best discussion of the ancient evidence for the use of pissa (pitch) or zopissa (a combination of wax, pitch and sea salt) on ships see, Morrison et al. 2000, pp. 186–188.

19 Lipke 2012, p. 205.

20 On the "drying out" of hulls see, Coates and Shaw 1993, pp. 87–90 and 134–41.

21 Modern study of the canal: Isserlin 1991 and Isserlin et al. 1994, 1996.

22 Pliny (*HN* 4.2) measures the Leukadian Isthmus at 4 stades, which makes it thirteen times smaller than the 5,600 m Corinthian Isthmus (cf. Pettegrew 2011, p. 553, n 14).

23 Evans 1972, p. 14.

24 Blackman 2001, p. 209; Wescoat 2005, p. 154, n 3; Lorenzo 2011, pp. 146–147 and esp. catalogue entry # I.B.0.

25 Snodgrass 1983, p. 17.

26 Casson 1971, p. 58–59 n 82; Morrison et al. 2000, pp. 40–41.

27 Brogan 1999, pp. 125–126 and esp. catalogue entry # II.B.7; Wescoat 2005, passim; Lorenzo 2011, p. 147 and esp. catalogue entry # I.B.4.

28 Brogan 1999, pp. 128–129 and esp. catalogue entry # II.B.11; Wescoat 2005, passim; Lorenzo 2011, pp. 148–9 and esp. catalogue entry # I.B.6.

29 Lehmann 1998, pp. 107–112.

30 Lianos 1999, p. 262, fig. 4. For the Athenian Acropolis, Gauer (1968, pp. 71, 73) and Korres (1994, p. 47) associate two blocks A and B with a bronze ship (catalogue entry # III.A.4),

but Raubitschek and Stevens (1946, pp. 107–114) have more convincingly assigned them to the Athena Promachos' base. I agree with the latter assignment of these blocks, but their reconstruction of trophies or inscribed stelai in the cuttings on the upper surfaces is not convincing, since the deep irregular cuttings were more likely created in the Middle Ages when the blocks were put to a secondary use of unknown nature.

31 Burford 1960, 1969; Raepsaet 1993, 2008.

32 Raepsaet 1993, pp. 255–256; 2008, pp. 591–592.

33 Werner 1997, p. 109.

34 Raepsaet1993, p. 247; 2008, pp. 591–92.

35 Morrison and Coates 1996, p. 345; Wescoat 2005, 169.

36 Mark 2008, p. 261.

37 One pair of oxen per ton is the liberal figure for traction capacity see, Burford 1969, pp. 184–191. One pair per 1/2 ton is the more common and standard figure for traction capacity see, Raepsaet 1993, 2008.

38 Mark 1991, p. 442, n 2.

39 Steffy 1994, p. 43–59.

40 The Panathenaic ship does not provide a useful parallel since it seems to have been an ornate ship-shaped float. For a thorough evaluation of all the evidence for the Panathenaic ship, see Shear 2001, pp. 143–155; updated evidence in Wachsmann 2012.

41 Pettegrew 2011, p. 571.

42 Pettegrew 2011, n. 38, p. 562–563.

43 These tentative figures are based on Raepsaet's more direct route as seen on Pettegrew's Fig. 10 (2011), which for the most part seems to follow the approximate path of the Corinth canal.

44 Thucydides notes a planned portage in 428 (3.8–14), and a completed portage in 412 (8.5–10). Polybius mentions two successful portages, by Demetrius of Pharos in 220 (4.19.7–9) and by Philip V in 217 (5.101.4). *CIL* 1(2) 2662 preserves as a Latin poem inscribed on a limestone slab the portage of Marcus Antonius, grandfather of the more famous Mark Antony, in his campaign against the Cilician pirates in 102–100 BC. Livy (42.16) and Dio Cassius (51.5) also relate stories of portages, but these are of doubtful historicity, while Strabo (8.2.1) and Pliny (*HN*. 4.9–10) offer summaries of the extraordinary portages of ancient heroes. For a recent and much fuller discussion of all these portages see Pettegrew 2011, pp. 565–570.

45 Gebhard 1995, p. 160.

46 Broneer 1971, pp. 3–13, 33–41, 53–56.

47 Gebhard 1995, p. 159.

48 Staïs 1900, pp. 113–150; 1917, pp. 168–213.

49 Coates 2012, pp. 139–141.

50 One pair of oxen per ton is the liberal figure for traction capacity see, Burford 1969, pp. 184–91. One pair per 1/2 ton is the more common and standard figure for oxen pair traction capacity see, Raepsaet 1993, 2008.

51 Salliora-Oikonomakou 2004, p. 40.

52 Abransom 1979, pp. 8–19.

53 Dinsmoor 1971, p. 42; Abransom 1979, n. 51, p. 9–10; Lippolis et al. 2007, p. 605.

54 Dinsmoor 1971, p. 8; Paga and Miles 2011.

55 Salliora-Oikonomakou 2004, p. 32.

56 Brogan 1999, p. 349.

57 Lorenzo 2011, p. 117.

58 Dinsmoor 1971, p. 16.

59 A modern comparandum can be found in the *Olympias*, a modern reconstruction of a fifth-century Greek trireme that is currently in a roofed but otherwise open dry dock in Palaio Faliro, Athens, Greece (see Rankov 2012).

60 *IG* II² 1006, lines 28–32 (123/2), 1008, lines 75–88 (119/8, 118/7), 1009, lines 38–9 (116/5) 1011, lines 16–8, 53–63 (107/6), 1028, lines 20–8 (100/99), 1029, lines 14–6 (94/3), 1030, lines 25 (post 94/3), 1035, lines 36 (1st century) and 1041, lines 20–1 (ca. 45/4); Agora I 286, lines 21–6, 129–32, 141–42 (127/6); Reinmuth 1955, pp. 220–239.

61 Culley 1977, p. 286 n. 10, pp. 294–95; Pritchett 1979, pp. 175–77. For the fullest treatment of the Aianteia, see Pélékidis 1962.

62 Gardner 1881, p. 316; Pritchett 1979, p. 176.

63 The order of the *Aianteia*, *Mounichia* and the *Diisoteria*, a festival of the Great Gods not connected to the Battle of Salamis (cf. Pritchett 1979, p. 175 n. 78), is not fixed in the inscriptions, but all three are usually mentioned. It is necessary to compare *IG* II² 1006, lines 28–32 where the order is *Diisoteria-Mounichia-Aianteia* with *IG* II² 1028, lines 20–28 where it is *Mounichia-Aianteia-Diisoteria* (cf. Culley 1977, p. 295 n. 44).

64 Autopsy.

65 *IG* II² 1035, line 4.

References

Abramson, H. 1979. "A Hero Shrine for Phrontis at Sounion?" *University of California Studies in Classical Antiquity* 12, pp. 1–19.

Basch, L. 1969. "Phoenician oared ships," *Mariner's Mirror* 55.2, pp. 139–162 and 55.5 pp. 227–245.

Blackman, D. 2001. "Ship dedications in sanctuaries," in *ITHAKI: Festschrift fuer Joerg Schaefer zum 75. Geburtstag am April 2001*, ed. by J. Schaefer, S. Boehm and K.-V. von Eickstedt, Würzburg, 207–212.

Blackman, D. and B. Rankov. 2013. *Shipsheds of the Ancient Mediterranean*, Cambridge.

Brogan, T. 2005. "Hellenistic Nike: monuments commemorating military victories of the Attalid and Antigonid Kingdoms, the Aitolian League and the Rhodian Polis ca. 307 to 133 B.C." (diss. Bryn Mawr).

Brunt, P. A. 1953. "The Hellenic League against Persia," *Historia* Vol. 2.2, pp. 135–163.

Burford, A. 1960. "Heavy Transport in Classical Antiquity," *The Economic History Review* 13.1, pp. 1–18.

Burford, A. 1969. *The Greek Temple Builders at Epidauros: A Social and Economic Study of Building in the Asklepian Sanctuary During the Fourth and Early Third Centuries B.C.*, Liverpool.

Carlson, D. N. 2009. "Seeing the Sea. Ships' Eyes in Classical Greece," *Hesperia* 78, pp. 347–365.

Casson, L. 1971. *Ships and Seamanship in the Ancient World*, Princeton.

Casson, L., and E. Linder. 1991. "The evolution in the shape of the ancient ram," in *The Athlit ram*, ed. by L. Casson and J. R. Steffy, College Station, pp. 67–75.

Cawkwell, G. 2005. *The Greek Wars: the failure of Persia*, Oxford.

Coates, J. 2012. "On Slipping and Launching Triremes from the Piraeus Shipsheds and from Beaches," in *Trireme Olympias: the final report: sea trials 1992–4, conference papers 1998*, ed. by B. Rankov, Oxford, pp. 134–141.

Coates, J. and T. Shaw. 1993. "Hauling a Trireme Up a Slipway and Up a Beach," in *The trireme project: operational experience, 1987–90: lessons learnt*, ed. by T. Shaw, Oxford, pp. 87–90.

Culley, G. R. 1977. "The Restoration of Sanctuaries in Attica, II," *Hesperia* 46.3, pp. 282–298.

Dinsmoor, W. B. 1971. *Sounion*, Athens.

Evans, J. A. S. 1965. *Procopius*, New York.

Gauer, W. 1968. *Weihgeschenke aus den Perserkriegen*, Tübingen.

Gardner, P. 1881. "Boat-Races at Athens," *Journal of Hellenic Studies* 2, pp. 315–317.

Hammond, N. G. L., and F. W. Walbank. 1988. *A History of Macedonia, Volume III 336–167 B.C.*, Oxford.

Herda, A. 1995. "B 12 Statue eines Kuros ('Sunion A')," in *Standorte: Kontext und Funktion antiker Skulptur: Katalog des Ausstellungs in der Abguss-Sammlung Antiker Plastik, an der Freien Universitaet Berlin, 29.11.1994–4.6*, ed. by K. Stemmer, Berlin, pp. 109–120.

Isserlin, B.S.J. 1991. "The Canal of Xerxes: Facts and Problems," *Annual of the British School at Athens* 86, pp. 83–91.

Isserlin, B. S. J., R. E. Jones, S. Papamarinopoulos, G. E. Syrides, Y. Maniatis, G. Facorellis, and J. Uren 1996. "The Canal of Xerxes: Investigations in 1993–1994," *Annual of the British School at Athens* 91, pp. 329–240.

Isserlin, B.S.J., R.E. Jones, S. Papamarinopoulos, and J. Uren. 1994. "The Canal of Xerxes on the Mount Athos Peninsula: Preliminary Investigations in 1991–2," *Annual of the British School at Athens* 89, pp. 277–284.

Korres, M. 1994. "The history of the Acropolis monuments," in *Acropolis Restoration: the CCAM Interventions*, ed. by R. Economakis, London, pp. 34–51.

Lehmann, K. 1998. *Samothrace: A Guide to the Excavations and the Museum*, Thessaloniki.

Lianos, N. A. 1999, "The Area of the ancient closed port of Thasos," in *Tropis V: 5th International Symposium on Ship Construction in Antiquity: Nauplia, 26, 27, 28 August, 1993*, ed. by. H. Tzalas, Athens, pp. 216–272.

Lipke, P. 2012. "Triremes and Shipworm," in *Trireme Olympias: the final report: sea trials 1992–4, conference papers 1998*, ed. by B. Rankov, Oxford, pp. 185–202.

Lippolis, E., M. Livadiotti, and G. Rocco. 2007. *Architettura Greca: storia e monumenti del mondo della polis dale orgini al V secolo*, Milan.

Lorenzo, K. 2011. "Ancient Greek and Roman Naval Victory Monuments" (diss. Univ. of Wisconsin, Madison).

Lovén, B. 2011. *The Ancient Harbours of the Piraeus Vol.1. The Zea Shipsheds and Slipways: Architecture and Topography*, Athens.

Macan, R. W. 1908. *Herodotus: The seventh, eighth, & ninth books Vol. 1 and 2*, London.

Morrison, J. S., and J. F. Coates. 1996. *Greek and Roman Oared Warships*, Oxford.

Morrison, J. S., and R. Williams. 1968. *Greek Oared Ships, 900–322 B.C.*, London.

Morrison, J. S., J. F. Coates and N. B. Rankov. 2000. *The Athenian trireme: The history and reconstruction of an ancient Greek warship*, New York.

Murray, W. M., and P. M. Petsas. 1989. *Octavian's Campsite Memorial for the Actian War*, Philadelphia.

Pettegrew, D. K. 2011. "The Diolkos of Corinth," *American Journal of Archaeology* 115.4, pp. 549–574.

Paga, J. and M. M. Miles. 2011. "The Archaic Temple of Poseidon at Sounion: New Discoveries," in *Archaeological Institute of America, 112th Annual Meeting Abstracts*, vol. 34, p. 98.

Pélékidis, C. 1962. *Histoire de l'éphébie attique des origines à 31 avant Jesus-Christ*, Paris.

Pritchett, W. K. 1979. *The Greek State at War: Part III*, Berkeley.

Raepsaet, G. 1993. "Le Diolkos de l'Isthme à Corinthe: Son tracé, son fonctionnement," *Bulletin de correspondance hellénique* 117, pp. 233–56.

Raepsaet, G. 2008. "Land Transport, Part 2: Riding, Harnesses, and Vehicles," in *The Oxford Handbook of Engineering and Technology in the Classical World*, ed. by J. P. Oleson, Oxford, pp. 580–605.

Raubitschek, A. E., and G. P. Stevens. 1946. "The Pedestal of the Athena Promachos," *Hesperia* 15.2, pp. 107–114.

Rankov, B. ed. 2012. *Trireme Olympias: the final report: sea trials 1992–4, conference papers 1998*, Oxford.

Reinmuth, O. W. 1955. "The Ephebic Inscription, Athenian Agora I 286." *Hesperia* 24.3, pp. 220–239.

Rice, E. E. 1993. "The glorious dead: Commemoration of the fallen and portrayal of victory in the late classical and hellenistic world," in *War and Society in the Greek World*, ed. by J. Rich and G.Shipley, London, pp. 224–257.

Rouse, W. H. D. 1902. *Greek Votive Offerings: an essay in the History of Greek Religion*, Cambridge.

Salliora-Oikonomakou, M. 2004. *Sounion*, Athens.

Shaw, T. ed. 1993. *The trireme project: operational experience, 1987–90: lessons learnt*, Oxford.

Shear, J. L. 2001. "Polis and Panathenaia: The History and Development of Athena's Festival" (diss. Univ. of Pennsylvania).

Snodgrass, A. M. 1983. "Heavy Freight in Archaic Greece," in *Trade in the Ancient Economy*, ed. by P. Garnsey, K. Hopkins and C. R. Whittaker, London, pp. 16–26.

Staïs, B. 1900. "Anaskaphai en Sounio," *Archaiologike Ephemeris*, pp. 113–50.

Staïs, B. 1917. "Souniou anaskaphai," *Archaiologike Ephemeris*, pp. 168–213.

Steffy, J. R. 1994. *Wooden ship building and the interpretation of shipwrecks*, College Station.

Strassler, R. B. ed. 1996. *The Landmark Thucydides: a comprehensive guide to the Peloponnesian War*, New York.

Taylor, A. 2012. "Battle Manoeuvres for Fast Triremes," in *Trireme Olympias: the final report: sea trials 1992–4, conference papers 1998*, ed. B. Rankov, Oxford, pp. 231–243.

Tzhos, E. E. 2002. "The Athenian Trireme: Form and Function of « Epotides »." in *Tropis VII Vol. 2: Proceedings of the 7th International Symposium on Ship Construction in Antiquity: Pylos, 26, 27, 28, 29 August 1999*, ed. by H. Tzalas, Athens pp. 775–789.

Wachsmann, S. 2012. "Panthenaic Ships: The Iconographic Evidence," *Hesperia* 81, pp. 237–266.

Wallinga, H. T. 1993. *Ships and sea-power before the great Persian War: the ancestry of the ancient trireme*, Leiden.

Walter, H. 1990. *Das griechische Heiligtum dargestellt am Heraion von Samos*, Stuttgart.

Werner, W. 1997. "The Largest Ship Trackway in Ancient Times: The Diolkos of the Isthmus of Corinth, Greece, and Early Attempts to Build a Canal," *International Journal of Nautical Archaeology and Underwater Exploration* 26, pp. 98–119.

Wescoat, B. D. 2005. "Buildings for votive ships on Delos and Samothrace," in *Architecture and Archaeology in the Cyclades: Papers in honour of J.J. Coulton*, ed. by M. Yeroulanou, and M. Stamatopoulou, Oxford, pp. 153–172.

West, W. C. 1965. *Greek Public Monuments of the Persian Wars*, Ann Arbor.

Whitehead, I.1993. "Mooring," in *The trireme project: operational experience, 1987–90: lessons learnt*, ed. by T. Shaw, Oxford, pp. 95–98.

13

Routes out of Attica

Sylvian Fachard and Daniele Pirisino

This paper reevaluates the importance of the routes leaving Attica and reaching Athens' main neighboring city-states. Their itineraries have been known since the 19th century, and their importance as "military roads" has been highlighted repeatedly since then. Based on new autopsy, we follow another approach and suggest that political, religious and economic factors justified the construction and maintenance of good roads and paths leading to the borderlands. These factors led to the development of a very dense and efficient communication network. This network was multifunctional, and road construction and maintenance were part of a multifaceted process which must be studied with a long-term view.

Introduction

Our knowledge of the Attic communication-network has never been so comprehensive as now. As a consequence of the major public works undertaken in Attica in the last two decades, rescue excavations have brought to light numerous stretches of ancient roads throughout the *chora*. The present picture is one of a fully developed and well-built network consisting of major and secondary wagon roads, coupled with a multitude of well-engineered paths and innumerable tracks.[1] This rich evidence has been studied and conveniently gathered in a recent monograph edited by M. Korres, which will serve as a reference for decades to come.[2]

In this paper, we focus on the routes leaving Attica and crossing the borders: to Megara, Plataia, Thebes, Tanagra, Oropos, the Amphiaraion, and Delphi. These routes have been known since the 19th century, but few of them have been studied in detail since E. Vanderpool and J. Ober.[3] Our approach is not topographical, for we do not detail their itineraries. We are interested in reevaluating the importance of these routes by assessing the purposes justifying their careful construction. The routes in and out of Attica have been most often studied from a military point of view, as potential invasion routes to be defended by forts or highways used for quickly dispatching reinforcements to the borders. Although military functions certainly played an important

role, others were also at stake. We suggest that political, religious and economic factors justified the construction and maintenance of good roads and paths leading to the borders of Attica and beyond. We believe these factors have not been sufficiently studied and deserve a new autopsy.

Routes out of Attica: the evidence

Six major routes radiating out of Athens exited Attica, leading to major towns or sanctuaries (Figure 13.1):[4]

1. The Sacred Way connected Athens to Eleusis and from there continued towards Megara, Corinth and the Peloponnese (Pausanias 1.39.1). From Eleusis, a northern alternative to the Megarid and the Corinthian gulf was a road through the Kantili pass, which provided the quickest way to Pagai.[5]
2. Via the Thriasian plain, a road served the border deme and region of Oinoe, continued to Eleutherai, the Kaza pass and then down to Plataia or Erythrai and Thebes.[6] This road is called a "direct road" or "highway" (*eutheia hodos*) by Pausanias (9.2.1).[7] From Oinoe, several alternative routes were available, mainly serving Aigosthena to the west and the Boeotian plain through the Portes path to the north.[8]
3. A route linked the Thriasian plain to the ancient deme at Kokkini (Azenia?). From there, an engineered path,

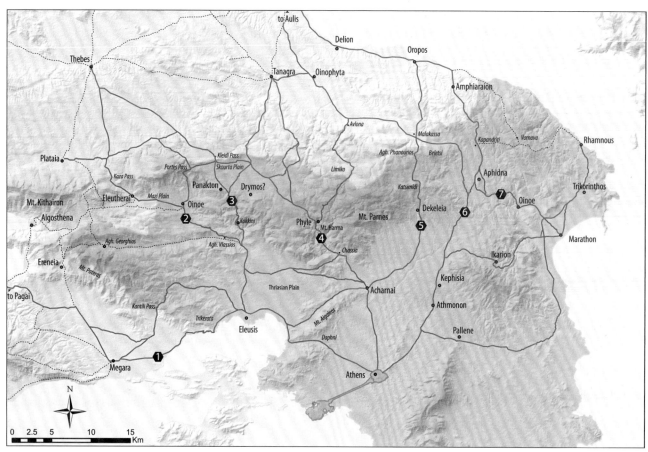

Figure 13.1 Main routes out of Attica. The extent of the Attic chora is highlighted; the borders are those for the years 366–335 BC. Modern names are in italics. Other main routes, not discussed here, are dashed. Map by Sylvian Fachard

discovered by E. Vanderpool, continued towards the Skourta plain.[9] A path went up to Panakton, but the main route crossed the plain and entered Boeotia, serving Tanagra to the northeast and Thebes to the northwest.

4. From Athens, a route served the deme of Phyle via Acharnai and the village of Chasia. The road was carriageable up to Chassia, from where two different routes, including a possible carriageable one, lead to Phyle.[10] Beyond the deme center, a route continued towards the Skourta plain, while many tracks skirted round the deme, serving Mt. Harma, the eastern portion of the Skourta plain (Drymos?), Limiko, and potentially descending to Tanagra, Oinophyta, the site at Avlona (Kakosalesi), and the Oropia.

5. From Athens, a road served the demes of Acharnai and Dekeleia, continuing due north to the Kleidi pass. The route continued to the old Aghios Merkourios pass (west of Beletsi) and descended towards Malakassa, and then to Oropos.[11]

6. A road linked Athens to Aphidna and continued towards the Amphiaraion, perhaps following a straight route through modern Kapandriti.[12] North of Aphidna, a branch turned west, crossed the southern fringe of the Oropia, continued towards Oinophyta and then served Tanagra, Delion and Chalkis.[13]

7. We include an important seventh route, connecting the plain of Marathon with Aphidna, the Oropia via Rhamnous and Varnava, and Boeotia.[14]

To these main axes we must add engineered paths and countless tracks crisscrossing the landscape and serving smaller demes, farms, fields, quarries, workshops, isolated cultivated dolines, terrace walls, orchards, olive groves, and zones of exploitation. Many of them provided shortcuts to Boeotia (Diod. Sic. 15.26.3). Such paths and tracks leave very few if no traces, but one might grasp a good idea of potential density by looking at the myriad of them mapped in the *Karten von Attika* (KvA).[15] The density of the 19th century network is stunning. Since Classical Attica was arguably similarly (if not more densely) occupied than in the 19th century, it seems fair to assume that the ancient communication network might have been even denser.[16]

Out of the first six routes, three, possibly five, were carriageable at least to the borders (and most probably beyond). The roads were all 3 to 6 meters wide, enough to accommodate the crossing of two-wheeled mule-carts, which were the commonest vehicle along these roads.[17] They all necessitated work and maintenance in order to be used by wagons, either by providing hard surface layers of composite materials, by carving the way in the rock, or by building retaining walls.[18] For example, past Eleusis, numerous traces of carving, wheel ruts and terracing have been recorded at the Kerata coastal road. Impressive retaining walls were built to support the road to Oinoe, between Aghios Vlassios and the Mazi plain (Figures 13.2, 13.3).

But a route did not need to be carriageable to be efficient. Pack animals (donkeys and mules) were more common than the wheel.[19] The "lords of the route" can transport 150–180 kg of wood, wine or charcoal over 20 km or 70–80 kg over 40 km in a day.[20] The surface of the path plays a role, as trekkers know. To accommodate pedestrians, carriers, mules and donkeys, considerable attention was also given to non-carriageable paths. Stretches of the route to Phyle were carved in the rock and supported by retaining walls (Figures 13.4, 13.5).[21] The Panakton route was not suitable for wagons on its entire stretch, but this engineered path was nevertheless an ambitious realization, as the steepest and most difficult stretches are supported by terrace walls and zigzags (Figures 13.6, 13.7).[22] All six routes required significant construction.

The building of the road-network was a piecemeal process. The communication axes Athens-Eleusis, Eleusis-Thebes, and Athens-Aphidna-Tanagra-Aulis were already in existence in the Bronze Age, as the archaeological sites known along these routes attest.[23] Different periods meant different needs and investments. In the long term, older routes could be revived, while others would have lost favor because of various circumstances.[24] Several roads were used in the Geometric period.[25] By the Archaic period, an already dense network connected the rural communities of Attica with the *asty*. Herms were placed by Peisistratos' son Hipparchos at mid-distance between the demes and the city (Plato, [*Hipparch.*] 228D).[26] This story suggests the existence of some one hundred routes in Attica in the 6th century BC, a great achievement in terms of civilian infrastructure. The Attic road-network would reach its fullest development in the Classical period, when the *chora* rose to its densest occupation. This was the greatest time of road construction in Attica, as most archaeological remains have been dated to this period. In the 4th century BC, a board of five *hodopoioi* was responsible for the maintenance of roads, employing public slaves as workmen (Aristotle, *Ath. Pol.* 54.1). Although their existence is not attested afterwards, road maintenance remained a necessity throughout the Hellenistic and Roman periods.[27]

Most axes described above are also very efficient, adopting the quickest route to their respective destination. This efficiency is demonstrated by superimposing least-cost paths generated using GIS.[28] The least-cost paths to Eleusis (19 km), Phyle (21.8 km), Tanagra (43.5 km), Oinophyta (47 km), Oropos (41.6 km) and the Amphiaraion (41.1 km) adopt the trace of the ancient roads with remarkable precision

(especially at saddles), very often running into deme centers and archaeological sites (Figure 13.8), thus providing very valid itineraries for supplementing stretches between known road segments. In contrast, the least cost paths to Thebes, Oinoe and Plataia follow only partially known routes and paths. The study of these "divergences" can be rewarding. For example, the suggested path to Thebes (56.8 km) does not cross the Dema pass, but cuts through the Kipoupoli saddle (320 m), west of the Aigaleos tower, and descends to Bouzaka (right by the "Grosses Hauss" noted on the KvA); it then crosses the Thriasian plain and chooses the Xirorema gorge up the slopes of Mt Psiloma (789 m) before reaching Stephani and the Skourta plain.[29] This direct route is not implausible. The quickest path to Oinoe correctly follows the Sacred Road up to the Daphni pass, but instead of continuing to the sanctuary of Aphrodite, it climbs west of Dasos and crosses Mt Aigaleos with difficulty at a height of 300m before descending into the plain, west of the Battala hill, in an area where many antiquities are mapped in the KvA. Last, the least-cost path to Plataia: between Magoula and the Mazi plain, it adopts a direct course through hilly country instead of following the Oinoe road. These three routes would not have been credible candidates for wheeled traffic, because they cross more difficult terrain and tend to avoid (known) localities, which were necessary stops along important itineraries – a requisite condition when traveling by land. However, all three represent credible "direttissime", most direct routes which could be used by messengers, scouts or good walkers eager to reach their destination as quickly as possible.

Functions of roads and engineered paths

The routes out of Attica were all major projects, involving extensive engineering and construction. They required maintenance and repairs, especially after the winter.[30] The fact that they still stand today in remote areas testifies to the quality of their construction. Vanderpool noted for the Oinoe and Panakton routes that they were not built by local residents: "They must have been built by the state and built to fill a special need," and according to him, this need was essentially military, although he recognized that the Oinoe road could have been used by civilian traffic as well.[31] Ober argued that military highways connected Athens with the "border fortresses" and that a "comprehensive program of road building was undertaken in conjunction with the fortification program."[32] In general, the military function of large roads leading to the borders of the *chora* has dominated research.[33]

In contrast, our study shows that these major Attic routes were not built to fill one specific need, but *several*. In this, we adopt as our starting point the *Annaliste* approach highlighted by L. Febvre in his seminal pages about circulation and routes written in 1922.[34] Febvre pushed

Figure 13.2 Stretch of the Oinoe road above the Ag. Vlassios valley. The road, supported by a solid retaining wall, is 5–6 m wide. Photo S. Fachard

Figure 13.3. The Oinoe road: wheel-ruts. Photo S. Fachard

Figure 13.5 Stretch of the Phyle route. The roadway is cut in the rock and supported by a retaining wall. Although this stretch is carriageable, others are clearly not. Photo S. Fachard

Figure 13.4 Stretch of the Phyle route. The roadway is cut in the rock and supported by a retaining wall. Photo S. Fachard

ahead the need to go beyond the topographical aspect of road construction and to consider their value as well as the reasons justifying their construction. We believe that a combination of many factors – political, religious, economic,

and military – justified the construction of such great roads and paths leading to the borders of the *chora* and beyond. These routes, therefore, play a much larger role in the wider phenomenon of connectivity of microregions discussed by P. Horden and N. Purcell.[35]

Political functions

State formation implies, almost naturally, the existence of a communication network, as L. Febvre asserts. He observes that the existence of a "state" depends on individuals' awareness of belonging to a collectivity and possessing common interests with the other members of this collectivity – a process in which routes play a fundamental role in connecting together the different locales.[36] By extension, large-scale road networks are major projects which can only be realized by strong states. Like other labor-intensive construction projects, they "tend to be coextensive with state powers and, by their very man-power requirements, testify to the state's ability to wrest significant surpluses from the

Figure 13.6 Stretch of the Panakton path. The roadway, supported by a retaining wall, forms a zig-zag. Compare the current state of the path with Vanderpool's picture (1978, Plate 3.2). Photo S. Fachard

Figure 13.7 The Panakton engineered path. Photo S. Fachard

polity at large."[37] There are political reasons for building and maintaining a solid road-network.

Good roads and paths made travel times shorter and journeys easier, linking communities and boosting state cohesion. This is particularly true (and needed) for large states such as Attica, with a diversified landscape divided between microregions. Such advantages were understood early. Hipparchos' positioning of herms at mid distance between the *asty* and the Attic villages/demes created a personalized link between each community and Athens. This operation might have enhanced by road-building. In

the Archaic period, the existence of a road-network linking perhaps as much as one hundred communities throughout the Attic peninsula helped cement the political unity of the polis. Beyond political maneuvering, the presence of such a high number of routes throughout Attica demonstrates an advanced level of state organization, arguably superior to that of the neighboring *poleis*. But the importance of a good road-network became even more vital after Cleisthenes' reforms.[38] The success of the new political organization, which included the wider participation of citizens and *bouleutai* from all over Attica, rested on the possibility of

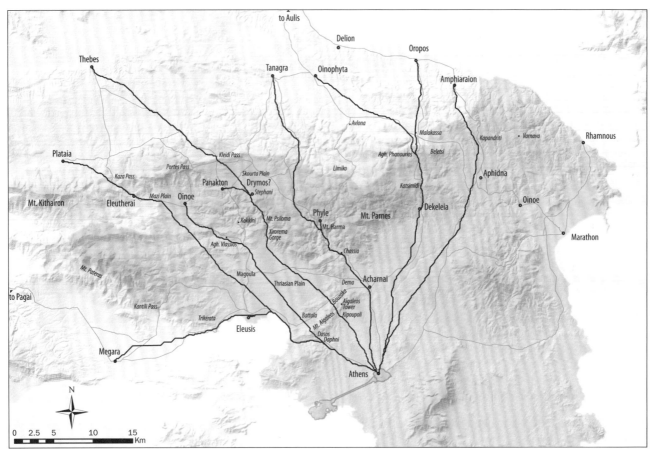

Figure 13.8 Least cost paths between Athens and main ancient localities outside Attica. Routes mapped in Figure 13.1 are in light gray. The extent of the Attic chora is highlighted; the borders are those for the years 366–335 BC. Modern names are in italics. Map by Sylvian Fachard

traveling to the city quickly and relatively comfortably in order to participate in the democratic debate and keep the institutions working. This is particularly true for the years closely following the reforms, when apparently a majority of Athenians lived outside the city. Is it too bold to claim that the absence of a good network would have undermined the participative factor of Cleisthenes' democratic system? Perhaps not. Had the road-network not been so developed, Cleisthenes may not have been in a position to design such an ambitiously participative scheme.

Moreover, political reasons provided strong incentives for building and maintaining solid routes towards one particular region of Attica, the borderlands. The six routes described above reduced traveling time between Athens and the most important border demes: Eleusis, Oinoe, Phyle, Dekeleia and Aphidna.[39] To this list must be added regions which never had a constitutional deme-status, such as Panakton and Drymos, occupying the southern fringe of the Skourta plateau, a highly contested piece of fertile land between Attica and Boeotia.[40] The inhabitants of the border demes, which had the peculiarity of sharing a common border with another *polis*,

would have felt isolated without good liaisons to Athens. They were also more exposed to foreign raids, which explains why the five above-mentioned had fortifications around their main settlement or a fort in their territory. The absence of roads might have even irremediably pushed some of them to develop stronger ties with their foreign neighbors, a reality inherent to border communities through the ages.[41]

It was, therefore, important, politically, to keep the borderlands as close as possible to Athens. One case is particularly telling, the more remote border-regions of Panakton and Drymos, which were settled and exploited by the Athenians in the 4th century BC, but always disputed by the Boeotians. The great engineered path serving this region might have well been a "military road," in that it was used by troops walking towards the homonymous garrison fort, but it additionally appears to us as a *political road*, a crucial link serving and bringing this disputed region closer to Attica. The construction of a direct route serving the communities living there was part of a political and territorial agenda, reinforcing Athenian claims over Panakton and Drymos. Similarly, as long as the territory of Oropos would remain so emotionally coveted by Athens, the maintenance of several direct routes to the Amphiaraion and the Oropia was part of a wider political agenda.

All in all, the construction and maintenance of a good and efficient road-network reinforced state cohesion and acted as an indication of state power. Attica was renowned for the highest level of infrastructure built throughout the *chora* (*Hell. Oxy.* 12.5), and the quality of its roads would have struck and impressed any visitor, ambassador, pilgrim, herald, merchant crossing the borders of Attica and walking to Athens. A developed road network was a sign of strong and unified political authority, and the construction of some routes to disputed regions of the borderlands assumed critical political functions.

Economic functions

As long as routes existed, they were used for transporting and exchanging goods. Febvre has shown that commercial routes are found in all civilizations, even in the most archaic and rudimentary.[42] Good roads boosted internal commerce and facilitated both imports and exports. The six main routes out of Attica acted as trading routes, vibrant commercial axes serving dozens of demes and connecting Athens with larger economic hubs such as Megara, Plataia, Thebes, Tanagra and Oropos. Although terrestrial routes have been traditionally deemed as costly and unpractical, especially when compared to the advantages of sea routes, it would be a mistake to underestimate the level of commercial traffic they could sustain. Xenophon reminds us that Attica received many goods by land (*Ways and Means*, 1.7). Some routes were essentially terrestrial: heavy traffic between Thebes, Plataia, Tanagra and Athens was only achieved through carriageable roads. Small-volume trade was well served by pack animals using a variety of roads, engineered paths and trails. The edible goods from Boeotia and Megara listed by Aristophanes (*Peace*, 1000–1005) must have been brought to the markets of Attica via these land routes, not by the sea.[43] And even were harbors were available, good and durable trading axes could reveal resilient and even beat the sea routes. A good example is the famous case of the Dekeleia route used to transport grain from Oropos to Athens during the 5th century. The episode related by Thucydides (7.28.1) is puzzling for two reasons: first, because the sea route would have appeared as cheaper than the land route; second, because the route appears to us as a difficult one for carts between Malakassa and Agh. Phanourios, especially when a much easier alternative existed through Aphidna. Yet, Horden and Purcell analyze this example to show that the importance of this land route during the Peloponnesian War reflects the persistence of an older network.[44] The study of roads must go beyond topography, as routes "are defined by local knowledge and current practice, not by physical peculiarities."[45]

Military functions have ignored or at best relegated economic functions to a position of secondary importance – wrongly in our opinion. Even in Sparta, the most militarized Greek city-state, roads would have served an economic agenda. The impressively dense network of cart-roads built by the Spartans, now well-studied by Pikoulas, certainly could have facilitated the quick movement of troops in and out of the Peloponnese.[46] Yet, scholars have argued persuasively that the network would have been built for transporting goods across the Taygetos range, "enabling the Spartans to enjoy the wealth of the Plain of Messenia."[47] Here as elsewhere, different functions do not exclude each other, but form a composite stimulus for building roads and paths through a difficult landscape.

The main routes radiating out of Athens and Attica were essential trading routes with neighboring states, and the demes found alongside them greatly benefited from their existence. Such important commercial axes encouraged economic interaction between the demes and other microregions. The route to the Amphiaraion crossed the territories of nine demes. In the 4th (or 3rd) century, the road was pleasantly lined with inns, allowing the travelers to get some rest and refreshments.[48] The route to Oropos connected nine demes along its route, including the market of Dekeleia, which, in times of peace, might have functioned as a cross-border commercial hub connecting microregions on both sides of the borders.[49] The Sacred road to Eleusis (and out to the Megarid) ran across a dozen demes, the two major sanctuaries of Aphrodite and Demeter, and the market of Eleusis itself. This was one of the busiest roads of Attica. The road to Oinoe connected 15 deme territories, before continuing towards Eleutherai, Plataia and Thebes. The Phyle route crossed 11 demes and served the Skourta plain and Boeotia. All in all, the six main roads radiating out of Athens, plus the road from Marathon to Rhamnous and Oropos, connected some 40 deme territories, close to one third of Attica. The level of trade and exchanges along these axes gives a good idea of their economic importance.

The main routes out of Attica also played another practical role, justifying their construction and maintenance: they contributed to the economic exploitation of the borderlands. The latter, dominated by mountains, offered almost unlimited resources for pasture. It seems reasonable to assume that the border demes exploiting these regions produced cheese, wool and leather, bred cattle (mainly sheep and goats, but some cows in the Skourta basin) and were active in beekeeping. The borderlands were also prime hunting country. The presence of many routes penetrating deep into the borderlands, completed by innumerable paths throughout the Parnes-Kithairon-Pateras ranges, stimulated these activities and facilitated the export of the above-mentioned products towards the plains of Attica and Athens itself. The routes were essential for the economic exploitation of the mountains of Attica.

Although the borderlands were dominated by mountains, non-negligible pockets of alluvial soil were available for grain production. Salient examples are the Mazi and Skourta basins. Here, grain production to the hectare would have been amongst the highest of the *chora*, resulting from a combination of rich soil, higher altitude and perhaps as much as twice the rain of southeastern Attica. The First fruits inscription reports grain from the Skourta plain (*IG* II² 1672).[50] The latter was partly marshy, but nowadays the surface suitable for agriculture reaches 15 sq km. In the Mazi basin, the area potentially dedicated to grain might have reached 1300 ha, a considerable surface which could have produced as much as 520 tons of grain, enough to feed over 2100 people. Besides grain, the Mazi basin has been a great wine country since antiquity, with suitable soil and gentle northern slopes facing south. The toponym of Oinoe speaks for itself, and it is from Eleutherai –occupying the western part of the plain– that the cult of Dionysos was first introduced to Athens (Pausanias 1.38.8). But both regions were bones of contention between Athens and Boeotia.[51] These disputes, territorial in nature, were no doubt fueled by economic motives. We already noted that the routes leading to these regions had a political importance, to which should be added an economic one. Indeed, grain and wine production might have surpassed the consumption of the communities exploiting these basins. Therefore, the many roads and paths leading to Oinoe, Skourta and Drymos played an active role in a chain of regional redistribution. Moreover, these economic routes also served the communities situated alongside (Phyle, the deme site at Kokkini, etc.) and gave incentives to build farms, terrace walls and plant orchards.

In the same way, the routes to the borderlands played a large role in the exploitation of woodlands, mainly for charcoal, wood and resin. Attic charcoal burners were obviously not confined to Acharnai.[52] Good routes facilitated the entire process of production in the woodlands, as well as the transportation to the main centers of demand: the demes in the lowlands as well as the city itself. Similarly, woodcutting was greatly eased by the presence of these roads and paths. Demand for charcoal and firewood would have been enormous, especially for the Attic pottery production.[53] A rational exploitation of the Attic pine forests was possible, if not necessary. The largest and darkest forests of Attica were in the Phyle region, up to the eastern part of the Skourta plain (Drymos?), Limiko and the northern slopes of Parnes (Figure 13.7). Even nowadays, one gets easily lost, and deer are a common spectacle. This represented a vast wooded region of some 190 sq km.

But without paths and roads, these woodlands could not be exploited. We believe they were, mainly thanks to the main axis linking Phyle to Skourta via the Harma saddle, from which radiated a multitude of paths through the woods.[54] Here, no engineering was necessary: axes replaced picks and terrace walls. From the slopes where the cutting

took place, mules and donkeys were used to carry their loads down to the paths and then to the city via the roads.[55] Perhaps this entire region was under the supervision of a board of specialized tax collectors responsible for levying taxes on wood production and sales, similar to the *hylonai* (if not the same) attested in the Oropia under Athenian rule.[56]

Another extremely valuable resource of the woodlands was pristine resin and its derived product, pitch – or more accurately, "conifer tar."[57] Its use for construction, shipbuilding and wine preservation would have required large quantities, involving the existence of vast pine forests and an organized *chaîne opératoire*. Such a vital production in the Ancient Greek world has been overlooked by research. In a luminous interpretation, D. Knoepfler showed that the word *das* (*dais*), attested in the Oropia by the Law on the Lesser Panathenaia, referred to "greasy wood" (splinters or resinous wood from which conifer tar was produced), whose sale and production were submitted to a tax.[58] Knoepfler suggests that this tax was levied throughout the entire Attic territory. And according to him, the control of the conifer tar-market – vitally important for the maintenance of the war fleet, for lighting, for preserving wine – was among the main reasons explaining the unremitting effort of the Athenians to keep the Oropia. We agree and suggest that conifer tar from the Oropian forests was produced and refined in seasonal workshops before being transported to Athens and the Piraeus on carts using the main road via Aphidna, rather than by sea.[59] Yet, possession of the Oropia proved to be a turbulent undertaking, and it eluded Athenian control for long periods. Conifer tar was too vital to be restricted to this region. If the production was indeed taxed throughout Attica, as suggested by Knoepfler, then the production was more widespread. Again, the forests of Phyle, Drymos and Parnes must have been the epicenter of Attic conifer tar production. This seasonal activity – conducted in "resin stations," perhaps occasionally part of isolated farms – would have been complementary to woodcutting and breeding.[60] A component of the *chaîne opératoire* was to open up paths and routes into the thick pine woodlands to collect *das*.[61] Land transport was key, from the forests to the production sites, and then to the city. Good roads and paths facilitated production. The Oinoe and Phyle roads, including the innumerable paths radiating from them, played an important role in this trade. A particular route was also very well situated for the production of resin and conifer tar: the engineered path from Kokkini to Panakton and the Skourta plain (n. 3, Figures 13.6, 13.7). The path skirts through thick forests which were still exploited for resin until a few decades ago.[62] In antiquity, these were the main pitch routes of Attica.

Religious functions

Some routes served religious purposes as well, since in addition to everyday travel, they were used by official *theoriai* to reach sacred destinations in order to conduct public rituals, or to fulfill individual devotional demands. Specific roads were the setting of ordered processions, both within and outside a city's territory. Due to the need to conduct processional items safely, these *pompikes* roads were built with particular care and were possibly the first (after certain Mycenaean roads) to develop as carriageable.[63]

Of these religious routes, a special role was played by those which extended beyond a city's territory. As a result of the increasing importance of Panhellenic sanctuaries, the network of outbound religious routes intensified. Some routes took on inter-regional relevance, as they stretched across different regions and became subject to different spheres of political influence. Among these religious routes, those leading to Delphi had a particularly relevant role as some of them were closely related to the myths surrounding Apollo.[64] For instance, the *Pythias Hodos* (Ael. *VH* 3.1) connected the region of Tempe to Delphi and was used during the celebration of the Septeria festival which imitated the killing of the dragon and the flight, expiation, and return of Apollo. Another example is the route that, according to a well known version of the myth recounted in the third Homeric Hymn, the god took on his first journey to Delphi.[65]

In Attica, a specific sacred *theoria* developed, which was intended as a re-enactment of the mythical journey of Apollo to his main oracular seat, according to a local form of the myth that, in contrast with the above-mentioned Homeric Hymn, had the god land in Attica on his way from Delos.[66] This overland pilgrimage to Delphi was known in Athens as the Pythaïs as early as the 5th century BC.[67]

The primal center of Apolline worship in Attica was the area of the Marathonian Tetrapolis. Here an early form of overland pilgrimage to Delphi developed, possibly in relation to the primeval religious routes that connected northern and central Greece to Delos across eastern Attica.[68] As with the later Athenian *theoria*, this sacred delegation was known as the Pythaïs.[69] However, the Athenian and the Marathonian Pythaïdes were two distinct rituals. The Athenian Pythaïs was an occasional pilgrimage, dependent on the appearance of lightning from the direction of Mount Harma (above Phyle) as a divine sign (Strabo 9.2.11). The delegation of the Marathonian *koinon*, on the other hand, was probably a more frequent ritual, propitiated through inspection of a sacrificial victim.[70]

Whereas the antiquity and relevance of Apollo's cult in the coastal regions of eastern Attica have long been recognized, it is difficult to understand fully the role of the Marathonian *koinon* with regard to the chronology of the introduction of the Pythian cult to Athens.[71] Apart from this unknown beginning, the Tetrapolis clearly kept some of its religious autonomy even after the unification of Attica, conducting its Pythaïs independently of Athens until the middle of the 2nd century BC, when it merged with the Athenian pilgrimage in 138/7 BC.[72] As long as

the two *theoriai* were dispatched separately, they followed two different routes.

The Marathonian Pythaïs moved from the Pythion at Aiantid Oinoe and entered Boeotia probably by way of Aphidna or through another route closer to the coast. From the Delion at Marathon, a further *theoria* was sent in the opposite direction to Delos.[73] The sacred delegation proceeded southwards and possibly stopped at Prasiai before setting off to the island. In fact, this pilgrimage route along the coastal region of east Attica might well reflect part of the primitive course of the Hyperborean offerings that, according to the version recounted by Pausanias, were handed down to Prasiai, whence they were carried to Delos by the Athenians (Paus. 1.31.2).[74]

The course of the Athenian Pythaïs was a subject of scholarly attention as early as the first decades of the 19th century and remains a much-debated topic.[75] The landscape offered individual travelers and small groups of pilgrims infinite combinations of routes into Boeotia. In contrast, the Pythaïdes were required to follow a pre-determined religious route, one that, according to local mythical tradition, had been used by the god when he first travelled to Delphi. The Athenians took great pride in the construction of this road and officially recognized it as a sacred way in its own right.[76]

A quick overview of the origin of the major steps in the study of the course of the Athenian Pythaïs helps to delineate the possible extra-regional religious routes to Delphi from Athens. Already in the 19th century scholars identified the following three potential itineraries across Attica.

1. A western route across Mount Kithairon
   In 1824, K. O. Müller provided the first, albeit brief, description of the entire extent of the overland route to Delphi. In Müller's view, the sacred way to Eleusis and the route leading thence into Boeotia through Eleutherai was the most likely itinerary for the journey of the *theoria* to Delphi across Attica.[77] This hypothesis found its best advocate in A. Boëthius's comprehensive study on the Pythaïs, and it is still enormously influential among current scholars.[78]

2. A central route across Mount Parnes via Phyle
   Because of the influence of W. M. Leake's 1829 *On the Demi of Attica*, a new approach to the relationship between the Pythaïs and its extra-urban setting was made from a principally topographic perspective. This approach lead scholars such as A. Milchhöfer to suggest a central route for the Athenian pilgrimage that would have traversed the deme of Acharnai and crossed Mount Parnes via Phyle on the way to Delphi.[79] The hypothesis of a pilgrimage route across Parnes has never been abandoned; the idea received renewed support from A. W. Parson's suggestion that the path of the pilgrimage might have followed the Eleusinian road in its initial stretch and then, past Daphni, sought Phyle through the Thriasian plain.[80]

3. An eastern route, across the territories of the Marathonian Tetrapolis

The actual connection between the routes of the Athenian and the Marathonian Pythaïs in Attica remains largely unknown; in short, it is uncertain if the course of the Athenian *theoria* assumed the route of the supposedly older Marathonian pilgrimage road, or if it took a completely different course. In 1855 E. Curtius was among the first to suggest that the Athenian pilgrimage could have reached the Asopos river valley through north-east Attica after merging with the Marathonian sacred road.[81] However, this possibility has not garnered much support in later research and A. Boëthius has convincingly suggested that these *theoriai* followed different routes[82] before joining the course of the "international" sacred road through Bocotia.[83]

In the first half of the 19th century, a dichotomy emerged which became common in later research. This dichotomy, constructed between alternative hypotheses concerning the first extra-urban stretch of the Athenian processional way to Delphi, framed the route as crossing either western or central Attica. This issue remains unresolved, and it will remain open until new, more compelling evidence is found.

The history of the research on the Pythaïs bears witness to a transition that gradually redirected scholarly approaches to religious routes in Attica; this transition stretched from the domains of philology and history of religion into the sphere of archaeology. Indeed, today's ever-increasing understanding of the rich road network in Attica lends renewed vigor to the investigation of pilgrimage and processional roads from a perspective which is mainly archaeological. As new road stretches are uncovered in the *pedion*, much can still be done for the study and precise contextualization of the routes that traverse the mountainous regions of northern Attica. Here, the remnants of ancient roads and paths can still be made out for very long distances, offering the opportunity for a better comprehension of their function in the wider context of the road network. This precise understanding of a route is best achieved through a first-hand experience of its course and the landscape it traverses. Happily, accurate surveying methods and modern mapping technologies have made targeted surveys and their results highly productive and accessible.

Conclusions

Much of modern scholarship on roads has emphasized their military functions or at best relegated economic functions to a secondary position. We are left with the impression of a militarized landscape in which only invading and defending armies were hitting the roads. Yet, how many times in the fourth century did the Athenian army move en masse to the borders to counter an exterior threat? Arguably, very few. Of course, small detachments were continuously sent to the borderlands for countering small raids and for reinforcing the garrisons located at Eleusis, Phyle and Panakton. Aristophanes' Lamachos was sent to Phyle during the night to guard the passes there (*Ach.* 1073–1077). Demosthenes

was sent to Panakton to reinforce the Athenian garrison there (54.3–5). Such limited troop movements did not need carts. Obviously, the efficiency of the Attic roads greatly facilitated troop movements. Ober rightly points out that, in case of an attack on a sector of the borderlands, reinforcements would be able to move quickly along such efficient routes. Similarly, a network of engineered paths and tracks in the densest forests and most remote areas of Parnes facilitated and dramatically enhanced border patrolling. In some cases, specific needs of the military command at Eleusis might have been incentives to open a track. In short, we firmly believe that a good communication network greatly contributed to the *phylake tes choras*.[84]

But the state had also many other reasons to build and maintain good roads and paths in the borderlands and out of Attica, and our goal was to highlight them. We are not claiming that the great roads and paths to Oinoe, Phyle and Panakton were built by resin gatherers and charcoal burners. They were built by the state to serve several needs. Road construction and maintenance were part of a multifaceted process which must be studied with a long-term view. The nature and intensity of traffic along a given communication axis would also evolve according to local traditions and habits, changing population densities, agricultural calendars, religious festivals, ever-evolving political situations and alliances, microregional conditions, changing economic realities, and seasons. The Phyle route probably was avoided from January to March because of snow and ice, diverting traffic to Oinoe. Possession of the Oropia would create renewed opportunities for the Aphidna axis. Open conflict with Thebes could result in the closing of the Oinoe route and the opening of alternatives.

Certain exceptional circumstances would have had an influence on processional routes and ritual traveling as well. During the Peloponnesian war, for example, the enemy's military presence on Attic soil drove the Athenians to conduct the annual procession for the Eleusinian Mysteries by sea (Xen. *Hell.* 1.4.20; Plut. *Alc.* 34.4). Indeed, the sense of insecurity in times of war played a substantial role in the choice of a processional route, and similar temporary disruptions must have especially affected extra-regional pilgrimage routes. In times of peace, if we were to take a daily sample of 1000 people using the Attic northern communication network, only a very small minority would have been soldiers or mercenaries. Along Attic roads, mules, donkeys, wine sacks and charcoal panniers were a more common sight than spears.

Acknowledgements

The authors are grateful to M.M. Miles, the editor of the present volume, for her constant encouragements and excellent suggestions. We also thank the peer-reviewers for their comments and recommendations. We thank the

Hellenic Ministry of Culture for granting permission to publish our photographs. Special thanks go to A. and A. Raya for providing a digital copy of the *Karten von Attika*. The research of Fachard was made possible thanks to the support of the Swiss National Science Foundation and the University of Geneva. Pirisino is thankful to his supervisors, J. Camp, N. Galiatsatos, and A. Leone for their invaluable support, as some considerations on the religious routes presented here were developed in the context of his PhD research (any errors or omissions are his).

Notes

1   For the sake of consistency, we use the term "route" as a communication axis between two points, regardless of its construction and size. A "road" describes a carriageable route; an "engineered path" is not carriageable, but supported by terrace walls and eventually carved in the rock. The term "track" refers to simplest form of route, requiring no construction but clearing. On the vocabulary of roads and tracks in Ancient Greek, see Lolos 2003.

2   Korres 2009.

3   Vanderpool 1978, Ober 1985, pp. 111–129, 181–188. More generally on Attic roads, see Chandler 1926; Philippson 1952; Young 1956; Edmonson 1966, pp. 3–29; Petropoulakou and Pentazos 1973; Siewert 1982, pp. 32–86; Ober 1985, pp. 111–129 and 181–188; Lohmann 2002. For recent studies of territorial communication networks outside Attica: see the impressive topographical work of Y. Pikoulas in Lakonia (2012); Lolos 2011, pp. 93–179 in the land of Sikyon; Fachard 2012, pp. 91–109 in central and southern Euboea.

4   On the gates of the city walls, now see Theocharaki 2011.

5   On these routes, see Ober 1985, pp. 128 and 188; Drakotou 2009; Papangeli 2009; Steinhauer 2009, pp. 41–43. For a 4th century BC bridge, probably over the Eleusinian Kephisos, see *IG* II² 1191, l. 21.

6   Ober 1985, pp. 117–121; Steinhauer 2009, pp. 43–44; Fachard 2013, pp. 83–84. There were three routes to the Thriasian plain, the first through Daphni and Rheitoi (see above), the other from Acharnai through the Dema gap (with three saddles, see Langdon 1994; Munn 1993, pp. 37–40 and map 2), and the last one (most difficult and longer) through Chassia.

7   γῆς δὲ τῆς Πλαταιίδος ἐν τῷ Κιθαιρῶνι ὀλίγον τῆς εὐθείας ἐκτραπεῖσιν ἐς δεξιὰ Ὑσιῶν καὶ Ἐρυθρῶν ἐρείπιά ἐστι. On the term *eutheia hodos*, see Lolos 2003, p. 140.

8   Vanderpool 1978, pp. 228–231; Ober 1985, pp. 117 and 186; Fachard 2013, pp. 83–84.

9   Vanderpool 1978; Ober 1985, pp. 117, 186; Steinhauer 2009, p. 44; Munn 2010, pp. 192–193. A Classical date has never been challenged, but we must admit that absolute elements for its dating are still lacking. Its excellent state of preservation over 2500 years in thick forestland would suggest that it was used and repaired at different periods.

10 According to Ober (1985, p. 117) "the Phyle route was probably not carriageable" after Phyle; we have found traces of two engineered paths and one probable roadbed leading to the saddle above the Skourta plain. On the Phyle route see Ober 1985, pp. 116–117 and 186–187; Steinhauer 2009, pp. 44–46.

11 On this road see Thucydides 7.28.1; Chandler 1926, 16; Wrede 1934, p. 31; Westlake 1948, p. 4; Ober 1985, pp. 115 and 184; Platonos 2009, p. 143; Steinhauer 2009, pp. 46–47. We have walked from the old church of Agh. Merkourios to the train station of Sphendale-Malakassa. Although no trace of an ancient road has been found during this quick autopsy, the terrain presents no major difficulty for the construction of a road. Two ancient sites with Classical (and Hellenistic?) pottery were observed along this route, although they seem too small to be identified with the remains of the ancient settlement of Sphendale, which would fit well in the area. On Sphendale, see Chandler 1926, pp. 3–4; Fossey 1988, pp. 41, 61.

12 Siewert 1982, pp. 76–77; Ober 1985, pp. 114–115 and 183–84; Steinhauer 2009, p. 47.

13 In the Oropia, a "road to Boeotia" is mentioned in an inscription (Woodhead 1997, 84, l. 142: ὁ[δὸ]ν [εἰ]ς τὴν Βοιωτί[αν]).

14 Siewert 1982, pp. 76–77; Ober 1985, pp. 112–114; Steinhauer 2009, pp. 48–49.

15 KvA; see also Milchhöfer 1895. The maps were reprinted in 2008 by Melissa Books, including an introduction and commentary by M. Korres. The KvA can be browsed online: http://digi.ub.uni-heidelberg.de/diglit/curtius1895a.

16 About the respective populations of Attica in the Classical period and the 19th century, see Hansen 2006, pp. 79–81. See also Bresson 2008, pp. 206–207.

17 Among the very rare representations of such carts, see the Classical votive relief from the Asclepieion in Athens (EM no 1341, Kaltsas 2007, p. 325). On carts, see Lorimer 1903; Pritchett 1965, pp. 181–196; Raepsaet 2002, pp. 168–189, 2008, pp. 588–598. Traffic rules and realities still elude us, and it is a pity that Philonides' *Apene* (the "Mule-Car") is lost.

18 Steinhauer 2009, pp. 65–66.

19 "By and large, the Mediterranean world before railways did not depend on the wheel. Pack animals have been the preferred solution, and their versatility is responsible for the complexity of the geography of communications in areas of high relief," state Horden and Purcell 2000, p. 131. On mules, see Raepsaet 2002, pp. 51–54, 68–71 and fig. 5. Across the Swiss Alps, the transport of merchandise (porterage) by mules had a long tradition, see van Berchem 1956, p. 203.

20 We owe this expression to Raepsaet (2002, p. 51). On the carrying capacities of mules and other animals, see Raepsaet 2008, p. 589, table 23.4. The *Onos Askophoros* ("Wine Pack Donkey") was a play by Leukon. For mules and donkeys carrying wood and charcoal, see n. 55.

21 This route was perhaps too narrow for carts after a certain point, but fieldwork is necessary in order to confirm this assumption.

22 On switchbacks and zigzags, see Gibson 2007, pp. 71–72, 73 fig. 8, and 80.

23 For a possible – yet contested – Mycenaean bridge in the Thriasian plain, see Langdon 1994; Lohmann 2002, p. 76; Hope Simpson and Hagel 2006, p. 167.

24 A good example is found west of Eleusis, where the passage between the slopes of Kerata and the sea is crossed by 4 different axes: the ancient road, the old Athens-Korinthos National road, the Athens-Kiato railway, and the new Olympia Hodos highway. One expects the latter to have eclipsed the

older road, but the high tolls which have been increased in 2014 have instead revived traffic along the *"palia ethniki,"* a good example of how traffic is influenced by external factors and circumstances.

25 Kakavogianni 2009, p. 182; Steinhauer 2009, p. 37.

26 For an exemplary found at Koropi (*IG* I³ 1023), halfway between the Agora and Kephale, see *SEG* X.345, XXXV.28; Jeffery 1961, p. 78, no. 35; Pritchett 1965, pp. 160–162; Whitehead 1986, pp. 14–15; Osborne [1985] 2010, pp. 341–367.

27 Recent excavations have uncovered roads rebuilt or enlarged in the Hellenistic and Roman periods: Drakotou 2009, pp. 115–116; Papangeli 2009; Platonos 2009, p. 141.

28 See Conolly and Lake [2006] 2011, pp. 215–224, 252 256. The operation was run on ArcGIS by ESRI, using an ASTER (30m resolution) digital elevation model. For the cost weighted surface, costs were based on slope and the effort of crossing the terrain, as calculated by Minetti et al. 2002. We thank A.R. Knodell for introducing us to cost-based territorial modeling in GIS. Fachard and Knodell are conducting a detailed study of least-cost paths in Attica using different softwares and digital elevation models in order to compare results and methods (in preparation).

29 A path through the Xirorema gorge to Stephani is mapped in the KvA, but it skirts round Mt. Psiloma instead of ascending its southern slopes. On the Aigaleos Tower, see Ober 1985, pp. 148–149. On the Dema Wall, see Jones, Sackett, and Eliot 1957; Munn 1993.

30 Rainfalls of the winter months would have eroded roadways and undermined retaining walls, just as they do nowadays in Greece.

31 "They are undoubtedly military roads, built to assure quick and easy movement of troops and supplies between the center and the border forts," Vanderpool 1978, p. 239.

32 Ober 1985, pp. 181, 196, 199, etc. See also Ober 1982, pp. 457–458.

33 According to Pikoulas, road-networks in the Peloponnese and Mainland Greece had essentially a military character (Pikoulas 1995, 2001, 2007). For a recent discussion of this issue (with focus on the land of Sikyon), see Lolos 2011, pp. 94–97.

34 Febvre [1922] 1970, pp. 343–365.

35 Horden and Purcell 2000, pp. 123–132.

36 Febvre [1922] 1970, p. 362. On page 343, he writes: "Le mode habituel de formation des Etats implique naturellement l'existence de routes et de moyens divers de communication. Car, sans routes et sans communications, comment les hommes parviendraient-ils à reconstituer, avec les debris d'unités naturelles dissociées par eux, des ensembles homogènes faits à leur convenance?"

37 Cherry 1987, p. 166.

38 On these reforms, see among others Lévêque 1964; Ostwald 1988; Ober 1999, pp. 32–52; Elden 2003, 2013, pp. 31–37.

39 We might also add a possible Attic deme at Agh. Georghios in the Koundoura valley – if indeed it belonged to Attica, which is uncertain (Edmonson 1966, pp. 33–39, 152–154; Lohmann 1989).

40 On Panakton and Drymos, see Munn 2010 (with references).

41 An echo of this ambivalent situation is found in Aristotle, who mentions a law banning the people living near the border to take part in deliberations about waging war against a neighboring state, "because their private interest makes them incapable of deliberating well" (*Pol.* VII 1330 a 20). For a possible concrete example of such a situation, regarding Drymos, see Munn 2010, p. 197.

42 Febvre [1922] 1970, p. 349.

43 On the modalities of land route imports between Attica and Boeotia, see Fachard 2013, pp. 103–105.

44 Horden and Purcell 2000, p. 128.

45 Horden and Purcell 2000, p. 130.

46 Pikoulas 1995, p. 351, 2001, 2007, pp. 84–85.

47 Christien 1989; Horden and Purcell 2000, p. 130.

48 Text attributed to Dikaiarchos, but probably the work of Herakleides Kretikos. For the text, see Pfister 1951, pp. 72–95.

49 For the market at Dekeleia, see *IG* II² 1237. The authors are grateful to E.M. Harris for this reference.

50 Bresson 2008, pp. 203–207.

51 Camp 1991; Munn 2010; Fachard 2013.

52 See Aristophanes, *Ach.* ll. 333–34, 178–85, 211–18, 665–75; on the production of charcoal at Acharnai, see Haussoullier 1884, p. 198; Jones 2004, p. 95; Kellogg 2013, pp. 122–126. For charcoal and firewood in Athens, see Olson 1991. For charcoal production and woodcutting in the mountains of the Oropia, see Robert 1960, p. 196–197.

53 We lack numbers for Attica, but studies in Roman Gaul have shown that 40 tons of wood were necessary for firing 25,000 vases in one kiln. Over some 40 years, 50 kilns would have necessitated 900,000 tons of wood, the equivalent of 100 sq km of forests (Trintignac 2003, p. 241, n. 1).

54 The Phyle sheet from the *Karten von Attika* gives us an idea of how dense a network of paths in this area might have been.

55 Perhaps larger volumes could have occasionally been transported by carts. See Euripides, fr. 283 N² for a mention of donkeys carrying charcoal baskets of wood from the mountains and Demosthenes 42.7 for donkeys bringing wood from the countryside to the city (Olson 1991, pp. 416–417). Nowadays, in the remotest and steepest areas of Mt. Pateras, mules are still used to carry wood down the slopes to the dirt roads, where they are collected by pickup trucks.

56 Papazarkadas 2011, p. 105; Knoepfler 2012, p. 448. The Oropia was an important woodland district although its control and exploitation were chronically outside Athenian jurisdiction: two Attic documents mention land in the Oropia as *ephylon* ("wooded"), see *SEG* III.117 and XXXVII.100 (Woodhead 1997, p. 84); Langdon 1987, pp. 47–58; Papazarkadas 2011, pp. 102–103; Knoepfler 2012, pp. 447–448.

57 "A brown to pitchdark product that can be obtained from the heating of coniferous," state Connan and Nissenbaum 2003, p. 709. See Theophr. *Hist. pl.* 9.2.6–7; Plin. *HN* 16.23 (57–58), André 1964, Vlau 1966. The use of conifer tar mixed with beeswax (to produce *zopissa*) is archaeologically attested in shipbuilding from the 6th century BC (Connan and Nissenbaum 2003). On the *chaîne opératoire* of conifer tar production in Roman Gaul, see Trintignac 2003.

58 Knoepfler 2012, pp. 452–453.

59 The sea route represented certainly a longer journey through Sounion. It also necessitated the transport of pitch down to the two harbors of the Oropia, as well as their loading and unloading (and for a portion of it, transportation from the

60 Piraeus to Athens). We saw that the land route from Oropos to Athens was preferred by the Athenians in the 5th century BC.

60 Trintignac 2003, pp. 241–242.

61 Once the conifer had been produced by pyrogenation, in terracotta urns or pits, it might have been transported to farms or workshops to be affined before it could be sold, as argued by Trintignac (2003).

62 Indeed, the excellent state of preservation of this path when Vanderpool discovered it can be explained by its intensive use by (modern) resin tappers. The widespread abandonment of resin in Attica is well attested in this area, and most of the path is now covered with vegetation.

63 Steinhauer 2009, p. 37.

64 This type of religious route falls under the first of the three categories of «sacred roads» identified by Curtius 1855, pp. 19–22.

65 The overland route followed by the god to found his oracular site is described in *Hymn Hom. Ap.* 182–285. The course on the "international" sacred road to Delphi possibly followed this route across Boeotia and Fokis. An amphictionic law (380/9 BC) makes reference to the maintenance of the roads leading to the temple of Apollo (*CID* I, 10). On the "international" sacred road to Delphi, see Davério-Rôcchi 2002.

66 Aesch. *Eum.* 9–14 provides the first certain mention of this Athenian version of Apollo's journey. According to J. Dörig (1967, pp. 106–109) Aeschylos' account would reflect the scene portrayed in the east pediment of the Alcmaeonid temple of Apollo at Delphi. An early reference to this form of the story might be found in a fragmentary paean ascribable to Simonides (*PMG* 519 fr.35; 11a Werner). Following the suggestion of Rutherford 1990, pp. 173–176, this paean should be connected with the celebration of a Pythaïs. We can identify certain places that were most likely, if not certainly, landmarks in the Athenian version of the overland route taken by Apollo to Delphi. These places are Athens, the region of Mount Parnes, Panopeus, and of course Delphi. Panopaeus was an important stop for the Pythaïs as well as for another Athenian ritual: that of the *thyiades* (Paus.10.4.3), see Camp et al. 1997. According to Pindar (Fr. 286 Snell), Apollo's escorted journey would have originated from Tanagra in Boeotia. Another Boeotian tradition identifies Tegyra, on the north edge of lake Kopaïs, as the actual birthplace of Apollo, and it sets the stories about the slaying of the Python and of that of Tityus in the in the region of mount Ptoüm (Callisthenes = Steph. Byz. s.v. Τεγύρα; Plut. Vit. *Pel.* 6).

67 The ceremony and the Pythaïsts, the officers in charge of conducting the rituals that preceded the sending of the Pythaïs, are featured among the entries of the fragmentary Athenian sacrificial calendar (F 1 A col. 2–3, ll. 26–30 Lambert; F 6 A, l. 11 Lambert). The Pythaïsts were obviously associated with this similarly-named procession (Strabo 9.2.11).

68 Farnell 1907, pp. 106–112.

69 On the cult of Apollo in Attica and the pilgrimage route from northern Greece to Delos across eastern Attica, see Farnell 1907, pp. 106–112; on the name of the Delphic pilgrimage from the Marathonian Tetrapolis, see Daux 1936, p. 535.

70 Philochoros, *FGrH* 328 F 75. See Boëthius 1918, pp. 38–51.

71 See for example Töpffer 1888. The cult of Apollo Pythios might have been introduced in the 6th century BC as it received particular impulse under Peisistratos and the Peisistratids: Suda, π3130; Phot., s.v. Πύθιον· Πύθιον· ἱερὸν Ἀπόλλωνος Ἀθήνησιν ὑπὸ Πεισιστράτου γεγονός...; Hsch: <ἐν Πυθίῳ χέσαι> Πεισίστρατος ᾠκοδόμει τὸν ἐν Πυθίῳ ναόν.... Peisistratos the Younger dedicated an altar in the sanctuary of Apollo Pythios (Thuc. 6.54.7). The inscribed crowning block of this altar came to light in 1877 (*IG* I³ 948). A fragment which belongs to the same altar has been recently found (Charami and Bardani 2011).

72 Daux 1936, pp. 532–540. There is no record of an Athenian Pythaïs in the 3rd century BC and the greater part of the 2nd century BC until the Pythaïs conducted by Timarchos in the year 138/7, where the delegates of the Marathonian Tetrapolis are featured along with the Athenians.

73 Philochoros, *FGrH* 328 F 75.

74 Pausanias' account would report an Athenian version of the Hyperborean itinerary (cf. Hdt. 4.33.1–3 with the comment of Corcella 1993, pp. 259–260). On the antiquity of the pilgrimage route through north-east Attica see Farnell 1907, pp. 106–112.

75 The course of the Pythais through Attica is currently being studied by D. Pirisino as the topic of his doctoral thesis. On this subject, see e.g., Karila-Cohen 2005, Rutherford 2013.

76 Aesch. *Eum.* 12–14; Aristid. *Panath.* 363 and scholium. In 1938 the American excavations in the Athenian Agora uncovered the boundary stone of this sacred way: ὅρος ἱερᾶς ὁδὸ δι' ἧς πορεύεται ἡ Πυθαῒς ἐς Δελφός. *Horos of the Sacred Way by which the Pythaïd journeys to Delphi* (*Agora* XIX, H 34).

77 Müller 1824, pp. 239–240. Müller proposed to look at Oinoe Hippothoöntis as an intermediate station along the journey of the Pythian pilgrimage; this is the Oinoe situated near the fortress of Eleutherai on the north-west border with Boeotia (Leake 1829, p. 276; Traill 1975, p. 52).

78 The best study on the Pythaïs remains Boëthius 1918. For a recent discussion on the course of the Pythaïs see the contribution of Ficuciello 2008, pp. 24–33.

79 Milchhöfer 1873, pp. 56–57, 1895, p. 14.

80 Parsons 1943, pp. 237–238.

81 Curtius 1855, pp. 20–27.

82 Boëthius 1918, p. 43.

83 Boëthius 1918, p. 43. For a reference to the Delphic sacred road across Fokis and Boeotia see Hdt. 6.34.2.

84 On this concept, see Munn 1993, pp. 25–33; Chaniotis 2008; Fachard 2012, pp. 279–294 (with references).

References

André, J. 1964. "La résine et la poix dans l'Antiquité. Technique et terminologie," *L'Antiquité classique* 33, pp. 86–97.

Berchem, D. van. 1956. "Du portage au péage: le rôle des cols transalpins dans l'histoire du Valais celtique," *Museum Helveticum* 13, pp. 199–208.

Boëthius, A. 1918. *Die Pythaïs. Studien zur Geschichte der Verbindungen zwishen Athen und Delphi*, Uppsala.

Bresson, A. 2008. *L'économie de la Grèce des cités (fin VIe–Ier siècle a.C.). II. Les espaces de l'échange*, Paris.

Camp, J. M. 1991. "Notes on the Towers and Borders of Classical Boeotia," *American Journal of Archaeology* 95, pp. 193–202.

Camp, J. M., M. Ierardi, J. McInerney, K. Morgan, and G. Umholtz.

1997. "An Athenian dedication to Herakles at Panopeus,"
    Hesperia 66, pp. 261–269.

Chandler, L. 1926. "The North-West Frontier of Attica," *Journal
    of Hellenic Studies* 46, pp. 1–21.

Chaniotis, A. 2008. "Policing the Hellenistic Countryside: Realities
    and Ideologies," in *Sécurité collective et ordre public dans les
    sociétés anciennes: sept exposés suivis de discussions par Hans
    van Wees ... [et al.]: Vandoeuvres, Genève, 20–24 août 2007,
    Entretiens sur l'Antiquité classique* 54, ed. C. Brélaz and P.
    Ducrey, Geneva, pp. 103–153.

Charami, C., and V. Bardani. 2011. "New Fragment from the
    Altar of Apollo Pythios," *Δελτίον της Ελληνικής Επιγραφικής
    Εταιρείας,* May [Online].

Cherry, J. F. 1987. "Power in Space: Archaeological and Geo-
    graphical Studies of the State," in *Landscape & Culture:
    Geographical & Archaeological Perspectives*, ed. J. M. Ed
    Wagstaff, Oxford, pp. 146–172.

Christien, J. 1989. "Les liaisons entre Sparte et son territoire
    malgré l'encadrement montagneux," in *Montagnes, fleuves,
    forêts dans l'histoire: Barrières ou lignes de convergence.
    Travaux présentés au XVIe Congrès International des
    Sciences Historiques, Stuttgart, août 1985*, ed. J.F. Bergier,
    St. Katharinen, pp. 18–44.

Connan, J., and A. Nissenbaum. 2003. "Conifer Tar on the Keel and
    Hull Planking of the Ma'agan Mikhael Ship (Israel, 5th century
    B.C.): Identification and Comparison with Natural Products
    and Artefacts Employed in Boat Construction." *Journal of
    Archaeological Science* 30, pp. 709–719.

Conolly, J., and M. Lake. [2006] 2011. *Geographical Information
    Systems in Archaeology*, Cambridge.

Corcella, A. 1993. *Erodoto. Le Storie. Vol. 4. Libro 4. La Scizia e
    la Libia*, Rome and Milan.

Curtius, E. 1855. *Zur Geschichte des Wegebaus bei den Griechen.
    Ein Beitrag zur Alterthumswissenschaft*, Berlin.

Daux, G. 1936. *Delphes au IIe et au Ier siècle, depuis l'abaissement
    de l'Étolie jusqu'à la Paix Romaine 191–31 av. J.-C.*, Paris.

Daverio Rocchi, G. 2002. "Topografia dello spazio internazionale.
    La *hierà hodós* da Atene a Delfi," in *Stuttgarter kolloquium
    zur historischen geographie des altertums*, ed. E. Olshausen,
    and H. Sonnabend, Stuttgart, pp. 148–159.

Dörig, J. 1967. "Lesefrüchte. III. Der Ostgiebel des Apollon-
    tempels in Delphi, " in *Gestalt und Geschichte: Festschrift
    Karl Schefold, zu seinem sechzigsten Geburtstag am 26. Jan.
    1965*, ed. M. Rohde-Liegle, H. A. Cahn, and H. Chr. Ackerman,
    Bern, pp. 102–109.

Drakotou, I. 2009. "Ιερά Οδός, ανατολικό τμήμα," In *Αττικής οδοί.
    Αρχαίοι δρόμοι της Αττικής*, ed. M. Korres, Athens, pp. 112–123.

Edmonson, C. N. 1966. "The Topography of Northwest Attica"
    (diss. Univ. of California, Berkeley).

Elden, S. 2003. "Another Sense of Demos: Kleisthenes and the
    Greek Division of the Polis," *Democratization* 10, pp. 135–156.

Elden, S., 2013. *The Birth of Territory*, Chicago.

Fachard, S. 2012. *La défense du territoire d'Erétrie: étude de la
    chora et de ses fortifications*, Gollion.

Fachard, S. 2013. "Eleutherai as the Gates to Boeotia," in *Pratiques
    militaires et art de la guerre dans le monde grec antique:
    études offertes à Pierre Ducrey à l'occasion de son 75ème
    anniversaire*, ed. C. Brélaz and S. Fachard, Paris, pp. 81–106.

Farnell, L. R. 1907. *The Cults of the Greek States* 4, Oxford.

Febvre, L. [1922] 1970. *La terre et l'évolution humaine: intro-
    duction géographique à l'histoire*, 2nd ed., Paris.

Ficuciello, L. 2008. *Le Strade di Atene*, Athens and Paestum.

Fossey, J. M. 1988. *Topography and Population of Ancient Boiotia*,
    Chicago.

Gibson, E. 2007. "The Archaeology of Movement in a Med-
    iterranean Landscape," *Journal of Mediterranean Archaeology*
    20, pp. 61–87.

Hansen, M. H. 2006. *The Shotgun Method: The Demography of
    the Ancient Greek City-State Culture*, Columbia.

Haussoullier, B. 1884. *La vie municipale en Attique: essai sur
    l'organisation des dèmes au quatrième siècle, Bibliothèque des
    Écoles françaises d'Athènes et de Rome* 38, Paris.

Hope Simpson, R., and D. K. Hagel. 2006. *Mycenaean Fort-
    ifications, Highways, Dams and Canals*, Sävedalen.

Horden, P., and N. Purcell. 2000. *The Corrupting Sea: A Study of
    Mediterranean History*, Oxford.

Jeffery, L. H. [1961] 1963. *The Local Scripts of Archaic Greece: A
    Study of the Origin of the Greek Alphabet and its Development
    from the Eighth to the Fifth Centuries B.C.*, Oxford.

Jones, N. F. 2004. *Rural Athens under the Democracy*, Philadelphia.

Jones, J. E., L. H. Sackett, and C. W. J. Eliot. 1957. "ΤΟ ΔΕΜΑ:
    A Survey of the Aigaleos-Parnes Wall," *Annual of the British
    School at Athens* 52, pp. 152–189.

Kakavogianni, O. 2009. "Αρχαίες οδοί στα νότια και δυτικά
    Μεσόγεια και τη Λαυρεωτική," in *Αττικής οδοί. Αρχαίοι δρόμοι
    της Αττικής*, ed. M. Korres, Athens, pp. 140–145.

Kaltsas, N. 2007. *The National Archaeological Museum*, Athens.

Karila-Cohen, K. 2005. "Apollon, Athènes et la Pythaïde. Mise
    en scène «mythique» de la cité au IIe siècle av. J.-C., *Kerbos*
    18, pp. 219–239.

Kellogg, D. L. 2013. *Marathon Fighters and Men of Maple:
    Ancient Acharnai*, Oxford.

Knoepfler, D. 2012. "L'occupation d'Oropos par Athènes au IVe
    siècle avant J.-C.: une clérouchie dissimulée?" ed. E. Culasso
    Gastaldi, *Gli Ateniesi fuori dall'Attica: modi d'intervento e di
    controllo del territorio, Atti del Convegno di Torino, 8–9 Aprile
    2010, Annuario della Scuola Archeologica Italiana di Atene* 88
    S. III, 10–2010, pp. 439–457.

Korres, M., ed. 2009. *Αττικής οδοί. Αρχαίοι δρόμοι της Αττικής*,
    Athens.

KvA = *Karten von Attika, mit Erläuterndem Text Herausgeben von
    E. Curtius & J. A. Kaupert. Kartenband*, Berlin 1904.

Lalonde, G. V., M. K. Langdon and M. B. Walbank. 1991. *The
    Athenian Agora, XIX. Inscriptions: Horoi, Poletai records,
    Leases of Public Lands*, Princeton 1991.

Langdon, M. K. 1987. "An Attic Decree Concerning Oropos,"
    Hesperia 56, pp. 47–58.

Langdon, M. K. 1994. "A Cyclopean Bridge and Rutted Road in the
    Thriasian Plain," *Studi micenei ed egeo-anatolici* 34, pp. 51–60.

Leake, W. M. 1829. "On the Demi of Attica," in *Transactions of
    the Royal Society of Literature of the United Kingdom* 1 (2),
    London, pp. 114–283.

Lévêque, P., Vidal-Naquet, Pierre. 1964. *Clisthène l'Athénien essai
    sur la représentation de l'espace et du temps dans la pensée
    politique grecque de la fin du VIe siècle à la mort de Platon*, Paris.

Lohmann, H. 1989. "Das Kastro von H. Giorgos ('Ereneia'),"
    in *Attische Festungen: Beiträge zum Festungswesen und
    zur Siedlungsstruktur vom 5. bis zum 3. Jh. v. Chr., Attische*

Forschungen 3, ed. H. Lauter, H. Lauter-Bufe, and H. Lohmann, Marburg, pp. 34–66.

Lohmann, H. 2002. "Ancient Roads in Attica and the Megaris," in *Ancient Roads in Greece, Proceedings of a Symposion Organized by the Cultural Association Aigeas (Athens) and the German Archaeological Institute (Athens) with the Support of the German School at Athens, November 23, 1998*, ed. H. R. Goette, Athens, pp. 73–91.

Lolos, Y. 2003. "Greek Roads: A Commentary on the Ancient Terms," *Glotta* 79, pp. 137–174.

Lolos, Y. A. 2011. *Land of Sikyon: Archaeology and History of a Greek City-State. Hesperia* Supplement 39, Princeton.

Lorimer, H.L. 1903. "The Country Cart in Ancient Greece," *Journal of Hellenic Studies* 23, pp. 132–151.

Milchhöfer, A. 1873. *Über den Attischen Apollon*, Munich.

Milchhöfer, A. 1895. "Karten von Attika. Heft VII–VIII, " in *Karten von Attika. Erläuternder text*, ed. Curtius, E., and J.A. Kaupert, Berlin, pp.1–37.

Minetti, A. E., C. Moia, G. S. Roi, D. Susta, and G. Ferretti. 2002. "Energy Cost of Walking and Running at Extreme Uphill and Downhill Slopes," *Journal of Applied Physiology* 93, pp. 1039–1046.

Müller, K. O. 1824. *Die Dorier* 1, Breslau.

Munn, M. H. 1993. *The Defense of Attica. The Dema Wall and the Boiotian War of 378–375 B.C.*, Berkeley.

Munn, M. H. 2010. "Panakton and Drymos: A Disputed Frontier," in *Attika: Archäologie einer "zentralen" Kulturlandschaft: Akten der internationalen Tagung vom 18.–20. Mai 2007 in Marburg, Philippika* 37, ed. H. Lohmann and T. Mattern, Wiesbaden, pp. 189–200.

Ober, J. 1982. "Edward Clarke's Ancient Road to Marathon A.D. 1801," *Hesperia* 51, pp. 453–458.

Ober, J. 1985. *Fortress Attica: Defense of the Athenian Land Frontier, 404–322 B.C*, Leiden.

Ober, J. 1999. *The Athenian Revolution: Essays on Ancient Greek Democracy and Political Theory*, Princeton.

Olson, S. D. 1991. "Firewood and Charcoal in Classical Athens," *Hesperia* 60, pp. 411–420.

Osborne, R. 1985. "The Erection and Mutilation of the *hermai*," *Proceedings of the Cambridge Philological Society* 31, pp. 47–73.

Osborne, R. 2010. *Athens and Athenian Democracy*, New York.

Ostwald, M. 1988. "The Reform of the Athenian State by Cleisthenes," in *The Cambridge Ancient History Volume 4: Persia, Greece and the Western Mediterranean, c.525 to 479 B.C.*, 2nd ed., ed. J. Boardman, N. G. L. Hammond, D. M. Lewis, and M. Ostwald, Cambridge, pp. 303–346.

Papangeli, P. 2009. "Ιερά Οδός, δυτικό τμήμα," in *Αττικής οδοί. Αρχαίοι δρόμοι της Αττικής*, ed. M. Korres, Athens, pp. 124–137.

Papazarkadas, N. 2011. *Sacred and Public Land in Ancient Athens*, Oxford.

Parsons, A. W. 1943. "Klepsydra and the Paved Court of the Pythion," *Hesperia* 12, pp. 191–267.

Petropoulakou, M., and E. Pentazos. 1973. *Αττικα. Οικιστικά στοιχεία – πρώτη έκθεση*, Athens.

Pfister, F. 1951. *Die Reisebilder des Herakleides, Sitzungsberichte, Österreichische Akademie der Wissenschaften (Wien), Philosophisch-historische Klasse* 227:2., Vienna.

Philippson, A., 1952. *Die Griechischen Landschaften: Eine*

Landeskunde. Der Nordosten der griechischen Halbinsel. Band I Teil 3: Attika Und Megaris, Frankfurt.

Pikoulas, Y. 1995. *Οδικό δίκτυο και άμυνα*, Athens.

Pikoulas, Y. 2001. "Το οδικό δίκτυο της Λακωνίας. Χρονολογήση, απαρχές και εχέλιξη," in *Forschungen in der Peloponnes: Akten des Symposions anläßlich der Feier "100 Jahre österreichisches Archäologisches Institut Athen", Athen 5.3.–7.3.1998*, ed. V. Mitsopoulos-Leon, Athens, pp. 326–330.

Pikoulas, Y. 2007. "Travelling by Land in Ancient Greece," in *Travel, Geography and Culture in Ancient Greece, Egypt and the Near East, Nottingham Studies in Ancient Society* 10, ed. C. E. P. Adams and J. Roy, Leicester and Oxford.

Pikoulas, Y. 2012. *Το οδικό δίκτυο της Λακωνικής*, Athens.

Platonos, M. 2009. "Οδικό δίκτυο βόρειας Αττικής," in *Αττικής οδοί. Αρχαίοι δρόμοι της Αττικής*, ed. M. Korres, Athens, pp. 140–145.

Pritchett, W. K. 1965. *Studies in Ancient Greek Topography, Part III (Roads)*, Berkeley.

Raepsaet, G. 2002. *Attelages et techniques de transport dans le monde gréco-romain*, Bruxelles.

Raepsaet, G., ed. 2008. "Land Transport, Part 2: Riding, Harnesses, and Vehicles," in *Oxford Handbook of Engineering and Technology in the Classical World*, Oxford, pp. 580–605.

Robert, L. 1960. "Sur la loi d'Athènes relative aux Petites Panathénées," in *Hellenika. Recueil d'épigraphie, de numistmatique et d'antiquités grecques* XI–XII, Paris, pp. 189–203.

Rutherford, I. C. 1990. "Paeans by Simonides," *Harvard Studies in Classical Philology* 93, pp.169–209.

Rutherford, I. 2013. *State Pilgrims and Sacred Observers in Ancient Greece. A Study of* Theōriā *and* Theōroi, Cambridge.

Siewert, P. 1982. *Die Trittyen Attikas umd die Heeresreform des Kleisthenes*, Munich.

Steinhauer, G. 2009. "Οδικό δίκτυο της Αττικής," in *Αττικής οδοί. Αρχαίοι δρόμοι της Αττικής*, ed. M. Korres, Athens, pp. 34–73.

Töpffer, J. 1888. "Die attischen Pythaisten und Deliasten," *Hermes* 23, pp. 321–332.

Theocharaki, A. M. 2011. "The Ancient Circuit Wall of Athens. Its Changing Course and the Phases of Construction," *Hesperia* 80, pp. 71–156.

Traill, J. S. 1975. *The Political Organization of Attica. A Study of Demes, Trittyes, and Phylai, and their Representation in the Athenian Council, Hesperia* Supplement 14, Princeton.

Trintignac, A. 2003. "La production de poix dans la cité des Gabales (Lozère) à l'époque gallo-romaine," *Reve archéologique de Picardie* 1–2, pp. 239–248.

Vanderpool, E. 1978. "Roads and Forts in Northwestern Attica," *California Studies in Classical Antiquity* 11, pp. 227–245.

Vian, F. 1966. "L'extraction de la poix et le sens de ΔΑΟΣ chez Quintus de Smyrne," *Revue des études grecques* 79, pp. 655–659.

Westlake, H. D. 1948. "Athenian Food Supplies from Euboea," *Classical Review* 62, pp. 2–4.

Whitehead, D. 1986. *The Demes of Attica, 508/7–ca. 250 B.C.: A Political and Social Study*, Princeton.

Woodhead, A. G. 1997. *The Athenian Agora*, XVI. *Inscriptions: The Decrees*, Princeton.

Wrede, W. 1934. *Attika*, Athens.

Young, J. H. 1956. "Roads in South Attika," *Antiquity*, pp. 94–97.

14

How to Look at a
Non-Peripteral Temple

Marya Fisher

In the study of Greek architecture, authors have emphasized different building types according to particular interpretive goals. This article investigates the diachronic treatment of the non-peripteral temple in three of the major approaches to the study of Greek architecture. The first, that of architectural development, often forefronts the role of the peripteral temple and, as result, obscures other architectural types. The second, that of architectural documentation, is fundamentally interested in form, and therefore admits a limited number of temples that lack peristyles. A third approach, which seeks to understand sacred architecture through the lens of cult and ritual activity, offers a greater opportunity to understand the importance of the non-peripteral temple within the wider Greek sacred landscape.

Architectural History at the Dawn of Modern Scholarship

The modern rebirth of interest in ancient Greek architecture is difficult to pinpoint, but the decade and a half beginning in 1749 marks a fresh start. Over the course of fifteen years, two voyages to Greece and the publications of their results heralded a return to a topic that had already fascinated Vitruvius.[1] These were the journeys of a Frenchman, Julien-David Le Roy, and two Englishmen, James Stuart and Nicholas Revett, which resulted in the publications, *Les ruines des plus beaux monuments de la Grèce* (1758) and *The Antiquities of Athens* (1762, Vol I).[2] Enabled by the newfound ability of scholars and gentlemen travelers to venture to Greece, still under Ottoman rule but more accessible to western Europeans, the authors sought to document the architecture of Athens and environs with first-hand authority.[3]

Even though they ostensibly share the same objective, these two major texts are radically different in their form and focus. The differences can be understood variously, but one which is illuminating is in the treatment of the non-peripteral temple. The non-peripteral temple, as the very term suggests, is defined by its lack of peristyle; the type varies in form, with both simple and complex plans, with

or without external or internal columns.[4] In their disparate attitudes towards these small sacred structures, these texts illustrate two approaches to Greek sacred architecture that have dominated scholarship: the developmental and the documentary. Both of these approaches stem from a fundamentally aesthetic appreciation of the structures discussed, with analysis centered on the form of the building, rather than its function.

Le Roy's is an ambitious volume, seeking both to document and to theorize, that is, to understand both history and form. Divided chronologically and geographically into two volumes, the "ruins" are considered first historically and then architecturally, with these two sections preceded by essays on the history and theory of architecture.[5] The format of the publication indicates the author's primary interest in theory, especially of the development of forms. Le Roy's method is best appreciated as an attempt to understand ancient architecture through the lens of Vitruvius with an emphasis on the Orders.[6]

This approach is most evident in Le Roy's essay on the history of architecture. Here he deals directly with architectural development, beginning with the sacred structures of the Egyptians, Hebrews and Phoenicians, next turning to Greek and Roman temples, and finally to

Christian churches. In his section on Greek and Roman temples, the architectural form of most interest to Le Roy is the peristyle. Indeed, the only mention of non-peripteral temples is in the context of a conjectural story about the origin of the column, introduced to support the roofs of early temples.[7] According to Le Roy, after this innovation, "the novelty of the spectacle produced by these columns ranged at equal intervals within the temples seems to have caught the imagination of the inventors of the peristyle."[8] What follows is a history of the development of the orders as they are displayed in peripteral temples. In this brief narrative of historical development centered on the peristyle, the non-peripteral temple is never treated as a distinct type, but only as a predecessor to *peripteroi*.

The primacy of the peristyle in Le Roy's understanding of Greek architecture is also reflected in the second of the two essays, on the "Theory of Architecture." In his explanation of the "beauty of architecture," Le Roy uses the peristyle as his primary example: "These three qualities – the pleasantness, the strength, and the variety of the sensations conveyed to us by architecture – though rarely combined in a single building, are the causes that make architecture beautiful. We shall show how they are to be found in peristyles in particular."[9] The section that follows is an encomium to the peristyle, its form and its grandeur. Le Roy's insistence on the peristyle as an example of the architecturally perfect form follows from his view of the development of Greek sacred building as outlined in the "Essay on the History of Architecture."

Stuart and Revett, in contrast, approach their subject quite differently. Their goals are reflected in the title of their book, *The Antiquities of Athens Measured and Delineated by James Stuart, F.R.S. and F.S.A., and Nicholas Revett, Painters and Architects.* They sought to document accurately the monuments of Athens, with an emphasis on precise measurements, not theoretical concerns.[10] This emphasis on accuracy is apparent not only in the title of the work, but throughout the plates and commentary. Stuart's insistence on systematic documentation may be read as a direct response to Le Roy's text, which he viewed as error-ridden. Stuart compares the accuracy of the two texts in his preface, "if nevertheless any one should doubt of the accuracy of the Measures, because they differ so greatly from those which Mons. Le Roy has given, I can only assure him, that in a considerable number of them, at the taking of which I assisted with Mr. Revett, and in many others, which occasionally I measured after him, I have always found reason to praise his exactness."[11] Stuart both underscores the accuracy in documentation of his own project, and undermines the legitimacy of Le Roy's text.[12]

The difference in the respective authors' methodology and its application to non-peripteral temples can be observed in the different ways in which they deal with the Temple on the Ilissos River in Athens. This temple, built in the third

quarter of the 5th century BC, exists today in drawings and its foundations; only a few blocks assigned to its frieze, and possible column bases are preserved.[13] The case of the Ilissos Temple, with its non-peripteral, amphiprostyle plan, is instructive because it is one of only non-peripteral temples in Athens or Attica which was known when Le Roy, and Stuart and Revett were in Athens studying the monuments.[14]

In his description of the Ilissos valley, Le Roy proceeds from the Arch of Hadrian and the Olympieion, west to the Panathenaic stadium, and finally, to the small temple on the banks of the Ilissos river.[15] Of the Ilissos temple, Le Roy writes, "A little way from the stadium, and likewise across the Ilissos, stand the scanty remains of a very small temple. I did not draw it; but I shall say a word on Diana Agrotera, or the huntress, to whom it was dedicated."[16] In this passage Le Roy indicates no interest in the temple. He does not mention its order, its incorporation into a church, or any other architectural detail. Indeed, Le Roy seems to emphasize the temple's insignificance by explicitly stating that he did not draw it. Instead, he uses the temple as a starting point to discuss the goddess with whom he associates the temple, based on a passage in Pausanias (Paus. 1.19.6). For Le Roy, the temple is of no interest architecturally, but serves only as a placeholder in the landscape of ancient sacred narratives.

Stuart and Revett, in contrast, dedicate the entire second chapter of their first volume to the temple. In the introduction to this chapter, Stuart underlines the importance of the small building, judging that its "forms are extremely simple, but withal so elegant, and the whole is so well executed, that it may doubtless be reckoned among those works of antiquity which best deserve our attention."[17] Building on this remark, Stuart and Revett fully document the temple, including both an impressionistic engraving of the contemporary state of the ruins and detailed measured architectural drawings of the plan, elevations, and numerous details; in all, there are eight plates devoted to the non-peripteral temple (Figure 14.1). Following the general structure of the volume, each plate is described in full, and thus, the building receives thorough visual and textual documentation.[18] The Ilissos Temple is given the same treatment accorded to the other buildings in *The Antiquities of Athens*; that the building lacks a peristyle does not preclude its documentation by the architects. If the section on the Ilissos Temple is shorter than others, this is perhaps because of its size rather than its significance.

Stuart ends his chapter on the Ilissos Temple with an attack on Le Roy and his treatment of the small temple. Stuart begins his criticism by enumerating the mistakes which appear in Le Roy's text, inaccuracies in the drawings which show the temple as a background element, and the attribution of the cult to Artemis Agrotera.[19] In addition to these perceived errors, Stuart belittles the lack of attention given the temple by the Frenchman, commenting, "at present it will be sufficient to observe that the little Grecian Temple [Le Roy] has here mentioned, altho' he omits to tell us

Figure 14.1 The Temple on the Ilissos River. Stuart and Revett 1762, Ch. 2, Pl. 1.

what Order it is of, is by its Situation apparently intended to represent the Ionic temple which has been treated of in this chapter."[20] Stuart even goes so far to suggest, at the conclusion of the chapter, that he believes that Le Roy, in mentioning the Temple on the Ilissos, is conflating two different buildings, the nadir of inaccuracy.[21]

Stuart himself considers the disparate treatments of this small temple emblematic of the different approaches taken by the authors of two texts. For Stuart and Revett, the non-peripteral temple is deserving of attention, but for Le Roy, it is not. Stuart's explanation of this difference centers on Le Roy's careless documentation and scholarship, his inaccurate drawings and analysis, but the issue is more fundamental. The difference in method and focus of the two texts make the non-peripteral temple important for Stuart and Revett, but of little interest to Le Roy. Le Roy's theoretical approach, with its emphasis on the development of the peristyle, marginalizes non-peripteral temples as the smaller predecessors of the *peripteroi*. Stuart and Revett's documentary approach treats the non-peripteral temples systematically, sometimes according them equal attention as *peripteroi*. Le Roy's emphasis on development precludes any interest in non-peripteral buildings of the Classical

period, while Stuart and Revett's interest in documenting makes the simple elegance of the Temple on the Ilissos a focus of their text. This case study from the dawn of the modern study of ancient Greek architecture illustrates the way in which methodology, approach and emphasis results in disparate treatment and valuation of non-peripteral temples in the scholarly narrrative, a phenomenon which has persisted through the 20th century.

Theories of Development and Narratives of Architectural History

Le Roy's text represents an example of the developmental approach to the history of Greek sacred architecture. Like most strains of the modern study of Greek architecture, it finds its origins in the text of Vitruvius, the 1st century BC architect and theorist, who, in his explanation of the origins of the Doric and Ionic entablatures, provides a narrative of development, tracing temple architecture from timber to stone construction (Vitr. 4.2.2–5).[22] The full expression of this approach, however, is found not in ancient texts, but in the Anglophone architectural histories of the 20th century.

Because of its importance to the study of Greek architectural history in the twentieth and twenty-first centuries, William Dinsmoor's *The Architecture of Ancient Greece: An Account of its Historic Development* serves as the prime exemplar of this strain of scholarship. Dinsmoor attempts to create a coherent narrative of the history of Greek architecture, just as Le Roy had done over a century earlier. Dinsmoor's history is based on an evolutionary theory of architecture, with Classical forms maturing from more primitive ones, a conceptual framework which owes much to the seminal work of J.J. Winckelmann. [23] For Dinsmoor, the Geometric and Archaic periods represent the birth and maturation of Greek culture and its architecture, the Classical period, its apex, and the Hellenistic and Roman periods, its decline. [24]

In Dinsmoor's narrative, non-peripteral temples, identified as "nondescript," fit into the birth phase of the life cycle. [25] Non-peripteral temples are the forerunners of the great peripteral monuments and are understood exclusively in this way within the context of the text. There is little interest in the continued construction and use of these buildings after the development of the peristyle. Dinsmoor does discuss exceptional examples (the Telesterion at Eleusis and the Erechtheion), and highly visible monuments (the Temple of Athena Nike), but these are exceptions. [26] This is not to say that Dinsmoor was not aware of the non-peripteral temples of the later Archaic and Classical periods, but only that they do not fit into his narrative of historical development and, as result, are not the focus of his text.

Dinsmoor's choice of emphasis is characteristic of his generation, and he gathered followers. Non-peripteral temples receive summary treatment in Robertson's 1945 handbook of Greek and Roman architecture, only appearing in the chapter on "The Earliest Temples." [27] They occupy just over a page at the beginning in Plommer's 1956 treatment of the architectural development of Greek temples, discussed exclusively as forerunners of *peripteroi*. [28] In Lawrence's *Greek Architecture,* the treatment of non-peripteral temples is particularly dismissive. Like his contemporaries, Lawrence introduces non-peripteral temples as primitive examples of the type, with only exceptional examples treated in later chapters of architectural development. Lawrence's comments, however, on these "primitive" examples are disparaging at best: "It would be fair to say that the architects at the end of the seventh century utilized all the elements of the later Classical Temples, without realizing either their structural or their aesthetic possibilities. The inheritance from centuries of bad building kept the engineering unnecessarily cautious and the design crude. But in both respects, experiment had proceeded far enough to enable the architects of the next century to discard obsolete traditions to produce buildings that were structurally sound and good works of art." [29] Since this passage concludes his chapter on "Primitive Temples," which Lawrence notes "as a rule [...] had no pteron," he clearly must refer to temples without peristyles when he writes of "crude" design and "obsolete traditions." [30]

For Le Roy, Dinsmoor and others trying to construct an overarching theory of the history of Greek architecture, non-peripteral temples must serve as a preliminary step, a necessary but "nondescript" phase, on the path to the great monuments of the Classical period. Including later non-peripteral temples in such a history would only serve to confuse the historical narrative constructed. The authors of such texts, read and followed by generations of scholars of Greek architecture, could not see the non-peripteral temple as anything but a forerunner, an ancestor.

A developmental approach to architectural history does not, however, necessarily preclude an emphasis on non-peripteral temples. Indeed, it is the focus of these developmental studies that determines the inclusion or exclusion of non-peripteral buildings. One notable example is Gottfried Gruben's emphasis on local regional building traditions in the development of architecture. His approach highlights the role of the non-peripteral temple, as apteral buildings dominate the sacred architecture certain regions, notably the Cyclades. [31] This is also true of the most recent Italian and French comprehensive scholarly works on Greek architectural history, which integrate temples without peristyles into the narrative of development, not simply as forerunners, but as representatives of an important building type that persists throughout the Archaic, Classical and Hellenistic periods. [32]

Documenting the Non-Peripteral Temple

The approach to Greek architecture exemplified by Stuart and Revett's text is also rooted in Vitruvius' *De architectura*. Like Stuart and Revett, Vitruvius, a working architect himself, is deeply interested in temple design, in plan and elevation; he lingers on details of planning and proportion in building. [33] Vitruvius' text interests itself in both peripteral and non-peripteral buildings without distinction. In his typology of temples, the Roman architect does not outline the difference between apteral and peripteral, but rather the different ways in which columns can be deployed in temple design. Vitruvius' approach is best illustrated by the introduction to his section on temple planning, in which he sets out his typology: "And first there is 'in antis', which is known as '*naos en parastasin*' in Greek, then prostyle, amphiprostyle, peripteral, pseudodipteral, dipteral, hypaethral" (Vitr. 3.2.1). [34] Vitruvius lists all these types altogether, proceeding from least to most complex, without creating a distinction between buildings with and without a peristyle. Yet all of Vitruvius' building categories are defined by external columns. He completely omits temples which have no external columns at all; the only non-peripteral types noted by Vitruvius are those with colonnaded porches on one or more sides.

Vitruvius' categories and omissions have had a dramatic impact on subsequent studies of Greek sacred architecture, effectively erasing temples lacking columns from some texts. This is true especially for Vitruvius' most faithful followers, the Humanist architectural theorists of the Renaissance, notably Leon Battista Alberti and Andrea Palladio, who mimic and expand upon Vitruvius in their treatment of the design of Greek temples. Some passages in these early modern texts that deal with the layout of sacred architecture are translations and condensations of Vitruvius, with little or no new information or interpretation offered (since none was then available).[35] Vitruvius and his Renaissance followers have no bias that fundamentally separates non-peripteral from peripteral; rather, the bias is against temples lacking external columns. For Vitruvius, the key formal element in Greek architecture is the external column, not the peristyle, as it would be for Le Roy.

Vitruvius' legacy is reflected in Stuart and Revett's text in the emphasis on certain architectural forms, such as the column, rather than on a certain type of building, as is the case in developmental studies of Greek architecture. That this emphasis on forms is present in Vitruvius, the Renaissance theorists, and modern documentarians of Greek architecture is to be expected. Unlike those scholars whose emphasis is on historical development, these texts are written primarily by working architects and are meant, at least in part, to provide models for other practicing architects, for whom forms, rather than historical narratives, are essential.[36] In the modern documentation of ancient building, exemplified by Stuart and Revett and their followers, the Society of Dilettanti's *Antiquities of Ionia* in particular, this emphasis on forms and accuracy is reflected in the inclusion of non-peripteral structures, but only those whose forms are compelling to the architect's eye; temples adorned with columns and entablatures, like the Temple on the Ilissos, therefore, receive more attention than simple, unadorned cult buildings.[37]

The act of sweeping historical architectural documentation, so important in the 18th and 19th centuries, has gradually lost centrality to the field of Greek architectural history, replaced functionally by archaeological reports and studies of individual buildings.[38] Authors of such texts continue to stress the crucial importance of accurate architectural documentation, still following the model of Stuart and Revett.[39] The non-peripteral temples that appear frequently in these volumes are included because of the approach and subject of the individual projects, be it a specific site or type of sanctuary, rather than exclusively for their formal attributes.

Columns and Cult: Ritual and the Non-Peripteral Temple

The two approaches to Greek architectural history exemp-

lified by Le Roy and Stuart and Revett are far from the only possible methods to examine Greek sacred architecture. Despite their clear differences, these two approaches are, in one respect, very similar: they focus on the form, rather than the function of buildings. Through these lenses, the role of these buildings as sacred space is largely unaddressed, effectively ridding ritual space of ritual. These aesthetic approaches are fundamentally alienating, as they present buildings as sterile spaces, agglomerations of formal elements, rather than the vibrant cult spaces they once were. In order to understand the Greek temple more completely, it is necessary to reintegrate the discussion of cult into the history of sacred architecture. Through such an approach, the non-peripteral temple is not marginalized or dissected for its composite forms, but, rather, represents a positive choice on the part of its builders.

Like the developmental and documentary approaches to Greek architecture, concentrated interest in ritual activity can find its roots in antiquity. Here the model is not Vitruvius, but Pausanias. In quantity, Pausanias gives us the most information about temples in the Greek world. Yet few of the temples he notes receive more than a cursory physical description; instead, he identifies them, and associates them with a given deity, perhaps adding some mythological or historical background. Pausanias' indifference to temple design is clear from both the brevity of his descriptions and his common and often infuriating omissions; the Ionic frieze of the Parthenon is only the most notorious of these lacunae (Paus. 1.24.5). Unsurprisingly, Pausanias tends to make no distinction, linguistic or otherwise, between temples with peristyles and those without.[40] His other interests, including the history of religion and ritual activities, mean that he only rarely describes the details of the buildings' plans and elevations.[41]

Pausanias' indifferent approach to the details of individual buildings is far from an ideal model for a history of sacred architecture, but his treatment of temples is revealing nonetheless. In a text focused on religion, temples, peripteral and non, are treated indiscriminately; for Pausanias, it is not the plan of the temple that makes it important, but its place in the religious topography of Greece. This is indicative that, for Pausanias, the presence or absence of a peristyle, colonnade or column does not make a temple more or less significant from a social, political, historical or ritual perspective. In this reading of Greek sacred architecture, non-peripteral temples are an integral element in the ritual landscape, one of the many ways people honored the gods and sought to communicate with them.

The interpretation of temples as ritual spaces is not new, but it is essential for understanding the omnipresence of non-peripteral temples in the Greek world.[42] The archaeological, architectural and literary evidence does not support the idea that these small temples are exclusively the result of chronology or economy, that they are solely the products

Figure 14.2 Temple of Demeter Malophoros, Selinous, Sicily, from the southeast. Photo M. Fisher.

of early architects or impoverished communities. There are far more non-peripteral temples than is generally commented upon, with *apteroi* accounting for more than half of all Greek temples.[43] These important sacred buildings occupied eminent positions in both urban and extra-urban sanctuaries, such as the Temple of Athena Nike on the Athenian Acropolis, to name just one striking example. Non-peripteral temples were built in the same years and in the same cities where some of the most monumental examples of the *peripteroi* were being constructed. One instance of this phenomenon is the second Temple of Demeter Malophoros at ancient Selinous, a non-peripteral temple that was built in the same years as Temple C, the first of the great peripteral temples on the city's acropolis (Figure 14.2).[44] In some instances, the construction of these small temples reflects strong regional preferences and traditions. But overall, the key to these buildings is their role in cult.

Because of the prevalence of the non-peripteral temple in Magna Graecia, in this region the type has received scholarly attention.[45] Valentina Hinz, in particular, has highlighted the connection between the *apteros* and cult, linking some of these small temples with the worship of Demeter and Kore in Southern Italy and Sicily.[46] In Magna Graecia, where

the importance of these deities is undeniable, the temples that populate the goddess' sanctuaries are overwhelming *apteroi*, not *peripteroi*.[47] Why were non-peripteral temples built for Demeter and Kore?[48] It is impossible at present to determine the precise cause. There is reason to believe, however, that there were specific motivations related to cult. The archaeological record reveals a wide range of concentrated ritual activities that took place within the walls of these small temples, including the offering of votives and the consumption of sacred meals.[49] It is possible that these rituals and the nature of the cult which inspired them may be related to the form of the buildings themselves.[50] In any case, the strong correlation between the worship of Demeter and Kore and the erection of non-peripteral temples in Southern Italy and Sicily is clear evidence that cult, rather than strictly chronology or economy, determined the way in which these sacred structures were designed and built.[51]

Conclusion

The perspective of ritual and cult provides a view of non-peripteral temples that reintegrates these important buildings into the religious landscape and illuminates their role in the sacred environment of ancient Greece. Ritual interpretations are essential to the understanding of sacred architecture; and a narrative that acknowledges the role of ritual in the construction of sacred buildings, in concert with other approaches, offers a freshly nuanced way of understanding the rich and varied repertoire of temples in the Greek world. With such an approach, the ancient Greek landscape can be repopulated with the full array of sacred structures that once dotted its hills and valleys, its cities and countryside. This more comprehensive view of the religious landscape of the ancient Greek world underscores its vitality and its variety.

Notes

1   The present essay would not have been possible without the help of M. M. Miles, C. Marconi and B. D. Wescoat, to whom I owe considerable thanks for their valuable feedback and encouragement. All translations fom ancient texts are my own.
2   The proposal for *The Antiquities of Athens* is reprinted and appears in Stuart and Revett's text (Stuart and Revett 1762, pp. v–vi, n. a). For reactions to the proposals, see Kelly 2009, p. 108; for the delay of the volume's publication, see Stuart and Revett 1762, pp. vi–vii; Kelly 2009, p. 162. On the impact of the publication of Le Roy's volume on *The Antiquities of Athens*, see Kelly 2009, pp. 165–167. That these two journeys occurred in such close chronological proximity is not a coincidence: Le Roy's mission was viewed as "a rival journey in the interests of France" by the Society of the Dilettanti (Cust and Colvin 1914, p. 79). The nationalist impetus for these expeditions is clear from the accounts of the Society (Cust and Colvin 1914, p. 159); for the role of nationalism in the work of the Society, see Redford 2008, p. 44.
3   Earlier documented accounts of Greece and its architecture existed, which serve as valuable testimonials to the state of the buildings as they were known from the Renaissance onward; for a review of this literature, see Middleton 2004, pp. 2–3; Beschi, pp. 338–358; Kelly 2009, pp. 104–105; Watkin 2007, pp. 21–22. In this period, exploration of Greece and other parts of the Mediterranean increased and yielded published accounts (Kelly 2009, pp. 101–104).
4   For the purposes of this paper, these buildings will be referred to as non-peripteral temples, apteral temples, and *apteroi*.
5   This methodological choice may have originated in the Enlightenment approach to architecture (as a science) and history as different disciplines (Kisacky 2001, p. 261).
6   For the relationship between Le Roy and Vitruvius, see Armstrong 2012, pp. 87–135.
7   Le Roy 2004, p. 218.
8   Le Roy 2004, p. 218. The absence of non-peripteral temples from Le Roy's text reflects the relative scarcity of such structures known in the mid-eighteenth century.
9   Le Roy 2004, p. 368.
10   For a comparison of the texts' approaches to accuracy, see Redford 2008, pp. 53–59.
11   Stuart and Revett 1762, p. viii. Kelly speculates that Stuart and Revett's emphasis on empirical study of the monuments was

a reaction both to Le Roy, and to the environment within the Society of the Dilettanti in the years of its production (Kelly 2009, pp.169–171).
12   Although not initially sponsored by the Society of the Dilettanti, Stuart and Revett were embraced by the group, and their methodology provided a model for subsequent expeditions; this is clear from the instructions issued by the Society to the expedition to Ionia, a journey inspired by the success of *The Antiquities of Athens* (Cust and Colvin 1914, pp. 81 and 153; Kelly 2009, p. 182).
13   Much of the scholarship on this temple is centered on its relationship to the Temple of Athena Nike on the Athenian Acropolis. There is a marked similarity in both architectural and sculptural forms of the two buildings. The architectural forms are so similar that the two buildings have been attributed to the same architect, Kallikrates (Mylonas Shear 1963). For discussions of the Ionic friezes of the two buildings, see Palagia 2005, Picón 1978. For the debate over the date of this temple, see Miles 1980.
14   Another non-peripteral temple in both texts is the Erechtheion, but because of the unique features of the plan and elevation of the Erechtheion, it is not a representative non-peripteral temple. Le Roy and Stuart and Revett were far from the first to deal the Temple on the Ilissos; it was well-known to travelers to Athens in the 17th and 18th centuries (Miles 1980, pp. 310–311).
15   Le Roy identifies this building not as the Olympieion, but as Hadrian's Pantheon; Stuart and Revett dispute this, and their differences on this issue were acrimonious. Although the correct identification as the Olympieion is offered by Stuart and Revett, Stuart modified the printed plan of the temple in order to display a standard decastyle plan (Middleton 2004, pp. 22–23).
16   Le Roy 2004, p. 425.
17   Stuart and Revett 1762, p. 7.
18   Stuart and Revett 1762, pp. 7–11, chapter 2, pls. 1–8.
19   Stuart and Revett 1762, pp. 10–11. Le Roy's attribution has been upheld by subsequent scholars (Travlos 1971, p. 112).
20   Stuart and Revett 1762, p. 11.
21   Stuart and Revett 1762, p. 11.
22   For a systematic discussion of the Vitruvian theory of the origins of the genera, see Vitruvius 1999, pp. 218–219.
23   Winckelmann 2006. For an analysis of Winckelmann's concept of art as a lifecycle, see Brendel 1979, pp. 15–24. In the present discussion, the 3rd edition of Dinsmoor is referenced (Dinsmoor 1950).
24   This is clear just from the titles of Dinsmoor's chapters, which speak of "Origins," "Culmination" and finally "Decadence" (Dinsmoor 1950, p. xiv).
25   Dinsmoor 1950, p. xiii.
26   The Telesterion (Dinsmoor 1950, pp. 113, 195–6); the Erechtheion (Dinsmoor 1950, pp. 186–194); the Temple of Athena Nike (Dinsmoor 1950, pp. 185–6).
27   Robertson 1945, pp. 51–61. As in Dinsmoor, a small number of exceptional non-peripteral temples do appear in the text: the Temple of Athena Nike and the Ilissos Temple (Robertson 1945, pp. 125–7) and the Erechtheion (Robertson 1945, pp. 127–135).
28   Plommer 1956, pp. 182–3.

29   Lawrence 1938, p. 98.

30   Lawrence 1938, p. 94.

31   Gruben 2001.

32   See Lippolis et al. 2007; Hellmann 2006, pp. 50–121.

33   For a discussion of Vitruvius' approach to design, see Rowland 1999, pp. 15–16.

34   For the Vitruvian meaning of these terms, see Vitruvius 1987, p. 283; Vitruvius 1999, p. 192.

35   We see this in the first architectural treatise of the Renaissance, *De re aedificatoria*, written by Leon Battista Alberti in the mid-fifteenth century (Alberti 7.4–5.) Of Alberti's relationship with Vitruvius, see Krautheimer 1969; for Alberti's reception of ancient building in his architectural practice, see Wittkower 1940–1941. This is true too of Palladio, with the interesting variation that in the typology of the temples, peripteral and non are distinguished (Palladio 4.3). Palladio was clearly reverent of both Alberti and Vitruvius (Wittkower 1944, p. 106).

36   The role of Stuart and Revett's text as a model for architects is clear from the Society of the Dilettantti's instructions to the Ionian Expedition, whose mission was modeled off of *The Antiquities of Athens*, that "it is the chief object of the Society to promote the progress of architecture by affording practical assistance to the architects of this country" (Cust and Colvin 1914, p. 153).

37   One key exception to this is to be found in Koldewey and Puchstein's treatment of the Greek temples of South Italy and Sicily, where temples lacking external columns are featured (Koldewey and Puchstein 1899).

38   Of great importance are the study of the ancient architecture of Sicily by Hittorff and Zanth (Hittorff and Zanth 1827), the study of the temples of South Italy and Sicily by Koldewey and Puchstein (Koldewey and Puchstein 1899) and the *Antiquities of Ionia*, produced by the Society of Dilettanti (Society of the Dilettanti 1769–1915).

39   For the continued importance of architectural documentation, see Barletta 2011, p. 612.

40   There are a small number of exceptions, where Pausanias does note the presence of a peristyle: the Temple of Zeus at Olympia (Paus. 5.10.3), the Heraion at Olympia (Paus. 5.16.1), the Philippeon at Olympia (Paus. 5.20.10), and the "old temple" in the agora at Elis (Paus. 6.24.10).

41   One of the rare examples is the Corcyraean Stoa at Elis (Paus. 6.24.4), discussed by Miles in this volume.

42   An active interest in this strain of scholarship can be found in the recent volume *Architecture of the Sacred* (Wescoat and Ousterhout 2012), as well as in the section on cult places in *Thesaurus Cultus et Rituum Antiquorum*, Vol. 4 [*ThesCRA* IV] (Sinn and Leypold 2005, pp. 87–112). For the ritual interpretation of interior spaces of temples, see especially Corbett 1970, Miles 1998–1999, and Mylonopoulos 2011.

43   Non-peripteral types represent about 54% of all Greek temples dating from the Archaic and Classical periods cataloged in Lippolis et al. 2007.

44   Marconi 2007, pp. 85 and 88.

45   Notably a study of the oikos-type temple (Isler 1984, pp. 27–60), a catalog of non-peripteral temples in Sicily (Romeo 1989), and an investigation of the cult of Demeter and Kore and its associated sacred buildings (Hinz 1998).

46   Hinz 1998.

47   Hinz 1998, pp. 51–52. The relationship between the worship of Demeter and Kore and non-peripteral temples is not limited to Magna Graecia. However, because of the preponderance of sanctuaries of the goddesses in this region, it is instructive to look to these temples as a case study. For a discussion of the form of temples of Demeter and Kore throughout the Greek world, see White 1993, p. 40, n. 70.

48   Not all the non-peripteral temples of Magna Graecia are dedicated to Demeter and Kore. Romeo associates non-peripteral temples in Sicily more generally with non-Olympian cult (Romeo 1989, p. 49).

49   Hinz 1998, p. 52. For the specific example of the votive dedications within Temple R at Selinunte, see Marconi 2014.

50   Romeo has suggested a link between the Eleusinian cult of Demeter and closed temple plans in Sicily (Romeo 1989, p. 49).

51   Hinz 1998, p. 52. Marconi also connects the architectural form of the Temple of Demeter Malophoros with its cult through the temple's role in the inspiration of awe (Marconi 2007, p. 86).

References

Armstrong, C. D. 2012. *Julien-David LeRoy and the Making of Architectural History*, New York.

Barletta, B. 2011. "Greek Architecture," *American Journal of Archaeology* 115, pp. 611–640.

Beschi, L. 1986. "La scoperta dell'arte greca," in *Memoria dell'antico nell'arte italiana*, Vol. 3, ed. S. Settis, Torino, pp. 295–374.

Brendel, O. 1979. *Prolegomena to the Study of Roman Art*, New Haven.

Corbett, P. E. 1970. "Greek Temples and Greek Worshippers: The Literary and Archaeological Evidence," *Bulletin of the Institute of Classical Studies* 17, pp. 149–158.

Cust, L., and S. Colvin. 1914. *History of the Society of Dilettanti*, London.

Dinsmoor, W. B. 1950. *The Architecture of Ancient Greece. An Account of its Historic Development*, 3rd ed., New York.

Gruben, G. 2001. *Griechische Tempel und Heiligtümer*, 5th ed., Munich.

Hellmann, M.-Ch. 2006. *L'Architecture Grecque*, Vol. 2, Paris.

Hinz, V. 1998. *Der Kult von Demeter und Kore auf Sizilien und in der Magna Graecia*, Wiesbaden.

Hittorff, J.-I. and L. Zanth. 1827. *Architecture antique de la Sicile; ou, Recueil des plus intéressans monumens d'architecture des villes et des lieux les plus remarquables de la Sicile ancienne*, Paris.

Isler, H. P., ed. 1984. *Der Tempel der Aphrodite; La ceramica proveniente dall'insediamento medievale: Cenni e osservazioni preliminari, Studia Ietina* 2, Zurich.

Kelly, J. 2009. *The Society of Dilettanti: Archaeology and Identity in the British Enlightenment*, New Haven.

Kisacky, J. 2001. "History and Science: Julien-David Le Roy's 'Dualistic Method of Architectural History'," *Journal of the Society of Architectural Historians* 60, pp. 260–289.

Koldewey, R., and O. Puchstein. 1899. *Die griechische Tempel in Unteritalien und Sizilien*, Vols. 1 and 2, Berlin.

Krautheimer, R. 1969. "Alberti and Vitruvius," in *Studies in Early Christian, Medieval, and Renaissance Art*, New York, pp. 323–332.

Lawrence, L. 1938. "Stuart and Revett: Their Literary and Architectural Careers," *Journal of the Warburg and Courtauld Institutes* 2, pp. 128–146.

Le Roy, J.-D. 2004 [1770]. *The Ruins of the Most Beautiful Monuments of Greece*, trans. D. Britt, Los Angeles.

Lippolis, E., M. Livadiotii, and G. Rocco. 2007. *Architettura greca, storia e monumenti del mondo della polis dalle origini al V secolo*, Milan.

Marconi, C. 2007. *Temple Decoration and Cultural Identity in the Archaic Greek World: The Metopes of Selinus*, Cambridge.

Marconi, C. 2014. "Two New *Aulos* Fragments from Selinunte: Cult, Music and Spectacle in the Main Urban Sanctuary of a Greek Colony in the West," in *Musica, culti e riti nell'occidente greco*, ed. A. Bellia, Rome and Pisa, pp. 105–115.

Middleton, R. 2004. "Introduction," in *The Ruins of the Most Beautiful Monuments of Greece*, trans. D. Britt, Los Angeles, pp.1–204.

Miles, M. M. 1980. "The Date of the Temple on the Ilissos River," *Hesperia* 49, pp. 309–325.

Miles, M. M. 1998–1999. "Interior Staircases in Western Greek Temples," *Memoirs of the American Academy in Rome* 43–44, pp. 1–26.

Mylonas Shear, I. 1963. "Kallikrates," *Hesperia* 32, pp. 375–424.

Mylonopoulos, J. 2011. "Divine Images 'Behind Bars.' The Semantics of Barriers in Greek Temples." In *Current Approaches to Religion in Ancient Greece*, ed. J. Wallensten and M. Haysom, Stockholm, pp. 267–291.

Onians, J. 1988. *Bearers of Meaning: The Classical Orders in Antiquity, the Middle Ages, and the Renaissance*, Princeton.

Palagia, O. 2005. "Interpretations of Two Athenian Friezes: The Temple on the Ilissos and the Temple of Athena Nike," in *Periklean Athens and its Legacy*, ed. J. Barringer and J. Hurwit, Austin, pp. 177–192.

Picón, C. A. 1978. "The Ilissos Temple Reconsidered," *American Journal of Archaeology* 82, pp. 47–81.

Plommer, H. 1956. *Simpson's History of Architectural Development Vol. 1: Ancient and Classical Architecture*, London.

Redford, B. 2008. *Dilettanti: The Antic and the Antique in Eighteenth-Century England*, Los Angeles.

Robertson, D. S. 1945. *A Handbook of Greek and Roman Architecture*, 2nd ed., Cambridge.

Romeo, I. 1989. "Sacelli arcaici senzi peristasis nella Sicilia greca," *Xenia* 17, pp. 5–54.

Rowland, I. D. 1994. "Raphael, Angelo Colocci, and the Genesis of the Architectural Orders," *The Art Bulletin* 76, pp. 81–104.

Rowland, I. D. 1999. "Introduction," in *Ten Books on Architecture*, trans. I. Rowland, Cambridge, pp. 1–18.

Rykwert, J. 1996. *The Dancing Column: On Order in Architecture*, Cambridge, Mass.

Salman, F. 2008. "Introduction: The Antiquities of Athens," in *The Antiquities of Athens*, New York, pp. v–xvii.

Sinn, U. and C. Leypold. 2005. "Tempel," in *Thesaurus Cultus et Rituum Antiquorum, Vol. 4.*, ed. V. Lambrinoudakis and J. Balty, Los Angeles, pp. 87–112.

Society of Dilettanti. 1769–1915. *Antiquities of Ionia*, London.

Stillwell, R. 1952. "Review: The Architecture of Ancient Greece, An Account of Its Historic Development by William Bell Dinsmoor," *American Journal of Archaeology* 56, pp. 158–160.

Stuart, J. and N. Revett. 1762. *The Antiquities of Athens*, Vol. 1, London.

Thoenes, C. and H. Günther. 1985. "Gli ordini architettonici: rinascita o invenzione?" in *Roma e l'antico nell'arte e nella cultura del Cinquecento*, ed. M. Fagiolo, Rome, pp. 261–310.

Travlos, J. 1971. *Pictorial Dictionary of Ancient Athens*, New York.

Vitruvius. 1997. *De Architectura*, trans. A. Corso and E. Romano, Torino.

Vitruvius. 1999. *Ten Books on Architecture*, trans. I. Rowland, Cambridge.

Watkin, D. 2007. "Stuart and Revett: The Myth of Greece and its Afterlife," in *James "Athenian Stuart 1713–1788: The Rediscovery of Antiquity*, ed. S.W. Soros, New Haven, pp. 19–58.

Wescoat, B. D. and R. G. Ousterhout. 2012. *Architecture of the Sacred: Space, Ritual, and Experience from Classical Greece to Byzantium*, New York.

White, D. 1993. *The Extramural Sanctuary of Demeter and Persephone at Cyrene, Libya: The Site's Architecture, Its First Six Hundred Years of Development*, Philadelphia.

Winckelmann, J. J. 2006 [1764]. *The History of the Art of Antiquity*, trans. H. Mallgrave, Los Angeles.

Wittkower, R. 1944. "Principles of Palladio's Architecture," *Journal of the Warburg and Courtauld Institutes* 7, pp. 102–122.

Wittkower, R. 1940–1941. "Alberti's Approach to Antiquity in Architecture," *Journal of the Warburg and Courtauld Institutes* 4, pp. 1–18.

14

The Vanishing Double Stoa at Thorikos and its Afterlives

Margaret M. Miles

The focus of this paper is the modern commentary on an unusual double stoa at Thorikos in Attica, built in the late 5th century BC. Although it was first discovered in 1754, its plan was not fully revealed until excavations by the Greek Archaeological Society in in the mid-1990s. Modified drawings are presented here with a new detail reconstructed: a central doorway in the crosswall. Parts of the stoa taken into the Agora of Athens and re-used in a Roman temple provide architectural details of the original building. The double stoa is then considered within the development of ancient Greek stoas.

The Initial Discovery at Thorikos

As Julien-David Le Roy was sailing in the Aegean Sea toward Istanbul in 1754, the wind suddenly shifted and his ship was forced to put into a small harbor some eight miles north of Sounion, on the east coast of Attica. For two weeks Le Roy and his crew explored the nearby site of Thorikos, where a few columns from a Doric building stood partly concealed behind thick, woody brush. Le Roy used the ship's marines as workmen to clear the brush and dig around the drums so that he could see them more closely and even measure some of them. The men uncovered what Le Roy took to be the remains of the colonnade of a classical temple, built of marble. Le Roy comments that although its remnants did not indicate it was a beautiful building, "I can attest that I took more pleasure in it than in many others more magnificent" (Figure 15.1).[1] It was the first ancient building he studied in Greece, and although he had not yet become a careful observer, his comments and illustrations are a valuable documentary record of early western European interest in the archaeology of Greece.

The colonnaded building at Thorikos first uncovered by Le Roy is remarkable for its innovative, double-faced plan, now much better documented thanks to the excavation of the mid-1990s carried out by the Greek Archaeological Society, which revealed the foundations for a long, central crosswall.[2] In this paper I trace the history of modern views about the

building, and I propose a significant modification to the most recent reconstruction of the original stoa, a central doorway; this structure likely served both as a stoa and a propylon. Also of interest is the later re-use of some of its superstructure in the Roman imperial period for a temple in the Athenian Agora: the stoa had an after-life providing a Classical aura for the imperial cult in the central city. It was recycled yet again in the Post-Herulian fortification wall of Athens. The original building dates to the last quarter of the 5th century BC, but its plan anticipates more sophisticated designs that reappear later in the Hellenistic period. The double stoa illustrates the great creativity in the architecture of the later 5th century BC in Athens, and subsequent creative use of this period's architecture in the later era. The history of investigation of the stoa provides a cross-section of the varying approaches and interpretations of ancient buildings over two and a half centuries, and the challenges that students have faced (and still face!) in interpreting them.

The marble Stoa at Thorikos was built just below the Velatouri hill, on an alluvial plain created by rivershed from the Adami and Potami rivers: today olive orchards, market gardens and beehives flourish on the good soil. Thorikos was a wealthy community in antiquity, thanks to the silver mines that fueled Athenian *arche* in the 5th century BC and her sometime hegemony in the following century. The

Vue de quelques fragments d'un Temple, situé dans un lieu de l'Attique appellé Thoricion.

Figure 15.1 Le Roy, view of Stoa. (Le Roy 1758, Vol. I, Pl. 2)

theater of the ancient deme of Thorikos and the industrial quarter that grew up around the entrances to silver mines are located above the stoa on somewhat higher ground, on the southern shoulders of the Velatouri hill. Since 1963, the the Belgian School at Athens has conducted excavations and study of the deme site, theater, industrial quarter and Bronze Age tombs of Thorikos.[3] The stoa, however, received systematic attention only in the mid 1990s, by the Greek Archaeological Society.

Early Modern Exploration of the Stoa

After LeRoy's initial discovery, his excavation of the stoa must have remained somewhat visible for some decades. The tops of some of the drums he exposed were defaced with graffitied names and dates, a record of a succession of visitors in the late 18th and early 19th centuries, when the drums stayed visible; these visitors no doubt learned of the stoa's existence from Le Roy's successful publication. Le Roy's romantic view of the site at Thorikos is attractive (Figure 15.1), but the scale of the human figures is wrong

(they make the columns look much larger than they actually are, and must have been added later).[4] His text, *Les ruines des plus beaux monuments de la Grèce*, appeared in print in 1758, four years before that of his rivals James Stuart and Nicholas Revett, and it won a wide readership in Europe. But Le Roy's book and especially his drawings were criticized for inaccuracy by Stuart and Revett, and other contemporaries.

Most significantly for documenting the Stoa at Thorikos, Le Roy missed some upper drums of the columns and reconstructs the colonnade with a shortened height, and he had not recognized that the columns were unfinished and their fluting not completed. Le Roy assumed the building was a temple, with six by thirteen columns, and he did not notice the widened intercolumniation on the long facades. The various oversights led him to suppose that the stoa was a very early temple in his posited history of Greek architecture, because of what he thought were short, stumpy, rough columns. Le Roy's purpose was to construct a narrative about the history of Greek architecture, and his approach had been to put things in order, from simple to complex, rough to polished. As an early pioneer in

Figure 15.2 View of Stoa at Thorikos, 1805, drawn by Simone Pomardi. (Dodwell, 1834)

the creation of an architectural history based on autopsy, inference, analogy and assumption (the tools we all use), he was misled by lack of comparanda and his own assumptions.

On September 5, 1805, Edward Dodwell, a scholarly-minded and careful recorder, traveled to Thorikos with artist Simone Pomardi.[5] Dodwell drew a fortified signal tower that stands still today on the southwest slope of the Velatouri hill, while Pomardi sketched the scene of their joint work at the stoa. His drawing, later engraved and published in 1834, shows that most of the stoa was covered by fill and bushes, but some of the drums and capitals were still accessible (Figure 15.2). In his publication and travel account of 1819, Dodwell illustrates a surface of one drum with guide-lines radiating from the center to the flutes, and he rather sharply corrects some of LeRoy's errors in his commentary on the site, in particular the assumption that the building was a hexastyle temple, with thirteen columns on the flanks.[6] Dodwell also mentions an entablature with a "ditrigylph," but it is not clear from his text whether he actually saw such a block, or, more likely, is simply suggesting how it should be reconstructed, based on subsequent fieldwork and publication by the Society of Dilettanti.

Dodwell regrets that he could not excavate, and he only illustrates what was visible when he visited in 1805. LeRoy's efforts to excavate at Thorikos were pursued further during 1813 by a party sent by the Society of Dilettanti, with strong financial backing. Sir William Gell led the party that included Francis O. Bedford and John P. Gandy (later Deering) as draughtsmen. The group traveled to Thorikos to study buildings that had not been drawn earlier by Stuart and Revett; they visited Eleusis, Rhamnous, Sounion and Thorikos.[7] Their fieldwork contributed three plates and commentary on the Stoa at Thorikos to the Society's *Unedited Antiquities of Athens* (1817).[8] Bedford dug under mastic bushes and fill five to six feet deep to locate as much as he could of the perimeter of the building, and he found 16 columns with lower drums in situ. He presents a plan of the building with 7 by 14 columns, and shows accurately the widened intercolumniation on the two long sides.

As archaeological documents, Bedford's precise drawings are far superior to Le Roy's: they provide an accurate and meticulous record of details of the blocks and of its Doric order, the best we have today. Bedford's plan of the "temple" at Thorikos (as it was generally called then) was unusual, as its 1:2 proportion and short facades with seven columns had no parallel.[9] Odd numbers of columns on facades are rare in Greek architecture, since ancient Greek architects preferred an intercolumnar space to a column in the center of a side peristyle. Bedford corrects Le Roy's assumption that the building was a temple, and states instead

Figure 15.3 View of excavated Stoa at Thorikos, 1893. Courtesy Deutsches Archäologisches Institut, Athens

that it must have been a stoa, with no walls (because none were then visible). Bedford, a well-informed architect, knew that ancient architects of the classical period did not typically use an odd number of columns on a side.[10] He provides an accurate reconstruction and excellent observations of details, such as capitals with differing annulets, and the elegant elevation of the columns. He had no information about the interior of the building, and simply presented what he was confident about, including the wider intercolumniation in the center of each long façade. The two studies, only 60 years apart, illustrate how quickly careful autopsy had improved the understanding and representation of Greek architecture. Interpretations could be built upon comparanda offered by actual examples, then being compiled with fieldwork and first-hand documentation, apart from the stale guidance of Vitruvius.

More Recent Excavation

After Bedford's visit in 1813, topsoil soon completely buried the stoa and it was lost to view until it was relocated again in 1893 by Valerios Staïs on behalf of the Greek Archaeological Society. His brief and partial excavation revealed more of its stepped crepidoma, and yielded a good documentary photograph (Figure 15.3). He dates the building to the beginning of the 5th century BC, and reports its dimensions as 14.70 × 31.96 m. Staïs mentions an inscription he observed on one of the two bases on the southeast side, placed on either side of the wider intercolumniation: "ἀνέθεκεν," and near the other was found a fragment of an Archaic statue of a female, "similar to the korai from the Akropolis."[11] Staïs notes also the existence of a *horos* inscription, brought to his attention by a local landowner.[12] He concludes that this must be a "sacred" building – because of the quality of the workmanship, the dedication and sculpture – and he suggests that the building was probably a temple or sanctuary to Demeter and Kore. This suggestion was amplified further in W.B. Dinsmoor's handbook of Greek architecture (1950), where the building is interpreted as a "telesterion."[13]

Since Bedford's visit in 1813 seventy years earlier, at least six and likely seven of sixteen lowermost drums had been lost: the fourth from the south corner; five along the northeast side, and (perhaps) on the north east side, the sixth drum from the west corner. Petrakos remarks that in connection with the re-opening of mines in the area during the later 19th century, material was scavenged from the ancient site for local building, and even earlier, lead and iron clamps likely were robbed out from the blocks.[14] No doubt many of the marble blocks were lost then. Once again soil washing in from the riversheds and brought by rain from the Velatouri hill covered the whole building.

In 1964, excavators from the Belgian School sank a small test trench, 2 × 4 m, and relocated the stoa under some 2 m of alluvial fill. R. Paepe, the geologist of the team, conducted a geophysical survey of the area and concluded that the sea levels nearby had fluctuated since antiquity: the ancient harbor might have reached somewhat closer to the stoa.[15] Because of its rectangular shape, and the high quality of the marble carving, the Belgian investigators left open the question of the buildings' function: a portico? a temple? a telesterion?[16]

Like Brigadoon, the stoa disappeared yet again after the Belgians dug their test-trench, until thirty years later a larger-scale excavation was carried out by the Greek Archaeological Society, under the direction of Basileios Petrakos and Maria Oikonomakou.[17] Their results are a wonderful surprise. At last, the whole plan of the building was revealed when workers exposed the foundations for a central cross-wall that divided the length of the building into two equal halves, so that we now know the stoa had two long outer faces with a shared central wall as the spine of the building. This excavation must have been arduous, as a massive amount of fill over the foundations had to be removed, and repeated rains during the excavation brought more mud, along with flooding from the adjacent stream-bed.[18] On a visit in 2014, I could see the active landscape still at work, already beginning to cover over the stoa yet again.

Roman Re-use of Building Parts from Thorikos

Interest in the building at Thorikos had intensified from 1959 onward when excavations in the ancient Agora in downtown Athens uncovered blocks of its superstructure in the Post-Herulian wall in the Agora, and nearby.[19] This wall, built soon after the Herulian sack of Athens in 267 AD, consists of two outer faces made of ancient blocks re-used from many buildings, with a variety of material as packing between them; the faces are set parallel to create a wall 2.50–3.5 m thick.[20] The wall was built hastily yet with some care after the sack, and just as for the Themistoklean Wall – built in an emergency some seven centuries earlier – many older buildings and monuments were dismantled to be re-used in the wall.

Many drums, set on their sides, comprised up to four columns brought from Thorikos, and at least ten wall blocks were set in the facings (Figure 15.4). Nearby were found eight triglyphs, epistyle blocks, and a backer block for an

epistyle that have nearly identical heights, and altogether belong to a reconstructed, Roman-period temple. W. B. Dinsmoor, Jr. determined that these blocks, assigned to the entablature of the Roman temple, derive from at least four other buildings, and the anta capital likely used for the Roman temple was probably made specifically for it, but was closely modeled on some other classical-period anta capital (Figure 15.5).

The blocks are distinctive for their marble and workmanship, and their identity as part of the building at Thorikos was recognized immediately. Many of them have masons' marks inscribed on joining surfaces, with letter forms that suggest they were carved in the Roman period, and keyed to their position. Eventually enough blocks emerged to provide the basis for a reconstruction, made initially (and mistakenly) with a hexastyle prostyle plan: it was called the "Southeast Temple." Meanwhile other architectural blocks from the Post-Herulian Wall were identified as belonging to the Temple of Athena Sounias at Sounion, yet another example of re-used 5th century BC material in a Roman temple, and they were reconstructed on foundations excavated on the opposite side the Agora, called the "Southwest Temple."[21]

The number of buildings (and one altar) transferred in whole or in part to the Agora from other locations during the 1st and 2nd centuries AD was growing in 1960: earlier studies of the Temple of Ares, moved from a deme in Attica to central Athens, had already been published. The transfer of temples, in part or whole, is now much better documented. Excavations at Pallene more recently uncovered the original foundations for the temple-blocks re-used in the Temple of Ares – the blocks were made originally for the Temple of Athena Pallenis.[22]

Thompson's interpretation for the blocks from the Post-Herulian Wall in the Agora stood for some years until Dinsmoor, Jr. restudied the attribution of the two sets of blocks to the two sets of foundations, and he demonstrated on the basis of careful measurements and a thorough review of the stratigraphy that the blocks from Thorikos belong to the temple on the west side, and the blocks from Sounion belong to the temple on the east side.[23] The blocks from Thorikos fit only the foundations of the Southwest Temple on the opposite corner of the Agora, and could not have been used for the Southeast Temple. Moreover Dinsmoor, Jr. clarifies the confusion surrounding the horos of the temenos of the Two Goddesses, for it cannot be associated with the marble building at Thorikos with any confidence: its findspot is unknown, and it dates to the 4th century BC. He thereby eliminates the association with Demeter (which was tenuous at best), and argues that instead the two Roman temples more likely were used for cults of the imperial family. He dates the Southwest temple to the first half of the 1st century AD, likely in the Augustan period, along with the Temple of Ares.[24] Dinsmoor, Jr.'s convincing interpretation of the blocks from Thorikos has not been superceded (Figure

Figure 15.4 Post-Herulian Wall in the Athenian Agora, from west, with column drums from Thorikos visible at right. Photo M. M. Miles

Figure 15.5 Capital, drums and anta capital from Thorikos, now in the Athenian Agora. Photo M. M. Miles

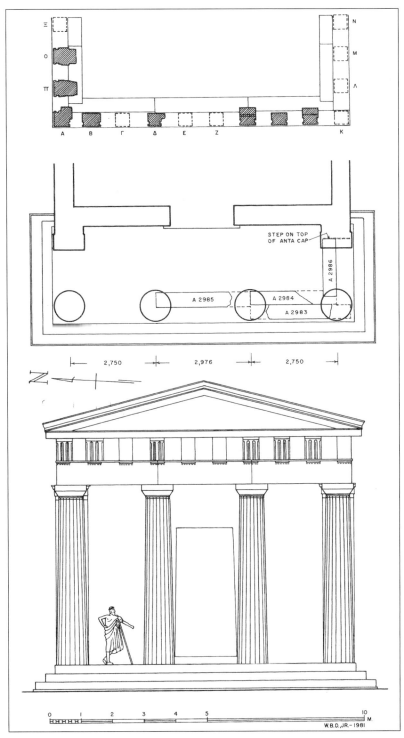

Figure 15.6 Southwest Temple in the Athenian Agora, drawn by W. B. Dinsmoor, Jr. Courtesy American School of Classical Studies at Athens: Agora Excavations

15.6). His study, and the subsequent discovery in the deme of Pallene of the original foundations for the Temple of Athena (whose blocks were re-used as the Temple of Ares) show that deities did not necessarily travel with blocks.

In the scholarly discussions of the transfers of the Roman imperial period, a general assumption prevails that the 5th century BC buildings were re-used simply out of economy or in desperation for building material, that is, what is referred to in discussions of spolia in later periods as the "discount solution." Instead, we should see the re-use of classical building-blocks as part of a nascent, deliberate classicism in the Augustan period, the roots of what becomes the Second Sophistic in Greece in the next century. Certainly it was not from ineptitude that blocks from buildings in Attica were re-used, for the masons of the Roman period were quite capable of imitating the original mouldings, as they did for the anta capital of the Southwest temple, to go with the columns from Thorikos.[25] Augustan-period masons in Athens were highly capable of creating new classicizing buildings too, such as the Temple of Roma and Augustus, and the Gate of Athena Archegetis, with columns modeled after the Propylaia and a classicizing sima.

The Double Stoa at Thorikos

As revealed by Bedford and again by Staïs, and confirmed in 1996/7, the columnar building has a rectangular plan, with a stylobate 14.70 × 31.96 m, and a two-step crepidoma.[26] The drawings of Bedford show a stylobate block still preserved in 1813 to the east of the southwest corner column, hence it is possible to restore two columns on each inner corner as part of the return on the two shorter façades.[27] A crosswall along the center of the building supported the pitched roof. The wall returns at both ends and provides a sheltered enclosure on both sides. Thus the overall plan of the building is now established. The stoa is noted briefly and illustrated with Petrakos' drawings by Goette, Hellmann, and Lippolis in their handbooks published since the excavation of its central wall.[28]

The marble fabric of the steps and columns has been described as "Agrileza" marble, quarried nearby in the Agrileza valley, or even closer to the building site. Vanhove suggests that a more particular quarry at Stephani, fairly close to the site of the stoa, was used as a quarry; she notes many small quarries throughout the length of the Agrileza valley and Souriza area.[29] The use of local stone for the stoa is paralleled by the use of Agrileza marble for the Temple of Poseidon at Sounion (from quarries at the southern end of the Agrileza valley), local marble from Agia Marina for the Temple of Nemesis at Rhamnous, Eleusinian limestone in various structures at Eleusis, and Pentelic marble for the Archaic statue of Dionysos at Ikarion (on the east slope of Mt. Pentele).

A notable feature of the plan is the widened inter-columniation in the center of the two longer facades, given by Staïs as 2.37 m. This was observed by earlier investigators, but puzzled them, since they assumed the structure was a temple, or a typical stoa, and such a wider intercolumniation seemed most unusual, in fact, unparalleled in that period except for the Athenian Propylaia.[30] Now that a central wall is established by the excavations of the 1990s, it becomes clear that the two widened intercolumniations

must frame a passageway through the central wall. Thus I reconstruct a doorway in the elevation (Figure 15.7).

The existence of a doorway is corroborated further by the vertical surface treatment of the stylobate blocks on the east center, both north and south sides, and the west center, south side. They indicate that no joining blocks were set there: they were intended to be finished, visible surfaces, and do not have anathyrosis.[31] Finally, the two bases originally found by Staïs on either side of the center intercolumniation on the east side also make sense as supports for objects that once framed the entraceway when the building was used. The doorway in the center provided convenient access to the other side of the double stoa, for if it had not existed, there would be no communication except by walking the length all the way around the end to the other side.

This unusual building served both as a stoa and perhaps also as a propylon, as its plan anticipates the much later (and more complex) propylaia to the Sanctuary of Athena at Lindos. It might have been intended to shelter paintings, dedications and other votives (Figure 15.8). We do not yet know what lay to the east or west of this stoa in antiquity, as all around it are unexcavated fields and orchards. Today the alluvial fill rises close to 2.5 m above the 5th century level on its west side, and about 1.5–2 m on the east. Like the earlier investigators of the 18th, 19th, and 20th centuries, I also assume that the monumental nature and overall high quality of the building indicate it was built for a religious or at least commemorative setting. The agora of Thorikos has not yet been found, and one possibility is that this stoa formed a part of it, analogous to its contemporary, the Stoa of Zeus in the central agora of Athens.

Beginning in the 20th century, the building has been dated consistently to the late 5th century BC, or last quarter of the 5th century BC.[32] Such a date is in keeping with its overall appearance and proportions, with the profiles of the echinos on the capitals, and the high quality of the precise tooling and workmanship of the building[33] (Figure 15.9). Numerous technical setting lines and guidelines are preserved on various blocks of the building and on the stylobate, and they illustrate the careful, practical application of geometry (rule, compass and chisel) used to set the columns precisely. Besides carefully chiselled guidelines for the preliminary fluting on a lowermost drum illustrated by Dodwell, guidelines for the fluting are partially preserved on the soffit of one the capitals brought into the Agora in the Roman period (Figure 15.9).

The construction of the double Stoa at Thorikos in the last quarter of the 5th century is yet another example of the continuation of construction in Attica even during the years of the Peloponnesian War.[34] Thucydides reports that the Spartans stopped at the Isthmos in the summer of 426 BC because of earthquakes, and decided not to continue on to ravage Attica (3.89.1). While that halt could have been temporary, the capture of 292 hoplites (120 of whom were

Figure 15.7 Plan of stoa, modified to include doorway (after Petrakos 1997)

full Spartan citizens) at Sphakteria in the following summer also was cause to suspend any further damaging invasions into Attica. The captives were held as prisoners, and the Athenians threatened to kill them if the Spartans invaded Attica again (Thuc. 4.41.1). Apart from those specific events that kept the Spartans from Attica from the summer of 426 BC onward until the occupation of Dekeleia, throughout the Peloponnesian War sanctuaries were generally respected by belligerents, and the contents of temples were not plundered.[35] Such pervasive, enduring respect for sanctuaries evidently permitted building construction in Athens and Attica to go on as usual during the last quarter of the 5th century BC.

Nonetheless the double stoa was left without full polish: the front and top surfaces of the stylobate still have protective panels and lifting bosses, and the columns were left unfluted for most of their height (in keeping with standard practice, the flutes were finished for a few centimeters on the lowermost drum, before the drums were

set, and just below the annulets of the capitals). In these details, the condition of the stoa is much like the Temple of Nemesis at Rhamnous. That temple was fully constructed in every other aspect, however, and received painted ornament, a cult image, and was fully used well into the Roman period as attested by both archaeological and epigraphical evidence. The incompleted surfaces did not at all prevent the use of the buildings, and they may not have seemed conspicuous or bothersome. The stoa-complex at Brauron in the Sanctuary of Artemis was also left incomplete with two sides unbuilt of a planned three for the colonnade, but the one completely constructed side was heavily used.[36]

At Thorikos there is no evidence for the upper entablature of the stoa. The top surface of the best preserved Doric capital from the stoa brought into the Athenian Agora is not completely smoothed to receive marble epistylia (although it is smooth enough to have satisfied the builders of the Roman period), nor were any identifiable pieces of the original

Figure 15.8 Perspective view of the Stoa at Thorikos (reconstructed with central door), drawn by Rocco Leonardis (2014).

entablature found in the Athenian Agora: this could indicate that there was no marble entablature to scavenge.[37] That the columns were fully standing is indicated by the series of Roman-period masons' marks, keyed to the proper position of each drum when they were disassembled; moreover, Le Roy reports finding a wooden empolion still preserved, after he pried apart two drums. From Staïs's observation of a dedicatory inscription on a base set against the steps, and a fragment of sculpture found quite nearby, it appears the building was in fact used in antiquity. A wooden entablature and wooden roofing support should be reconstructed; the superstructure of the entablature, even if wooden, helped to secure the overall framing of the building, and rendered it quite useable. The roof offered protection to its contents and visitors.[38]

Dinsmoor, Jr. was uncertain about the original use of the wall blocks still in the Post-Herulian Wall in the Agora, since he did not know about the stoa's interior wall, but we may now assign them to the stoa; they provide the width of the interior wall as 0.625 m (with protective surface) (Figure 15.10). The other blocks may be constructed in pairs for the side walls of the stoa to a maximum width of ca. 0.993, equivalent to the average bottom diameter of the columns.[39] The height of the columns of the stoa was 5.616 m, and on top of them in the Athenian Agora the Roman rebuilders

used an epistyle with an average height of 0.766 m, and a frieze with an average height of triglyphs 0.696 m.[40]

The precise drawings of columns left unfluted (because they were unfinished) provided inspiration to architects as late as the 19th century (Figure 15.11). The unfinished columns of the Stoa at Thorikos as drawn by Bedford, of the Temple of Nemesis at Rhamnous as drawn by Gandy, and of the Temple of Apollo on Delos (drawn by both Le Roy and Stuart and Revett) became models in the Classical Revival period of building in England, Scotland and Ireland where they were used for churches, private houses, and public monuments.[41] Architects could express the academic detail of the beginning of the flutes at the bottom and under the capital, but retain the convenience and reduced expense of unfluted columns, as they were following such notable ancient exemplars. One such Greek Revival example is the Presbyterian Church in Portaferry, County Down (1841). With hexastyle amphiprostyle facades, the architect John Millar recalled the three unfinished Doric buildings, known so well through published drawings.[42] He included Ionic columns in the interior, on the model of Iktinos' complete Temple of Apollo at Bassai: thus in one church, the visual essence of four monuments of the 5th century BC are used to express a subtle theological statement (Figure 15.12).

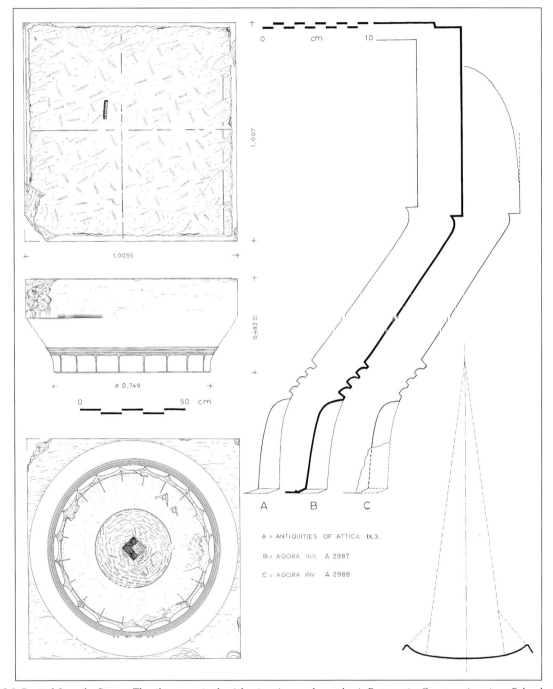

Figure 15.9 Capital from the Stoa at Thorikos, now in the Athenian Agora, drawn by A. Petronotis. Courtesy American School of Classical Studies at Athens: Agora Excavations

How Distinctive is the Design of the Stoa at Thorikos?

By the later 5th century BC, the versatility of stoas as a building type had long been exploited, and stoas were prominent in sanctuaries and agoras in many Greek cities.[43] I discuss here only the most obvious examples suitable for comparison with the Stoa at Thorikos. In central Athens,

the closest *comparandum* in date and likely function is the Stoa of Zeus in the Athenian Agora. Built ca. 425–410 BC and dedicated to Zeus Eleutherios, the plan of the Stoa of Zeus is strikingly innovative, with two temple-like facades on each end, complete with pediments, the first Greek stoa to have two symmetrical projecting "wings" in front. In his analysis of the design, J. Coulton remarks upon the

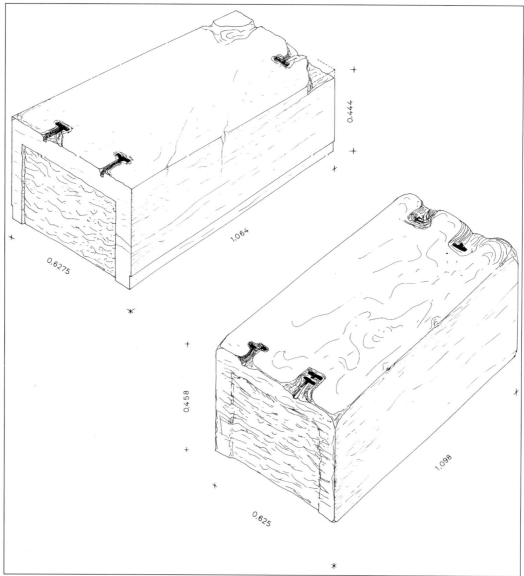

Figure 15.10 Two uninventoried wall blocks from the Post-Herulian Wall in the Athenian Agora, drawn by A. Petronotis. Courtesy American School of Classical Studies at Athens: Agora Excavations

careful solutions to the problems posed by the unusual plan: two wings treated as hexastyle facades; precise, related proportions of its various parts; unfluted Ionic columns used for the interior; a three-metope span for the center front; a re-etrant design for the Doric frieze in the interior corners of the wings, with a geison above it with a square mutule bearing nine mutules at the corners.[44] The overall length of the stoa is 43.56 m.

The excavator Thompson, Coulton, Camp and others have commented on the salient religious quality evoked by the temple-like wings, with a statue of Zeus Eleutherios immediately in front; when viewed at some distance, the wings echo the façade of the Hephaisteion on the hill above and behind the stoa. The stoa replaced a small Archaic

temple likely destroyed by the Persians, but its altar continued to be used even in the lifetime of the stoa.[45] I suggest the new stoa likely was palliative for the treatment of Plataians, just beseiged by Spartans (429–427 BC, Thuc. 2.71–78, 3.52–68); Athenians shamefully did not support them as they had sworn to do. The temple-like stoa recalled the oaths to Zeus Eleutherios all participating Greeks swore at Plataia at the time of the Persian invasion. It also provided a ceremonial focal-point for Plataian refugees, who were granted *isopoliteia*.[46]

The Stoa of Zeus Eleutherios demonstrates the ingenuity and creativity of the architect, who saw the potential of merging two genres, temple and stoa, into a successful hybrid. The design, with forward-facing side wings, lived

Figure 15.11 Elevation of the Stoa at Thorikos, drawn by Francis Bedford (Unedited Antiquities of Athens 1817, Ch. 9, Pl. II)

on in many stoas built later, although not at this scale or with the great depth of the wings in the Stoa of Zeus. The stoa had an interior bench, was decorated with paintings by Euphranor, received dedicated armor and other memorabilia, had statues and inscriptions set up in front of it, and was a setting for Socratic dialogues.[47] As a commemorative monument dedicated to Zeus Eleutherios, it provided a shady retreat in a conspicuous and central part of the Agora, and attracted passers-by at leisure. Documentation for the function of the double Stoa at Thorikos is lacking, but likely it served the public in very similar ways.

In Attica, the stoa-complex in the Sanctuary of Artemis at Brauron, built ca. 420 BC, offers structural points of comparison to the double Stoa at Thorikos. Although intended as a three-sided complex, the one side that was fully constructed has at its core a double-sided arrangement much like that at Thorikos.[48] The outer Doric façade faces an open square on the side opposite the Temple of Artemis, with a pitched roof that rises to a central wall. The wall is pierced with six doors leading to a series of six dining rooms, in turn backed by a solid wall of the same height as the outer façade (rather than a second colonnade as at Thorikos). The back wall of the dining room on its outer, northern side forms one side of a long open-air corridor, enclosed with doors at both ends. The corridor was used to display votive offerings under a partially roofed section parallel to the back wall of the dining rooms. In the center of the stoa, a small passageway between two dining rooms

and through the supporting cross wall permitted direct access to the corridor. The critical structural element in this complex is the central wall that supports a pitched roof, supported by the outer Doric façade on one side, and the back wall of the dining rooms on the other. This structural core is much like that of the double Stoa at Thorikos. The reconstructed height of the Doric column of the façade at Brauron, built in a mixture of local limestone and marble (for metopes and capitals), is about 29% smaller than that of the Stoa at Thorikos. The length of the stylobate of the façade is ca. 29.19 m.

While the two contemporary stoas in Athens and Brauron offer parallels in date, likely function, structural support and notably innovative design, outside Attica the double design is not used until the mid 4th century BC, at Molykreion (near Antirrhion, west of Nafpaktos), where a simple double stoa, ca. 11.40 × 38.80 m, was built without actual columns, instead with wooden posts on stone bases 0.60 m square, spaced ca. 2.55 m apart within the side walls. The stoa was set adjacent and parallel to the Temple of Poseidon on the acropolis of Molykreion, with one side facing the temple, and the other out toward Naupaktos.[49] The original excavator A. Orlandos opines that the slight walls and general quality of the remains of the structure indicate it may have been built as a temporary workshop while the temple was under construction, analogous to the workshop of Pheidias at Olympia. If he is correct, the stoa provided shade for workmen in both morning and evening light,

Figure 15.12 Presybeterian Church, Portaferry, County Down. Photo M. M. Miles

given its northwest-southeast orientation. The sanctuary's perimeter around the temple commands extraordinary views both eastward into the Gulf of Corinth and westward toward the Gulf of Patras; today trees block a potential viewshed south over the Antirrhion-Rhion crossing. The temple and the double stoa, even if intended as a temporary building, were positioned in a highly visible location.

Elsewhere beyond Attica the most striking comparison for the double stoa is the Corcyraean Stoa in the agora of Elis, described by Pausanias with unusual (for him) attention to its design (6.24.4):

> Near the stoa where the Hellanodikai spend the day is another stoa; between them is a street. This one the Eleans call the Corcyraean stoa, for they say the Corcyraeans came by ship to their land . . . and carried off a share of booty, but they themselves took many times as much booty from the Corcyraeans and built the stoa out of a tenth of the spoils. The construction of the stoa is Doric and double, with columns on one side facing the agora, and on the other, the far side of the agora. In the middle of it are not columns, but there is a wall

supporting its roof, and there are statues dedicated along the wall on each side. In the stoa on the side that faces the agora stands a statue of Pyrrho, son of Pistokrates, a sophist who did not adopt a fixed position on any topic.

Excavations at Elis have uncovered exiguous remains of this double stoa, some 30 × 99 m overall, with a central wall and two colonnaded sides.[50] What has been excavated seems to date mostly to a Roman-era rebuilding (1st century BC/AD), but traces of an earlier structure have been noted by the excavators, and are dated to the last third of the 5th century BC. The occasion of the dedication noted by Pausanias (acquisition of spoils from Corcyra) is assumed to be a series of confrontations in the late 430s BC between Elis and Corcyra described by Thucydides (3.29.2, 3.79–80). Likely the original name and occasion was retained for a later rebuilding of this stoa; we cannot know whether the original stoa also had the same double design.

The convenience for agoras of the double design was already recognized at Mantinea in the late 4th century BC;

on the side of its agora a double stoa with two shallow "wings" on the side facing inward to the agora was backed with an Ionic colonnade. The two sides are linked by a room that crosses both at one side, rather than a doorway through the cross-wall.[51] The Middle Stoa in the Athenian Agora (2nd century BC), some 147 m long, features the convenient double design, but with columns as center supports rather than a cross-wall as at Thorikos and Elis; screen walls between columns were used to block off areas with the huge stoa.

A double design was created in secondary construction at Delos in the tight setting of its agora, in the 71.08 m long Stoa of Philip V, dated to his ascendency ca. 210 BC. The stoa was originally an ordinary one-aisled single stoa, but a second colonnade was added about three decades later on the opposite side to form a double stoa with an exedra on its north end.[52] Like the double stoas at Elis and Molykreion, the double design suits its topographical position very well: in the agora of Delos, the original stoa faces the main foot traffic passing through the agora to the Sanctuary of Apollo, while the later addition faces the sea and harbor.

At Lindos on Rhodes we find the potential of a double stoa brilliantly expressed within the elaborate propylaia (or upper stoa) to the acropolis, where it provides a dramatic entrance to the Sanctuary of Athena Lindia. A fire in 392/1 BC had destroyed the temple and after it was rebuilt, in the Hellenistic period a series of terraces with monumental steps and stoas completed the whole complex.[53] The propylaia or upper stoa is a double stoa in plan, with five doors reconstructed through a central cross wall, recalling Mnesikles' Propylaia to the Athenian akropolis.[54] On each end of the propylaia are two symmetrical projecting wings (as in the Stoa of Zeus in the Athenian agora). Their scale, Doric order and tetrastyle prostyle plan anticipate the design of the façade of the Temple of Athena within the sanctuary for the visitor walking up toward the top level; the total length is 36.20 m. The colonnade on the inner side of the door wall forms one side of a surrounding open courtyard, with the temple at the opposite end. As any visitor to the akropolis of Lindos will attest, walking up and into the sanctuary still induces awe, even today when the experience is inevitably shaped by the happenstance of preservation or restoration. The magnificence of the framing of spectacular landscape by serried Doric columns, with contrasting shaded and open passageways offered in the double stoa, on a high akropolis rising from the sea, make the complex at Lindos one of the great achievements of Greek architecture.

Conclusion

Within its historical context, we see that the double Stoa at Thorikos was unusual for its time, and remained so: even though there are points of similarity with other stoas, the design itself, a discrete building with a central doorway, was

not repeated. The columns of the stoa had great longevity since they were re-used for a Roman temple in Athens, and again in the Post-Herulian Wall. Because they were drawn faithfully by Bedford, along with other unfinished columns at Rhamnous and Delos they became models for still-living buildings.

The double design at Thorikos is ingenious, but it only becomes compelling when there is a reason to have a janiform passageway, as at Lindos, where it serves also as propylon, marking the transition in a liminal zone. We cannot appreciate fully how it suited its setting until further excavation is carried out in adjacent areas to reveal what lead to and away from the stoa – this will be left to a future generation. Today it remains a lone monument in a pastoral landscape, much as Le Roy first found it.

Notes

1   Le Roy 2004 [1770], pp. 238–240, quotation p. 240; he traveled in the suite of Antonio Donà, the Venetian ambassador to the Sublime Porte. Le Roy had the men pry apart two of the drums that were in situ, and discovered perfectly preserved wooden empolia in their centers, "of some red wood, quite hard and well preserved," p. 240. This essay is based on study of published information, and autopsy at Thorikos and in the Athenian Agora. Translations below are my own. I thank Rocco Leonardis for drawing the perspectival reconstruction of the stoa (Figure 15.8), based on published measurements.

2   Petrakos 1994, 1995, 1996, 1997; Goette 2001, pp. 216–219; Hellmann 2006, pp. 248–249; Lippolis et al. 2007, p. 607.

3   Their earlier publications were under the name Belgian Archaeological Mission; see *Thorikos* I–X (1964–2011); specifically on the stoa, Mussche 1967, Paepe 1968, Vanhove 1994, p. 44. For the theater at Thorikos, Paga 2010, pp. 355–356.

4   Middleton (2004, p. 11) quotes a contemporary of Le Roy who remarks on the employment of the artist Louis-Joseph Le Lorrain in Paris to redraw Le Roy's sketches before they were engraved; the human figures may have been added then.

5   On Dodwell and his visits to Greece, Camp 2013, p. 7; I thank J. Camp for the specific information about the visit to Thorikos.

6   Dodwell 1819, pp. 535–536. He describes the site as "covered with dense and almost impenetrable foliage of the lentiscus" (p. 535, and Dodwell 1834, p. 15).

7   This party had originally intended to travel within Ionia, but were forestalled at times by the threat of pirates near Asia Minor, and outbreaks of plague near some intended sites there; during two lengthy delays, they went first to Eleusis (1812), and then to Rhamnous, Sounion, and Thorikos (1813): details in Cust and Colvin 1914, pp. 149–164. The work they did accomplish in Asia Minor was published in 1840 (*Antiquities of Ionia*).

8   Chapter 9, pp. 57–59 and plates I–III, referred to here and below as Bedford 1817.

9   The plan of the building at Thorikos as drawn by Bedford

had great longevity: its outline was repeated as recently as Dinsmoor, Jr. (1982, fig. 6) and Travlos (1988, fig. 561), since no new knowledge about it had yet been added. Dinsmoor, Jr. states that the building is a stoa (p. 415), while Travlos describes the building as a temple.

10 Bedford could have known about the enneastyle Archaic Temple of Hera I (then called the "Basilica") at Paestum. Writing after Bedford's publication, Col. Leake refers to the building simply as a "quadrangular colonnade," and notes that the length of the building compares to the width of the Parthenon; he says it is a ἑκατόμπεδος στοά (Hekatompedos Stoa) and may have been a stoa in the agora of Thorikos (Leake 1841, pp. 69–70 [first edition, 1821]). For his comparison with the Parthenon, he uses Stuart's measurements of the Parthenon and Bedford's of the stoa.

11 Staïs 1893, p. 17, 1895, pp. 221–234.

12 Staïs 1893, p. 17. It reads: ὅρος|τεμένους|τοῖν θεοῖν ("boundary of the temenos of the Two Goddesses") = *IG* I² 869 [and *IG* II² 2600], cf. *IG* I³, p. 972. The inscription, now in the Louvre, Paris, is excluded from *IG* I³ as it is dated to the 4th century BC; there are duplicate entries in the older epigraphical references. Staïs transcribed it incorrectly as one line, with three-barred sigmas. See Dinsmoor, Jr. 1982, pp. 451–452, for a summary of the circumstance of its finding, and a photograph of a squeeze of the inscription on pl. 95; the finding place of the inscription in or near Thorikos is not known (= *SEG* XXXII.231).

13 Dinsmoor 1950, p. 196; Boersma (1970, pp. 78–80, 188) discusses and catalogues the building as a Temple of Demeter and Kore.

14 Petrakos 1995, p. 21, 1997; Dinsmoor, Jr. remarks that the ground around the area at Thorikos "is covered with fragments of this material [marble]," which also suggests later breaking-up of the blocks (1982, footnote 14 on p. 418).

15 Paepe 1963[1968], 1966/1967[1969], 1968[1971].

16 Mussche 1964[1967], pp. 73–76.

17 Petrakos 1994, 1996, 1997.

18 Petrakos 1995, p. 21, 1996, pp. 19–20; Petrakos suggests the building might have been abandoned even in antiquity as the unsuitability of the site was realized.

19 Thompson 1960, p. 342, Thompson and Wycherley 1972, p. 167.

20 Detailed descripton in Frantz 1988, pp. 125–141; updated finds in Athens and plan in Theocharaki 2011. The fill of the wall included many smaller architectural pieces, such as ceiling coffers from the Temple of Ares, stray capitals, bases, working chips, and earth. Its circuit tightly enclosed the ancient city on the north side of the Akropolis, with part of its northern line founded along the south side of the Library of Hadrian (Frantz 1988, pl. 5).

21 Thompson and Wycherley 1972, pp. 167–168. Thompson associated the temple with Demeter because of its position on the Panathenaic Way, below the City Eleusinion, and because he believed the cult of the deity would be transferred along with the blocks; cf. Miles 1998, p. 49.

22 Dinsmoor 1939, McAllister 1959, Dinsmoor, Jr. 1974, Miles 1989, *passim*; moved from Attica: the original suggestion was that it was moved from Acharnai, because there was a cult of Ares there, but its foundations were uncovered at Pallene, as

demonstrated by Korres 1992–1998; for an Archaic temple moved into Thessaloniki in the Roman period, Grammenos 2003, pp. 80–82; for other examples of transferred buildings known from epigraphical or archaeological evidence, Petronotis 1980; Hellmann 2006, pp. 108–111.

23 Dinsmoor, Jr. 1982.

24 Evidence for date: Dinsmoor 1982, p. 434; attributions: Dinsmoor (1982, pp. 437–438) considers attributions to Athena or an imperial cult; discussed further in Baldasarri 1998, pp. 202–208. A sanctuary possibly associated with Demeter has been excavated by M. Oikonomakou (1994) at Agios Georgios near Thorikos (ca. 1.5 km distant from the stoa).

25 Careful imitations were also made for repairs to the east front of the Temple of Nemesis at Rhamnous: Miles 1989, pp. 235–239.

26 Bedford 1817 (in feet and inches); Staïs 1893, 17; Petrakos 1994, 24; Lippolis et al. 2007, p. 607: 14.70 × 32 m.

27 Petrakos 1996, p. 22. The stylobate block drawn by Bedford no longer exists.

28 Goette 2001, pp. 216–219; Hellmann 2006, pp. 108–111, 248–249; Lippolis et al. 2007, 607.

29 Goette 1991, p. 213, 2001, p. 217–219; Vanhove 1994, p. 44. Goette (1991, p. 213) notes that it is dificult to differentiate between "Thorikos" marble and "Agrileza" marble (visually), and that there are quarry marks within 150 m of the building site. Dinsmoor, Jr. (1982, p. 418) refers to the stone as "Thorikos" marble.

30 Dinsmoor 1950, 196.

31 See Figure 15.3 for the lifting bosses in the intercolumniation on the east flank.

32 Lippolis et al. 2007, p. 607, with earlier bibliography. No ceramic evidence for the date has been published.

33 The following proportions compare the height of the Doric column to its expression in lower diameters, a proportion that changes over time, and is an element of design prescribed by Vitruvius (4.3.4); Le Roy himself attempts this (the figures are derived from Dinsmoor 1950, pp. 337–339; Miles 1989, p. 223; for the Stoa at Brauron, Bouras 1967, p. 35, 45–46; for the stoa at Thorikos, Dinsmoor 1982):

Olympia, Temple of Zeus	1:4.635, 1:4.719
Bassai, Temple of Apollo	1:5.13, 1:5.31
Propylaia, west wing	1:5.4483
Parthenon	1:5.476
Delos, Temple of Apollo	1:5.50
Hephaisteion	1:5.611
Propylaia, central building	1:5.6636
Temple of Ares (estimate)	1:5.7045
Double Stoa, Thorikos	1:5.6129, 1:5.7099
Delos, Temple of Athenians	1:5.7125
Temple of Nemesis	1:5.7422
Temple of Poseidon	1:5.7756
Stoa at Brauron (reconstructed)	1:5.946
Nemea, Temple of Zeus	1:6.3607

34 For discussion and a survey of construction both in the city and in Attica during the war, see Miles 1989, pp. 227–235; earlier views in Boersma 1970, p. 80.

35 Miles 1989, p. 229, Miles 2008, p. 36–37.

36 For other unfinished buildings, Kalpaxis 1986.

37 Dinsmoor, Jr. 1982, p. 416, footnote 9. The ever-increasing evidence for reusing architectural blocks on other sites should teach us caution about assuming this; possibly the entablature, if it existed, was used elsewhere.

38 Le Roy was the first to suggest a wooden entablature, which he regarded as an indication of an early date (2004 [1770], p. 240).

39 Dinsmoor, Jr. 1982, p. 418 (origin of wall blocks), pp. 450–451 (catalogue; five are in the wall, three were in a tower of the wall, and other are in fragments). The two preserved bottom drums are A 3010d (l.d. 0.984 m) and A 3011d (l.d. 1.001 m).

40 The dimensions of the entablature selected for the Roman rebuilding yield a proportion identical to that of the Temple of Zeus at Nemea (H. of epistyle : H. of frieze, 0.909 in both). My figures are based on the blocks brought into the Agora and studied by Dinsmoor, Jr. (1982).

41 A selection is conveniently illustrated in Watkin 2006, pp. 46–50.

42 Brett 2002, pp. 62–63.

43 Coulton notes that war booty is known to have financed some 5th century stoas, notably the Stoa Peisikl at Spartan, described by Pausanias (3.11.3), and the Stoa of the Athenians at Delphi (1976, pp. 39–41).

44 Coulton 1976, pp. 41–42, 222 (date for Stoa of Zeus on p. 222); excavation of the Stoa: Thompson 1937, pp. 5–77, 225–6; description of stoa: Thompson and Wycherley 1972, pp. 96–103; Camp 2010, pp. 73–75.

45 Persian destruction debris: Thompson 1937, pp. 12–14.

46 On the issue of *isopoliteia*, Hornblower 1991, pp. 448–450 (commenting on Thuc. 3.55.3)

47 Testimonia in Wycherley 1959, pp. 25–30.

48 Bouras 1967, fold-out sections 7, 8.

49 Orlandos 1924–25, p. 63; Coulton 1976, p. 261, fig. 88 on p. 262; temple: Knell 1973; topography: Freitag 1999, pp. 58–67; sources for Molykreion and futher bibliography in Hansen and Nielsen 2004, p. 385.

50 Coulton 1976, pp. 14, 45, 79, 237; Mitsopoulos Leon 1983, 1990; Pochmarski 1990 (with full earlier bibliography); Lippolis et al. 2007, pp. 650–651. Pochmarski argues for the earlier phase of the building and retains its identification with the "Corcyraean" stoa described by Pausanias. The remains consist of robbing trenches, parts of foundations, fragments of the superstructure, and elements of its terracotta roof.

51 Formerly this stoa was considered to have been built in two phases, with the back added as a much later afterthought, but a restudy of its foundations shows that it more likely was built all at once, in the late 4th century BC, with a deliberately planned double design: Lauter 1986, pp. 116–121; Lauter et al. 2004.

52 Coulton 1976, pp. 60, 233–234; Bruneau and Ducat 2005, pp. 165–167.

53 Dyggve 1960, pp. 180–184, 247–258, dates the construction of the lower stoa later than the upper stoa/propylaia of ca. 300 BC; Lippolis (1988–89), and Pakkanen (1988) argue the entire complex was planned together, whereas Winter (2006, pp. 217–218) and Hollinshead (2012, p. 40) see an evolving plan. For the fire, Higbie 2003, pp. 256–258.

54 The features recalling Mnesikles' Propylaia should be seen as a deliberate homage; earlier observers thought they indicated a date in the 5th century for at least parts of the propylaia at Lindos, discussed by Dyggve (Dyggve 1960, pp. 180–184).

References

Baldassari. P. 1998. *Σεβαστῶι σωτῆρι : edilizia monumentale ad Atene durante il saeculum Augustum*, Rome.

Bedford, F. O. 1817. Drawings and commentary in *The Unedited Antiquities of Athens, comprising the arhcitectural remains of Eleusis, Rhamnus, Sunium, and Thoricus*, Chapter 9. Published by The Society of Dilettanti, London.

Boersma, J. 1970. *Athenian Building Policy from 561/0 to 405/4 B.C.*, Groningen.

Bouras, Ch. 1967. *Η αναστήλωσις της στοάς της Βραυρώνος. τα αρχιτεκτονικά προβλήματα*. Athens.

Brett, C. E. B. 2002. *Buildings of North County Down*, Ulster Architectural Heritage Society. Belfast.

Bruneau, P. and J. Ducat. 2005. *Guide de Délos*. Paris.

Camp, J. M. 2001. *The Archaeology of Athens*, London.

Camp, J. McK. 2010. *The Athenian Agora. Site Guide*, 5th ed., Princeton.

Camp, J. McK., II. 2013. *In Search of Greece. Catalogue of an Exhibit of Drawings at the British Museum by Edward Dodwell and Simone Pomardi*, Los Altos, Cal.

Coulton, J. J. 1976. *The Architectural Development of the Greek Stoa*, Oxford.

Cust, L. and S. Colvin. 1898. *History of the Society of Dilettanti*, London.

Dinsmoor, W. B. 1940. "The Temple of Ares," *Hesperia* 9, pp. 1–52.

Dinsmoor, W. B. 1950. *Ancient Greek Architecture*, 3rd ed., New York.

Dinsmoor, W. B., Jr. 1974. "The Temple of Poseidon: A Missing Sima and Other Matters," *American Journal of Archaeology* 78, pp. 211–238.

Dinsmoor, W. B., Jr. 1982. "Anchoring Two Floating Temples," *Hesperia* 51, pp. 410–452.

Dodwell, E. 1819. *A Classical and Topographical Tour through Greece during the years 1801, 1805, and 1806*. London.

Dyggve, E. 1960. *Fouilles de l'Acropole, 1902–1914 et 1952*. Vol. III.2. *Le sanctuaire d'Athana Lindia et l'architecture lindienne*, Berlin.

Frantz, A. 1988. *The Athenian Agora*, XXIV. *Late antiquity, A.D. 267–700*, Princeton.

Freitag, K. 1999. *Der Golf von Korinth: historisch-topographische Untersuchungen von der Archaik bis in das 1. Jh. v. Chr.*, Munich.

Goette, H. R. 1991. "Die Steinbrüche von Sounion im Agrileza-Tal," *Mitteilungen des Deutschen Archäologischen Instituts, Athenische Abteilung* 106, pp. 201–222.

Goette, H. R. 2001. *Athens, Attica and the Megarid: An Archaeological Guide*, London.

Grammenos, D.V., ed. 2003. *Roman Thessaloniki*, Thessaloniki.

Gruben, G. 2001. *Griechische Tempel und Heiligtümer*, Munich.

Hansen, M. H. and R. H. Nielsen. 2004. *An Inventory of Archaic and Classical Poleis*, Oxford.

Hellmann, M.-C. 2006. *L'architecture grecque*, Vol. 2, Paris.

Higbie, C. 2003. *The Lindian Chronicle and the Greek creation of their past*, Oxford.

Hollinshead, M. 2012. "Monumental Steps and the Shaping of Ceremony," in *Architecture of the Sacred. Space, Ritual and Experience from Classical greece to Byzantium,* ed. B. Wescoat and R. Ousterhout, Cambridge, pp. 27–65.

Hornblower, S. 1991. *A Commentary on Thucydides, I, Books I–III,* Oxford.

Humphreys, S. 2004. *Strangeness of the Gods,* Oxford.

Kalpaxis, T. E. 1986. *Hemiteles: akzidentelle Unfertigkeit und "Bossen-Stil" in der griechischen Baukunst,* Mainz am Rhein.

Knell, Heiner. 1973. "Der Artemistempel in Kalydon und der Poseidontempel in Molykreion," *Archäologischer Anzeiger,* pp. 448 461.

Korres, M. 1992–1998. "Από Σταυρό στην αρχαία Αγορά," *Horos* 10–12, pp. 83–104.

Lauter, H. 1986. *Die Architektur des Hellenismus,* Darmstadt.

Lauter, H., H. Lauter-Bufe, and P. Becker. 2004. "Die reifklassische Doppelstoa in Mantineia. Neue Daten," *Mitteilungen des Deutschen Archäologischen Instituts, Athenische Abteilung* 119, pp. 317–338.

Leake, W. 1841. *The Topography of Athens and The Demi. II: The Demi of Attica.* 2nd ed. London.

Le Roy, Julien-David. 2004 [1770]. *The Ruins of the Most Beautiful Monuments in Greece,* introduction by Robin Middleton, trans. David Britt, Los Angeles.

Lethaby, W. 1908. *Greek Buildings Represented by Fragments in the British Museum,* London.

Lippolis, E. 1988–1989. "Il santuario di Athana a Lindo," *Annuario della Scuola archaeologica di Atene e delle missioni italiane in Oriente* 48–49, pp. 97–157.

Lippolis, E., M. Livadiottti, and G. Rocco. 2007. *Architettura greca. Storia e monumenti del mondo della* polis *dalle origini al V secolo,* Milan.

Lupu, E. 2009. *Greek Sacred Law. A Collection of New Documents,* Leiden.

McAllister, M. H. 1959. "The Temple of Ares at Athens: A Review of the Evidence." *Hesperia* 28, pp. 1–64.

Middleton, R. 2004. "Introduction," in Le Roy, Julien-David. 2004 [1770], *The Ruins of the Most Beautiful Monuments in Greece,* Los Angeles, pp. 1–199.

Miles, M. M. 1989. "A Reconstruction of the Temple of Nemesis at Rhamnous," *Hesperia* 58, pp. 131–249.

Miles, M. M. 1998. *The Athenian Agora,* XXXI. *The City Eleusinion,* Princeton.

Miles, M. M. 2008. *Art as Plunder. The Ancient Origins of Debate about Cultural Property,* Cambridge.

Mitsopoulou Leon, V. 1983. "Die Südhalle von Elis." *Jahreshefte des Österreichischen Archäologischen Institutes in Wien* 54: pp. 41–102. Mussche, H. F. 1964 [1967]. "Le Batiment dorique," in *Thorikos II,* ed. H. F. Mussche, Brussels, pp. 73–76.

Mussche, H. F. 1994. "Thorikos During the Last Years of the 6th c. B.C." in *The Archaeology of Athens and Attica under the Democracy,* ed. W. Coulson et al., Oxbow Monograph 37, Exeter, pp. 211–215.

Oikonomakou, M. 1994. "Άγιος Γεώργιος Θορικού (οικόπεδο Χρυσ. Ρώμα)." Αρχαιολογικόν Δελτίον 49, pp. 64–66.

Orlandos, A. 1924–25. "Μολύκρειον." Αρχαιολογικόν Δελτίον 9, p. 63.

Paepe, R. 1963 [1968]. "Le Cadre régional du site de Thorikos," in *Thorikos I,* ed. H. F. Mussche, Brussels, pp. 11–26.

Paepe, R. 1966/67[1969]. "Geomorphic Surfaces and Quaternary Deposits of the Adami Area (S-E Attica)," in *Thorikos IV,* ed. H. F. Mussche, Brussels, pp. 7–52.

Paepe, R. 1968[1971]. "Geo-electrical Prospection of the Temple Site Area in the Adami Plain," in *Thorikos V,* ed. H. F. Mussche, Brussels, pp. 9–16.

Paga, J. 2010. "Deme Theaters in Attica and the Trittys System," *Hesperia* 79, pp. 351–384.

Pakkanen, J. 1988. "The Column Shafts of the Propylaia and Stoa in the Sanctuary of Athena at Lindos," *Proceedings of the Danish Institute at Athens* 2, pp. 147–159.

Petrakos, B. 1994 [1995] "Θορικός." *To Ergon tes Archaiologikes Etaireias,* pp. 22–27.

Petrakos, B. 1995 [1996] "Θορικός." *To Ergon tes Archaiologikes Etaireias,* pp. 20–23.

Petrakos, B. 1996 [1997] "Θορικός." *To Ergon tes Archaiologikes Etaireias,* pp. 19–23.

Petrakos, B. 1997 [1998] "Θορικός." *To Ergon tes Archaiologikes Etaireias,* pp. 23–34.

Petronotis, A. 1980. "'Wandernde' Tempel I," in ΣΤΗΛΗ, *τόμος εἰς μνῆμην Νικόλαου Κοντολέοντος,* ed. V. Lambrinoudakis, Athens, pp. 328–330.

Pochmarski, E. 1990. "Zur Chronologie der S.-Stoa in Elis." *Jahreshefte des Österreichischen Archäologischen Institutes in Wien* 60, pp. 7–17.

Redford, B. 2008. *Dilettanti: The Antic and the Antique in Eighteenth-century England.* Los Angeles.

Shear, T. L. 1981. "Athens: from City-state to Provincial Town," *Hesperia* 51, pp. 356–377.

Staïs, B. 1893. "Ἀνασκαφαὶ ἐν Θορικῷ," *Praktika tes en Athenais Archaiologikes Etaireias,* pp. 12–17.

Theocharaki, A. M. 2011. "The Ancient Circuit Wall of Athens: Its Changing Course and the Phases of Construction," *Hesperia* 80, pp. 71–156.

Thompson, H. A. 1937. "Buildings on the West Side of the Agora." *Hesperia* 6, pp. 1–226.

Thompson, H. A. 1951. "Excavations in the Athenian Agora: 1951," *Hesperia* 21, pp. 83–113.

Thompson, H. A. 1960. "Activities in the Athenian Agora: 1959," *Hesperia* 29, pp. 327–368.

Thompson, H. A. 1981. "Athens Faces Adversity," *Hesperia* 50, pp. 343–355.

Thompson, H. A. and R. E. Wycherley. 1972. *The Athenian Agora,* XIV. *The Agora of Athens,* Princeton.

Travlos, J. 1988. *Bildlexikon zur Topographie des antiken Attika,* Tübingen.

The Unedited Antiquities of Athens, comprising the architectural remains of Eleusis, Rhamnus, Sunium, and Thoricus. 1817. London.

Vanhove, D. 1994. "The Laurion Revisited," in *Studies in South Attica II,* ed. H. F. Mussche, Gent, pp. 30–75.

Watkin, D. 2006. " Stuart and Revett: The Myth of Greece and Its Afterlife," in *James "Athenian" Stuart, 1713–1788. The Rediscovery of Antiquity,* ed. S. Soros, New Haven, pp. 19–57.

Winter, F. 2006. *Studies in Hellenistic Architecture,* Toronto.

INSCRIPTIONS CITED

INDEX